THE COLLECTED WORKS
OF HERMAN DOOYEWEERD

Series B, Volume 14

GENERAL EDITOR: D.F.M. Strauss

Time, Law, and History

SELECTED ESSAYS

Herman Dooyeweerd

Paideia Press
Grand Rapids
2017

Library of Congress Cataloging-in-Publication Data

Dooyeweerd, H. (Herman), 1894-1977.
Time, Law, and History
Herman Dooyeweerd.

p. cm.

Includes bibliographical references and indexes
ISBN 978-0-88815-202-2 (soft)

This is Series B, Volume 14 in the continuing series
The Collected Works of Herman Dooyeweerd
(*Paideia Press*)
ISBN 978-0-88815-202-2

The Collected Works comprise a *Series A,* a *Series B,* a *Series C*
and a *Series* D

Series A contains multi-volume works by Dooyeweerd,
Series B contains smaller works and collections of essays,
Series C contains reflections on Dooyeweerd's philosophy
designated as: *Dooyeweerd's Living Legacy,* and
Series D contains thematic selections from Series A and B

A CIP catalog record for this book is available
from the British Library.

PAIDEIA PRESS
Grand Rapids, MI 49507
www.reformationalpublishingproject.com

Printed in the United States of America

Time, Law, and History

Herman Dooyeweerd

SELECTED ESSAYS

All articles in this volume are translated by
Daniël Strauss

Edited by
Harry Van Dyke (Entire work)
Roy Clouser (Chapter 7)
David Hanson (Chapter 7) and
Deon Van Zyl (Chapter 4)

General Editor
Daniël Strauss

Foreword

From a systematic and genetic point of view this Volume of Selected Essays is exceptional in various respects. The problem of time dealt with in the first part of this Volume could be seen as the fourth Volume of his magnum opus, *De Wijsbegeerte der Wetsidee* (1935-1936 – see page 1, footnote 1). After a penetrating assessment of the diverse conceptions of time found in the history of philosophy and the special sciences, Dooyeweerd explains his own unique understanding of "cosmic time". While traditional conceptions of time by and large defined one aspect of time only, Dooyeweerd's view acknowledges the fact that cosmic time comes to expression within each modal aspect in accordance with the nature of the aspect concerned. According to Dooyeweerd there is a strict correlation between the law-side and factual side of cosmic time – evinced in the difference between time-order and time duration. The time-order in the first three aspects is reversible, but in the physical and post-physical aspects it is irreversible. Succession reflects the numerical time-order and should be distinguished from the (irreversible physical) relation of cause and effect (causality). There is a succession of day and night and night and day, but neither is the day the cause of the night, nor the night of the day.

The article on legal principles shows elements of the intellectual development of Dooyeweerd's thought – even that at this stage he contemplated distinguishing between the kinematic and physical aspects. Of importance is also his reflections on the element of positivity in the structure of the post-historical norm-spheres. The scope and depth of this article stretches beyond merely looking at jural principles, for it addresses key elements of Dooyeweerd's developing social philosophy as well.

In his discussion of Michael Wilhelm Scheltema's dissertation, *Beschouwingen over de vooronderstellingen van ons denken over Recht en Staat* (1948), Dooyeweerd is mainly interested in the problems generated by historicism. It is followed by an equally penetrating investigation of Aristotle's concept of justice, this time in the form of a review article devoted to a study by Peter Trude, *Der Begriff der Gerechtigkeit in der aristotelischen Rechts- und Staatsphilosophie,* that started as a dissertation prepared under the supervision of Ernst von Hippel and published in 1955 in the series *Neue Kölner Rechtswissenschaftliche Abhandlungen.* Dooyeweerd positions his discussion against the background of a general characterization of Greek philosophy.

In the next article Dooyeweerd engages in a discussion of a problem that is very much alive today, namely "The Debate about the Concept of Sovereignty." Of particular importance for a proper understanding of the idea of a *just state* (Rechtsstaat) is the way in which he compares the traditional concept of sovereignty with the theory of sphere-sovereignty.

These issues are continued in his reflection on the "Relationship between Individual and Community in the Roman and Germanic Conceptions of Property," positioned in the context of the prevailing contrast between the Roman and the Germanic conception of property. Some of the initial sections of this article enter into a most insightful exposition of the nature and differences between the spheres of public law, civil (private) law and non-civil private law (see pages 345-350).

The culmination-point of everything discussed in this work up to this point is indeed found in the last article on "Law and History." It takes the criticism on historicism to a new level, particularly because it brings the basic distinctions of his philosophy to bear upon the inherent problems of historicism – and then he contrasts this with a novel understanding of the process of disclosure in cultural development and legal life.

Daniël Strauss
20-04-2017

Table of Contents

I

My Philosophy of Time

Part A

The Problem of Time and Its Antinomies on the Immanence Standpoint

Part B

The Problem of Time in the *Philosophy of the Cosmonomic Idea*

(v)

II

The Structure of Jural Principles and the Method of the Science of Law in Light of the Cosmonomic Idea

III

Presuppositions of Our Thought about Law and Society in the Crisis of Modern Historicism

(vii)

IV

A New Study of Aristotle's Concept of Justice

V

The Debate about the Concept of Sovereignty

VI

The Relationship between Individual and Community in the Roman and Germanic Conceptions of Property

VII

Law and History

I

My Philosophy of Time[1]

Part A

The Problem of Time and Its Antinomies
on the Immanence Standpoint

1. Dependence of the insight into the problem of time upon the Archimedean point of a thinker

Right from the beginning the *Philosophy of the Cosmonomic Idea* related the problem of time to that of the true character of reality, the *being of what is*.

Since this insight into the "being of what is" is entirely dependent upon the choice of the Archimedean point or the transcendent starting-point of philosophical thought, and since the latter in turn determines the understanding of the cosmonomic idea as a foundation for philosophy, it should not be surprising as well that the philosophical treatment of the problem of time will faithfully mirror the assumed cosmonomic idea.

On the immanence standpoint the problem of time necessarily becomes a wellspring of antinomies.

The basic antinomy of all immanence philosophy, after all, is the choice of the Archimedean point within temporal reality itself. This antinomy must then be camouflaged through the primary absolutization of temporal aspects of meaning in which the thinker believes he can find its time-transcendent starting-point. But this primary absolutization, through which the aspects or modalities concerned are apparently elevated above the universal temporal coherence prevailing between them,

---

1 [A compilation of four articles on time as a problem for philosophy, published in *Phil. Ref.* 1 (1936): 65–83; 4 (1939): 1–28; 5 (1940): 160–82 and 193–234. The first article was originally intended by Dooyeweerd to be a shortened version of the Introduction to a planned fourth volume of his *Wijsbegeerte der Wetsidee*, the third volume of which had appeared early 1936. In the years that followed he added three more articles on the topic. A fourth volume of his magnum opus never materialized.]

causes one to disregard the *cosmic universality* of time. The result is that time, which indeed embraces all aspects, must be closed off in one or a few law-spheres in which time merely comes to expression in a particular *modus* or *modality*. In this way mechanistic, psychologistic, historicistic and other conceptions of time emerge.

Immanence philosophy never realized that the theoretical abstraction which lies at the foundation of its absolutization of a temporal aspect to become an Archimedean point, itself presupposes cosmic time which overarches all aspects of meaning.

And yet this is the case. Theoretical thought, in its logically deepened meaning, can only lead to knowledge through a combination or synthesis with a non-logical "Gegenstand" of this thought. This synthesis is founded in a supra-modal cosmic intuition of time.[1]

Every absolutization of a temporal aspect of temporal reality, such as we encounter, for example, in a mathematicistic, psychologistic, historicistic or moralistic philosophy, actually rests upon a theoretical synthesis in the above intended sense. And such a synthesis is possible only through cosmic time which universally binds together all aspects. This cosmic time cannot be grasped in a concept, since it makes possible all concept formation in the first place.

2. The basic antinomy of immanence philosophy. The temporality of the logical thought-structure

No single absolutization of a temporal aspect into a supra-temporal, self-contained resting point for philosophical thought, can indeed elevate that thought above time. This is the basic antinomy of metaphysical immanence philosophy, which, for all its attempts to break through the bondage to time by means of metaphysical concepts, is itself only possible by the grace of time.

Similarly, every theoretical attempt to enclose time within specific aspects presupposes universal cosmic time, which holds all these aspects in a continuous cosmic coherence.

1 [The problem of knowledge is treated at length in *WdW*, 2:359-473 (cf. *NC*, 2:429-541); see also *Reformation and Scholasticism in Philosophy*, 2:94-137.]

In idealistic Greek metaphysics the absolutization of theoretical ideas into supra-temporal *noumena* (intellectual objects) resulted in breaking apart the temporal coherence of reality, causing a denial in principle of cosmic time which made possible this absolutization by human reason to begin with.

The reification of the *noumenon* (the reason-idea) into a "timeless substance" requires that the metaphysical "ideal reality" ought to be conceived as supra-temporal. Only the physico-psychical *phaenomena* of the "world of the senses" could then be acknowledged in their temporal character.

With this idealistic basic attitude there immediately arises a thoroughly antinomic problem: What is the relationship between the timeless *noumenon* and the temporal, changeful *phenomenon*?

From the beginning of Greek metaphysics this problem was acknowledged as an *ontological problem* regarding the relationship of *being* and *becoming*.

Even before the emergence of the authentic theory of ideas this problem revealed its inner antinomic character in two mutually exclusive standpoints: the static metaphysics of being of Parmenides, and the dialectic absolutization of time in Heraclitus' dynamistic basic thesis: "everything is changing and nothing endures."

3. Time structure (the horizon of time) and temporal duration

In order to gain proper insight into the problem of time, it is of primary importance to remember that universal time, which embraces our entire temporal cosmic reality in all its modal aspects of meaning, may not be identified with *becoming*, with *continuously being subjected to change*.

One can say that all genesis, all becoming and passing away, do take place within time, but not that *time itself* is *becoming*. Rather, within cosmic time, an initial distinction is required between (a) a law-side, and (b) a factual side[1] subject to the former. These two sides co-exist in an unbreakable coherence.

According to its law-side cosmic time is the structural time-order embracing the entire temporal reality. As such, time bears a constant and transcendental character, that is to say, it makes possible temporal reality in its immanent structure.

This invariant cosmic time structure serves as the foundation both for the constant structures of the temporal modalities of reality (those of number, space, motion, organic life, feeling, and so on), and for the individuality structures of things, events, societal relationships, etc. etc. The individuality structures overarch the aspects and group them in different ways into individual totalities.

The *Philosophy of the Cosmonomic Idea* designates this time structure as such as the *temporal horizon* of all of empirical reality.[2] As to its factual side time in its universal cosmic character is indeed a flowing continuum (*fluidum*), the continual mutual fusion of moments, which are temporal moments of subjective states, acts, events and so on.

According to its factual side time can be called *duration in moments*, and it soon becomes apparent that this "duration" can never be "empty": it can never be separated from the factual side of temporal reality, no more than it can exist outside the universal *time-structure*, outside the *horizon of time*. On no account should this duration be identified with *one* of its modal aspects, such as the duration of *motion*, *emotional* duration or *historical* duration. On the contrary, its cosmic continuity is of a supra-modal character which pervades and overarches all law-spheres.

---

1 [The term "factual side" here translates the composite noun "subjectszijde" in the original. In order to avoid ambiguity in the use of the term "subject," which could mean (i) that which is involved in subject-object relations or (ii) whatever is correlated with the law-side, the correlate of the latter may be designated as the "factual side." This enables a distinction between the *factual subject-side* and the *factual object-side* – thus liberating us from ambiguity in the use of the term "subject."]

2 See my *WdW*, 2:474-534 [cf. *NC*, 2:542-98].

The whole of temporal reality, within its time-structure, has a certain cosmic duration which flows through its modal aspects in a supra-temporal continuum.

This cosmic duration within the time-structure can only be experienced by the human being, who has a supra-temporal center of its temporal existence, the heart, in which eternity was placed.

Time can only be experienced in its relation to *created eternity* (the *aevum*, as it is called in Scholasticism, in opposition to the *aeternitas increata*, the uncreated eternity of God).

All immanent temporal time-measurement, for example in hours, minutes and seconds, in the final analysis remains *external* and as such cannot provide us with an awareness of time. Our intuition of time, which itself cannot be grasped conceptually, is undeniably rooted in the identity of our selfhood, in the transcendent center of our existence. All that restlessness in our experience of time, as Augustine already realized from a truly Christian point of view, derives from the heart, from the stirring of time and eternity in the innermost depths of our existence.

4.   The subject-object relation in time duration

In connection with the distinction drawn between *time structure* and *factual time duration* we still have to add the following.

According to the insights developed by the *Philosophy of the Cosmonomic Idea*, a subject-object relation presents itself both within the modal structures and within the individuality structures of cosmic time, a relation that is entirely determined by these structures.[1]

For example, an entity qualified by its physico-chemical aspect, such as a mountain or a lake, has a cosmic time-duration which functions in all modes of time. But within the sensitive-psychic aspect of its reality, for instance, this time-duration does not display a subjective, but an objective character. For this thing does not have a subjective sensory function, but is only observed as an object by beings which themselves function as sub-

---

1   See my *WdW*, 2:301-42 and 3:71-128 [cf. *NC*, 2:366-413 and 3:104-53].

jects within the psychical law-sphere.[1] However, the objective psychical time duration in this aspect is indissolubly related to the subjective psychical time duration of the sensitive consciousness.

Take another example. A monument, which is symbolically qualified and which has its foundation in free, historical form-giving, displays an objective modal time duration within historical development.[2] It does not function as a freely forming subject, but only as something *formed*, as an *object*.

But also here this objective modal time duration is strictly related to the time duration within the subjective historical consciousness, which belongs only to the human being.

5. The immanence standpoint fails to appreciate this time structure

On the immanence standpoint, where the thinking selfhood searches for its Archimedean point *within* time, it is impossible to fathom the true nature of cosmic time.

That there are constant transcendental[3] structures embedded within the cosmic horizon of time eludes the apprehension of the immanence standpoint. These constant structures make possible all subjective change and alteration in time. But this occurs only in the temporal structural coherence of all aspects taken collectively, which is never given as timeless, in themselves closed, "substances" or "forms." At most, within modern humanist philosophy, thinkers arrive at the one-sidedly rationalistic conception of time as *a piori* subjective form of sensory intuition (Kant), as a result of which they fail to recognize the many-sidedness of cosmic time, both with regard to its horizon

1 According to its (physico-chemically qualified) individuality structure as a thing, however, it does have a subjective duration within its typical time structure. Here the physico-chemical *subject-function* indeed takes on the role of the guiding, qualifying or destinational function.

2 According to its individuality structure as an entity a monument merely has *an objective* time duration, because its typical qualifying function is not subjective but objective in nature.

3 In the *Philosophy of the Cosmonomic Idea* "transcendental" always refers to that which, in the structure of cosmic time itself, forms the foundation of all of temporal reality. This foundation first makes possible the variable forms and shapes taken on by temporal reality. The transcendental temporal structure of reality points *beyond* time to its transcendent root and the Origin of creaturely reality. See my *WdW*, 1:51-53 [cf. *NC*, 1:86-88].

(or structural character), and to its factual side as "cosmic duration."

Greek metaphysics already only considered the variable sensory appearances (*phaenomena*) as being intrinsically temporal, but it reified[1] the constant structural laws of temporal reality to timeless ideas or timeless ontic forms. Before anything else this meant that what is arrived at is the theoretical absolutization of the logical structural functions of temporal reality.

The logical essence[2], so the argument went on, cannot have any *becoming* or *genesis* within time. Therefore the world of thought of necessity evinces a supra-temporal character.

From its inception this was the position taken by "realistic" metaphysics. In opposition to *nominalism* in all its nuances it clung to the objective metaphysical reality of the ideas of reason.[3]

Realistic metaphysics, which understood the so-called *objective ideas* as supra-temporal substances (*ousiai*), regardless whether or not it ascribed to them an existence prior to that of individual entities, necessarily arrived at the construction of a so-called "thing in itself," apart from subjective functions of consciousness. This construction rested upon enclosing the temporal reality of an entity within the pre-logical law-spheres as well as upon reifying the structure concept of such a thing into a supra-temporal substance.

The inner antinomy entailed in this metaphysical realistic conception becomes evident as soon as one realizes that the entire "thing in itself" with its supposed supra-temporal substance of "essential law" is nothing but the product of a subjective theoretical abstraction which in itself is possible only within the horizon of time.

1 [Dooyeweerd coined a Dutch word, *"hypostaseeren,"* (here rendered *reify*) to mean: making independent, ascribing to something the nature of a *timeless substance.*]

2 What is intended is the concept of functional or individuality structures which lie at the basis of perishable shapes or forms of temporal reality.

3 Nominalism, in all its variations, denies the reality of these universal "ideas" except within the subjective thought-function. In other words, it denies that within reality itself logical structures have an *objective* existence.

6. The expression of cosmic time within the structure of the modalities

If our temporal thought-function indeed transcended time, if it could really rise above the boundary of time, then it would have to commence with an elimination of the temporal coherence within the diversity of law-spheres.

But this attempt immediately dissolves itself in insoluble antinomies. Indeed, human thinking in all its forms presupposes this temporal coherence between the *logical* and the *non-logical* aspects.

The logical modality itself has an *immanent temporal structure*. Its irreducible nucleus, *analysis*, cannot maintain its *logical* character outside the temporal coherence with modal moments which on the one hand refer back to cosmically earlier modalities, and on the other hand point ahead to cosmically later modalities. In the second volume of my work *De Wijsbegeerte der Wetsidee* I have explained at some length this transcendental-temporal structure of the logical modality. The general theory of the law-spheres that I worked out in this volume revealed this temporal structure in all modalities or aspects of our cosmos. It was done in respect of both their *subjective* and *objective* functions.

What was the result of our analysis? It appeared that the structure of a modality, which delimits a law-sphere and guarantees its inner condition and irreducibility, displays an architectonic composition of moments. The mutual order of these moments is a reflection of the temporal succession of the law-spheres themselves.

7. The temporal structure of the modality of logical analysis

Within the comic order of time the logical law-sphere is grounded in various other law-spheres in the sense that it presupposes them.

The truly qualifying kernel or nucleus of the logical modality consists in *analysis*. Within cosmic time this original and therefore irreducible core in the first place presupposes the modality of *number*, which has as its nucleus *discrete quantity*.

Within the logical modality this temporal succession of the logical law-sphere in relation to that of number comes to expression in a moment which points *backwards* to number. We have designated it as a *retrocipation* or an *analogy* of number. This numerical analogy within the analytical is that of a logical *plurality* or *multiplicity*, which is displayed by every subjective concept as to its logical side. Every concept according to its logical aspect is a *synthēsis noemāton*, that is an *analytical unity* in the multiplicity of conceptual moments.[1]

This analogy of number cannot originate in the meaning of the logical itself, as is claimed by *logicism*. Why not? The reason is that although it appears within the logical aspect it does not belong to the original and irreducible nucleus of the logical mode. Its meaning as a multiplicity is indeed only determined by the *analytical* itself. In other words, the entire determination of multiplicity must be derived from the nucleus of the analytical, which as such presupposes discrete quantity in its original, numerical modal meaning. For multiplicity is *original* only within the meaning of number. Within the meaning of the analytical, by contrast, multiplicity only functions *analogically*, that is to say, as a moment pointing back to the nucleus of the numerical aspect. Furthermore, a numerical analogy appears not only within the logical aspect. The latter also occurs in all those law-spheres which succeed the numerical within the cosmic time-order. There is indeed a multiplicity within the meaning of space, in that of movement, in the meaning of the organic-biotic, in the meaning of feeling, in that of analysis, in the historical, in symbolical signification (language), in the economic, the aesthetic, the jural (just think of legal relationships!), and so forth and so on.

But there is only one multiplicity in its *original* meaning: namely, discrete quantity as the original and irreducible nucleus of number.

Similar to its numerical analogy, the logical mode also displays within its temporal structure analogies or retrocipations of the nuclei of space ("thought space"), of movement (the "movement of thought" with its logically earlier and later), and

---

1 Correlated to this, within the logical object-function of reality, is the objective-logical *systasis* of analytical moments.

9

so on. Within the cosmic order of time all these moments point back to earlier law-spheres.

But, one may ask, is it the case that we here indeed have a time-order? Can one not argue that a cosmological presupposition of the meaning of logical analysis is something *timeless*?

The answer is: No. One can call it timeless only by falsifying the cosmic intuition of time which lies at the basis of all logical concept formation and by entangling thought in unsolvable antinomies. Interpreting the transcendental-theoretical synthesis that lies at the basis of all thought as though it were a unity of consciousness which transcends time in its logical aspect (Kant) presupposes a primary reification of the logical modality, an act that we have identified as being in conflict with its intrinsically temporal structure. All such interpretations are possible only on the immanence standpoint. The basic antinomy entailed in its point of departure is given with its choice of Archimedean point in the theoretical *cogito* (I think). Nonetheless, this choice *presupposes* the cosmic time-order. We shall demonstrate this from yet another viewpoint.

Within the transcendental structure of the logical modality there are also moments which do not point back to aspects positioned earlier in the time-order, but which point ahead to law-spheres that appear later in the order of aspects. These moments unfold in a different direction of the cosmic time-order, and in the general theory of the law-spheres they are designated as *anticipations* of a modality.[1]

Anticipatory moments *deepen* and *disclose* a modality in approximation of later meaning-nuclei. For example, the meaning of number is deepened by the infinitesimal approximating function of so-called "irrational numbers" (such as the square root of 2, of 3, and so on), in which the nucleus of *space* – that of continuous extension – is anticipated, without ever transforming this infinite approximating function of number into the original meaning of space.

---

1 [Dooyeweerd eventually explained the inter-modal coherence between the different aspects by grouping both *retrocipations* and *anticipations* together as *analogical structural moments*. Systematically one should therefore distinguish between retrocipatory and anticipatory *analogies* (cf. NC, 2:75.)]

In the same way anticipatory moments can be found within the modality of the logical law-sphere. This shows that according to the internal time-order of this law-sphere it certainly is not the *last*, since it is followed, rather, by still *later* ones.

The general theory of the law-spheres discovered the following anticipations within the logical modality: *logical control* (historical anticipation), *logical symbolism* (lingual anticipation), *thought economy* (economic anticipation), *logical harmony* (aesthetic anticipation), the *logically legitimate ground* (jural anticipation), and so on.

Yet the question is: how do we know that these moments are indeed pointing forward in an anticipating sense rather than being retrocipating moments in cosmic time referring backwards? This is indeed a crucial point in the theory of the law-spheres. With regard to the logical modality we start out by establishing that the structure of this modality reveals itself both in *naive, pre-scientific* and in *theoretic, scientific thought*.

The analytical structure expresses itself also in the pre-scientific concepts of things, events, and so on. Pre-scientific concepts like these display all those analogical moments that we have discovered as *analogies* or *retrocipations* in the logical modality. Yet these concepts display nothing of *logical control*, of *though-economy*, of logical harmony, or a search for the *just* ground of a logical argument. It is only in *systematic theoretical thought* that the logical structure begins to unfold these anticipatory moments. Through this unfolding the meaning of the analytical mode is disclosed and deepened.

This disclosure concerns the nucleus of the analytical aspect and all its analogies. Thus the logical structure can express itself both in a not-yet-disclosed form and in a disclosed and deepened shape. All those non-original moments which are necessarily contained in the first mentioned form of the logical structure are of an *analogical* or *retrocipatory* nature. By contrast, all the non-original moments that come to expression only in the *disclosed* or *deepened* meaning of the logical are of an *anticipatory* or forward-pointing character.

Remark: *on the misconception regarding a Christian logic*

Once one has really understood this insight into the transcendental temporal structure of the logical aspect, which is rooted in the Christian transcendent starting-point of the *Philosophy of the Cosmonomic Idea*, one also starts to realize what this philosophy has in mind when it speaks about a *Christian logic*.

Speaking about the "necessity of a Christian logic" also within our own circles caused much controversy because it was not immediately clear what the meaning of this statement might be. One could already hear people drawing the presumptuous and absurd conclusion that this new philosophy would postulate totally different structural laws for logical thinking than those generally accepted until now.

Of course the truth is that the structural laws for logical thinking cannot be dependent upon the vantage point from which they are investigated. Only the *theoretical insight* gained into the nature of these structural laws – and along with it *theoretical logic* itself – is completely determined by the choice of an Archimedean point.

On the immanence standpoint the structure of logical thinking is conceived as something timeless, as being separated from its coherence with the other aspects of the cosmos. In this way a so-called "pure, formal" logic emerges which is often interpreted in such a way that its *principles* acquire a false theoretical bent. This issue is discussed in Vollenhoven's essay *De Noodzakelijkheid eener Christelijke Logica*.[1]

In my work *De Wijsbegeerte der Wetsidee*[2] I have explained the sense in which alone a so-called "formal logic" ought to be understood from a Christian standpoint. On the immanence standpoint it is inevitable that the transcendental structure of the logical is absolutized, for without making it independent, that is, without this primary absolutization, the immanence standpoint cannot maintain itself.

A Christian approach discloses a particular insight into the many-sided determination of the thought-structure by the *temporal order* of reality. It turns out that, in the anticipatory direction of time,[3] logical thinking necessarily functions under the guidance

---

1 [D. H. Th. Vollenhoven, *De Noodzakelijkheid eener Christelijke Logica* [The necessity of a Christian logic] (Amsterdam: H. J. Paris, 1932), pp. viii, 110. See also Vollenhoven's later, book-length treatment of "Hoofdlijnen der Logica" [Outline of logic] in *Phil. Ref.* 13 (1948): 59-118.]

2 *WdW*, 2:397-98 [cf. *NC*, 2:464-65].

3 The Philosophy of the Law-Idea calls this direction of time the "transcendental" direction because it points beyond time to the Root and Origin of all temporal meaning.

of *faith* and that in the final analysis logical thinking too proceeds from the religious root of human existence, from the *heart* in the biblical sense of the term.

Those who are of the opinion that it is possible, on a Christian standpoint, to defend the *neutrality* of the *theory of logic*, will have to reconsider their position as soon as they engage in a serious study of the extremely divergent conceptions about the character and limits of formal logic. (Just compare the position of Aristotle with that of the modern discipline of logic!) And they should particularly be careful not to confuse the universally valid structure of logical thinking with its theoretical interpretation. This confusion also caused tremendous misunderstanding with regard to the effects of sin upon human thinking.

The conviction that human thought was excluded from the fall into sin is clearly in conflict with the Bible – to such an extent, in fact, that it is hardly conceivable that someone would defend it from a Scriptural standpoint. The statement by Paul regarding man's "fleshly mind" (Col. 2:18) must prevent this misconception.

It is also mistaken to attribute this conception to Kuyper, for no one opposed it more vehemently than he did with his much disputed theory concerning the relation between regeneration and scholarship. *The Philosophy of the Cosmonomic Idea* made this conviction its own starting-point.

Kuyper certainly did not mean to claim that the structure of logical thinking is abolished or changed in principle. This is only correct. Whoever would accept that would no longer be able to speak about sinful thinking, for fallen thinking is only possible within the constant structure of the logical thought-function. Christians therefore do not respond to a kind of *esoteric* logical laws for thinking that would not also apply to non-Christians and which would in principle have to remain hidden to the latter. Together with those who do not share in regeneration, Christians are enclosed within the same temporal world- order. They do not have a monopoly on doing science. Yet the insight of Christians into the temporal order is disclosed by the divine Word-revelation which also determines their conception of the theory of logic.

Indeed, a difference in principle between a truly Christian and a non-Christian attitude manifests itself not only in the *theory* of so-called formal logic, which aims at theoretical insight into and scientific interpretation of logical principles. The difference should also become manifest in the manner in which we are subjectively involved in certain fields of investigation by means of logical thinking.

13

In the second and third volume of my *Wijsbegeerte der Wetsidee* I have demonstrated this extensively with regard to the method of concept formation. The cosmonomic idea from which one consciously or unconsciously proceeds makes a huge difference with regard to the method of forming concepts. For example, when one assumes a purely logical origin of the concepts of number and space, then of necessity one logically relativizes the modal boundaries of meaning between these two aspects of our temporal cosmos, for then in an a priori sense one will be not inclined to settle for the implicit theoretical antinomies and prefer to be satisfied with pseudo-solutions for them.

Consequently, one should not consider the peculiar method of concept formation postulated by the *Philosophy of the Cosmonomic Idea* as an idle play with words. For example, this philosophy opposes the traditional manner in which the jural is distinguished from other normative areas according to the method of looking for a higher logical concept (the so-called *genus proximum*), that is supposed to encompass all of these areas, followed by determining the specific differences (*differentia specifica*) obtaining between law, social norms, morality and so on.

For that matter, this philosophy did not simply postulate its own Christian method of concept formation. It dedicated an important part of its philosophical labor to an elaboration of this method and *demonstrated* how an alternative starting-point affects the very method of scientific thinking in a practical way.

8.   The urge towards the Origin of all temporality

Thus the cosmic order of time, according to its two basic directions – the foundational or retrocipatory direction and the forward-pointing or anticipatory direction – comes to expression in the very structure of the modalities, while their nuclei express the *boundary point* or *criterion* of these two directions of time (the present as boundary between the earlier and later). An understanding of this state of affairs turns out to be of tremendous importance for Christian thought.

For it is in this context that we understand also philosophically what those believers who are secured in Christ can know with absolute certainty in the light of God's Word: namely, that there is nothing within time in which the heart can come to rest, because whatever is embraced by time does not rest in itself but points above and beyond itself, in a dynamic restlessness, to the creaturely – in truth *transcendent* – Root and the eternal, self-sufficient Origin of all things.

For the entire view of cosmic time in which every modality, in complete non-self-sufficiency, points backwards and forwards to all the other modalities, and in the final limiting aspect of temporal meaning, that of faith, points beyond time itself, is only possible on a scripturally Christian standpoint which reveals to us every absolutization of temporal, creaturely meaning as sinful apostasy from the true God – as idolatry.

Not until we adopt this standpoint do we experience, also in philosophy, that powerful urge in all temporality towards the Origin, an urge that is concentrated religiously in our heart, whence are the issues of life according to the testimony of Scripture.[1] And only in Christ Jesus, the new Root of Creation, does this restless striving after the Origin acquire its direction towards the only true God who has revealed himself in his Word.

Theoretical thought which has fallen away from its true Origin in idolatry – the "fleshly mind" in Paul's sense – searches within time for a self-sufficient point of rest. It performs this search on the basis of an absolutization which sets apart theoretical thought in its transcendental structure by lifting it out of its cosmic coherence without realizing that this transcendental structure lies at the basis of all real thinking in the sense of making it possible.

This concludes our elucidation of the basic antinomy of this immanent standpoint. We shall now turn our attention to the contradictions entailed in the conception of time that flows from this basic antimony. In the present context a single example will have to do.

9. The inner antinomies of the Eleatic concept of being in connection with a denial of the temporal structure of space. Spatial simultaneity

Parmenides already realized that when the essence of reality, the being of what is, has to be viewed as completely *timeless*, then one must also exclude the whole temporal diversity and coherence from this metaphysical concept of being. Since this

---

1   [Cf. Prov. 4:23.]

15

a-temporal being can only be grasped by theoretical thought in its logical structure, it cannot have a character distinct from this thought. Thus he teaches that "thought and being are identical" (Diels-Kranz, 1960, B. Fr. 3). This concept of being is absolute, supra-temporal, without becoming, imperishable, without multiplicity or movement – it is one continuum.

It is obvious that this concept of being would dissolve itself in a logical nothingness if its postulated self-sufficiency were to be taken seriously. In itself it is purely *negative*; it avoids all positive content. It even avoids *logical multiplicity* which alone makes possible *logical unity* and with it the nature of a concept as such. That is to say that it indeed entails the eradication of the meaning of analysis itself, because no analysis is possible without an analytical multiplicity which has to be gathered into the unity of a concept.

An *absolute unity* lacking all multiplicity is the negation of all logical meaning. Yet, already the negative predicates employed by Parmenides establish an *immanent relation* with *multiplicity*, *movement*, and so on – and in a deeper sense with *time* itself.

The statement: "only *absolute being* is" presupposes the analytical *principium identitatis*, which can only maintain its relative temporal character, its meaning, in coherence with the *principium contradictionis* and the *principium rationis sufficientis* (the principle of contradiction and the principle of sufficient reason). In addition, logical identity displays its identity only within *logical diversity*, just as logical unity is nothing but the *unity* of a *logical multiplicity*.

Parmenides, as we know, did not stop at his logically negative predication of his concept of being. The "timeless being" is identified by him with spherical *filled space*, an everywhere dense and limited continuum.

However, we have noted that cosmic time has a universal structure that embraces all law-spheres and functions in each law-sphere in a peculiar modality. Within the law-sphere of number it expresses itself in a *quantitative earlier and later* which determines the position of each number in the succession of numbers. And in the original modality of space, cosmic time comes to

16

expression as *spatial simultaneity*.[1] Thus, the conception of an a-temporal space lacking all multiplicity is *internally antinomic*. Space does not exist without an analogy of number and without the simultaneity of a spatial multiplicity. Every subjective spatial figure displays an inner multiplicity in the sense of continuous extension and can exist only in a simultaneous extension of this multiplicity. A straight line already presupposes a spatial multiplicity as it is bounded by two points. Even a point, although it lacks actual extension, is not defined except through the intersection of two simultaneously extended straight lines or curves.

Thus, by identifying *being* with the spherical shape of a limited and fully filled space Parmenides in any case abolishes the predicate *timelessness*. The "eternity" and "immobility" of his concept of being in a positive sense indeed is nothing but that of *simultaneity*, the *at once* in the *modal meaning of space*. As the Eleatic thinker expresses it: "It [i.e., *being*] was never and never will be, because it is all of this simultaneously in the present as one and indivisible." [B Fr. 8:3–6]

Zeno, the pupil of Parmenides, follows his teacher in his attempt to demonstrate the impossibility of continuous temporal succession. He does that with the aid of his famous paradoxes, which identify continuous temporal succession with *motion*. His argumentation dissolves temporal succession into moments of time which he deems *timeless* but in reality identifies with *static spatial points* that are given *at once* without any true succession. Zeno adopts the three time phases of past, present and future, first theoretically distinguished by Parmenides, and he agrees with his teacher that only the present fits metaphysical *being*.[2] This stance actually disproves the claim that this concept of being is *timeless*, since *spatial simultaneity* is not timeless, but rather presupposes *cosmic time*.

1 This naturally cancels the traditional *coordination* of space and time. Time belongs to a deeper layer of reality than space, because it expresses itself in the latter as one of its *modalities*.

2 Cf. Werner Gent, *Das Problem der Zeit. Eine historische und systematische Untersuchung*, (Frankfurt am Main, 1934); J. A. Gunn, *The Problem of Time* (London, 1929), pp. 18 ff.

Furthermore, the modal meaning of space contains anticipations of the nucleus of motion. Under the guidance of the latter these anticipations of motion are disclosed whenever a projectile travels through space. Such anticipations of movement within the modal meaning of space, which never actually take on the original meaning of motion, are systematically investigated by two sub-disciplines of modern mathematics: projective geometry and group theory.

Thus, through his identification of metaphysical *being* with the spherically limited and everywhere dense space, Parmenides implicitly relativizes his concept of being in terms of movement, which he actually, as a logical *nothing*, explicitly wanted to exclude from his concept of being.

Heraclitus had indeed absolutized the aspect of motion of temporal reality to be the metaphysical essence of reality. Parmenides, by contrast, in his metaphysical concept of being absolutizes *static space*.

When Parmenides' pupil Zeno attempts to demonstrate the logical nothingness of multiplicity and movement, he actually does no more than provide a strict proof for the *irreducibility* of the original meaning of space to that of *number* and *movement*. But implicitly he also demonstrates the inner antinomies entailed in a reification of the modality of space to the root of reality which transcends the temporal coherence. Thus the attempt to demonstrate the logical nothingness of time, with the diversity and coherence entailed in it, definitively failed.

Subsequent philosophical developments had to abandon this negative assessment of time. Whoever traces the history up to the most recent times (to Einstein, Bergson and Heidegger) will have to acknowledge the correctness of our contention that it is impossible for the immanence standpoint to grasp the cosmic universality of the horizon of time and the many-sidedness of its aspects. The latter constantly drives theoretical thinking into a position where it encloses the horizon of time within one or another aspect. This occurs invariably, whether a Newton defends a purely *objectivistic* notion of time or a Berkeley and Bergson hold to a purely *subjectivistic* conception, that is to say, whether time is conceived as *order* or merely as *subjective duration*, as an *actual state* or merely as an *ordering form* for *sensory impressions of consciousness*.

But this only ensures that the problem of time at once turns into a veritable wellspring of all the antinomies which continue to characterize the course of development of immanence philosophy.

The *Philosophy of the Cosmonomic Idea* holds that the origin of these antinomies is grounded in the basic antinomy of the immanence standpoint itself. And this deepest origin is not philosophic but *religious* in nature.

10. Eternity, time and *aevum*

Thus far in our treatment of the problem of time and its antinomies on the immanence standpoint, our aim has been to show that the philosophical problem of time is inextricably linked to one's conception regarding the structure of reality. What is more, both the philosophical conception of time and that of reality truly reflect one's choice of an Archimedean point within the cosmonomic idea lying at the foundation of these views.

The problem of time lies on a much deeper and more fundamental level than that of space – with which it was associated for a long time without sufficient justification. Time indeed concerns the entire structure of the cosmos and of the horizon of human experience. It entails the basic question at what point human consciousness *transcends* the horizon of time. For without this transcendence time cannot be made a philosophical problem.

If we did not transcend time at the deepest concentration point of our existence, our consciousness of necessity would be exhausted by time, which would cancel the possibility of *religious self-concentration*. The *problem* of time would have been unknown to us, because time essentially only becomes a problem to us if we are able to take distance from it in what is supra-temporal, which we experience in the deepest core of our being. Only because eternity (the *aevum*) has been laid in the human

19

heart,[1] notwithstanding the fact that the entire functional "mantle"[2] is contained within time, is it possible for human beings to have an *awareness* of time. If being human were fully absorbed by time, such an awareness of time would have been lacking.

Yet, the supra-temporal concentration point in human self-consciousness, which can only actualize itself in the religious concentration of all our functions on eternity, should not itself be called *eternal*.

Since my conception gave rise to much misunderstanding regarding this point, it is necessary to explain it in more detail.

Already in Christian synthesis philosophy of the patristic and scholastic era it was realized that one has to accept an intermediate position between time and eternity. The *created eternity* (*aeternitas creata*) was designated with the term *aevum*.

This concept was introduced by Boethius in his *Consolatio philosophiae*, and Thomas Aquinas gave an elaboration of it in his *Summa Theologica*,[3] concurring in the main with the conception of Siger of Brabant.[4]

It must be remembered that Thomas Aquinas – in following Aristotle – conceived time only as the *measure of movement*. He distinguishes also between *actual* motion and *potential* motion (*movability*).[5] His predecessors defined the *aevum* as the "measure of the spiritual substances."[6] Some of them applied the following criterion in order to distinguish between time and eternity: time has a beginning and an end; eternity lacks both; the

---

1 For the moment I leave aside the question whether or not the well-known text from Eccl. 3:11 ought to be understood in this sense. The entire Bible teaches us that the consciousness of eternity forms part of the created nature of the human heart.
2 [This is one of the few places where Dooyeweerd uses the term *"functiemantel"* which is basic to the anthropology of his close colleague Vollenhoven. Tol/Kok translate it as: "the entire cloak of the functions."]
3 Thomas Aquinas, *Summa Theologiae*, I, Q. 10, artt. 5 and 6.
4 Compare Werner Gent, *Das Problem der Zeit* 1934, p.7, and *Die Philosophie des Raumes und Zeit*, 1926, p.60.
5 Ibid., I, Q. 10, Art. 4.
6 Ibid., I, Q. 10, Art. 5.

aevum does have a beginning but no end. Thomas did not consider this distinction to be essential, but merely accidental.[1]

Others located the difference between time and eternity in that eternity lacks an earlier or later while time does display an earlier or later, accompanied by renewal and ageing, while the *aevum* knows an earlier and later without innovation and ageing (*"prius et posterius sine innovatione et veteratione"*).

According to Thomas this position is contradictory because "earlier and later" entails renewal.[2] His own conception assumes that eternity is the *measure of steady and enduring being* (*"mensura esse permanentis"*). The reason why some creatures lack eternity is because their essence (*esse*) is subject to change (*transmutatio*) or because they are constituted by change. These creatures are measured by time, as is the case with the movements as well as the essence of all corruptible things. Others are less far removed from the *permanent essence* (*permanentia essendi*) because their essences exist neither in change nor in being subject to change. However, they do have, whether actually or potentially, an adjunct transmutation, i.e., an accidental "added" change. These creatures are subject to measurement in a dual sense: with regard to their essential nature (*esse naturale*) they are measured by the *aevum* and in respect of their "*transmutatio adjuncta*" by time.

Thomas calls these creatures "*aeviterna*" and limits them to celestial bodies and angels. Celestial bodies cannot change except in their position; angels can change not only in their position but also in their emotions and insights which display succession.

In the meantime it does not seem doubtful that Thomas must apply the *aevum* also to the "*anima intellectiva*" (intellectual soul) of the human ontic form. After all, time for him is restricted to

---

1 Ibid. In Art. 4 a similar argumentation is pursued in order to demonstrate that the criterion for distinguishing between time and eternity, according to which time has both a beginning and an end and eternity lacks both, merely concerns an accidental difference. For even if time were without a beginning and an end, as it is taught by those who hold on to the mistaken teaching that the movement of celestial bodies is lasting for ever, then the difference between time and eternity would still be valid. Boethius is correct in pointing this out in his *De consolatione phil.* (4, 5). Indeed, eternity as *mensura esse permanentis*, as Boethius holds, is a *tota simul* (all at once), which is a property not applicable to time as *mensura motus* (temporal measure). Time always has a succession of moments.

2 Ibid.

21

bodily movement, whereas the human *essence*, as immaterial form, is not subject to change. Furthermore, *reason*, as Aristotle taught, in deviation from the material substantial forms, is implanted by God into the body from *the outside* and is therefore not indissolubly connected with matter.

Thomas Aquinas summarizes his view regarding the relation between time, eternity and *aevum* as follows: Time has an earlier and later; the *aevum*, however, does not have an earlier and later, although it can be connected to it; eternity neither has an earlier and later, nor is it compatible with it.[1]

11. The meaning of the *aevum* in the *Philosophy of the Cosmonomic Idea*

It is now clear that this conception of the *aevum* stands in an immediate relation to the Aristotelian understanding of eternity and time as well as with his conception of "soul" and "body." If time is merely the measure of movement, then the *"animae intellectivae"* as such – i.e., according to their essence – cannot be subject to time.

The Christian transcendence standpoint can hardly accept this view, because it cannot position the center of human nature in *"reason"* and consequently cannot conceive of the human soul – the "inner person" or the "heart" of human existence – as a reification of a functional complex that is abstracted from the temporal cosmic coherence of aspects.

Yet I would like to take over the term *"aevum"* in the sense of an intermediate state between time and eternity. It may be less objectionable because it arose within the context of a Christian world of thought which felt the need for a distinction between the supra-temporal in a creaturely sense and eternity in the sense of the being of God.

In human self-consciousness as center of the religious concentration of all temporal functions we indeed encounter the supra-temporal meaning of this *aevum*. As an *actual condition* the *aevum* therefore is nothing but the creaturely concentration of the temporal upon eternity in the religious transcendence of the boundary of time.

---

1   Ibid. It appears from Art. 6 that Thomas assumes just one *aevum* for all spiritual substances. These substances partake of eternity in the *"visio gloriae."*

With eternity laid in the heart of the human being, this *aevum* condition inherently belongs to the created structure of the human selfhood. It has to be actualized each time our self-consciousness becomes active in religious concentration, even if this *aevum*-consciousness manifests itself in an apostate direction owing to attempts to search for the eternal in time. The absolutization of what is temporal is indeed possible only in the religious transcendence of the time limit, even though this transcending, as concentration of temporal functions, maintains its bond with time as the boundary. In this life the *aevum* condition therefore remains bound to time. To speculate about the *aevum* condition at the separation of soul and body, or with regard to angels, is fruitless in a philosophical sense. It would be, in Calvin's phrase, a *"meteorica et vacua speculatio,"*[1] because it concerns "mysteries" that are not yet revealed to us. All our representations, concepts and ideas in this life are bound to time and even our self-consciousness, although it transcends time in the *aevum*, remains focused on the horizon of time.

12. The horizon of time on the immanence standpoint

We have seen that the immanence standpoint in philosophical thinking necessarily leads to a position in which the transcending concentration point of human consciousness is sought within the temporal horizon of our cosmos itself.

The possibility of finding the Archimedean point within theoretical thought itself is fully dependent upon the possibility entailed in our theoretical thought activity to transcend the cosmic horizon of time. If indeed theoretical thought as such is completely embraced by the horizon of time and within this time horizon is indissolubly intertwined with all non-logical aspects of reality, then it cannot be determined by its logical structure alone but much rather by the temporal world-order.[2] The postulate of the inner self-sufficiency of theoretical thought as Archimedean point of philosophy can then no longer be maintained and with it immanence philosophy loses its foundation.

---

1 [*Institutes* 1.10.2.]

2 This is altogether different from Kant's acknowledgment that our (in themselves timeless) thought categories are necessarily *geared to*, and so are *restricted to*, a merely sensory horizon of time.

Understandably, traditional philosophy constantly attempted to delimit the time problem in a functionalist manner. Time and again it mistook universal cosmic time, which expresses itself at once in all modal aspects of reality because it provides the foundation for them all, for *one* of these modal aspects of time.[1]

Indeed, theoretical thought as such remains enclosed within the modal diversity (the "modal horizon") of the cosmos. Since it is itself characterized by logical meaning it cannot transcend this diversity and can therefore conceptualize cosmic time only in its modal aspects.

Cosmic time in its supra-modal continuity allows theoretical thought to form only a transcendental *idea* of it – i.e., to arrive at knowledge of it that transcends the limits of concept-formation.[2] Such a transcendental idea must remain theoretically open because it is nothing but an approximation of and reference to the supra-modal time horizon within the modal boundaries of the logical. It represents the critical direction of the movement of thought towards its cosmic time-limit. It is no longer possible to define the latter in a theoretical-logical way.

A theoretical *concept* of time therefore always remains restricted to the modal aspects of time. Thus the initial absolutization of a theoretical abstraction, basic to all immanence phi-

---

1 Only after completing my work *De Wijsbegeerte der Wetsidee* (1935-1936) did I learn of the above-mentioned work by Werner Gent, *Das Problem der Zeit*. I am thankful to note that Gent presents the rich modal diversity of time in a manner similar to my own conception. However, the reader will immediately realize that it lacks the *core* of my conception of time: the cosmic structure of time in its modalities, of which the deeper unity is guaranteed by the idea of time. Gent actually did nothing more than trace the various temporal modalities as they unfolded historically in the distinct conceptions of time of philosophers. But he did that without coming to a closer reflection upon what this meant. His approach therefore did not provide a new basis for the problem of time.

2 [In this context the Dutch and German languages employ the terms "*grensbegrip*" and "*Grenzbegriff*." Literally translated it ought to be rendered as a *limiting concept*. Yet, what is actually intended is not what falls within the limits of a concept, but a kind of knowledge transcending the limits of concept-formation. For that reason it would seem more appropriate to translate the Dutch word "*grensbegrip*" with the phrase "*concept-transcending knowledge*." Cf. D. F. M. Strauss, *Philosophy: Discipline of the Disciplines* (Grand Rapids: Paideia Press, 2009), p. 430, et passim.]

24

losophy, blocks any insight into the cosmic horizon of time. On this standpoint an *idea* of time can only end up being modally enclosed[1] and so lead to the absolutization of a modal concept of time that entangles thought in antinomies which by themselves follow from every theoretical over-extension of a modally delimited concept.

It is then dependent upon a more precise specification of the cosmonomic idea to determine which particular direction will be taken by the philosophy of time on the immanence standpoint.

13. Once again the distinction between time as structural order and time as subjective duration

Thus far we have sharply distinguished between the cosmic order of time as structural law of all temporal reality, and the subjective temporal duration which is correlated with this time-order, in the sense that the latter delimits and determines whatever is subjected to it. At the same time we observed that, in respect of the unbreakable correlation of law and subject, the law-side of time does not have any meaning or reality without the subject-side, and vice versa.

Also in its philosophy of time immanence philosophy is driven, now to the extreme of absolutizing the law-side of time, then again to the absolutization of its subject-side. In the former case we speak of a *rationalist* conception of time and in the second case of an *irrationalist* one. Newton's conception of absolute time in the sense of a mathematical *"ordo successionis"* is an example of the former, while Bergson's understanding of time as absolute psychical *"durée"* or *"evolution créatrice"* and Spengler's view of time as historical *"Schicksal"* (fate) are examples of the latter.

Furthermore, within immanence philosophy both a metaphysical and a merely phenomenal conception of time are possible. The former assigns to time, whether taken in a rationalist or

---

1   This applies equally to a theory of time and a theory of reality which, as is the case with Aristotle, orients itself entirely to the metaphysical concept of substance in an attempt to eliminate the modal horizon altogether. In the end, after all, the "substantial forms," at least in respect of their *genus*, remain modally determined. See below, sec. 23.

irrationalist sense, an *essential* character that determines the nature of reality. The second, by contrast, considers time to be restricted to the *world of phenomena*, behind which the existence of a timeless true reality may or may not be assumed. Within this contrast it is possible to discern further conceptions of time by distinguishing between subjectivistic and objectivistic views.

14. The subject-object relation in the order of time in its inter-modal and modal structure

These different views can only become clear when we focus upon the cosmic subject-object relation which has been subjected to an extensive analysis by the *Philosophy of the Cosmonomic Idea*. This relation reveals itself in all those aspects whose modal structures contain analogies of earlier aspects.

Since a model object-function of reality is nothing but the objectification of modal functions of *earlier* aspects appearing in *later* ones, it follows that cosmic time itself comes to expression in these modal subject-object relations.[1] his consideration explains why things and events that have, say, only an object-function within the sensitive-psychical aspect also display only an objective temporal duration within this aspect. Although this objective duration is necessarily correlated with subjective temporal duration within this aspect, it ought to be strictly distinguished from possible sensations.

It is in no way possible to reduce this objective temporal duration to the subjective temporal duration of sensations correlated with it, even though objective temporal duration exists only in connection with *possible* subjective sensations. Its objectivity within cosmic time is grounded in a subjective time duration that applies to the perceived thing or event in an earlier law-sphere in which it functions as a subject.

This *inter*-modal subject-object relation within temporal duration, which embraces at least two different modal aspects, must be distinguished sharply from the *intra*-modal subject-object relation that appears within the structure of a single aspect. Both

---

1   At the same time, modal object-functions themselves may disclose objective *anticipations* of later modal functions of reality.

these relations are determined by the comic time-order as structural law.

15. Subjectivistic and objectivistic time conceptions

Immanence philosophy entirely eliminates the inter-modal subject-object relation in the temporal duration of an observed thing or event. Since this relation can be understood from the cosmic horizon of time only, it is from the outset disregarded on the immanence standpoint. The effect is that on the immanence standpoint any adequate insight into the intra-modal subject-object relation is also precluded.

With regard to the latter relation there are two options: either one attempts to reduce objective time duration completely to subjective duration, or one attempts to come to a complete separation of the two, thus depriving objective duration of its *relative* character.

In the case where a subjectivistic conception of time may want to escape from an irrationalist and fully skeptical time-phenomenalism, or from an irrationalist, mystical time-metaphysics, an attempt could be made to provide a foundation for objective time duration of perceived sensory objects in a mathematical or psychical law-conformity of the subjective sensation – in which case, however, subjective consciousness itself has to be raised to the status of law-giver. This then is a rationalist form of a subjectivistic conception of time: object and law are identified and both are traced back to the knowing subject as law-giver.

16. The influence of a modal basic denominator for the diversity upon the conception of time

Finally, the choice made on the immanence standpoint with regard to the basic philosophical denominator in terms of which the attempt is made to conceive all of temporal reality in its deeper unity and mode of being will of course also influence its conceptions of time. Therefore the well-known *isms* – such as mathematicism, mechanicism, biologism, psychologism, and historicism – will manifest themselves also in the various time conceptions.

Depending for a good deal upon the question whether or not immanence philosophy has engaged in any critical self-reflection, it may subsume *all* aspects of reality under one absolutized aspect, or, alternatively, it may limit time to a so-called *phenomenal* world while assigning certain aspects (such as the mathematical, logical, ethical and aesthetical) to a supra-temporal *"noumenal"* world.

17. The uncritical character of theoretically dissolving human self-consciousness in time

The denial of every possibility of transcending time in human self-consciousness always rests on a lack of a truly critical assessment of the problem of time. We have seen that the problem presupposes this possibility.

If the Archimedean point of philosophy is indeed to be found in human "reason," then a properly critical consideration of the consequences of such a starting-point will hardly escape from being trapped in the metaphysical distinction between a supra-temporal *noumenon* and a temporal *phenomenon*.

18. The dialectical nature of the time problem on the immanence standpoint. The dialectics of reason and decision making

Ever since Parmenides and Heraclitus, philosophical thinking has never managed to free itself from the old dialectical problem of the relation between *being* and *becoming*. Essentially this was the problem of time itself: the relation between temporality and what is supra-temporal. This problem acquires its *dialectical character* as a result of the attempt, either to transcend the boundary of time in *thought* by viewing "reason" as the synthesis of time and eternity, through which both in a deeper sense were drawn onto the same level; or else to separate time and eternity absolutely, in the sense advanced by Kierkegaard. The latter completely negates the creational link between the horizon of time and the transcendent horizon of God's revelation. The result is either *"Vernunftdialektik"* (the dialectic of reason) or existential *"Entscheidungsdialektik"* (the dialectic of decision-making).

Meanwhile we should remember that the dialectical ground-motive itself drives the conceptions of time of immanence philosophy from the one extreme to the other, such that in a deeper sense they are linked together.

19. Kant's conception of time is entirely contained within the boundaries of his "*Vernunftdialektik*"

In order to explain this dialectical ground-motive in Kant's philosophy of time a brief overview is required of the state in which Kant encountered the problem of time. Despite Heidegger's attempt to interpret Kant's conception of time in the first edition of his *Critique of Pure Reason* as an "existential time dialectics," it needs no argument that Kant's thought harbors only a "*Vernunftdialektik*." We can also leave aside the fact that Heidegger's time metaphysics is foreign to Kierkegaard's semi-Christian "leap of faith" across time's "boundary line of death" into the wholly other *Jenseits*. Kant's conception of time remains completely within the traditional opposition between *phaenomenon* and *noumenon*.

20. The dialectical tension between science ideal and personality ideal in the humanistic philosophy of time

The particular direction taken by this philosophy of time in a deeper sense is determined by the philosophical ground-idea of humanistic thought. Within it the time problem evinces the tension between the personality ideal and the science ideal. The personality ideal acts as the dialectical pole of the awareness of transcendence, of the religious experience of the supra-temporal, of freedom in its opposition to the limited horizon of time. By contrast, the science ideal is the counterpole of the awareness of being bound to time; it constitutes immanence in time, the lack of freedom in the face of the all-determinative law of causality, notwithstanding the fact that the origin of this law is sought in "reason" which is the supra-temporal sovereign of time. As long as this "reason," as center of the free personality, is still concentrated in theoretical thought, the science ideal maintains its primacy, with the effect that the personality ideal can only operate within the boundaries of the science ideal.

It was under the primacy of the science ideal in the rationalistic types of humanistic philosophy since Descartes that a conception oriented to the natural sciences acquired the upper hand.

Initially the problem of time did not occupy a place of central significance in humanistic thought. Particularly in the thought of Descartes and in the philosophy of Spinoza, who is only methodologically connected to the new humanistic mode of thought, the problem was entirely pushed into the background.

The basic principles of Descartes' mechanics were not yet adapted to the method introduced by Galileo. They were constructed in an aprioristic mathematical manner,[1] and they lack the unbreakable connection between mathematics and experiment – although Descartes did not want to eliminate observation. Yet his thought is thoroughly permeated by the new science ideal, which assumed in his thought a mathematical mechanistic form.

If one merely takes notice of the terminology one could come to the conclusion that Descartes simply took over the well-established Aristotelian definition of time as it was accepted by Scholasticism: time is the measure or number of movement according to an order of earlier and later.[2]

21. The influence of the new substance concept on the humanistic conception of time

In the meantime the interpretation of this definition is immediately affected by the *new metaphysical substance concept* which shares no more than the name with the Aristotelian-Scholastic concept. The latter was teleologically conceived as an inner metaphysical unity of *form* and *matter* which is realized in an individual thing. In the pre-Kantian phase of humanistic philosophy, however, the substance concept was entirely oriented to the mathematical science ideal. This science ideal could only de-

---

1   Cf. *Discours de la Méthode*, Part 6 (*Oeuvres choisies*, Paris, p. 48: "... and it appears to me that, in this way, I have found heavens, stars, and earth, and even on the earth, water, air, fire, minerals, and some other things of this kind, which of all others are the most common and simple, and therefore the easiest to know." All of this is supposed to be derived from a few known *a priori* principles!

2   Aristotle, *Phys.* IV, 11, 219 b 2.

clare war on the Aristotelian-Scholastic theory of the *"formae substantiales"* (form substances).[1]

The humanistic substance concept was simply an over-extension of the method of mathematical natural science in order to have it serve as a cosmological method for constructing reality. This method left no room for the idea of an inner teleological structure. The new causality concept of physics was essentially a *modal concept of function* which brings to expression the external lawful relations of things in the sense of a strictly mathematical equivalence of their changes which are interpreted in a mechanistic way.

Remark: *about Kant's substance concept*

Apparently this is entirely overlooked by the Thomist, P. Hoenen, in his work *Philosophie der anorganische natuur* (1938, pp. 165 ff.) where he argues against the category of substance in Kant's philosophy. Hoenen considers it to be the *fate* of Kant that he did not know Aristotle and Scholasticism, otherwise he would never have claimed that all change is purely accidental and that substance is what remains the same under all changes.

However, Kant undoubtedly did know the Aristotelian substance concept, but he had to reject it on principle, just as all his humanistic predecessors did, since their substance concept was also oriented to the new science ideal.

From his claim that substantial change is impossible it is clear that Kant's substance concept is essentially intended as a modal function concept. He does not deal with individual "substances" but instead with "matter" as functionally lawful coherence of physical relations. What was at stake here for Kant was not the inner structure of things, but their external physical coherence.

Taken by itself this substance concept surely is not a "false principle," as Hoenen asserts. Only its rationalist conception, and in relation to that its absolutization by neglecting the individuality structure of things, made the function concept problematic for modern physics.

It is actually the main shortcoming of the Aristotelian-Thomistic nature philosophy that it dissolves the modal aspects of reality in a theory of substances which as such can never account for the modal structure of reality. As a consequence it also cannot do justice to the individuality structures of reality as I

---

1 I have shown at some length in *WdW*, 1:178–217 [*NC*, 1:223–60] that even Leibniz in no way went back to this conception.

have shown in Volume III of my work *De Wijsbegeerte der Wetsidee*.[1]

Carrying through this causality concept required that one had to abstract completely from the inner individuality structure of things subsumed under this concept of causality. A thing or entity had to be resolved into a mathematical physical function. The new substance concept as applied to "material things" was nothing but a metaphysical absolutization of the modern concept of function, turned into the *noumenal essence* of corporeal reality.

That this new functionalistic causality concept of substance entails an essentially new perspective on the problem of time speaks for itself. Because the Scholastic idea of causality took the Scholastic substance concept as its point of orientation, it essentially displayed a metaphysical teleological character. In terms of this approach, time was seen as the measure of movement, and in general as the measure of the internal movement of things – from potentiality to actuality. It was only toward the end of the Middle Ages that the nominalistic school in Paris developed a Scholastic mechanistic concept of time. But this modern branch of the Scholastic understanding of time is by no means the traditional line of thought. The latter maintained the teleological concept of causality and the substance concept. In this context "movement" is not understood in terms of the modal aspect of movement, since it is taken as *concrete* "natural" movement or as motion according to the inner essential nature of things. This *natural motion* has a final, teleological character: it concerns the structural development of things from potentiality to actuality, from potency to ripened form.

The conception of time of the humanistic science ideal, by contrast, is completely oriented to the modern *functionalist* concept of causality and substance. Any hint of an inner teleological development from potency to actuality is removed from it. The time conception of mathematical physics is here elevated to be the cosmological conception of time. To the extent that humanist philosophers increasingly become aware of the connection between the time conception and the functional causality con-

1 [See *WdW*, 3:151–54 (*NC*, 3:218–22, 707–13). Today, see also *Reformation and Scholasticism in Philosophy*, 2:323–41.]

cept, largely under the influence of the new natural-scientific method founded by Galileo, the problem of time acquires a more central place.

The question whether, on this standpoint, philosophers consider time to belong to the *noumenal essence* of reality or merely ascribe to it a phenomenal character, and whether they conceive of time in a subjectivistic or objectivistic frame of mind, is dependent in the first place upon their conception of the actual substance of "natural reality," that is, upon their choice of basic philosophical denominator for their theory of reality.

That Descartes denies the metaphysical nature of time by ascribing to it only a *modus cogitandi*,[1] is directly connected to his view that the material substance of "bodies" is exclusively determined by the attribute of a rigid, timeless, three-dimensional spatiality.

A consistent application of this substance concept would consider changes in matter merely as *modes of continuous extension.* For Descartes these *modi* are restricted to *divisibility* and *motion*, where the former results from the latter.

22. Two fundamental questions in respect of Descartes' concept of space and motion

In terms of the theory of law-spheres two basic questions emerge:

(1) Did Descartes conceive extension in its original modal meaning? and

(2) Did he understand motion in its original sense, or did he, rather, intend it as an anticipatory function of space, that it to say, as an anticipation of motion in a spatial sense?

The entire aprioristic mathematical method of Descartes would seem to argue for an affirmative answer to the first question and

---

1 *Principles of Philosophy*, I, 57: "Thus, for example, time, which we distinguish from duration taken in its generality and call the measure of motion, is only a certain mode under which we think duration itself.) [See also the last sentence of sec. 57: "hence what is so designated is nothing superadded to duration, taken in its generality, but a mode of thinking."]

an affirmative answer to the second part of the second question.[1]

However, what may apparently count against this argument is Descartes' rejection of an "empty space" and the fact that he understood extension in a material sense. It is evident that the foundations of his mechanical theory labored under a serious confusion, which exacted its price in his later thought.

How is it to be explained that Descartes, in spite of his orientation to the new function concept of the humanistic science ideal, nonetheless thought of spatiality only in "bodily" and "material" terms?

23. After-effect of the Aristotelian-Scholastic theory of material extension

To my mind this can only be explained from the continued influence exerted on his thought by Aristotelian Scholasticism.

The truth of the matter is that Aristotle (and with him Aristotelian-Thomistic Scholasticism) did not know the modal horizon of reality and so also did not know the modal structural principles of reality. He accepted the modal functions merely within the structures of individual *entities*. His entire theory of reality was oriented to the teleological concept of substance, which was exclusively directed towards understanding the internal structure of *individual things*.

In this line of thought there also was no room for the spatial aspect of reality with a modal structure that is independent of the inner nature of material things. "Space" acquired an entirely secondary position vis-à-vis the primary concept of the concrete bodily place of a thing. As such it is purely a product of

---

1 Compare also the answer Descartes gave to an objection made by Gassendi, namely that his concept of space is merely a mathematical thought-entity which cannot directly be transferred to natural reality. Descartes replied that if mathematical extension, of which we have an exact concept, did not exist outside our mind in nature, all our knowledge would be fictional and imaginary. (Lettre à M. Clerselier, *Oeuvres choisies*, p. 171).

thought,[1] existing merely in the realm of thinking,[1] a so-called "abstraction of the second degree."

In the fourth Book of his *Physics* the Stagirite extensively elaborates his conception. As he defines it there, the place of a body is the real, first (i.e., immediate), unmovable, encompassing surface. A body is moving when it changes place, where the latter is understood as defined above. "Place" according to Aristotle is therefore something real. It is extended in a material sense and it is different from the subject occupying it.[2]

Furthermore, place is relative. A body only then has a place if there exists yet another body which is the place of the first one, where the first body finds itself. According to Aristotle[3] the localization system of bodies, in which all individual material substances have their "place" is the material universe outside of which there does not exist another material reality, which therefore cannot be "somewhere" and therefore cannot have a place.

Secondly, it follows from Aristotle' definition that *immediate contact* is required between the body occupying its place and the surrounding "material extension" in which it is situated. From this Aristotle even draws the conclusion that "if outside a body there is another one surrounding the first, then that other body is at a place; if not, then not."[4]

---

1 Space is here always conceived as the recipient of material bodies. Obviously, in our theory of the law-spheres, space as a *modal aspect* of reality cannot fulfill this odd role. Of course, all the arguments raised by Aristotle in following the ideas of his predecessors such as Zeno of Elea against the reality of space as a recipient do not affect our conception in the least.

   However, together with this internally contradictory concept of space as recipient, Aristotle – and in his footsteps Aquinas – also eliminated the modal structure of space as a substrate of the physical aspect of reality. The modal relations (which are independent of the individuality structure of things) in the sense of continuous extension are not recognized here in their true nature as fundamental for concrete reality. In part this also explains the basic difference between Aristotelian-Scholastic thought and the Platonic-mathematical school followed by Descartes.

2 Similarly in the case of Thomas Aquinas, *Summa Theologica*, I, Q. 8, art. 2, where place is designated as "res quaedam."

3 Cf. *Phys.*, 5, 212 b 14.

4 *Phys.*, IV, 5, 212 a 31.

This theory is defined further by Aristotle's view regarding the structure of the universe as an all-encompassing material extension, which, according to him, is constituted by spheres that encapsulate each other. This universe presumably finds its immobile center in the earth, as the sphere of the first element earth, while the last sphere is formed by the fixed stars.

24. The localization and contact theory of Thomas Aquinas

This Aristotelian theory was refined with acuity by Thomas Aquinas in his remarkable localization theory.[1]

According to Thomas the spatial position (proximity or distance) of bodies is dependent on their *contact*.[2] The contact between real bodies is the only source of local relationships: *immediate* contact effects spatial proximity, *mediated* contact effects spatial *distance*.

Thus Thomas, too, in principle denies the existence of space as a *basic modal aspect* of reality. He only acknowledges concrete positional relations as the resultant of mediate or immediate *bodily contacts*. It would not be correct to say that the Aristotelian-Thomistic theory conceived matter as a "filling of space." After all, such a conception would presuppose the primary character of space, which is explicitly denied by Aristotle and Thomas. They know only material, real extension, no immaterial modal extension. As conceptual abstractions ("of the second degree"), geometrical relationships are here conceived as derived from materially extended things.

25. The form-matter scheme as violating the sphere-sovereignty of the modal aspect of space

According to the Aristotelian-Thomistic conception no exact (i.e., original) spatial relationships can exist within real things, i.e., "in res." It is not allowed by the *metaphysical scheme* of form and matter.

On this view, the "substantial form" of the entity penetrates the entire matter that receives this form. Just as the "vegetative soul" of the plant and the "sensitive soul" of the animal pene-

1 In connection with this theory, see Hoenen, *op. cit.*, pp. 136 ff.
2 Cf. e.g., *Summa Theol.*, I, Q. 8, art. 2 ad 1; Q. 52, art. 1; *Quodlib.*, 1, art. 4 and VII art. 8. For other references, cf. Hoenen, *op. cit.*, pp. 137 ff.

trate the whole material body of these entities – while maintaining the basic dualism of form and (primary, i.e., "not yet determined") matter – such that all pre-biotic and pre-psychical functions lose their modal sphere-sovereignty by being reduced to modes of the essential form,[1] so also the modal spatial relationships abdicate their original character to the physically qualified material bodies. Through the essential physical form, continuous extension is formed into *physical, material space*.

Notice the difference between the Aristotelian-Thomistic theory of substantial forms and the theory of individuality structures of the *Philosophy of the Cosmonomic Idea*. It is also understandable why Aristotle, in Book VI of his *Metaphysics*, reckons mathematical space among *intelligible matter*. According to him extension never belongs to the *ontic form* of things.[2]

26. The Cartesian compromise between the humanistic science ideal and the Scholastic concept of space

Descartes produced an internally antinomic fusion of the Aristotelian-Thomistic theory of material extension and the conception of space as the essential property or attribute of a material substance.

On the one hand he reduced all the other modal aspects of the material body to that of continuous extension, while, in line with the function concept, he radically abstracted from the in-

---

1 This explains also why the Aristotelian-Thomistic conception of the living organism is essentially *vitalistic*. It does not leave room for the approach, defended by the *Philosophy of the Cosmonomic Idea*, that the atomic structure of bodily matter maintains its sphere-sovereignty vis-à-vis the structure of the cell. In other words, there are atomic material entities which as such are qualified in a physico-chemical way and therefore are not actively alive or animated. They are only enkaptically bounded within the living organism. When the living organism disintegrates these material components are once again released. Both Aristotle and Thomas thought of "primary matter" as in itself totally undetermined; as "primordial" matter it receives all its determination from the "vital form." Cf. Hoenen, op. cit., p. 313.

2 As a matter of principle the *Philosophy of the Cosmonomic Idea* acknowledges that the aspects of number and space never serve as the *qualifying function* of individuality structures. Yet these aspects nonetheless maintain their irreducible *modal* character also within the individuality structure of things, even though these functions are here typically disclosed by the "guiding function."

ternal individuality structure of things. On the other hand he accepted the traditional theory that extension displays a "material," bodily character. As we have seen, this theory cannot be reconciled with the independent modal character of space. Indeed, he accepted the contact theory to the point of absurdity by denying the possibility of mediated contacts.

In line with the modern modal concept of function Descartes considered space to be *primary*, lying at the foundation of physical entities. At the same time he adhered to the meaning of space as postulated by the metaphysics of Parmenides, namely that it is filled (*tō pleon*) with corpuscular matter which has a fine structure and which is infinitely divisible. And this fine matter is supposed to embrace and permeate all bodies.[1]

As primary modal function, continuous extension can only possess an original spatial meaning. In the sense of filled space, by contrast, it can be of a physical nature only, hence can present a spatial analogy only within the meaning of motion. We shall soon return to this point.

To what extent Descartes' substance concept is essentially a pseudo-modal concept of function becomes clear from his reaction to the theory of atoms defended by Gassendi as well as in his assumption regarding the infinite divisibility of matter, which does not contradict his particle theory.[2] This conception is directly linked to another one according to which three-dimensional continuous extension is the sole ontic property of matter. The mathematical continuum is infinitely divisible; mathematical extension is the essence of the material substance; ergo ...

This "extended matter" is totally stripped of its individuality structure since it is conceived of in a purely *functional* sense. Neither Democritus nor Gassendi thought about it in this way. According to them an "atom" after all is "indivisible" and this "in-

---

1 Cf. *Lettres* CIV, 2:474: "These tiny bodies, which enter when something evaporates and leave when it condenses, and which pass through the hardest entities, are of the same nature as those that see and touch each other. Yet one should not think that they are atoms and that they have any duration: they are an extremely fine fluid substance that fills the pores of other bodies."

2 *Principles of Philosophy*, II, No. 20; IX, 74. In principle, matter is thus made into a continuum of points. See also ibid., II, No. 31-35; IX, 81-83.

divisibility" is essentially another "qualitative" property which can apply only to an *individual whole*.

Descartes' nominalistic mathematical substance concept really demanded a complete reduction of "matter" and motion to space. Movement would then not be understood in its original modal distinctiveness but merely as an anticipation of the aspect of motion from within the modality of continuous extension. However, Descartes' dependence on the Aristotelian-Scholastic theory regarding the *material* nature of extension did not allow for this implication.

Observe here the series of antinomies flowing from the attempted synthesis between two mutually exclusive conceptions of reality. The leveling tendency of the humanistic science ideal alone cannot explain this tension.

27. The Aristotelian-Thomistic view of time. Its objectivistic and rationalistic character

This lack of clarity present in Descartes' nature philosophy also explains why his understanding of time, in spite of its functional mechanistic and subjectivistic orientation, could not occupy that central place in his thought which it acquired in the humanistic science ideal since Newton.

An internally contradictory synthesis between the humanistic science ideal and Aristotelian Scholasticism also worked itself out in Descartes' conception of time.

According to the latter, time is strictly an *objective order* of corporeal reality itself. This view is inextricably linked to the Aristotelian-Thomistic understanding of *place* and *time*.[1] Here the real character of time is primarily grounded in its so-called topological structure[2] as an order of earlier and later in the parts of a movement. "Motion" is here taken as a *change of place* which is assumed to be "natural" in the sense of answering to the essence of things.

According to Aristotle and Aquinas, time and movement are not at all identical. After all "motion," on their view, exists

1 Cf. Aristotle, *Phys.* IV, 10, 14.
2 This term is introduced into the understanding of time by the Thomist Hoenen (op. cit., p. 281).

39

merely *in the things moved*. But the same does not apply to time! Two movements taking place adjacent to each other occur in "the same time." Furthermore, the speed of movements may differ and a movement may be accelerated or decelerated. But this also does not hold good for time, which always flows uniformly as a dynamic continuum.

Both place and time are *extrinsic* to whatever happens in them. As to its "metrical structure" time is an extrinsic *measure* for the intrinsic flowing *duration* of a concrete event. In his aforementioned work Hoenen remarks, half in jest, that to the question: "When and how long did Aristotle live?" one can only give a nonsensical and pseudo-witty answer: "He lived in the duration of his life." This is exactly what we established with respect to "place": just as "place" belongs to what is "positioned," so "time" is something extrinsic to that which occurs at a specific time and is measured by it.[1]

28. The Cartesian view of time. The rationalistic distinction between time and duration

When we compare the Cartesian conception of time with the briefly discussed Aristotelian-Thomistic view, then it is immediately apparent that Descartes no longer can view time as a real objective order for reality. The essentially nominalistic and functionalistic substance concept of Descartes compels him to dissolve time into a subjective *"modus cogitandi."* This *"modus cogitandi"* is in no way identical with the "merely imaginary time" of Aristotelian Scholasticism. After all, Descartes too conceives of time merely as the measure of motion. In rationalist fashion he also identifies *time* with *time-order* and almost literally copies the Aristotelian argument that one has to draw a strict distinction between the *intrinsic duration* and the actually (extrinsic) *time* as *measure of duration*.

For Descartes, the intrinsic duration of bodies is independent of their movement, but we *measure* the intrinsic duration of bodies through a comparison with certain maximal and regular mo-

---

1   Hoenen, op. cit., p. 281. That this argument entails a *circulus vitiosis* stands to reason. Clearly, this argument, by equating *time* and *time measure*, is caught in a vicious circle.

40

tions, namely those which generate years and days. Thus we acquire a common yardstick for measuring the duration of all things, and this measure we call time.[1] Notice that the latter merely adds a (mathematical) mode of thinking to the concept of *duration*. It does not belong to the attributes of reality and therefore as such it exists merely within human thought.

If spatiality is the sole (modal) property of material bodies and if as such it is a-temporal, then it is impossible to ascribe an *objective reality* to time. In the rationalist frame of mind this means that it cannot exist as *ordo successionis*. In the context of his subjectivistic nominalistic thought the only option for Descartes is to account for the objectivity of time in terms of an *ideal mathematical rational order*.

If Descartes had drawn the consequences of his substance concept and oriented his time concept to the meaning of modal extension, he would have had to reduce time to an absolute, modal mathematical time, as was done later by Newton. But here again we notice the negative after-effect of the Aristotelian-Scholastic mode of thought in the context of modern functionalism. Descartes continues to understand time in a one-sidedly *concrete* sense oriented to the empirical movements of celestial bodies, albeit in contrast to the *merely mechanical* understanding of the latter by Aristotle.

Gunn is justified in his remark that Descartes failed to distinguish properly between physical and psychical time.[2] Gunn is justified in his remark that Descartes failed to distinguish properly between physical and psychical time.[2] This distinction, however, could not be made within the Cartesian framework of thought. Rigid spatiality, after all, provided this thought with a

---

1 *Principles of Philosophy*, I, 57: "for indeed we do not conceive the duration of things that are moved to be different from the duration of things that are not moved: as is evident from this, that if two bodies are in motion for an hour, the one moving quickly and the other slowly, we do not reckon more time in the one than in the other, although there may he much more motion in the one of the bodies than in the other. But that we may comprehend the duration of all things under a common measure, we compare their duration with that of the greatest and most regular motions that give rise to years and days, and which we call time."

2 J. A. Gunn, *The Problem of Time* (London, 1928), p. 47.

philosophical basic denominator for the pre-psychical aspects of reality. Moreover, Descartes could acknowledge motion only as an *external* mode of extension given to bodies by a veritable *deus ex machina*, not as an irreducible modality of reality grounded in God's temporal creation *order*. He also logicized the numerical aspect into a logical cognitive relation, while at the same time reducing the psychical aspect of time entirely to a logical mathematical aspect. In Descartes' world of thought there was no room whatever for an intermodal temporal connection between space and motion. Space as such was conceived as a timeless attribute of material substance.

29. The principle of relativity in Descartes' mechanics

This perspective explains why it is apparently possible to discern a point of contact in his thought for the modern theory of relativity. Descartes contemplated the relativity of movement. He thought of matter as a *filling of space* and on principle rejected the idea of empty space. He believed that this space-filling matter received motion from God externally and that God kept the total quantum of it constant. In terms of the argumentation followed by Descartes, motion therefore had to be given to matter *within* space.

However, when the movement of matter takes place within space and when this space itself is material, then it is impossible to find a fixed reference system in terms of which an "absolute movement" could be calculated. Movement and rest are then completely relative.

30. The general theory of relativity in the light of the *Philosophy of the Cosmonomic Idea*

Descartes' view on the relativity of motion could have been quite fruitful if it had been grounded in a truly *physical* concept of space, for in such an understanding motion, time and space are realized at the same time, as indeed occurs in Einstein's theory. In this physical concept of space, after all, the latter indeed is not conceived of in its *original* modal sense but only as a spatial analogy within the meaning of *movement*.

This spatial analogy, according to the *Philosophy of the Cosmonomic Idea*, reveals itself in a subject-object relation within the modal aspect of movement. Within the cosmic time-order this modal relation is grounded in the intermodal subject-object relation between space (in its original sense) and motion. What does this mean?

Within the modal meaning of movement a distinction is required between a *subjective* and an *objective* analogy of space.

The former is the *subjective* path of movement as a *successive* continuous change of position and the latter as the so-called *objective space of movement*.[1] Einstein has demonstrated that the latter, in the concrete form of "world space," can only be understood as the physical correlate of material motion (gravitation), because its properties are determined by the latter. This indeed reveals a subject-object relation within the aspect of movement. For this objective world space, which cannot itself be a *subject* of movement, since all movement takes place *within it*, has meaning and existence only in relation to the subjecttive motion of matter.

Yet this modal subject-object relation is grounded *intermodally* in cosmic time. For this dynamic world space has its *subjective*-(original) *spatial correlate*, of which it is merely an *analogical objectification*.

Strict simultaneity, viewed from a modal perspective, exists in the *original* sense of *spatial* time. Within this original modal meaning, movement can never have an original meaning, since it can only function as an *anticipation*. Within the modal aspect of *movement*, on the other hand, simultaneity can only function analogically. Here simultaneity on principle is *relativized* within

---

1 The "path of motion" and the objective "space of movement" as such are not yet determined except in a *modal* sense only. The gravitational and electromagnetic fields, by contrast, as well as the "world space," are co-determined by the individuality structure of reality.

the modal meaning of movement.[1] The speed of light, which functions in the general theory of relativity as the constant c, naturally is only a relative, "empirical" constant in the meaning of motion.

In the mathematical foundations of the theory of relativity motion and the modal time-order inherent in it must be absorbed in the rigid scheme of the four-dimensional Minkowski space, where time is added as the forth dimension, essentially transformed into the simultaneity of *spatial* time, and where curved space in a geometrical sense anticipates the gravitational movement. But this geometrical scheme, which once again understands space in its original subjective modal meaning – albeit within the physically qualified individuality structure of "matter"[2] – remains indissolubly bound to the modal subject-object relation within the meaning of movement that we have indicated above.

Neither the four-dimensional geometrical space of the general theory of relativity nor the (dynamic) objective physical world space – of which the former is only the geometrical correlate – is identical to the objective-psychical space of sensory per-

---

1 The fact that Einstein makes an appeal to the sensory time of perception remains a weak point in his argumentation regarding the relativity of physical simultaneity as he does in his "popular" booklet: *On the special and general theory of relativity* (Sammlung Vieweg, no. 38). The entire account of a person who is standing on the station platform and the traveller on the train who each have different time perceptions regarding two light signals, simply does not fit the general theory of relativity as a theory of mathematical physics. The same applies to Einstein's psychological definition of simultaneity: "I take two events to be simultaneous for a given observer when they are perceived at the same time by the observer who is located at the same distance from both." Einstein here enters the slippery (for him) area of psychology where he cannot advance any cogent arguments against the objections raised by Bergson and Maritain. In his mathematico-physical demonstration of the general theory of relativity, as published in his famous study "Zur Elektrodynamik bewegter Körper," *Annalen der Physik* 17 (1905): 891–921, the psychological concept of time does not play any role.

2 Of course this has to be denied by those who elevate the Euclidean character of space to an essential property of space. Cf. e.g. Eduard May, *Die Bedeutung der modernen Physik für die Theorie der Erkenntnis* (Leibzig, 1937), p. 104. To the non-Euclidean geometries he assigns no more than "formal logical" significance. Certainly this is patently incorrect in the case of the Einstein-Riemann space!

ception. And "curved space" simply does not belong to the space of sensory perception, although its objectivity has largely been established through experimentation.

31. Why Descartes' conception of relativity had to remain fruitless in a scientific sense

However, this whole complexity cannot be accounted for by Descartes' theory regarding the total relativity of motion.

He knows after all only one kind of space, his geometrical, three-dimensional space. As we shall see below, this is only a spatial anticipation of the sensory space of touch and sight. He does not know anything about a subjective and objective movement space. Within this geometrical space Descartes assumes that matter in motion completely "fills space" in a way that is dense throughout. This conception is internally contradictory, for within the original meaning of space genuine movement is not possible.[1] For this reason he succeeds in relativizing only rest and motion but not space in movement. No wonder his unclear and internally antinomic conception had to make room for that of Newton, whose theory of absolute motion consistently linked up with the theory of absolute space and absolute time, which had a strong influence on Kant.

32. More's conception of time

It is important to remark here that Newton's conception of absolute mathematical time – already prepared as it was by Gassendi[2] – leaned directly on the view of time of his tutor Barrow as well as on that of Henry More, the neo-Platonist from Cambridge who was heavily influenced by the Renaissance philosopher Ficino.

In the thought of More we find a complete break with both the Aristotelian and the Cartesian conception of time as the mea-

---

1 The modal structure of the spatial aspect exhibits only anticipations of movement.

2 Cf. Pierre Gassendi's definition of time as *incorporea duratio,*a *corporibus independens* (W.W. Florence, 1:195). [This work could not be identified.] On his understanding, too, time flows uniformly, independent of whatever content, also of the movements of the stars: "tempus quiescente coelo perinde fluere intelligi, ac fluit donec movetur coelum" (W.W. 1:199), quoted by Gent, op. cit., p. 11.

sure of movement. In More, time is *reduced to geometry*.[1] It is turned into a modality of extension and identified with duration: *"per tempus intelligo Durationem."*[2]

The contrast between More and Descartes reaches, as Cassirer has correctly observed,[3] its climax in the theory of space. Descartes *materialized* space: for him extension and matter were identical. More, on the other hand, aims at an understanding of absolute space which, in transcending its geometrical concept, is viewed as an immaterial, spiritual attribute of the divine substance. It participates in the attributes of God: his unity and simplicity, his immovability and eternity, his immeasurability and omnipresence, his attribute of being all-encompassing, and his independence from corporeal things, and so on.[4]

In a similar way More conceives of "absolute time" as a mode of absolute space independent of the movement of material bodies. As *"duratio successiva finita"* ("finite successive duration") *absolute time* is for him merely the image of God's eternity, of his *"duratio permanens infiniti"* (permanent infinite duration).

---

1 *Epist.* II, H. *Mori ad Cartesium,* Op. tom., 2:245.

2 *Antidoton adversus Atheismum,* Appendix c. 7 § 2, Op. tom. 2:162.

3 *Das Erkenntnisproblem,* 2:443.

4 *Enchiridium Metaphysicum,* P. I, cap. VIII. 8: "Neque enim reale dumtaxat, sed Divinum quiddam videbitur hoc Extensum infinitum ac immobile ... postquam Divina illa Nomina vel titulos, qui examussim ipsi congruunt enumeraverimus ... Ut Unum, Simplex, Immobile, Aeternum, Completum, Independens, A se existens, per se subsistens, Incorruptibile, Necessarium, Immensum, Increatum, Omnipraesens, Incorporeum, Omnia permeans et complectens" (quoted in Cassirer, ibid., 2:445).

Part B

The Problem of Time in the *Philosophy of the Cosmonomic Idea*

1. The experience of time and the limits of a concept and a definition of time in theoretical knowledge

"What is time? If you don't ask me, I know; but if you ask me to explain it I no longer know."[1] This well-known statement of Augustine contains a truth with a general implication. In philosophical discussions about the problem of time this truth is often forgotten as soon as an attempt is made to grasp time in a theoretical concept.

That we have an awareness of time is beyond dispute. However, the crucial question is whether or not this awareness is rooted in a deeper layer of experience than what is accessible to theoretical conceptualization. That such a deeper layer really exists must be clear to everyone who reckons with the peculiar limits of the theoretical attitude of thought as compared to the immediate non-theoretical experience of reality. Definitions and theoretical analysis have their intrinsic limits – delimitations that make them possible to begin with. Whatever is theoretically *irreducible* is also *indefinable* and every proper definition ultimately finds its foundation in such irreducible elements. In the absence of immediate *insight* into what is indefinable we cannot speak of a real *concept* of what is definable. Any "insight" remains rooted in a final bottom layer of *experience* which transcends the boundaries of the theoretical attitude of thought and precludes a strict separation between theoretical and pre-theoretical experience. It is only through experience that this knowledge is made *our own* – and this awareness constitutes the primary condition of true knowledge. Whatever in principle remains foreign to the knowing selfhood also resides in principle outside the limits of the human ability to know.[2]

Anyone who is versed in modern philosophy and who takes notice of the above will immediately tend to think of the role of

---

1 [Augustine, *Confessions* 11.17.]
2 For more on this, see my *WdW*, 2:414–20 [cf. NC, 2:479–85].

intuition or an "intuition of the essence," or alternatively about "empathy" or what is "lived-through" – as these are contrasted with abstract thought forms by, respectively, phenomenology and philosophy of life. The former are posited as *immediate* ways of knowing in contrast to the *mediated* or *symbolic* ways of knowing.

A proper insight into the nature of time, as we shall see, indeed requires a correct understanding of what we live through in our concrete time experience which transcends the limits of theoretical abstraction. In other words, what is required is a correct insight into what theoretical abstraction necessarily subtracts from our full experience.

Yet a strange vicious circle is hidden in the attempts to transcend the limits of an abstract theoretical concept in philosophical investigation by means of intuition or experience as long as the self-sufficiency and autonomy of theoretical knowing is maintained. This is done both by modern phenomenology and by the metaphysical philosophy of life of Bergson. The former does so by requiring a theoretical reduction or the methodical *ēpochē* of the entire "natural world picture" with the pretension of gaining an adequate grasp of the *true essence* of what is given in experience, while the latter pretends to enter fully into the metaphysical essence of true time by requiring the elimination of whatever falls outside the *évolution créatrice* of the psychical *durée*. In both instances this whole elimination or reduction is possible only through a theoretical abstraction that is absolutized when it claims to be able to unveil what is essentially given in our experience of time.

In order to give an account of this state of affairs we must briefly pay attention, first of all, to the difference between the theoretical and the non-theoretical or naive attitude of thought.

The theoretical attitude of thought, which is a *sine qua non* not only for the special sciences but also for philosophy, is characterized by the theoretical distance which logical thought takes in respect of its field of investigation. This "taking distance" essentially turns that which is investigated into a "Gegenstand" of thought. This theoretical distance gives rise to the awareness of "problems" that are typical only of theoretical thought.

Naive experience, by contrast, is not aware of any problem in a theoretical sense because naive thought does not have a "Gegenstand." The "Gegenstand" is that which is theoretically *opposed* to logical thought – is that which is the product of a theoretical setting apart of temporal reality. Also as to its logical side naive experience remains completely *embedded* in temporal reality; it does not know a dualism between knowing and what is known. Also the logical and post-logical functions of things in *structural subject-object relations* (to be discussed later) are grasped by naive experience as they give themselves. Naïve experience apprehends reality in an integral way and not as set apart. The setting apart of temporal reality is performed only in theoretical analysis and synthesis, without which no proper theoretical knowledge of what is investigated is possible.

The analysis in question engages our logical function as it takes on the theoretical attitude of thought, which as such can never liberate itself from the grip of theoretical concepts.

Theoretical analysis can only set apart temporal reality as given in naïve experience by proceeding in an *abstracting* way. Something is abstracted from full temporal reality and this abstraction is necessary in order to acquire an articulated insight in a particular structure of this reality. Within our naive experience this structure never comes to consciousness explicitly, but only implicitly.

2. The two basic structures of temporal reality

This last mentioned structure will be designated as the *modal aspects* of temporal reality. As we shall see, this is not the only structure of temporal reality, since it is *implicit* in a second, more concrete structure in which reality immediately presents itself to naive experience.

The latter structure will be designated as the individuality structure of temporal reality. In it, concrete things, events, deeds, acts and societal collectivities are revealed as concrete totalities functioning within the modal aspects.

Insight into the fundamental difference between these two structures and into their mutual coherence will turn out to be of critical importance for a proper treatment of the problem of time. For this reason we will first have to analyze these structures successively. As we do this it will become evident why time *as such* is not accessible to theoretical thought since it forms the essential *presuppositum* of all theoretical knowledge. This presupposition alone give access to that depth layer of our experience which transcends the limits of theoretical concept formation. At the same time it will protect us from the mistaken orientation of phenomenology and philosophy of life which, without really intending to do so, once again try to press the intuition of time and the experience of time into the framework of a *theoretical abstraction*.

3. The modal aspects of time and their cosmic continuity

Temporal reality *functions* in a diversity of modal aspects which themselves are not subject to change in time but instead form a constant and basic modal framework within which the individual changeable entities, events, acts, deeds and societal relationships display their variable functions. The modal aspects *make possible* this variable functioning.

The modal structure does not exhibit the the concrete *what* that is typical of individuality structures, since it reveals the *how* of reality. Each modal aspect is a functional *way* of being, a *modality* or a *modal aspect* of reality.

In the general theory of modal aspects the *Philosophy of the Cosmonomic Idea* provisionally brought to light fourteen such modal aspects of temporal reality. According to their law-like structure they are designated as *law-spheres*. They are that of quantity, spatiality, the aspect of movement, the biotic aspect, the feeling (psychical) aspect, the analytical (or logical) aspect, the historical aspect, the aspect of symbolical signification, that of social intercourse, the economic, the aesthetic, the jural, the moral and the faith aspect.

In theoretical-philosophical analysis these modalities are essentially set apart in a theoretical *discontinuity*. However, within temporal reality they are fitted into a *continuous cosmic coherence* and, as we shall see, this cosmic coherence is a *temporal coherence*.

As modal aspects of temporal reality they are implicitly modal *time-aspects*. In other words, within each modality of reality time comes to expression in a distinctive way without being exhausted by any one of them. The modal structure of reality itself is enclosed within cosmic time.

4. The customary opposition of time and space and the general theory of relativity. Is the opposition between time and time-measurement logically sound?

Those who are accustomed to the abstract views of reality found in prevaling philosophy may find this statement highly problematical.

One of the most deep-seated prejudices embedded in the predominant view of time is that time expresses itself only in *motion* and *change*. Here, *time* and *space* are opposed either as equal and distinct (though mutually related in motion) ordering schemes of what we can experience in reality, or as mutually exclusive "streams of experience" or "mathematical conceptual constructions." To be sure, the widespread view that space as such is timeless is confronted with a serious problem by the theory of relativity. Yet until now the philosophical conception of time does not seem all that willing to accept the view of Minkowski and Einstein, namely that time and space cannot be separated. The argument is that the distinction between *time* and *time-measurement* is incontestable. The general theory of relativity therefore informs us only about the measurement of time without teaching us anything about time itself. The conception of time as "fourth dimension" is merely a perspectival mathematical mode of representation which is partially explicable from the fact that the theory of relativity accepted the propagation of light as the physical measure of time, thus identifying the light waves with time itself.[1]

Yet, the question is: Can a time-measure be anything other than a specific time duration and can time-measurement happen outside time? If the answer is negative the opposition be-

1   Cf. e.g. Gunn, *The Problem of Time*, p. 206.

tween time and time-measure or time-measurement loses its exclusive character and thus, without closer specification, becomes logically useless.

If an exclusive opposition between time and time-measurement is accepted notwithstanding, then, as we shall see, one gets entangled in unsolvable antinomies.

As it turns out, the opposition between time and time-measurement is not at all logically incontestable, because in the second case the word "time" must have a more restricted meaning than in the first instance, at least if the entire concept of time-measurement is not to collapse under internal antinomies. At any rate, distinguishing in principle between time and time-measurement does not support the correctness of the view of space as timeless found in classic physics.

5. The connection between the standard opposition between time and space and the metaphysical substance concept. All "definitions" of time are essentially definitions of modal time aspects

To the contrary, in this conception time turned out to be an indispensable presupposition for the definition of space itself.[1] At the same time it became apparent that a genuine definition of time was not possible. Rather, the supposed definition of time is no more than a mathematical approximation of the modal aspect of motion in which time once again is presupposed.

After all, when the difference between time and space is accounted for with reference to a continuous flow of *successive* moments of equal duration as opposed to *static continuous extension*, then it is clear that the concept of *flow* incorporates the concept of motion, which in turn is possible only *in time*. For that matter, the concept of "static continuous extension" hides that of spatial *simultaneity* which likewise presupposes time. Moreover, simultaneity is not only possible within the static meaning of space, but also, *albeit in a different way*, in the modal meaning of motion, of organic life, of feeling, logical analysis, historical de-

1 This was shown even before Minkowski by the Hungarian intellectual Melchior Palálgyi (*Ausgewählte Werke*, vol. III: *Zur Welt-mechanik: Beitrag zur Metaphysik der Physik* (Leipzig, 1925), p. 2. For that mater, Palálgyi later turned into a decided detractor of general relativity theory.

velopment, and so on. As we shall see, however, in all these instances *spatial* simultaneity is presupposed.

Finally, from the beginning the notion that space as such is timeless was closely linked to the metaphysical concept of matter as extended substance. The latter was supposed to be timeless in and of itself, and subject to time only in its "effects."[1] It is precisely this conception that was threatened in principle by the general theory of relativity, which, linked with quantum theory about the emission of energy, no longer separated space and time in any physical sense.

The truth is that all so-called definitions of time are merely definitions of modal *aspects of time*, where time itself constantly remains the indefinable presupposition. From the outset it must be viewed as impermissible to accept a modal definition of time as a definition of time itself.

This holds equally for Newton's "absolute" *mathematical* time as for Einstein's relative physical "movement time." It holds no less for Bergson's "feeling duration," for Spengler's or Heidegger's *"historical* time," and similarly for Kant's conception of time as "transcendental sensory form of intuition" and Hobbes's *empirical sensory* conception of time as phantasm of motion.

6.   Within each one of the modal aspects time expresses a peculiar meaning

The *Philosophy of the Cosmonomic Idea* has shown that time indeed comes to expression within *all* modal aspects in a unique way. By successively looking at the various aspects in what follows I merely intend to provide a brief *indication* of the modal properties of time.

In the *aspect of quantity* time assumes the modal meaning of *numerical relationships*. In the number sequence there exists an ir-

---

1   Cf. Bernhard Bavink, *Ergebnisse und Probleme der Naturwissenschaften*, 5th ed. (Leibzig, 1933), p. 179.

reversible time-order of earlier and later,[1] which is in no way dependent upon our subjective counting since it is rather implied by the *lawful structure* of the arithmetical aspect itself.

Nor does "earlier and later" express a kinematical succession, but rather a *quantitative* temporal value: "in the number sequence, 2 is *earlier* than 3" means: $2 < 3$.[2]

In the *aspect of space* time assumes the modal meaning of continuous extension. The static *simultaneity* of spatial parts differs modally both from the time-order of *numbers* and the *succession of motion*.

Spatial *simultaneity* has nothing to do with *supra*-temporality or timelessness. Already Parmenides fell prey to this confusion in his conception of timeless "being." Spatial simultaneity can only exist within the cosmic time-order embracing all aspects. It coheres in a temporal sense both with numerical time and with kinematic time. (In an "anticipatory function" spatial simultaneity can *approximate* kinematic succession.)

1 This modal order of earlier and later is, as we see below, necessarily related to subjective time duration, thus revealing its essential time character. It is incorrect to say that the order of succession of a sequence of numbers, which we here essentially understand as a time-order, could be reversible. Of course we can count backwards just as well as forwards. But then the irreversible modal time-order of numbers remains presupposed. The number 3 presupposes the number 2 and 1, but the reverse is not true. Counting backwards remains a counting in reverse and cannot be seen as counting forwards. Nor should this sequence be interpreted in a purely logical way. The logical order of prius et posterius as such is not a sequence in the meaning of quantity. We shall see that it, too, is a modal time-order. The view that the sequence of numbers is *timeless* leads to a striking antinomy in the so-called *measurement of time*. Time duration cannot be measured by something timeless, and yet within every measurement of time the numerical order plays an essential role. The same applies to the order of spatial parts. [Later on, Dooyeweerd altered his view by accepting that the time-order within the first three modal aspects is reversible.]

2 In his *Logik der reinen Erkenntnis* (Berlin: Cassirer, 1914), p. 155), Hermann Cohen designates the + symbol of arithmetic as the "symbol of anticipation" and "the harbinger of time." This anticipation is according to him characteristic of time and therefore he does acknowledge, unlike Paul Natorp, the time character of the principle of a number sequence, although he *logicizes* the arithmetical time-order. Kant saw number as a schematization of the category of quantity in time as "transcendental form of intuition."

Without static spatial time, kinematic time would have been impossible. The truth of this position is seen from the fact that Newton's conception of "absolute motion," to which his mathematical time concept was oriented, requires the static simultaneity of the spatial coordinates for his concept of the uniform duration of moments of movement.

In the *aspect of movement*, which definitely should not be understood in the mechanistic sense of classic mechanics and in which for example the qualitative electro-dynamic phenomena function, time reveals itself in the modal sense of *kinematic succession*. It has no room for static spatial simultaneity, since all forms of simultaneity – according to the modal meaning of motion – exhibits only a *relative* character. "Absolute rest" is only possible within the original meaning of *spatial extension*. Yet *motion* presupposes this static spatial extension. Not *within* spatial extension,[1] but only *on the basis of* the latter is motion possible as a new, irreducible *aspect* of temporal reality.[2]

In the *biotic aspect* time reveals itself in the modal sense of an *organic development of life*, in which the phases of life-development play an important role. This biotic developmental time cannot in any way be reduced to modal kinematic time. Vital development is not motion itself but can only appear on the *basis* of modal functions of movement. In respect of the biotic time-order, mathematico-physical time-measures remain necessarily *external*. They do not touch the *internal* biotic time phases of birth, maturation, ageing and passing away. These phases do not display a homogeneous character and can therefore not be delineated from each other in a mathematical way.

The question: When is an individual born? is intrinsically a biotic time question. Consequently it can only be answered from a

---

1 Every attempt to eradicate the boundaries between space and motion by reducing the dynamic path of movement to a static line necessarily leads to the paradoxes of Zeno of Elea. Every attempt to reduce one modal aspect to another, must, as the *Philosophy of the Cosmonomic Idea* has shown, lead to typical antinomies.

2 Spatial extension and movement are here intended in their original meaning as distinct modal aspects. They must not be confused with the space of sensory experience and the sensory movement *image*, which are analogies of space and movement within the psychical aspect.

biotic perspective, although it is clear that we are here confronted with difficult boundary questions.

In the *psychical aspect* time reveals itself in the modal meaning of feeling life.[1] The modal time-order to which emotional life is subject impresses upon the succession of emotions a peculiar character. Feelings or sensitive impressions experienced earlier do not simply fade away like the moments of a movement. Rather, they live on in consciousness within the totality of a mood for a shorter or longer period of time, or they are repressed to the sub-layer of consciousness, the so-called subconscious or unconscious, from where they can continue to be operative within conscious emotional life.[2] In a dream or a recollection – albeit in a modified way – it can also be absorbed reproductively in the conscious stream of feeling. This modal time-order reveals itself also in the order of feeling associations. In no way can this order be explained mechanistically,[3] because it has its own *feeling quality.*

Emotional time, according to the subject side, is a non-homogeneous *feeling duration*[4] in the sense intended by Bergson. Within this duration, feelings interpenetrate in a continuous stream that is no more divisible in a mathematical sense than the development of biotical duration. Also in the subject-object relation of sensitive duration as it presents itself within our awareness of time,[5] the subjective moments of feeling are not time points, such as the moments in spatial time, but indivisible

---

1   Feeling ought not to be understood here in the predominant sense in which it is taken in psychology, but in the sense of a *modal aspect* with a *modal nature.*
2   The same applies, as is well known, to logical thought-life.
3   See A. Prandtl, "Assoziations-psychologie," in Emil Saupe, ed., *Einführung in die neuere Psychologie*, 2nd and 3rd ed. (Osterweck am Harz: Zickfeldt, 1928), pp. 88 ff.
4   The relation between time-order and subjective and objective time duration is explained in more detail below.
5   We shall return to this below [see Remark, pp. 61 ff.]

time phases (compare the so-called "*specious* present"[1]) which are essentially phases of a sensitive motion in the perception of sensory objects in sensitive space.[2]

In the *logical aspect* time expresses itself either in the modal analytical sense of the logical *prius et posterius*, or in logical *simultaneity*. The time order here assumes a modal normative character, which is also maintained in the post-logical aspects. The predominant conception that one cannot speak of a genuine *time-order* in this context suffers from the preconceived opinion that logical relations as such are time-less. The *logical* earlier and later is then explicitly opposed to the *temporal* earlier and later.

Yet the logical *prius et posterius*, just as the order of logical simultaneity, is a genuine *modal* time order. Within the logical thought process or movement of thought it maintains its *normative* character vis-à-vis the psychical and pre-psychical aspects.

Just as the simultaneity of logical features manifests itself in every subjective conceptual synthesis and in every logical predication, so also does the logical earlier and later (of grounds and conclusions) come into play in every logical argumentation.

---

1   Cf. Gunn, *The Problem of Time*, p. 291: "From the point of view of mathematics the present is a point without duration; it is the last instant of a series going back into the past and the first of a series into the future. But from the point of view of psychology the matter is very different. The present is essentially a duration, brief but having an extension in time, a breadth of a temporal character. The moment of experience or the specious present is always a definite slice or span of duration."

2   That this "specious present" is real *feeling time* or *sensitively experienced time* – and not traceable to memory, as was suggested by Thomas Reid in his *Essays on the Intellectual Powers of Man* (1785) – is emphatically demonstrated by H. Wildon Carr in a paper read to the Aristotelian Society in its session of 1915/16, as quoted by Gunn. In his paper Carr provided a critical analysis of the experience accompanying our sensation of a falling star and then remarked: "The line is sensed, not memorized. The whole series is within the moment of experience, and is therefore a present sensation." Bergson, too, emphasized this in his contrast between "emotional duration" and the mathematical time concept. A similar view is found in the thought of William James as well as J. A. Gunn (op. cit., p. 394 et passim).

That the abstract discursive form of the syllogism manifests itself only in theoretical thought[1] in no way supports the thesis that the logical *prius et posterius* plays no role in pre-theoretical thinking. Whoever wants to hold on to this position will have to demonstrate that the *principle of sufficient reason* does not find any application in normal thinking, which of course is impossible.

The principle of sufficient reason cannot be applied outside the modal time-order of the logical *prius et posterius*.[2] In a logical sense the reasons [premises] *precede* the conclusion, and not *vice versa*. This is also known to naive thought.

In the *historical aspect* time reveals itself in the modal sense of *cultural development*.[2] Historical "periods" are periods in the execution of the human task of formation and control. They are not mathematically demarcated from each other; the vital cultural factors of an earlier period are absorbed into those of the later cultural period. It is in *tradition* that historical developmental time fuses past, present and future. This time-order bears, similar to those present in all the subsequent aspects to be discussed, a *modal normative* character. It imposes on humankind a normative task to be culturally formative: it confronts the inertia of resting in the present or vegetating on the past with the demands of the *future*. A *reaction* in history is an anti-normative reaching back to a dead past; in an reactionary way it positions itself against the norm of historical development.[3]

In the *lingual aspect* time reveals itself in the modal sense of *symbolical signification*. The pause between two speech acts, the

---

1 Cf. A. Messer, *Psychologie*, 5th ed. (Leipzig: Meiner, 1934), p. 259: "That the drawing of conclusions in our normal thinking as a rule does not follow the pattern of a major premise, a minor premise, and a conclusion, as might seem to take place according to the rules of logic, hardly needs mentioning. Most of the time we apprehend the relation of thought contents immediately without an awareness of a mediating concept." The subsequent statement of the author is infected by the criticistic view of reality with its *separation* in principle of "ought" and "is": "It (i.e., logic) says nothing about the process of thinking itself."

2 According to its subject-side "culture" is "formative control."

3 For a more detailed explanation of the normative character of the historical aspect, see my *WdW*, 2:126–300 [NC, 2:181–365] and my essay "Recht en History" [included as the last chapter in the present volume].

deceleration or acceleration in the tempo of speech or a gesture, carries with it symbolic significance, similar to the objective duration of a light or sound signal. The subjective duration of symbolical signification and the objective duration of a sign are subject to the normative time-order of the lingual aspect. The normative meaning of this modal time-order is apparent when it is realized that it could also be applied in an incorrect manner, violating lingual norms.

In the *social aspect* time assumes the modal meaning of forms of social intercourse. Letting a person of higher social status "go first" signifies social politeness or courtesy. *Tact* requires that one does not express a specific request at an *inconvenient time*. *Politeness* forbids those invited to dinner to show up *too late*. Celebrations are of an explicitly social character when the demands of conviviality assert themselves. The normative character of time is immediately apparent also in this modal aspect.

In the *economic aspect* time assumes the modal meaning of *frugality*. "Time is money," says the businessman, and he is using more than a metaphor. The economic time-order saves time in a normative weighing of values. The entire phenomenon of interest rests on a higher evaluation of *present* goods over equivalent *future* goods. The distinctions between hourly wages and piece work, between fixed and floating capital, practices like offering discounts and trading in futures make sense only within the economic time-order, an order that cannot be reduced to any other modal aspect of time.

In the *aesthetic aspect* time reveals itself in the modal meaning of *beautiful harmony*. The classic norm of unity of time (and place) for a drama is meaningful only aesthetically. The aesthetic time-order does not tolerate aesthetically empty moments. When a novelist loses sight of the distinctive modal character of the aesthetic time-order and confuses it with the historical time-order, he may be able to produce a reliable historical narrative, but not a genuine work of art.

In the *jural aspect* time reveals itself in the modal meaning of *law* or *retribution, in the* retributive harmonization of interests.[1] Truly modal juridical configurations of a normative jural nature are found in instances such as: the willful delay (*mora*) in default of an obligation; the acquisition of property rights by prescription [i.e., through continued use of a property over a period of time]; the expiration of outstanding claims or contractual obligations; a time stipulation in contracts; and the change in status from minor to adult. The same applies to the limited time of validity of a law or ordinance; think also of the legal concept of "retroactive force" in a right of transfer.

When a merchant in Amsterdam places an order by telephone or telegraph which is accepted in London or New York, then the question concerning the time of the agreement [when it was concluded] is truly a question of *juridical time*, a question that can only be answered according to legal norms, because only within the juridical time order is there room for *legal* consequences.

In the *moral aspect* time comes to expression in the normative sense of neighborly love.[2] Holding back available support or help that is within reach when it is urgently needed shows a lack of love and is immoral. The whole of time in its moral aspect is pervaded with the demand for love: in times of danger the fatherland demands the duty of love of country. The duties of parental love, of marital love, of camaraderie, and so on, all *make demands on our time*. The statement of Jesus that "you have the poor with you *all the time,* but Me you do not" [cf. Matt 26:11] pertinently highlights the special sacrifices that *"love time"* demands in the face of death.

In the *faith aspect* time finally reveals its transcendental boundary function as it points from within time to what is hidden beyond time – towards eternity. In the majestic opening words of

---

1 [Within the universal scope of the jural aspect, retribution should not be restricted to revenge or to penal law. The classical Roman jurists (Ulpianus and others) captured this meaning of retribution with their time-honored phrase: give every person his or her due (*ius suum quique tribuere*). "Giving a person his or her due" is simply synonymous with the "tribution" part of *retribution.*]

2 This temporal aspectual meaning of love ought not to be confused with the religious fullness of love, which is the "fulfilment of the law."

the book of Genesis: "In the beginning God created the heavens and the earth," pistical time points to God's act of creation, which first called time itself into existence.

When we as Reformed people believe that regeneration precedes conversion, then naturally it is not the temporal succession within the sensorially perceivable aspect of clock time that is intended, but rather a time-order that has meaning only within the boundary function of faith. If the heart, as the religious center of the human being, is not first of all reborn through God's spirit, then the turn-around can also not manifest itself within the temporal issues of life. But regeneration itself can be apprehended only in pistic time as the mystery of God's work in a sinner's heart, which lies hidden behind its temporal existence.

7. The necessity of abstracting from the cosmic continuity of time in the theoretical attitude of thought. The difference with the naive attitude

In the preceding brief description of the modal aspects of time we actually have done nothing more than provide a *theoretical explication* of what one already *implicitly* knows in the pre-theoretical understanding of time. The predominant philosophical views of time, which attempt to identify time with one modal aspect of time (for example the physical aspect of motion, the psychical aspect or the historical aspect), positively contradict what is given in naive experience. In order to avoid confusion in what follows we shall refer to time in its full scope, as distinct from its aspects, as *cosmic time*.

However, in our theoretical analysis we have to suspend *cosmic time itself* in its all-encompassing continuity in order to be able to set apart its modal aspects such that they can be apprehended in a theoretical concept. This is precisely what the naive experience of time *cannot* do. Even in its logical-analytical aspect, naive experience remains fully *embedded* in time; it does not, in its logical thought-function, confront the abstracted modal aspects as its "Gegenstand" or problem. To naive experience, precisely because it lacks every form of an opposing attitude of thought and has its logical function fully embedded in time, the modal aspects remain completely *implicit* within the continuous unity of the cosmic experience of time. In naive experience the continuity of time completely encompasses the diversity of modal aspects.

When I look at my watch I experience intuitively – perhaps in part only subconsciously – the cosmic continuity of time in its diverse aspects, even though these aspects do not stand out with any distinction in my experience. Particularly the *normative* aspects cannot be left unaccounted for without turning time into a theoretical abstraction totally foreign to life. That the watch reminds me of my duties is one of the most elementary givens of naive experience. Only a scientific theory that disregards its boundaries could advance the idea that these normative aspects fall outside time.

But why is it necessary that the theoretical attitude of thought has to eliminate the cosmic continuity of time, and with it time itself, in its conceptual content? This is necessary because time itself is a *transcendental presupposition* for theoretical analysis and synthesis – in other words, because it determines theoretical concept formation and makes it possible to begin with.

8. Cosmic time and the problem regarding the possibility of the knowledge-producing synthesis. Why Kant could not bring this problem to a genuine solution

The epistemological problem regarding the theoretical synthesis was raised for the first time in Kant's critical question, *How are synthetic judgments a priori possible?*

However, on his standpoint he was unable to bring this problem to a solution. The synthesis of our theoretical epistemic activity is always a synthesis between the *logical-analytical conceptual function* and the *nonlogical*, opposing modal aspects of reality that are theoretically analyzed in the concept. How is such a synthesis possible?

Undoubtedly as a consequence of his criticistic standpoint Kant posed this problem far too narrowly. He addressed it solely in terms of the "transcendental-logical categories"[1] and *psychical* sensitivity, where only the latter can present us with the "matter of experience," ordered by space and time as transcendental forms of intuition. Moreover, in all of this he proceeded from the prejudice of the self-sufficiency of the theoretical attitude of thought.

Consistent with the preceding position he restricted time to the modal structural function of the a priori sensory form of intuition, while for him the logical "thought-forms" as such were timeless.

As a result, he sought a "third," extra-sensory category of experience that would have to make possible the synthesis between these modal aspects of consciousness which after all are by nature completely different. As this "third" instance he introduced time, in which the categories, with the aid of the "transcendental imagination," could be schematized.

But as a pure *modal* aspect, a *sensory* form of intuition, time naturally cannot mediate between "understanding" and "sensibility." If the structure of the logical forms of thought is itself completely timeless, then they remain irreconcilably opposed both to the "sensory matter of experience" and to time as the "sensory form of intuition."

Only when all aspects without distinction, including the logical-analytical, are embedded in time, can time indeed be conceived as the *transcendental condition* for the theoretical synthesis.

9.   The immanence standpoint in the prevailing philosophy

Yet this state of affairs cannot be appreciated and acknowledged unless the immanence standpoint in philosophy is aban-

---

1   That these categories already entail a synthesis between the logical aspect and the non-logical aspects (quantity, space, movement) cannot be conceded on Kant's standpoint. To concede this would imply giving up his transcendental-logical starting-point which locates the origin of all determinations of the "matter of experience" in the freely formative activity of the " transcendental thinking subject."

doned. This standpoint is characterized by the fact that one attempts to find the starting-point of philosophy,[1] from which the diversity of aspects is to be apprehended in a theoretical "totality view," *within theoretical thought itself*. The immanence standpoint, once critically examined, is at odds with the recognition that theoretical thought in its transcendental-logical structure is enclosed *within time* and therefore determined by the cosmic time-order. It implies instead the postulate of the self-sufficiency, the autonomy, of theoretical "reason."

Proceeding from its Christian starting-point, the *Philosophy of the Cosmonomic Idea* not only radically distanced itself from this immanence standpoint but also demonstrated that its postulate regarding the so-called autonomy of theoretical thought is uncritical and dogmatic. The truth is that the immanence standpoint, too, is not a purely theoretical standpoint: the postulate of the self-sufficiency of theoretical thought is a dogmatic assumption, at bottom a preconception of a *religious* kind which flagrantly contradicts the entire structure of the temporal cosmos. The postulate of the self-sufficiency – the "unconditionality" – of theoretical thought, even if qualified by adding "within its own domain," implies a *primary absolutization of the theoretical synthesis*, that is to say, of a theoretical abstraction whereby all of reality is "theoreticized" by denaturing the big *datum* of naive experience.

That this postulate is abandoned in the modern irrationalist philosophy of life only *seems* that way. The psychic "*durée*" of Bergson is nothing but a theoretical abstraction, the product of a theoretical analysis of the feeling aspect of time according to its subject-side. By virtue of the primary absolutization of the theoretical (in this case the psychological) synthesis, it is presented as the *true* and *complete time*. The same applies to Heidegger's (phenomenological) "historical time" as the "horizon" of thought: it absolutizes a "phenomenological" abstraction which itself can only be the product of theoretical analysis and synthesis. Heidegger too proceeds from the self-*sufficiency* of the *theoretical*, to be more precise: of the *phenomenological* cognitive

---

1 [In the *Philosophy of the Cosmonomic Idea* this starting-point is designated as the Archimedian point of philosophy.]

attitude, interpreted by him in an irrationalist sense. He rejects every acknowledgment of the supra-theoretical conditionality ("*Bedingtheit*") of a phenomenological investigation.

10. Only in the religious center of his existence does the human being transcend time. The uncritical character of the immanence standpoint

Why is the prejudice of the "self-sufficiency of theoretical thought within its own domain" uncritical and dogmatic? Because theoretical thought in its modal logical aspect (and this is intended here) cannot unilaterally determine its relationship to the other modal aspects of reality. In the "cogito" the thinking *selfhood* is active, functioning not only in the logical-analytical aspect but equally in all other aspects of reality and so functioning at the same time as the individual *concentration point* of all these aspects of temporal human existence. Since all aspects are equally embraced by cosmic time and therefore are intrinsically *temporal* in nature, the concentration point of the human being, where all temporal aspects coincide as in one focal point, cannot itself be of a temporal but only of a supra-temporal, transcendent character. The theoretical synthesis is determined both by cosmic time and by the supra-temporal transcendent selfhood.

The immanence standpoint only *seems* to succeed in maintaining itself by abruptly, in line with "critical" philosophy, identifying the thinking selfhood with the so-called transcendental-logical epistemic subject (in Kant the "transcendental-logical unity of apperception"). What actually happens is that the selfhood collapses into a *transcendental-logical form-unity* which is then sharply distinguished from the *individual, temporal,* "empirical" *psychological* I-ness. This "transcendental thinking subject" then serves as *theoretical-logical* concentration point. As subjective thought-pole (Theodor Litt) it can never be turned into the "Gegenstand" of thinking because it is the necessary, universally valid condition for all thought directed towards a "Gegenstand."

The dogmatic character of the "transcendental-logical" conception of the selfhood is apparent as soon as one realizes that it is a *theoretical abstraction* and as such a *thought-product* of the thinking selfhood. The thinking selfhood identifies itself uncritically with its own thought product.

Neither a "transcendental-logical" selfhood nor an "empirical-psychological" selfhood exists. Of course the selfhood does display modal psychic and modal logical *functions*; nevertheless it is the necessary *transcendent concentration point*, not only of the psychical and logical, but at once also of all its other temporal modal functions.

A transcendental-*logical* unity *above* the theoretical diversity of thought-categories, as Kant believes to have found in his transcendental thinking subject, does not exist. Within the modal structure of the logical aspect only a logical unity in a logical multiplicity is found. This unity cannot be transcendent in nature.

The theory of the transcendental thinking subject is nothing but the nominalistic, epistemological formalization of the old theory of Scholastic psychology concerning the *anima rationalis* (rational soul) as substance. This metaphysical psychology located the soul's "unity and simplicity" in the intellect as its *essence*, its substantial center, which imprinted a *rational* character on all the other "capacities of the soul."

This view of the soul derived from Aristotelian psychology and here corresponded with Aristotle's view of divinity as "pure reason" (*actus purus*). Scholasticism attempted in vain to accommodate this view to the Christian doctrine of the simplicity and indivisibility of the soul.[1]

In vain, I say, for the "rational soul" lacks the essential unity that Christian doctrine justifiably ascribes to the "soul." As a metaphysical abstraction it remains caught up in the diversity of temporal functions. Thinking, which is supposed to constitute its essential nature, in the final analysis is but one of the modes in which the soul manifests itself. Neither the will nor the life of feeling admit of being reduced to mere *modes* of thinking. Only in the religious concentration point of the human being are

---

1 Compare in this regard my treatise "Kuyper's wetenschapsleer," *Phil. Ref.* 4 (1939): 193-232, at 203.

all temporal functions and acts brought together in their deeper unity.

Yet the immanence standpoint, by virtue of its starting-point, is forced to search for its starting-point within thinking itself. On the basis of this view of the concentration point of the human being, it was impossible to gain insight into the nature of *cosmic time*. In Aristotelian-Thomistic Scholasticism time is merely conceived as "measure of movement." On this view the "rational soul," to which it ascribed "incorruptibility," is subject to time only in an "accidental" sense, namely in connection with the *material body*. According to its "rational essence" it is "supra-temporal," where it can only be measured by the "*aevum*"[1] (Thomas Aquinas).[2]

11. A true awareness of time presupposes a transcendent center for time experience. *Kuyper's* view of the transcendent center

It is indeed correct to say that we would not have a genuine awareness of *time* if we did not *transcend* time in the deepest core of our being. All merely temporal creatures lack an *awareness of time*. Every instance of absolutizing time rests on a *lack of critical self-reflection*.

But the true concentration point, the *supra-temporal root* of our existence, cannot be known on the basis of an autonomous philosophy; for the latter, in its theoretical character, necessarily remains enclosed *within the horizon of time*. It is only the divine Word-revelation that discovers us to ourselves. True self-knowledge, as Calvin remarks in his *Institutes*, is acquired only

---

1 Since Boethius the "*aevum*" was conceived as an intermediate state between time and eternity, from which it therefore had to be distinguished. According to Thomas, time has an earlier and later; the *aevum* as such, by contrast, does not have any earlier and later, though the latter can be combined with it; eternity has neither an earlier nor a later, nor can it be combined with them (*Summa Theologica*, I, Q. 10, art. 5).

2 *Summa Theologica*, I, Q. 10, art. 5: "Sed aevum dicitur esse mensura spiritualium substantiarum." More on this in my treatise "*Het Tijdsprobleem en zijn antinomieën op het immanentiestandpunt*," *Phil. Ref.* 4 (1939): 1-28. [This treatise is included in the present volume as Chapter I, Part A, sections 10-32.]

through true knowledge of God. I call this the *religious concentration law* of human existence.

The "soul" of the human being, which according to the testimony of Scripture is not affected by the *temporal* death since it continues to exist even after laying down the "body" – that is, after laying down the *entire temporal form of existence* enclosed in the individuality structure – is the *religious root* of the human being, also designated by Scripture as the "inner man" or the "heart" of a person, from which flow the "issues of life" and in which "eternity is laid." It is, as Kuyper expresses it in his *Stone Lectures on Calvinism*, "that point in our consciousness where our life is still undivided and where it is still bound together in its unity." According to Kuyper this concentration point is not found in "the spreading vines but in the root from which the vines spring. That point cannot be found anywhere but in the antithesis between all that is *finite* in our human life and the *infinite* that lies beyond it. Here alone do we find the common source from which the different streams of human life spring and separate themselves."[1] Kuyper employs not only the image of a religious *root* but also that of a *focus*: "Personally it is our repeated experience that in the depths of our hearts, at the point where we disclose ourselves to the Eternal One, all the rays of our life converge as in one focus, and there alone regain that harmony which we so often and so painfully lose in the stress of daily life."[2]

However, this religious root of the individual human existence ought not to be understood in the sense of an "autonomous individual," since it is created by God participating in the *religious root-community of humankind*. In Adam it found its first head falling away from God, but in Christ as its second head this religious community with God is *restored*. This religious root-community of humankind is the true *supra-individual* con-

1   On this, see my treatise "Kuyper's wetenschapsleer," *Phil. Ref.* 4 (1939): 193–232, at 211.
2   This view of the religious center of human existence is irreconcilable with the traditional Scholastic concept of the soul, one that Kuyper worked with in his dogmatics, as he also did [in his anthropology] with the traditional view of dichotomy.

centration-point of the entire cosmos. It also explains why the fall in Adam not only affected the total human race but drew with it also the entire temporal cosmos, as in Christ the *whole* mos is saved in its root.

A truly Christian philosophy of time is therefore impossible when theoretical thought is not directed towards the genuine supra-temporal concentration-point of the temporal comsos. Theoretical thought in philosophy is never self-sufficient. Rather, by virtue of the structure of creation itself it is necessarily *religiously determined,* whether in an apostate direction or in a directedness towards the true Origin of everything, as revealed in Christ Jesus.

12. Law-side and subject-side of cosmic time. Time as time-order and time as duration

The time-transcending character of the religious concentration point of the temporal cosmos is also manifest in that it transcends the diversity of modal aspects which are enclosed within the horizon of time. The deeper root-unity of the modal aspects cannot be found *in time.* Given its cosmic continuity, time cannot itself be the root-unity of these aspects.

In order to understand this properly we must begin by making a sharp distinction between two *sides* of time which mutually presuppose each other and which therefore cannot be separated from each other, namely the *law-side* and the *subject-side* of time.

According to its law-side, (cosmic) time presents itself as *time-order;* it manifests itself within the modal aspects and typifies itself within the individuality structures. According to its subject-side, time is individual duration. Every creature, insofar as it has a temporal mode of being, is subject to the time-order. The time-order, in its *cosmic* character encompassing and grounding all modal aspects and individuality structures, is the *same* for every subject. The individual and subjective *time duration,* however, is different for every individual temporal existence.

Remark: *on aspects and the time order*

This is also the case within the modal aspects. Numerical and spatial relationships acquire a distinct subjective duration within the context of concrete entities, events, and so on. Five people, for example, are together for five minutes within the same square room. After the fifth minute one of them moves to an adjacent space, leaving four people in the first room. The first numerical and spatial relationship lasted only for five minutes. The modal aspects of this time duration follows the modal time-orders: the numerical duration follows that of the numerical time-order, and the spatial duration follows that of the spatial aspect (simultaneous extension).

Within the modal aspectual structures of number and space we find only modal time-order and no subjective duration. The same applies to the logical aspect of time. That the logical *"prius en posterius"* was not appreciated as a genuine configuration of time can be explained in part from the fact that the subjective logical movement of thought, through which the logical time aspect reveals its subjection to the logical time-order as logical duration, was supposed to be conceived of as a kind of "psychical natural event" which needed only a "causal explanation." However, a discursive logical process implies a subjective logical time-duration in which the logical time-order manifests itself in subjectively diverse ways (one person reaches a conclusion more quickly and accurately than another person) and in which inferences may also be drawn illogically (which is not the same as a-logically). If the *logical* meaning of subjective time *duration* is eliminated, the thought process itself is cancelled and then it is no longer possible to speak of the duration of a thought-act. And that logical meaning is indeed eliminated whenever an attempt is made to separate the duration of thinking from the logical time-*order*.

According to their objective logical properties, entities have an objective logical duration. Embedded in their temporal individual existence, these properties indeed come into existence and pass away – in contrast with the constant individuality structures (and the logical types implied by them) in which they function.

The logical object-function of a thing should not at all be identified with a subjective logical concept. Nor should it be identified with the constant individuality structure which enables the coming into being and passing away of an individual entity or, for that matter, with the constant structure of the logical aspect within which it functions with its objective logical properties. Of course the subjective concept which I have formed of a certain thing is independent of the continued existence of that thing. The same applies to the sensory representation. But the actual logical object-function of a thing is, in combination with the entire entity, just as transient as its objective historical, economic, aesthetical or juridical functions. Just as an entity, when passing away, ceases to be a beautiful or economically valuable thing, or a cultural or legal object, so it will also lose its characteristics as a logical object. A pile of rubble no longer displays the features of the building prior to its collapse.

A subjective concept has its subjective logical duration and is equally perishable in time. However, in human society the contents of such a concept allows for its objectification in lingual symbols, whereby it is preserved for later generations. In this way an objectified concept acquires through its acceptance by a relatively constant intellectual community a logical duration in a social sense. This duration is independent of acceptance by individual persons and only ceases to exist when the thought community changes its mode of thinking. However, it is never the case that a concept is timeless, as was taught by idealism.

The issue turns out to be totally different as soon as one brings into play the truth value of propositions. Truth is essentially not logical in nature. Rather, it is of a supra-temporal, religious nature, because Truth is by nature central and total. The proposition *Socrates was a man* is not true "in itself." It is definitely *untrue* if our understanding of "man" proceeds from a false and unbelieving conception, such as when the term "man" is simply employed to designate a higher form of animal. Similarly, the proposition $2 \times 2 = 4$ is not *true in itself*, because it immediately acquires a false sense if it is withdrawn from the truth value of God's creational sovereignty.

13. The criterion for the order of time

Time-order in the true sense of the term is necessarily related to subjective (or: subjective-objective) time duration. It is an *order for time duration*. Every order of before and after, of earlier and later, which necessarily manifests itself on the subject-side of reality as time duration, is time-order. In the absence of this relation to time duration one cannot assign a truly temporal character to before and after. For example, this can certainly not be done with respect to the priority relationship between the Creator and his creation.

Although of course it does not constitute a definition, the above description serves as the genuine criterion for time-order.

71

In immanence philosophy, which after all looks for its Archimedian point within theoretical thought,[1] this necessary two-sidedness of time is not appreciated, since it cannot properly understand the true meaning of law and subject.[2] Law and subjectivity in their mutual relation can only be understood in a proper way from a Christian standpoint which looks for the origin of creation in God's sovereign creational will. God has subjected every creature to His law. The creature is in this sense *sujet* (subject) to God's creation-order.

The law belongs to creaturely reality as its *determination* and its essential *delimitation*. Therefore no subject exists without a law. But the opposite is also true. The law has meaning only as determination and delimitation of creaturely subjectivity. Therefore there is no law without a subject. Only God is not a subject, because God is not subject to the law, which after all finds its origin in His divine creational will. The law-side and subject-side are therefore the two sides of created reality without which no creaturely being is possible.

Since the entire temporal reality is embraced by time, this two-sidedness of law and subjectivity must also come to expression within time itself.

14. Rationalistic and irrationalistic conceptions of time

It is therefore in principle mistaken to reduce time one-sidedly either to the law-side or to the subject-side. The time conceptions of immanence philosophy made this mistake as a matter of principle and as a consequence oscillated between these two opposites. The absolutization of the law as general order or rule already was characteristic of *rationalism*, whereas the absolutization of individual subjectivity, by contrast, gives rise to the *irrationalistic* trends within traditional philosophy.

It is therefore no surprise that the conceptions of time alternatively manifest rationalistic and irrationalistic orientations. A truly rationalistic orientation is found, for example, in Newton's conception of absolute "mathematical" time. As objective order for earlier and later in movement, in contrast with the so-called

---

1 It is, as we have seen, the concentration point of thought from which the thinker has to understand the modal aspects of reality in a theoretical totality view. The Archimedian point is the starting-point of philosophical thought and must transcend time with its modal refraction points.
2 Another source of confusion about the subject concept was the identification of subject and substance in Scholastic metaphysics.

empirical time, this absolute mathematical time implies a completely uniform duration[1] of its flowing moments. In its progression it is supposed to be *completely independent of any subjective event*. Newton entirely separates uniform movement from the subjective duration of reality.

A standard example of an alternative, *irrationalistic* position is Bergson's view of time as subjectively experienced emotional duration ("élan vital"). It is opposed to all law-conformity because the latter is considered a conceptual abstraction that falsifies true reality. This conception is typically *modal psychologistic* in nature because it erases the boundaries between the biotic and the psychical.

15. Time as horizon of temporal reality

When time is viewed according to its law-side, i.e., when it is seen as *order*, then it constitutes the *horizon* both of temporal reality and of our entire temporal experience, making these possible to begin with through its determining and delimiting character that embraces the whole of temporal reality.

Both structural orders of reality are grounded in this horizon of time, namely the earlier mentioned order of modal aspects and the order of individuality structures. We will return to the latter in more detail below.

16. The time-order of the aspects as law of refraction. The prismatic character of this time-order

As horizon of the modal aspect structures the order of time truly is a *law of refraction*. The meaning-totality of our temporal cosmos, which constitutes the essential *unity* and *fullness* of the meaning of all aspects of creation, cannot be given within time. It has a *transcendent, supra-temporal* character.

This applies to both the law-side and the subject-side of reality.

According to its religious *fullness* and *meaning-totality*, the law of God is *one* and *indivisible*: the demand to serve God wholeheartedly. According to the religious fullness and meaning-totality of the subject-side of reality, the temporal creation, since the fall, is completely concentrated in the religious root-community of the new humanity in Christ. However, *within time* this re-

1 This "duration" is here simply transformed into a dependent reflex of the mathematical time-order.

ligious fullness according to its law-side and subject-side is re-fracted into the modal aspects in which the wisdom of God's plan for creation unfolds in a rich diversity of modal ordinances and subject-functions. Just as unbroken sunlight is refracted through a prism into the multicolored richness of the spectrum, so the religious fullness of meaning of creation is refracted in the wealth of modal aspects which do not find their transcendent root-unity within time itself.

17. The individuality structures of reality lack this prismatic character

In the second place, this religious fullness of meaning differenti-ates according to the law-side and subject-side into the individ-uality structures of the temporal creation. We have seen that the individuality structures imply the modal aspects. As we shall demonstrate, the individuality structures, which in essence are structures of individual *totalities* that function equally in all modal aspects of reality, are essentially *time-structures* em-braced by the horizon of time. Yet, as we shall see, unlike the modal aspects they are not *refraction points*.

18. The idea of time as an element of the transcendental ground-idea of philosophy

In its general theory of the modal aspects the *Philosophy of the Cosmonomic Idea* has shown, by means of theoretical analysis, that the modal-aspect structures essentially are *time-structures*.

As we have seen, cosmic time, which in its continuity em-braces and overarches all modal aspects, refuses to be theoreti-cally analyzed, because it is a transcendental pre-supposition of theoretical analysis. Therefore, the only access open to the philosophical investigation of the cosmic time-order is by way of analyzing the *modal structures* of time. Within the transcen-dental ground-idea of philosophy, cosmic time itself serves as philosophy's basic presupposition.

This ground-idea (or cosmonomic idea) is a foundational *lim-iting concept* of philosophy. Through it, philosophical thought, in the process of critical self-reflection, gives an account of its own necessary presuppositions which are themselves non-theoreti-cal in nature and which make possible philosophical investigation to begin with. This basic idea contains, in addition to an idea about the *origin* and deeper *unity* of the modal aspects of temporal reality, also an idea about the interrelation or *coherence* of these aspects.

It is striking that these three transcendental ideas, which in their internal linkage are comprehended in any cosmonomic idea, lie at the foundation of every philosophical system, whether a thinker shows a *critical awareness* of it or not. Yet the immanence standpoint cannot concede that one's philosophical ground-idea is determined by non-theoretical presuppositions.

19. The method employed in the theoretical analysis of the time-order of the modal aspects

If the modal aspects are intrinsically *time* aspects, then their orderly *succession* in time, too, must be a real time-order, an order that comes to expression within the modal structure of each aspect.

Remark: *on the temporal order of the modal aspects*

If our earlier exposition of the distinction and correlation between time-*order* and time *duration* is properly understood, it will not be difficult to accept this understanding of the essential *temporal* character of this succession. Although the order of the modal aspects is *constant* within time, just as they are with respect to their modal structure, this does not detract anything from the temporal order as such. It forms a part of the temporal world-order and is contained in God's world-plan. It should not be viewed as eternal, or as an order which *transcends time*.

In the genesis or process of becoming of the temporal world, this order was related to subjective temporal duration, which continues in the most universal sense in relation to the developmental process of the human individual in society. This process is indeed a temporal cosmic process and cannot be conceived of in a purely biological way. What is undeniable is that life can develop only *after* the physico-chemical conditions are formed in time; that feeling develops only after a period of totally unconscious embryonic life in which all actual independent sensitive processes are absent; that the logical thought-function develops only after the genesis of actual sensory feeling life; that the cul-

75

tural-historical function unfolds only after the first rudimentary differentiation of logical thinking; that the lingual function[1] reveals its initial development prior to the social function; etc.

It should be remembered, however, that the time-order of the modal aspects is related only to subjective duration within the individuality structures of concrete creatures and that these individuality structures themselves determine and make possible the individual process of development. Temporal duration is not inherent in the modal aspects and individuality structures themselves, but only in their subjective realization. In themselves they are merely *orderings* of time.

This tie to subjective duration undoubtedly stamps the *before* and *after* in the order of aspects as a *time*-order. Time-order and time duration, after all, are necessary correlates.

The general theory of law-spheres investigated this cosmic time-order in the following way. When analyzing these structures it appeared that each one of them contains a *modal nucleus* which in its original sense is proper only to that specific aspect. It guarantees the *modal irreducibility* or *modal sphere-sovereignty* of the aspect under consideration. The same cosmic time-order which externally binds the aspects together in a continuous coherence and determines their succession also brings this coherence and succession to expression in their inner structure. All law-spheres which in the cosmic time-order have other law-spheres preceding them reveal, in accordance with their *internal* modal structure, moments that hark back to these earlier aspects. In the general theory of law-spheres they are designated as *retrocipations* or *analogies*. Unlike the nucleus of an aspect, these retrocipations or analogies do not display an *original* character, for in them the modal nucleus harks back, rather, to the meaning-nuclei of the modal aspects that appear earlier in the cosmic time-order. On the other hand, those aspects which in the cosmic time-order are followed by others that appear later in this order display within their inner structure certain moments that anticipate these later aspects. In the general theory of the law-spheres they are designated as *modal anticipations*. These an-

---

1 Messer acknowledges that a child's lingual function develops only after its rudimentary logical development. He writes: "The absorbed representations, which function in cognition as concepts, are present in the child in large numbers before it acquires the corresponding words" (*Psychologie*, p. 245). Even in the case of an adult "a concept may already be present even as he is still thinking about the word" (ibid., p. 250).

ticipations too do not display an *original* character since in them the nucleus of an aspect rather *points forward in time* to the meaning-nuclei of those aspects that appear *later* in the cosmic order.

Obviously, given this state of affairs there must be two boundary aspects of temporal reality where one does not display any analogies within its modal structure and the other does not display any anticipations. These boundary aspects are that of *quantity* and that of *faith*, because the former is not preceded by any law-sphere and the latter is not followed by any law-sphere.

20. The *refraction point* within the respective directions of the time-order

In all the other modal structures the modal nucleus actually is the *refraction point* of cosmic time. The two directions of time here manifest themselves by pointing backwards and pointing forwards. The *Philosophy of the Cosmonomic Idea* designates the former direction as the *foundational* and the latter as the *transcendental* direction of time.

Within the structure of a particular aspect it is the modal nucleus that qualifies the retrocipations and anticipations. The latter therefore do not take on the meaning of the modal meaning-nuclei to which they point backwards or forwards.

In the general theory of relativity, for example, the space of (physical) movement is not space in its original modal sense, but only an analogy of space within the meaning of movement which is founded in the original meaning of space. This explains why, in the general theory of relativity, the properties of this space are dependent upon those of "matter" as a function of gravitation. Naturally this would not have any meaning for so-called geometrical (non-physical) space. Similarly, in the irrational and differential functions of number we find modal anticipations of the meaning of *space* and *movement*.

21. The time-structure of the psychical and the logical aspects

Thus, take the modal structure of feeling.[1] In the moment of *sensibility* we find an analogy of the nucleus of organic life. In the moment of *emotionality* (from *"movere"*: to move), where the awareness is correlated with the objective images of movement

1   See the Remark below on the modal meaning of feeling.

in the "outer world," we meet an analogy of the original nucleus of the kinematic aspect. In the subjective sensory space, which in an objective sense answers to the sensory spatial awareness, we see an analogy of the original nucleus of space. In the moment of sensory multiplicity (once again both in a subjective and an objective sense), we meet an analogy of the original nucleus of quantity.

Remark: *on the modal meaning of feeling*

The modal meaning of feeling certainly embraces more than what psychology usually means by this term. Without any doubt it includes the so-called *"Empfindungen"* or sense impressions. A sensory impression of a visual, tactile or other typical structure, when viewed according to its *modal* character, is just as much a sensory phenomenon as a feeling of pleasure or pain. Since J. N. Tetens, psychology is tainted by the prejudice to deny the sensitive nature of sensory impressions merely because of their normal subject-object relation and to assign it merely to the purely subjective feelings of pleasure and pain. As we know, Tetens himself was still not consistent in his distinction between "feelings" and "sense-impressions," since he ascribed both to the same experiential ability. Kant was the first to pursue this line consistently since he no longer subsumed *"Empfindungen"* under sensibility but under the cognitive faculty.

No doubt a one-sided epistemology with a natural-scientific orientation and theory of reality played an essential role here. The modern psychological conception of *"Empfindung"* as a "relatively simple observational content"[1] is derived from the atomistic association psychology, which attempts to construct the entire consciousness from simple elements.

However, until now the attempt to specify a *modal* difference between "feeling" and *"Empfindung"* has been unsuccessful. In naive experience, as it finds expression in the so-called psychology of everyday life, such a basic distinction is not found. Neither the criterion of subjectivity, nor that of polarity and "affectivity," nor that of so-called *actuality* (Oswald Külpe) is adequate for differentiating modally between feeling and *"Empfindung."* The first and the third criterion are disqualified because they are not oriented to the structure of an aspect but in general to the subject-object relation. But neither is the second criterion useful in this regard. Just consider the impressions of pain and temperature, which are counted as *"Empfindungen"* although they undoubtedly display a polar and affective character.

At the same time, one should not confuse the modal element of emotionality (sensitive movement) with the *typical* affectivity of pleasure and pain – as is done by Messer. In a modal sense the subjective sense of color also inherently displays the moment of sensitive movement, otherwise we would be unable to become aware of the greater or lesser *intensity* of colors, because this awareness presupposes sensory movement in a sensitive sense. On the other hand, logical feeling can hardly be classified within the scheme of affective feelings of pleasure and pain.

Lack of insight into the modal structure of feeling life is the reason why within the scheme of mental feelings (as worked out by Messer, following Jodl) essential normative feelings, such as formative (cultural) feeling, lingual feeling, social sensitivity, economic sensitivity, and so on, are left totally unexamined. Except for the so-called "personal feelings" (*Persongefühle*), attention is paid only to logical, aesthetic, ethical and religious feelings, the so-called "objective feelings" (*Sachgefühle*).

Conversely, in the following concepts we evidently find anticipations of the modal meaning of the psychical aspect: logical sensitivity, historical sensitivity, lingual feeling, social feeling, aesthetic, jural and moral feeling as well as certitudinal feeling (the feeling of trust in a firm foundation or – in combination with the logical anticipation – the feeling of confirmation or assurance).

Remark: *on the psychical aspect*

Schopenhauer enumerates all such anticipatory feeling functions alongside the retrocipatory (sensory) functions in order to demonstrate that the concept of *feeling* throughout "has only a *negative* content, namely that something which is present in consciousness is not there as a concept or as abstract rational knowledge. For the rest, whatever it may be, it belongs to the concept of *feeling*, whose extremely broad domain encompasses the most heterogeneous entities. One will never understand how they come together so long as one fails to see that they are only similar in the *negative* respect that they are *not abstract concepts.*"

If Schopenhauer had been aware of the principle of sphere-sovereignty, he would not have written this sentence. Messer (op. cit., p. 127) comes close to this negative conception of Schopenhauer: "One may therefore say, half in jest: *Was man nicht definieren kann, das sieht man als ein Fühlen an* [What cannot be defined is taken to be a feeling]." The reason why the nucleus of the aspect of feeling cannot be defined is made clear in my theory of the law-spheres. The nucleus is indeed the *irreducible* element in the modal structure of an aspect. Yet, in this respect the sensitive aspect does not occupy an exceptional position. The same applies

79

even with regard to the nucleus of the logical aspect. On the other hand, the absence of any insight into the modal structure of the aspect of feeling avenges itself when an internally undetermined "universality" is assigned to it and when feeling is assumed to be, in line with the developmental psychology of Felix Krueger, the originally undifferentiated origin of all other "experiences," such as thinking and willing (thus Messer, ibid., p. 119).

Apparently the anticipatory feeling functions, which indeed in the early developmental phase display a largely undifferentiated form, are here confused with concrete "acts," which, as we shall see, can never be exhausted by one aspect.

Similarly, the analysis of the modal structure of logical thinking has undeniably demonstrated the *temporal* character of this structure. At the same time it has shown the untenability of all attempts at locating a time-transcending Archimedean point for philosophical thought in the logical aspect.

Within the modal structure of the logical aspect we find, according to the cosmic time-order of the modalities, the following *analogies*:

1. The arithmetical analogy in the moment of a logical multiplicity, which is inherent in every concept as its *synthesis noematon*.
2. The analogy of space in the moment of cognitive space, in which the multiplicity of conceptual properties are juxtaposed in order subsequently to unite them in a concept.
3. The analogy of movement in the logical movement of thought to which we have alluded in an earlier context.
4. The analogy of the biotic nucleus in logical thought-life.
5. The psychical analogy in the conceptual representation (the pretheoretical conceptual *image*) which is still attached to sensory feeling impressions but nonetheless succeeds in fixating logical characteristics.

The following anticipations are discerned:

1. The historical anticipation is present in the formative logical control,[1] which can only reveal itself in scientific thought by virtue of its systematic character. (This differs from naive, pre-theoretical thinking where concepts are still attached to sensory impressions.)

---

1   In the theory of the law-spheres the nucleus of the historical aspect (according to its subject-side) is analyzed as "free formative control" (culture).

2. The lingual anticipation in the form of logical cognitive symbolism – through which theoretical thought liberates itself from its restrictive bondage to sensory representations.
3. The social anticipation reveals itself in the moment of disclosed logical interaction, in which the logical argumentation continually has to defend itself in opposition to counter-arguments (which is likewise typical only of scientific thinking).
4. The economic anticipation is seen in the moment of logical thought-economy. It is absent in naive thought. In its structure it may be viewed as a theoretical deepening of the principle of sufficient reason.
5. The aesthetical anticipation appears as the moment of logical (system) harmony.
6. The jural anticipation comes to the fore in the moment of the logical legal ground – which has to justify itself in the interaction of argument and counter-argument.
7. The moral anticipation reveals itself in the moment of theoretical *eros* (Plato).
8. The certitudinal anticipation is present in the moment of logical certainty, as it reveals itself in the logical axiom – which points forward to a supposition of faith.

In the coherence of nucleus and analogies a modal aspect reveals itself only in a closed or restrictive structure. Through its anticipations, by contrast, the structure of an aspect reveals its deepened or disclosed function,[1] while the process of disclosure itself is a cosmic temporal process.

22. The criterion for the distinction of the retrocipatory and anticipatory directions of time within the modal structure of an aspect

Because the process of disclosure within the modal structures of reality essentially bears a *temporal* character, we also have a criterion for establishing whether the non-original moments within an aspect are analogical or anticipatory in character. As we have seen, the directions of referring backwards and for-

---

1 This also establishes the correct relationship between naive and scientific thought. Scientific thought is not *detached* from naive thought; rather, it is essentially a *deepening* and *disclosing* of pre-theoretical thought, a process that can be activated in accordance with the nature of logical analysis only via theoretical abstraction and opposition.

wards in the succession of moments, after all, have to be related to *genetic time duration* if they are to count as true directions of *time*.

It is possible to show that within concrete reality the modal structure reveals itself in a closed condition before the process of disclosure commences in the anticipatory direction of time. Disclosure, by contrast, cannot occur before a modal function has realized itself in a *closed form*.

Thus the modal function of motion first of all realizes itself in a closed structure within inorganic entities. Moreover, in the "directed" movements of a living organism they are realized in a disclosed structure, which, in the time-order of creation, can only develop *after* inorganic creatures appeared. But even in the still closed movements the temporal coherence with the numerical and the spatial aspect necessarily comes to expression in an arithmetical and a spatial analogy. In the directed movements, namely those guided by their biotic destination, the process of disclosure involves the entire modal structure in its closed condition. In other words, the disclosure concerns both the nucleus as well as the modal analogies.

For example, the sensitive function realizes feeling *first* in a closed form in the so-called sensory feelings *before* feeling life is disclosed by the normative aspects. Animal feeling life does know a greater or lesser degree of differentiation in restrictive bondage to the biotic differentiation of sensory organs, but it does not know a genuine disclosure of normative feelings. With this we have also established the temporal succession between the analogical and the anticipating moments within the modal structure of the aspect of feeling.

The modal structure of the logical aspect also realizes itself *first of all* in a closed function, namely in pre-scientific thinking – where all the analogical moments are present, but where no single modal anticipation of the later aspects is present. In *naive* logical thinking one does not find a logical control of thought--contents by means of systematic concepts, or a logical thought-symbolism, or thought-economy, or logical harmony, or the jural anticipations in the weighing of logical legal grounds against their counter grounds, or any theoretical *eros* (a moral anticipation) or any logical axiomatics [accepted on faith].

In the same way one can determine which moments within later aspects, such as the historical aspect, the lingual aspect or still later aspects, are of an analogical or anticipatory nature. In a primitive legal order, for example, the entire analogical structure of the modal jural aspect is realized, including the *economic analogy*[1] (as in legal action against any excessive pursuit of subjective legal interests according to the primitive *talio* principle[2]). But here every moral anticipation is absent. Governing primitive law is the principle of *Erfolgshaftung* (strict liability), which pays attention exclusively to the *consequences* of a deed. It does not yet know the anticipatory concept of juridical fault, through which juridical causality and unlawfulness [illegality] is deepened.

Remark: *on the closed condition of primitive societies*

That the whole of primitive society in all its aspects finds itself in such a closed condition, despite the undeniable fact that all of its life is typically guided by faith, is a state of affairs that has been subjected to an extensive examination by the *Philosophy of the Cosmonomic Idea.*

The key to understanding this fact is found in the boundary character of the pistical function. In a truly primitive society apostasy actually reaches a transcendental limiting point where heathendom divinizes undisclosed natural forces (cf. the *mana* belief). Under the guidance of such an apostate faith all the earlier normative functions necessarily remain in a "closed form," because through the absolutization of natural forces they are rigidly bound to their prelogical substrate functions. Compare for exam-

---

1   The structure of the aesthetical aspect also contains an economic analogy. Beautiful harmony cannot reveal itself without observing the principle of aesthetic frugality. Applying too much paint also in the case of a primitive work of art results in an ugly painting. By contrast, the logical, historical, social and lingual aspects of reality can reveal their temporal coherence with the economic aspect only in the *anticipatory* direction. Primitive language, for example, still lacks every form of symbolical economy. In the subjective development of a child the lingual function without any doubt unfolds itself before the economic function.

2   This is the economic analogy according to the law-side (norm-side) of the jural aspect. On the subject-side [factual side] this analogy reveals itself in a subjective right and in the structure of a legal object. Here the legal object is nothing but the juridical objectification of an economic evaluation (for that reason free air cannot be a legal object).

ple the rigid bondage of contracting parties to the words of an agreement (think of the stipulation of the primitive Roman *ius civile*), which leave no room whatever for the application of the disclosed legal principles of good faith, equity, moral cause, and so on. The magical conception of the spoken word, whereby a person can put a spell on someone, dominates everything.

Consider also the rigidifying power exerted here by tradition over culture. Every change in the old ways is denounced as sacrilegious.

23. The sphere-universality of the modal aspects of time

In this way every modal aspect according to its modal time-structure is in fact a mirror of the entire cosmic time-order in all its modal refraction points. The *Philosophy of the Cosmonomic Idea* has designated this state of affairs as the *sphere-universality* of the aspects, which is simply the sphere-sovereignty or modal irreducibility of the modal aspects.

This state of affairs also explains the possibility to carry through all the isms within immanence philosophy such as mathematicism, mechanicism, biologism, psychologism, logicism, historicism, and so on. All these isms essentially flow from a necessity implicit in the immanence standpoint, namely to find the *root-unity* of the aspects in one specific aspect of temporal reality – abstracted and absolutized by theoretical thought – such that all other aspects are then considered to be merely modalities of the absolutized aspect.

24. The meaning-character of temporal reality

What comes to expression above all in this state of affairs is the *meaning-character* of reality. Nowhere in reality do we find an *absolute point of rest*, an *autonomous anchor*.

Throughout temporal reality *every aspect* points *beyond itself* toward the temporal coherence of modal aspects. In the transcendental limiting aspect of time, i.e., the faith aspect, this temporal coherence of aspects points beyond time to their religious root, which in turn demonstrates its non-self-sufficiency through its relation of religious dependency with respect to its *Divine Origin*.

This character of reality guarantees the tendency of all of created reality towards the Origin, because no creature can find rest in itself. And this tendency is concentrated in the human

84

heart. Augustine said: "Our heart is restless until it finds rest in Thee."[1] To "our heart" we may add: "and the world in our heart."

25. The perspectival structure of cosmic time and the awareness of transcendence

Only through this meaningful relatedness of temporal reality to the creaturely center and the Divine Origin does the perspectival structure of cosmic time reveal itself. In relation to concrete events, human beings experience this structure as the *past*, the *present* and the *future*.

This perspectival structure presupposes a *directedness* of time. As we have seen, this is already manifested by the modal structure of temporal reality which according to the Divine order of creation can find its ultimate point of orientation only *beyond* time. In the measure that the awareness of transcendence declines, human self-awareness also diminishes, and with it the ability to experience the perspectival structure of time.

This comes to expression in a very strong form among so-called primitive peoples. The absence of a disclosed *historical* time awareness in primitive cultures has been sufficiently demonstrated by ethnological investigations.[2]

Yet it is incorrect to identify this perspectival time-structure – in a historicistic sense – with the historical aspect. It properly belongs to cosmic time as such and only expresses itself in a particular modal sense as the historical aspect of past, present, and future.

26. The subject-object relation in time duration

In order to shed even more light on the *meaning-character* of temporal reality (and with it, of time as such) – which cannot be closed off – we are obliged to take a closer look at the subject-object relation within time. In traditional views of time this relation is not properly understood, as is evident from the fact that

---

1 *Confessiones* 1.1.
2 See e.g. Maurice Leenhardt, "Le temps et la personalité chez les Canaques dans la Nouvelle-Calédonie," *Revue philosophique* 62.9/10 (1937): 49 ff.

subjectivistic and *objectivistic* conceptions are used interchange-ably.[1]

The subject-object relation is a fundamental relation within the structure of temporal reality. Therefore it should never be confused with the epistemological relation of subjective theoretical thought and its *Gegenstand*.[2] Since Kant, this confusion has generally pervaded immanence philosophy.

In addition, the object in the sense of *Gegenstand* is often, in a typical rationalist manner, identified with what is law-conformative in our knowledge (compare Kant's description of the "Gegenstand" of experience).

In order to demonstrate the incorrectness of identifying object and "Gegenstand" it is sufficient to point out that naive experience is completely familiar with the subject-object relation while, as we have seen, an abstract "Gegenstand" is completely foreign to the naive attitude of thought.

The subject-object relation appears both within the modal and the individuality structure of reality. We shall first look at this relation within the structures of the modal aspects. It is found in all those law-spheres where it is possible to discern analogies within their modal structures.

Remark: on modal subject-object relations

Already in the spatial aspect there exists such a relation between a *subjective spatial figure* and its *points*. A spatial point does not have actual subjective extension in any dimension. It is simply an objective analogy of the irrational (infinite) numerical function within the aspect of space. The modal spatial time-order is revealed in the point as an objective moment (time-point) within simultaneous extension. Dependent upon points is also the *objective magnitude* (a numerical analogy) of a spatial figure.

Similarly, in the aspect of movement we find the subject-object relation in the relation between the subjective (actual) movement with its actual path and its objective movement-space. The properties of the latter depend upon those of motion and it exists only

---

1 Irrationalist time conceptions are always subjectivistic and view every instance of objective time duration as a conceptual abstraction that falsifies reality.
2 Equally disastrous for insight into the subject-object relation is the identification of the subject concept with the metaphysical substance concept.

in relation to the possibility of subjective movement. (Compare the "curved space" of the general theory of relativity.)

In the biotic aspect there is a subject-object relation between the subjective vital function and its biotic object, which is itself but an *object* of vital functions. Compare food as object of the biotic processes involved in feeding, or inhaled air as vital object of the process of breathing; and so on. The same applies in general to the relation between subjective life and objective living space.

Again, in the psychical aspect of feeling the subject-object relation is present in the relation between the subjective feeling of space and the objective sensory space (visual space, tactile space and audible space) in which the sensory objects present themselves to sensation.

The subject-object relation in the logical aspect is present in the correlation between a subjective concept and the objective-logical characteristics of an entity.

In the lingual aspect the subject-object relation comes to expression in the relation between the subjective act of signifying and the objective sign (e.g., a letter, a light signal, a sound signal, a banner).

In truth, full temporal reality has both modal subject and modal object-functions in all aspects succeeding the first boundary aspect. In the modal structure of the subject-object relation we find a one-sided (irreversible) relation of dependence between object and subject-functions. This must be understood properly. The existence of the modal object does not in any way depend upon a concrete, individual subject-function within the same law-sphere. The objective sensory properties of a blossoming rose in its actual existence is not dependent upon an individual subjective impression from A to B. But it is certainly dependent upon a *possible* subjective observation.[1] In other words, the dependency relation in question ought to be understood in a *structural* sense and should therefore not be viewed as something individual and subjective.

---

1   The same state of affairs manifests itself in the relation between subjective spatial extension and a point. This explains the inner antinomic nature of the attempt to construct actual exension through a "continuum of points." The subject-object relation is here inverted in an antinomic fashion.

Furthermore, the modal object-functions are by no means the *product* of the subject-functions, for in that case they could not have an *objective* existence. A color *dreamed of* differs in principle from a color *observed*. The former does not have a real objective existence since it merely displays a so-called intentional or an apparent objectivity. In the final analysis it remains *subjective* in character.[1]

The modal subject-object relation in question necessarily comes to expression also *in time* in the relation between *subjective* and *objective* time duration. The latter never coincides with the former.

For example, the duration of so-called present time (the "specious present") in the subjective sensory awareness differs from the objective sensory phases which correspond with the observed events – such as the collapsing of a house, the falling of a stone, the firing of a gunshot, and so on.[2] What is observed as *simultaneous* within the present moment (as immediate emotional duration) may occur objectively as *successive*. Yet the objective duration of an event could only be observed in the psychic aspect of reality by means of the emotional duration of our subjective awareness – where the so-called time-measurement serves to establish the objective duration as accurately as possible.

1 The reflection of a subjective emotional mood onto objects around us therefore also remains subjective in character. Messer (op. cit., p. 129) counts them among the "objects of feeling." This is clear from the fact that the emotional qualities radiated onto these objects vary fully in consonance with our emotional moods. Nonetheless, a living room or a landscape, for example, may essentially also display an *objective* mood which affects our subjective mood. Finally, subjective feelings can essentially *objectify* themselves in facial expressions, in words or gestures, in a cry of joy, in sobbing, etc. etc. Yet this does not primarily concern a subject-object relation within the emotional aspect of feeling, but one within the lingual aspect. Such an objective expression of feelings functions as a symbolic sign and requires interpretation.

2 The term "specious present," as we know, was introduced by E. R. Clay and given currency in the language of psychology particularly by William James in his work *Principles of Psychology* (1:609 ff.) Objectifying the present in clock time, according to more recent experiments, yields a variation from 0.5 up to 4 seconds. This shows that the duration of observational time differs between individuals and that it is strongly influenced not only by the intensity of attention and interest, but also by fatigue, alcohol, drugs, and so on.

For the sake of the so-called time-measurement it is also possible to objectify the subjective emotional duration in a mathematical approximation of the time duration of the psychical ob-
ject- function of an event. This is done, for example, when the
subjective duration of pain is "measured" against the objective
sensory duration of moving images described by the hands of a
clock over the dial. The psychology of dreams tells us that the
objective (or rather: objectified) dream tempo is normally extremely rapid, whereas the subjective emotional duration does
not at all leave that impression. Actually, we do not measure the
inner subjective emotional duration itself but only its
objectification in the physical aspect of clock time. In its inner nature the subjective emotional duration cannot be measured (the
kernel of truth in Bergson's conception of time). This is so because all time-measurement (that is, duration measurement) –
unlike the subjective estimation of time – rests on *objectification*.
In addition, insofar as the measurement concerns an actual
event, it can never be a merely modal objective time-measure,
since it concerns, rather, an objective time measure within an individuality structure of reality which as such can never be exact
in the abstract mathematical sense.

With that, we have made the transition to the individuality
structures of time. In particular the so-called clock time will now
occupy our attention.

27. The individuality structures of time and the metaphysical substance concept

The individuality structures of reality, unlike the modal structures, do not relate to the *how* or the *mode* of being, but to the *concrete what* of reality.

As we noted earlier, individuality structures are time-structures of individual totalities such as things, concrete events or
acts, societal forms (family, state, church, business enterprise),
and so on. However, they are not – as is the case with the modal
aspects – refraction points of cosmic time, since they are genuine
totality structures that encompass and embrace the refraction
points of the modal aspects in a *cosmic continuity*. In this respect
they represent a deeper layer of the time horizon than the modal
aspects.

A concrete entity, such as this tree in front of my house, is
more than the sum of its modal functions of number, space,

89

movement, organic life, and so on. Before all else it is a *temporal individual whole with a relative persistence* that lies at the basis of all its modal functions. Traditional metaphysics used to speak in this context of a *substance*.

The *Philosophy of the Cosmonomic Idea* distanced itself on principle from the philosophical substance concept, and it did so on solid grounds.

The substance concept was meant to account for an undeniable *given* of naive experience, namely the relative *endurance* or *persistence* of an entity in spite of the exchange of its parts and its sensorially perceptible shapes and properties. Given its substance concept, however, metaphysics, misled by the immanence standpoint, in principle detached itself from what is actually given in naive experience and set out to find an abstract "essence" of things, supposedly accessible only to theoretical thought. In this way metaphysics arrived at its *theoretical* construction of a "substance" as a self-contained "thing-in-itself," which is then *opposed* by the subjective perception and apperception of human consciousness.

Although it does allow for the most diverse conceptions depending on further theoretical specifications of the immanence standpoint, the metaphysical substance concept in all its forms was therefore nothing but the absolutization of a *theoretical abstraction.*[1] It was always predicated on the elimination of the cosmic horizon of time and a theoretical *breaking apart* of reality into a *noumenon* and a *phenomenon.*[2]

The "thing-in-itself," in whatever way it is conceived, is nothing but a theoretical abstraction from temporal reality which is *reified* into an independent substance. This also comes to expression in the prevalent definition of medieval scholasticism which was also taken over by Descartes: a substance is "something which exists in such a way that it does not depend on the existence of any other thing."

Since the *Philosophy of the Cosmonomic Idea* has distanced itself from the immanence standpoint and its absolutization of the theoretical synthesis rooted in it, it cannot maintain the sub-

1 At this point the *theoretization* of reality avenges itself. It finds its philosophical origin in the immanence standpoint, in the attempt to find the Archimedian point of philosophy within theoretical thought.
2 [Into what is *intelligible* and what is *observable*.]

stance concept. Over time, as immanence philososophy developed, it was precisely this substance concept which, by enclosing the *true* reality of a thing within a particular modal aspect of reality, proved to be one of the major obstacles for doing justice theoretically to the time structure of reality.

It is understandable that modern functionalism, which aimed at replacing the substance concept with the function concept in an anti-metaphysical fashion, in this respect brought little gain. With its substance concept metaphysics at least aimed at giving an account of the totality structure of entities. Anti-metaphysical functionalism, by contrast, remains entirely caught in the modal-aspect structure of reality. In addition it fundamentally misinterprets this structure on the basis of the immanence standpoint. (Compare for example the positivistic psychologistic functionalism of Mach and his followers, his followers, the transcendental-logical functionalism of the Marburg school of neo-Kantianism, and so on).

In order to acquire a proper insight into what is presented to naive experience regarding the relative persistence of an entity in spite of the exchange of its parts and of the sensorially perceptible shapes and properties of such things, it is first of all necessary to account for the fact that all individual totalities presented in time can exist only in a typical time-structure. This concerns the structure of an individual whole and not that of a merely modal structure. The modal structures as such are indifferent with respect to individual totalities that function within them.

The causality concept of classical physics was a genuine *modal concept* insofar as it was indifferent toward the individual nature of things. Classic physics attempted to understand the behavior of entities according to their physical aspect in terms of the law of causality. The scope of Newton's law of gravitation applied to a falling pencil in my room as well as to the movement of celestial bodies.

It is precisely this which distinguishes the *modal* concept of causality from Aristotelian physics with its *substantial* teleological concept of causality. The latter attempts to explain movement as something flowing from the *inner nature* of things. This inner nature is found in the "substantial form" as the inherent

91

teleological principle of a thing, through which it strives towards its own perfection.

28. The individuality structures and their typical grouping of the modal aspects

What then constitutes the basic difference between the individuality structures of temporal reality? Without a doubt it is found in the typical *totality character* of these structures. Ultimately this character remains inaccessible to scientific analysis, for the same reason that cosmic time in its *continuity* cannot be theoretically analyzed. The inner nature of an individual totality simply impinges itself upon our experience. The moment one attempts to enter into a theoretical analysis of such a totality one is dependent upon the *modal aspects* in which that totality functions but which can never exhaust its existence. In this analysis, the totality, just like cosmic time, remains that which is *presupposed.* In its totality it *precedes* theoretical analysis and one can never afterwards construct it from "elements."

The philosophical substance concept therefore only *appeared* to be successful at penetrating behind the modal horizon of theoretical analis into a depth layer of reality. As soon as metaphysics tried to define the "substance" theoretically it had to take recourse to *modal* distinctions. The modal aspect which was then chosen to characterize the *essence* of the substance was absolutized to become the sole determining ground for the existence of such a thing.[1]

Thanks to the immanence standpoint, the dialectical totality concept, too, as introduced by German idealism, led to an absolutization of a specific *aspect* of the totality. Take the concept of *Volksgeist* (folk spirit), which was viewed essentially as the *historical* potential of an entire "culture," where "culture" was supposed to embrace all normative aspects of temporal society.

1 Compare for example the Aristotelian distinction between the *vegetative, sensitive* and *rational* soul – where the substantial difference between these three is sought in the aspects of life, feeling and logical thinking. The higher function successively absorbs the lower one and impregnates upon it a new essential character. Compare also Descartes' definition of the body substance as res extensiva (extended thing) and the soul as *res cogitans* (thinking thing).

Is it then impossible for theoretical analysis to teach us anything about the individuality structures of temporal reality? This is certainly possible, just as the theoretical analysis of the modal-aspect structures ultimately furnishes us with theoretical insight into the cosmic time-order insofar as the latter reveals itself as an order of its modal *refractions*. But the *sine qua non* for a truly fruitful and correct analysis is to base it on the idea of an individual totality as a transcendental limiting concept. Similar to the way in which the cosmic time-order expresses itself within the modal aspect structures, so it also comes to expression within the modal aspects of an individual whole. This may concern the individuality structure of an entity, a concrete event or a concrete societal relationship.

What is striking in the first place is that the modal functions within an individuality structure are *grouped in a typical way*. This grouping does not affect the cosmic time-order of the aspects as such as we have discussed them earlier; this order maintains itself also within an individuality structure of reality. The latter structure also does not affect the *modal irreducibility* or *sphere-sovereignty* of the aspects. Also within the individuality structure of, say, a tree, the modal numerical function is irreducible to the spatial function and the movement function. It is not possible to reduce anyone of these three functions in a so-called "holistic" sense to mere modalities of the organic function of life or to the (objective) psychical function of an entity.

However, when our theoretical analysis follows the cosmic time-order of the modal aspects within the inner structure of the tree it strikes us that only with the biotic aspect does it become meaningful to speak of this entity as a tree, and at the same time that the organic aspect of life is the last modal aspect in which the tree still functions as a *subject*. In all later aspects it does not have *subject-functions* but only modal *object-functions*. The organic function of life is the typical *destinational function* or the *qualifying function* of the internal tree-structure. This qualifying function within the individuality structure also unlocks or discloses its earlier modal functions in the *anticipatory direction* towards its typical biotical destination. This enables us to detect within the aspect of movement *internally directed* motions, such as those of the metabolic and growth movements (which are different from the external motions of a tree, for example when it is struck by a gust of wind).

Yet this does not transform these internal movements into something intrinsically biotical. They merely deepened their biotic anticipations under the typical guidance of the qualifying function of the tree.

It is the individuality structure of the tree and not the time-order of the modal aspects which guarantees this typical grouping of the modal functions within an individual whole.

The individuality structure is a *typical* structure of cosmic time. When the subjective biotic function of the tree is harmed it can no longer exist as an individual whole. Yet it cannot be said that this biotic function is the *essence* of the tree, because the modal biotic function does not constitute the totality principle of the tree. The opposite is much rather the case: the totality character determines that the biotic function is the directing and guiding function of all the other functions. In other words, the totality itself does have a modal character but equally embraces all aspects of the tree in their typical grouping. If any one of these aspects were lacking, the tree would cease to exist as a *tree*. The individuality structure also fully accounts for the relatively persistent character of the tree as its parts and sensory properties are replaced.

While functioning in its typical individuality structure the tree remains identical to itself. Loss of this structure, for example when it is felled and sawn into boards, will give rise to a number of other entities with radically different structures.

29. Why also the individuality structures are truly time-structures of reality

But the structure itself does not come into being and pass away, for as such it is a *constant*, lawful cadre within which individual totalities exist with a certain individual time-duration. Nonetheless it remains the time-structure of an individual totality, because without its relation to subjective (or objective) time-duration it does not have any meaning. The individual time-duration related to it is determined by the time-structure in a law-conforming way.

For example, the lifetime of a plant, by virtue of its structural type, is bound to the typical life-span of the latter. In the case of a work of art it is bound to the typical aesthetically qualified objective form, and in the case of a state it is bound to the maintenance of an independent public legal organization on the basis of an autonomous organization of the sword power; and so on, and so forth.

30. The differentiation of individuality structures and enkaptic structural interlacements

In the theory of individuality structures the *Philosophy of the Cosmonomic Idea* brought to light the impressive diversity of structural types displaying a totality character. Like the modal structures, these structural types are not disconnected, since the cosmic time-order groups them into a set order and intertwines them through so-called enkapsis. It is possible to distinguish between *radical types, genotypes* and *variability types.*

Within the radical types, which delimit entire "kingdoms" of individuality structures, the so-called radical functions, i.e., the typical structural functions that characterize the individual totality, are as yet determined only in a *modal* sense.

Remark*: on radical functions*

Different radical types have not one but two of these radical functions. In addition to the typical qualifying or destinational function they also have a typical foundational function. Such a typical foundational function is present in all those individuality structures whose qualifying function does not display an *original* type but points backward to an original type within an earlier modal aspect of reality. Among the natural individuality structures a typical foundation is found in all cases where the individuality structures are enkaptically interlaced with other structures such that they cannot exist without the latter. The psychically qualified animal soma, for example, is typically founded in a biotically qualified somatic organization. The former may temporarily be dysfunctional, while the latter continues to function – but the reversal is not posssible. In the third volume of my work *De Wijsbegeerte der Wetsidee*, where the theory of individuality structures is extensively explained, I was mistaken in denying that the radical type of the animal kingdom lacks a foundational function.

95

Furthermore, all human artifacts are typically founded. For example, a plastic art work such as Hermes of Praxiteles is typically founded in an objective material form which is realized through the free historical form-giving of the artist. The aesthetic individuality of Hermes indeed is that of this incomparable form of a god depicted in the marble material as a result of free formative control.

All human societal structures are also typically founded. Marriage, nuclear family and extended family typically are *biotically* founded, respectively in sexual union and blood ties. State and church, by contrast, typically are *historically* founded in a historical power-organization. In the case of the state it is given in the organization of the sword power, and with respect to the church it concerns the power of the Word and sacraments.[1]

We can therefore say that the radical type of the plant kingdom is biotically qualified, that of the animal kingdom is psychically qualified with a typical biotic foundation, while the realm of art works has an objective aesthetic qualification which is founded in a typical objective cultural form.

In the geno-types of a kingdom these radical types are differentiated in an ever increasing individualization. Radically different individuality structures are are intertwined in cosmic time through *enkapsis*. This *enkapsis* leaves the distinctive *inner nature* of the intertwined structures intact and distinguishes itself in this respect in principle from the simple part-whole relation which is determined by a single structural principle. The marble material, for example, used by the artist in bringing to expression his aesthetic conception, maintains its inner nature also in its enkaptic bond within the art work. As natural material it does not turn into a part of the art work. Parts of Hermes are only the aesthetically qualified marble bodily forms. In the inner structure of the natural material (i.e., the aggregate of calcite crystals) the physical-chemical functions maintain their qualifying role. The external enkaptic bond within the art work exclusively concerns the external form of the marble. In this form the physico-chemical operations of the marble are bound so that they no longer have the leading role, in order that the marble – in this enkaptic function – can serve as the material expression

1   See *WdW*, vol 3, Deel II, hfst. iii–iv [cf. *NC*, vol. 3, Part II, chap. iii–iv].

of the aesthetic conception. It is possible to speak of an "enkaptic totality" or a "intertwinement totality" consisting of radically different structures, as long as the part-whole scheme is not applied in an inappropriate way by calling the natural material a part of the art work. Rather, both the natural material and the art work are parts of the enkaptic structural whole where the (cultural) form of the marble statue functions as the nodal point of the interlacement.

The variability types bring to expression those peculiarities which do not derive from the inner structure itself, but which owe their origin to the interlacement with other individuality structures. Wood and marble plastics, for example, are variability types of the plastic art work. Similarly a church-state and a state-church are variability types of the genotypes state and church, while the arctic fox and the polar bear respectively represent variability types of the already highly differentiated genotypes of fox and bear.

31. The enkaptic configuration of the human body

According to the *Philosophy of the Cosmonomic Idea* the human body, too, is structured as an interlacement of individuality structures. In this sense it is the enkaptic structural whole of man's entire individual *temporal* existence which itself is intertwined with a multiplicity of societal structures. In lieu of a distinction often made in modern psychology between "body," "psyche" and "spirit" which are at bottom nothing but abstract function complexes of temporal human existence, we ought to recognize three mutually interlaced individuality structures of the body: the biotically qualified *soma*, the psychically qualified *soma*, and the pistically qualified body,[1] thus taking into account *the individual structural whole of all the modal functions* of the hu-

---

1 The nervous system and the entire sensory equipment undoubtedly fall outside the inner limits of the biotically qualified (vegetative) soma-structure. They belong partially to the second and partially to the third structure of the body. [Dooyeweerd soon realized that one cannot accept a single modal aspect (such as the "pistical") as the qualifying aspect of human bodily existence. His ripened conception therefore holds that the (normative) "act"-structure, though in itself not qualified by any normative aspect, qualifies the human body in a structural way. See *Reformation and Scholasticism in Philosophy*, 2:342–432.]

man body. The traditional problems as to the relation between "soul" and "body" then turn out to be pseudo-problems. In its unity, indivisibility and incorruptibility, the soul remains the transcendent spiritual religious center of the human being which en-souls the entire body in its temporal structure and stamps the body as human.[1] But the soul as such is not susceptible to scientific investigation, because it is the *presupposition* of all scientific activities. Only the temporal manifestations of the soul in the corruptible body are open to such investigations. Our theory of the enkaptic configuration of the human body certainly can account for the experiential fact that our sensitive feelings and perceptions, our biotical drives and physico-chemical motions can be controlled or guided only within definite structural limits. The different bodily structures after all maintain their internal sphere-sovereignty in their structural interlacement. The human being controls the sub-logical functions of the biotically and psychically qualified soma-structures only insofar as they function enkaptically within the so-called spiritual bodily structure (which is qualified by the function of faith).

32. The significance of the distinction between modal and individuality structures for psychology. The distinction between "act" and modal function

The distinction between modal and individuality structures is also of fundamental importance for psychology as a special science. It still frequently happens that knowing, willing and feeling are coordinated as functions of the "soul" (in the terminology of faculty psychology: as "faculties" of the soul), whereby at once every meaningful delimitation of psychology's field of investigation is lost while the door is opened wide for all possible forms of "psychologism."

The *Philosophy of the Cosmonomic Idea* began by introducing a sharp distinction between the *modal aspect* which delimits the field of investigation of the discipline of psychology and the *individuality structures* which express themselves also within this aspect. The modal aspect delimits the subject matter of the field

---

1 [Evidently, Dooyeweerd's thought here is still in the grip of the metaphysical scholastic concept of the soul which he eventually criticized so severely. See *Reformation and Scholasticism in Philosophy*, 3:165–88.]

of investigation. At the same time the "sphere universality" of this aspect at no point compels genuinely psychological problems to be assigned to other disciplines.

A first fruit of this distinction is insight into the proper relation between "acts" and their "modal aspects."[1]

Feeling is not an "act" but a modal function of the latter. Knowing and willing are by contrast true *acts* which as such cannot be reduced to one particular modal subject-function since they are directly related to the central root of temporal existence (the "selfhood").

Genuine "acts" of the selfhood always reveal themselves within time in an individuality-structure and they function equally in all aspects of reality.[2] Concrete acts of knowing and willing do not involve an abstract "soul" (as supposed substantial complex of rational ethical functions), but involve, rather, the entire temporal human existence in the enkaptic interlacement of all its individuality structures, which always proceed from the selfhood as existential center.

Psychology as a special science can investigate these "acts" in their individuality structure only, according to the modal psychical aspect, similar, for example, to the science of law, which observes societal structures such as the state or the church only according to a *jural* point of view. Nevertheless, the special sciences need to base their research on the idea of a totality-structure.

33. The problem of time measurement

In the present context we only want to shed further light on the problem of the so-called measurement of time and contemplate its place within the entire problem of time.

1 "Act" and "action" may be distinguished as *internal* and *internal-external* activity. It is not the case that an "act" differs" from an "action" in the sense that it operates entirely with an abstract "psyche" or "psyche" and "spirit," for also in an "act" our biotically qualified soma is jointly operative. The distinction merely entails that according to its temporal side the act entirely functions within the internal enkaptic structural whole of the ensouled body, whereas it only projects itself to "the outside" in the action.

2 This state of affairs explains also why the disciplines of law and ethics understand the will in another modal aspect than what is done in psychology. Feeling itself never displays different *modal* aspects. As such it is a modal function.

The neo-Platonist Plotinus may well have been the first to point out that the concept of "time-measurement" is internally contradictory within the context of the then prevailing object-ivistic conception of time. Aristotle, as we have noted in an earlier context, tried to define time as the measure of movement (*arithmos kineseos kata to proteroi kai hysteron*).

However, when time itself is only the measure of movement, how then is it possible to measure time itself through movement?

In the modern era this problem entered a critical phase through the introduction of Einstein's general theory of relativity. It is indeed impossible to arrive at a satisfactory solution as long as immanence philosophy causes one not to distinguish properly between the modal and individuality structures of cosmic time and as long as these two structures are not viewed in their mutual coherence.

In the light of our preceding considerations it must be clear that the cosmic time-order cannot be measured. After all, every measurement occurs within this time-order and is only *possible* through this time-order.

Only time-*duration* in the context of subject-object relations can be measured. Furthermore, the time-measure is necessarily itself a duration of time in a subject-object relation. The time-measure, after all, must be objective in relation to all subjective measurements.

As time-duration an objective time-measure cannot exist "by itself," for it can only exist in correlation with a possible subjective measurement of time-duration. Furthermore, every actual act of measurement has its own subjective time-duration.

It is a very inaccurate expression to call an objective time-measure [as on a clock] an act of measuring time. An objective time-measure cannot function as the subjective agent of measuring time. The actual measuring of time is an act presupposing a subjective *concept* of measure and number; an objective time-measure is merely the object of this concept.

Meanwhile, all concrete time-duration occurs within the individuality structures of reality. A *purely* modal time-duration does not exist in reality. Even the modal aspects of a concrete time-duration remain aspects of time-duration within an individuality structure. As a consequence, the only way to measure time-duration is by means of a time-measure within an individuality structure.

An experimentally useful time-measure has to be perceivable in an objective sensitive sense and must contain an objective sensory image of movement on an instrument with numbered segments. This modal sensory object-function of the time-measure acquires a concrete shape through the individuality structure of the latter.

What does this mean? In everyday life Westerners measure time with the aid of a timepiece. The division in days, months and years is derived from the time-duration of the rotation of the earth around its axis and its revolution around the sun. On the basis of this time-measure we construct our *chronology*. Not the time-measure itself but only the mathematical processing of it bears an exact mathematical character. In this we simply follow the modal numerical time-order with which these movement images are correlated. This is how our modern *clock* came into existence. Various clocks with their respective particular time-measures are regularly adjusted in accordance with the universal time-measure of the chronometer, which in turn is dependent upon the most universal time-measure: the so-called astronomical day that is based upon astronomical observations.

It is clear that clock time and calendar time are human designs formed to satisfy the needs of human society. Practically we use them as a universal ordering scheme through which all events and actions of the past, present and future are located with respect to their simultaneity or degree of succession. The artificially objective time-measure, even though it is a sensorially perceptible *measure* displaying an objective sensory character, still functions within an individuality structure of time which as such embraces all modal aspects of reality.

This individuality structure of our societal time, however, is enkaptically interwoven with the natural individuality structure of so-called astronomical time, that is, the daily duration of celestial movement. The latter continues to form the foundation upon which the former is built.

The time-measure of our societal time is read from an instrument, a cultural object. This subjective measuring does not just involve our sensory perception but no less our logical function, our historical and lingual function, and in fact the entire complicated structure of human existence, including the transcendent selfhood.

The objective (experimental) time-measure is, as we have seen, one-sidedly dependent upon *possible* subjective measuring by a human being. It exists only in structural correlation with measuring.

Is it possible for this objective time-measure to display a purely *modal* mathematical exactness? Of course not. The sensorially perceived face of a clock, divided into numbered segments, is not a spatial figure in its original (geometrical) sense, but an objective sensory spatial image which describes the objective sensory images of the hands that are brought into correspondence by the mechanism. The subjective trajectories of the moving hands acquire a sensory objectification in a spatial image which itself is bound to the instrument. In the original meaning of space as simultaneous extension in dimensions, as we have seen earlier, there is no movement in its original meaning. In fact, the objective sensory image of the clockface with its moving hands merely objectifies *sensory analogies* of space and movement. It is only within the sensory awareness-space that we can *see* moving images. The sensory spatial image indeed constitutes the structural *condition* for the sensory image of motion. This is so because in the cosmic time-order the aspect of motion is founded in the aspect of space and not vice versa. Neither the calibrated images, nor the objective sensory duration of the moments in the moving images of the hands, bear an original mathematical character. In the objective sensory duration of the moments, original subjective moments of movement are objectified. Even a minimal acceleration of their motion would cancel their uniformity in duration. No more exact is there uniformity in the objective sensory duration of the earth's rotations.

102

One may aim for a certain degree of accuracy in the time-measure, but this can never be exact in a purely mathematical sense, simply owing to its objective sensory perceptibility.

The same naturally applies to the use of more universal time measures, such as the so-called astronomical day used in the chronometer (i.e., the duration of the rotation of the earth around its axis in relation to the fixed stars), as well as to more primitive time-measures such as hourglasses, sun dials, and so on. The fact that the time-duration used for measuring actually functions in the individuality structure of a real event, and that the experimental objective time-measure has to be a sensorily perceptible (i.e., objectively psychological) measure, on principle forbids physics as an experimental, mathematical natural science from working with a theoretically constructed, purely modal objective mathematical duration of motion in formulating the laws of mathematical physics (which does not mean, of course, that physics ought to abandon its mathematical foundations). An example of such a constructed objective mathematical duration of motion with an abstract modal meaning was Newton's "absolute mathematical time." This was not time itself, but an objectification of a meticulously constructed mathematical time-duration within the modal meaning of motion. It was a purely modal objective *possibility* within the meaning of movement which formed the basis for the classic principle of inertia.

The intended objective mathematical duration of movement is not at all real time-duration but only an imagined duration, a theoretical abstraction from the modal time-order of movement which is synthetically constructed in relation to number and space.

Newton's absolute mathematical time stood or fell with his conception of "absolute space" and "absolute movement," where the three-dimensional Euclidean space served as the strictly static coordinate system of absolute movement. The reason why it could not be used as an empirical time-measure is that it was theoretically abstracted from every individuality structure of time. The discrepancy which was thus caused between the formulation of laws of physical motion and experimental time-measurement contributed to a crisis in the foundations of classic mechanics.

103

Although physical movement time as such displays a modal prepsychical time-aspect, the experimentally useful time-measure remains a sensorially perceptible individuality structure. This individuality structure naturally expresses itself also in the aspects of movement, space and number, which entails that also the mathematical formulation of this time-measure ought to take this individuality structure into consideration. The general theory of relativity did this in respect of the relativization of the time-measure in relation to the assumed constancy of the velocity of light and in giving up a privileged coordinate system. All of this resulted in a relativization of the concept "simultaneity" within the meaning of movement. In the mathematical foundations of this physical theory it is not time *itself*, but only the subjective speed of light as the fourth dimension in the so-called Minkowski space that is geometrically anticipated. In a similar way the so-called *curved space* brings to expression in a geometrical way the dependence of the objective world space upon gravitational fields.

34. Hoenen's criticism of Einstein's denial of an absolute simultaneity

The Thomist philosopher of nature, Peter Hoenen, S.J., professor at the Gregorian University in Rome, attempted to expose a logical error in Einstein's relativizing of the physical concept of objective simultaneity. According to Hoenen, absolute simultaneity occurs automatically the moment the following situation obtains within two systems of the theory of relativity that move towards each other while each has attached to it an unmoving coordinate system. When two arbitrary points P and Q as arbitrary moments of movement coincide, absolute simultaneity is a fact. Presumably, Einstein neglected one clock and one bearer of time: the movement itself of his two systems. Once we view this in the light of "the evident principle of the instantaneous occurrence of distances" then it would indeed appear that an (absolute) objective simultaneity does exist.

Hoenen illustrates this statement with the following example. Suppose a material point moves in a path perpendicular to a line A–B. Then consider the moment at which the moving point intersects line A–B at point P which lies at a distance *a* from point A. We now can see that the moving point finds itself *at once, at the same time*, at a distance *a* from A; and conversely, that

A is at the same distance from the moving point. A moment earlier, those distances were different; but from the contact of the moving point with P the new distance results at once from the contact.

The same would then apply to points P and Q in the two first mentioned moving systems of the theory of relativity at the moment when point P of the first system coincides with point Q of the second system.

If an arbitary point A is chosen from the second system, then, according to "the principle of the immediate occurrence of distances," point P will be at the distance Q–A from A *at the very same moment* (Q–A being constant), and conversely, point A will be at the same distance from P – but only at this one moment. It is not required that the distance has been measured or that someone has to measure it; it is there. And what is valid for an arbitrary point of the second system applies to all points.

The author concedes that this objective simultaneity cannot be *measured* by observers at a distance, because that would require signals coming from a distance. Yet this does not detract anything from the *existence* of an absolute, objective simultaneity, since it only affects the possibility of our subjective perception of it. Intellectually we can grasp the existence of an absolute, objective simultaneity.

35. Criticism of Hoenen's critique

In the light of our preceding explanations this argumentation is highly instructive with regard to the objectivistic "time concept" of Aristotle and Thomas Aquinas, as well as with regard to the modal shifts in meaning that it is guilty of. In the example of a moving material point that intersects a line A–B at a point P the apparent assumption is objective sensory space within which the trajectory and the spatial straight line function only as objective analogies. After all, in the original meaning of space, movement is impossible and consequently there cannot be a spatial intersection of a trajectory and a perpendicular straight line. What is lost sight of is that an objective sensory time-measure does not exist "by itself" but only in a structural relation to possible sensory perception. Hoenen has eliminated the entire subject-object relation.

Furthermore, without any thought he transfers the strict objective simultaneity that occurs in the intersection of straight lines and a spatial plane, to the objective simultaneity within the aspect of movement and to the objective sensory image of the movement. The crucial question surely is whether or not an absolute objective time-measure is possible independent of a moving system. Only in the latter case would we be able to speak of *absolute* simultaneity. The same, correspondingly, holds for the objective sensory image of movement within the psychical aspect of reality.[1]

In the footsteps of Aristotle and Aquinas, Hoenen indeed is of the opinion that this is the case. He proceeds from the notion that time is the "possible enumeration of motion according to its topological and metrical structure" or a system of concrete numbers with ordinal and cardinal values, a system present in reality itself in the succession of the segments of a movement which makes numeration possible according to the series of successive numbers.[2]

On his standpoint he can claim that in every arbitrary movement, even according to Augustine's remark about the rotation of the potter's wheel,[3] an absolute time is realized, although the one *universal* time is realized only in the daily movement of celestial bodies.

> If the movement of the clock [Hoenen argues] is not fully uniform – and in practice it never is – then as a measuring instrument it is imperfect. Yet its movement remains the possible bearer of another numeration (even a changeful one) in which equal differences of successive numbers would correlate with equal segments of a genuinely uniform movement. This means that movement thus continues to constitute real time, although as a measuring instrument it is imperfect, like all our instruments.[4]

What does all this reveal? From the system of concrete numbers which is present in reality itself in the succession of the segments

1 Of course, on an objective sensory level there does exist a mutual simultaneity of sensory spatial images. But this simultaneity remains relative to the level.
2 *Philosophie der anorganische natuur*, pp. 283-284.
3 [See *Conf.* 11.23: "If the celestial lights should cease, the whirlings of a potter's wheel would still mark intervals of time . . ."]
4 Op. cit., p. 292.

of a movement (which as real movement cannot ever occur out-side an individuality structure), we are unexpectedly trans-ferred to a purely *imagined* system of numbers that serves to quantify the mathematical segments of a "genuinely uniform" movement – to a mathematical concept of a purely *modal possibil-ity* of movement! As we have seen, however, the latter can never serve as the objective time-measure of concrete movements.

Remark: *on "uniform movement"*
In Newton's understanding, a genuine uniform movement is one upon which no external forces exert an influence, hence in which the principle of inertia can manifest itself in strict independence from gravity.

In reality, however, the so-called inert mass – that is to say, the resistance to acceleration – is never without heavy mass, i.e., gravitation. In the theory of relativity, as is well known, the two *are equated* – entailing an implicit rejection of "absolute move-ment" as *real* motion. What physics accepts as genuine uniform movements are really never exact. They are only movements whose deviations from the mathematical probability concept – at least in the case of macro events – are negligibly small.

In micro events (e.g., the movement of electrons) exact time measure is fundamentally impossible in consequence of Heisen-berg's uncertainty principle.

Now it cannot be denied that we have a *concept* of a mathemati-cally defined movement. The same applies to the concept of the strict objective spatial simultaneity of points in spatial exten-sion. However, these are modal concepts that have consciously been abstracted from the individuality structure of reality. Though in this sense they may be structural *conditions* for the physical measurement of concrete movements, on principle they cannot be used as objective *time-measure* of actual time-du-ration.

As we have seen, Hoenen does acknowledge the impossibil-ity of measuring with this time-measure (the abstract "quanti-fied movement"). He writes:

Einstein's formulae imply that if we had signals of "infinite speed," that is to say, if we could perceive immediately at a dis-tance, then we would be able to establish absolute simultaneity. Similarly, since distances result with "infinite speed," i.e., im-mediately, this simultaneity does exist and we have an intellec-tual grasp of it, even though we cannot experimentally establish

107

which events are simultaneous, just as we cannot perceive the existing length relationships with absolute accuracy.[1]

However, the existence of a structurally modal (that is, merely possible) simultaneity is something fundamentally different from the existence of a *strictly individual simultaneity* of *concrete events*. The former can be grasped intellectually from the modal structure of the aspect in question, independently of experimental measuring. In the case of the latter this is impossible, because it does not merely concern a mere modal aspect but a concrete event within a temporal individuality structure of time. Here, to infer from a modal concept to concrete reality were patently false because it would be based upon a fundamental confusion of time-structures.

Celestial movement as a universal time-measurement is as such only given within a physically qualified individuality structure (which for the rest, as we have seen, has its typical object-functions in the post-physical aspects). Although the instrumental clock time of our modern society is enkaptically interwoven with this "natural" individuality structure of time, its own internal individuality structure nonetheless displays a normative social qualification and a typical historical foundation. For this reason its objective time-measure is normatively determined such that all clocks are to conform to this time-measure. Thus the physical relativity of the time-measure is practically compensated for by a general normative measure.

As a general statement the positivistic conclusion: "what in principle cannot be measured does not exist" is certainly incorrect. This can be conceded to Hoenen unreservedly. Einstein no doubt went too far when he later dropped the restriction of his relativity principle of simultaneity to the physical. But in the present case the quailfication "in principle" indeed refers to the quantified uniform motion itself which was proclaimed to be the time-measure. Yet as a mathematical concept of an objective mathematical analogy within the modal aspect of movement it cannot *exist* as a time-measure for concrete movements within the individuality structure of time.

In the light of our preceding analysis is must be clear that "clock time," in which, as we have seen, two temporal individuality structures of time are mutually interwoven, simply does

1   Op. cit., p. 396.

108

not affect the inner nature of the other time-structures. Consequently it cannot be identified with cosmic time.[1]

Insofar as psychology works as an empirical science with a modally delineated field of research (and not as a speculative metaphysics), it will have to give an account both of the modal time aspect in which the phenomena it investigates function and of the temporal individuality structures that come to expression within this aspect. In its use of clock time psychology will have to maintain an awareness of the intrinsic limits of the latter.

As they debate the correct view of time, Einstein and Bergson argue past each other, because the one party absolutizes the objective physical and the other the subjective psychical aspect of time.

The one cosmic time-order, equally valid for all things and events, does not entail – as Newton believed in his rationalist view of time – a single, truly uniform objective duration divorced from the individuality structure of reality. All concrete time-duration, including that of a time-measure, remains bound to this latter structure and continues to be determined by it.

The problem of time acquires its proper foundation only when the insight is gained that it essentially concerns the problem of creaturely reality itself and that the manner in which it is posed is entirely determined by the ultimate religious starting-point of a thinker.

---

1   This is implicitly conceded by Hoenen when he remarks that "the time *in* which an event occurs and which is a measure for its duration ... is something extrinsic, in opposition to the intrinsic flowing duration of the event" (op. cit., p. 279). However, this is only valid for the *time-measure*. Hoenen's mistake lies in his identification of the latter with *time* itself.

II

The Structure of Jural Principles and the Method of the Science of Law in Light of the Cosmonomic Idea[1]

THE QUESTION CONCERNING the possibility of a Calvinistic legal science must have a curious ring for all those who adhere to the requirement of "neutrality" for scientific thought as something self-evident.

Yet this fact in itself is not sufficient to reject the question or to assume in advance that it entails an oxymoron. On the contrary, a truly critical reflection on the history of legal science suggests that the question should be reversed: Is it possible for the science of law to be *neutral*? Thus far it has not even been able to establish the object, method and problems of the science of law apart from a worldview.

1. The prejudice of naive positivism

Only naive positivism, for which the case for positive law no longer posed a problem, honestly believed for a while that it had severed all connection between the science of law and worldview. But this naive positivism was unmasked long ago by modern "critical" positivism: its entire basis turned out to be one big political prejudice: the dogma of law as the will of the state and of the state as a pre-legal and supra-legal reality. This dogma burdened both its naive conception of legal sources as its theory of legal validity and its logicistic hermeneutic.

Naive positivism believed only in positive law, and it did it not want to concern itself with anything else but positive law. Yet a moment's scientific reflection tells us that positive law is given to us only in a cosmic coherence and that its *meaning* can only be understood in the context of that coherence. Under-

1 "De structuur der rechtsbeginselen en de methode der rechtswetenschap in het licht der wetsidee," in *Wetenschappelijke bijdragen aangeboden door Hoogleeraren der Vrije Universiteit ter gelegenheid van haar vijftig-jarig bestaan* (Amsterdam: De Standaard, 1930), pp. 225–266. Trans. D. F. M. Strauss, eds. Natexa Verbrugge and Harry Van Dyke.

111

standing its meaning, therefore, cannot but hinge upon the view we have of this coherence.

If law is the "will of the state" or "the will of the legislator," what then is that mysterious "will of the state legislator"? Is it something extra-legal? Is it perhaps a psychic drive or representation? Then the will has to be interpreted in a psychological way, implying that the science of law has to be incorporated into psychology. Or is it perhaps a system of logical propositions subsumed to each other? In that case a legal system has to be interpreted as a system of logical concepts where what is particular ought to be deduced from the general with the means of Aristotelian subsumption logic. Or is the "will of the state" perhaps a function of a society and its history? Then sociologists and historians are the ones to interpret the will of the state.

In any event, conceiving law as the product of an extra-legal will of the state, naive positivism already took sides unintentionally in an issue of worldview, namely in respect of the meaning of law within the coherence of life and the world.

Its naturalistic attitude, which affects all basic questions of legal scientific thought, is simply masked by its anti-philosophical image.

2. "Critical" positivism as an explicit reaction to the modern neutrality postulate

Modern critical positivism from the school of Hans Kelsen no longer attempts to camouflage the connection between its formalistic, normlogical methodology and a specific type of the humanistic worldview—in spite of its radical rejection of every last vestige of natural law from the domain of the science of law. It openly acknowledges that the strict separation of the domains of "natural being" and "ought to be" represents an unverifiable postulate of the idealistic worldview.[1]

1 See Kelsen's foreword to the first edition of his *Hauptprobleme der Staatsrechtslehre entwickelt aus der Lehre vom Rechtssatze* (Tübingen, 1911), page v: "With respect to method in this context I only want to highlight the starting-point I have chosen in order to find a solution to the challenge I have set for myself. This is therefore the appropriate place to mention my starting-point, because in the final analysis it concerns presuppositions that are rooted in a worldview and are therefore subjective, non-debatable presuppositions."

From a philosophical perspective, this acknowledgment in itself is an important positive development. Positive law[1] is once again made into a *problem* and this can never happen without *transcending* positive law and in doing so implicitly giving up the basic thesis of positivism. According to Kelsen, the science of law has the task to eliminate from the material of positive law all "ethical-political" value judgments about its *content*, in order to understand it as a system of formal logical propositions. Legal science has to proceed from a pre-positive, basic or original legal norm as the highest source of validity of positive law, positing this original norm as the hypothesis of all legal experience.

In the case of an absolutistic legal order this original norm, for example, would be: Force ought to be exercised under all conditions commanded by the monarch. From this (transcendental-logical) basic principle of natural law, as Kelsen himself concedes, positive law now ought to be interpreted as a fully consistent, functional system of logically deduced norms.

Critical positivism is oriented to the theory of natural law and so it acquired a natural-law twist. Yet this natural-law system is purely formal-logical in nature. It sets itself off sharply from binding positive law to jural principles in any truly material sense of the word. It is a natural-law positivism that wages an irreconcilable war against every scientific orientation that advocates natural law in any material sense.

In the meantime, regardless how large the influence of this critical positivistic trend may still be at the moment, if signs are not misleading its sun is already declining. The Marburg school of neo-Kantian philosophy, to which the norm-logical school of legal thought is oriented, exhibits a noticeable transition towards a materialist-idealist trend of thought, and its initial formalistic orientation hardly has any influence today. On the horizon of legal philosophy the signs of a revival of a material idea of natural law are multiplying.

This change, which was accelerated by the spiritual revolution following the end of the [first] world war, did not escape the attention of Kelsen. In one of his most recent publications he acknowledges that the current spiritual climate is no longer very sympathetic to legal positivism. "Earlier than was to be ex-

---

1 [The distinction between positive law and pre-positive law is equivalent to the everyday distinction between a principle (pre-positive) and its application (positivization).]

pected, a reaction that promises to be a *renaissance of metaphysics*, and therefore also of natural-law theory, has set in."[1]

In his remarkable rectorial oration of 1925 on the theme: "What is our current position in respect of Natural Law?" Professor Manigk stated openly that natural law in its various historical manifestations had been a methodological misconception. And yet, he added, "conceptions of natural law have survived to this day. Behind the appearances of natural law there must be an unconquerable *Idea of Natural Law*."[2]

3. The possibility of a Calvinistic science of law is dependent upon a distinct orientation with regard to the pre-positive foundations of law

The question "How do we currently assess natural law?" impresses itself also upon the Calvinistic view of law and it demands an unambiguous answer on the basis of its own cosmonomic idea.

It cannot be doubted that the method of the science of law is fully dependent upon the point of view assumed in respect of the pre-positive foundations of law. A formalistic norm-logical method as developed by critical positivism is naturally unacceptable to anyone who rejects Kelsen's norm-logical starting-point and who sets out to search for the pre-positive foundations of positive law in *material jural principles*.

Once the *negative* conclusive force of the neutrality postulate has been conquered *in principle*, the possibility of a Calvinistic Science of Law is dependent upon a positive answer to the above question. The answer will determine whether or not the Calvinistic theory of law is able to provide the science of law with a fruitful method through which it can demonstrate its right of existence.

4. The refutation in principle of the neutrality postulate through the illumination of the cosmonomic idea lying at its foundation

We started our treatise with the question: Is it possible to deny the possibility of a Calvinistic science of law by means of the

1 H. Kelsen, *Die philosophischen Grundlagen der Naturrechtslehre und des Rechtspositivismus* [The philosophical foundations of the theory of natural law and legal positivism] (Charlottenberg, 1928).

2 Alfred Manigk, *Wie stehen wir heute zum Naturrecht?* (Berlin-Grunewald, 1926).

neutrality argument? This question has lost its force for anyone who accepts the theory of the cosmonomic idea.

Since positive law is given only in the cosmic coherence of the law-spheres, it naturally follows that every theory of law is rooted in a cosmonomic idea in which a stand is taken with respect to the two basic questions of *every* worldview: (i) How is one to view the mutual relationship and coherence between the various law-spheres; and (ii) What is the ultimate origin of all law-spheres?

The theory of the cosmonomic idea in itself is the refutation of every scientific theory that pretends to be without any presuppositions.

The *petitio principii* of the neutrality postulate is obvious even in one of its most ingenious philosophical defenses recently launched by Heinrich Rickert. Rickert defends the idea that theoretical thinking must be without presuppositions. According to him, philosophy, as a theoretical "world-view theory," must, in order to provide scientific clarity about the different worldviews, avoid every connection with worldviews and be guided solely by "theoretical truth-value." Denying the validity of this value, says Rickert, will terminate all knowledge in a disintegrating scepticism.

At the same time, theoretical value is by no means the only value in the "realm of values." Next to it are other values, such as the ethical, aesthetical, religious, and so on, all of equal validity even though they cannot be proved theoretically. In an unprejudiced way theoretical philosophy has to investigate the possible groupings of these values (each of which represents a unique type of worldview) without making a choice between them. The choice is left to the autonomous personality who cannot allow theoretical thought to dictate which worldview ought to be accepted.[1]

The fallacy in this argument is contained in the reification of theoretical truth. As if theoretical truth is not tied in with the organic coherence of our temporal cosmos! And as if the meaning assigned to this truth is not entirely dependent upon the view one has of this coherence in one's cosmonomic idea!

1   See Rickert, *System der Philosophie* (1921), 1:24 ff., in connection with p. 407.

No one can quarrel with Rickert's assertion that "the objective validity of theoretical truth can be stringently proved to everyone"[1] provided it claims to be no more than an *analytical* judgment. But this analytical judgment can never contain anything more than the tautology that all theoretical thought is bound to theoretical truth. In a similar fashion one can assert that all aesthetics is bound to aesthetic norms, that all morality is bound to moral norms, and so on and so forth.

But as soon as the above assertion that theoretical thought is stringently provable is presented as a synthetic *material* proposition, and (as is Rickert's intention, judging by the whole set-up of his work) if it serves to provide the ground for theoretical philosophy's independence of worldviews, it is clearly false. The material concept of truth is so little independent of a worldview that the history of philosophy provides us with a veritable catalogue of the most divergent conceptions regarding the material sense of truth. These conceptions demonstrate as clear as day that they are based on an underlying cosmonomic idea.

As an illustration one may compare the realistic concept of truth of Aristotle with the nominalistic concept of truth of Hobbes, Kant's transcendental-idealistic concept of truth, the pragmatist truth concept of William James or Henri Poincaré, or the critical-ontological concept of truth found in the thought of Nicolai Hartmann.

Rickert's "idealistic" characterization of theoretical truth as a "value" with timeless validity, totally independent of subjectivity, already contains the *petitio principii* of humanistic value philosophy whose cosmonomic idea is grounded in the sovereignty of reason.

"Value" conceived in a humanistic sense is nothing but an idealistic reification or an absolutization of normative functions abstracted from their unbreakable coherence with human subject-functions (in the sense of *sujet, being subject to*). The reified normative functions are abstracted into timeless "ideas" serving as the ultimate ground for every form of normative validity for human subjectivity.[2]

1   Op. cit., p. 150.
2   Ibid., p. 136.

116

In this idealistic type of the humanistic cosmonomic idea in which this "value philosophy" is based, a position of apostate revolt is chosen in opposition to the absolute religious truth, of which "theoretical truth" is only a temporal refraction of meaning. According to this apostate position, God's will is not the ultimate ground of norms, but human reason in its absolutized ideas or "values."

However, in the face of the absolute religious truth there is also within theoretical thought no *neutrality* possible.

In the neutrality postulate one makes a stand against God's creational sovereignty by absolutizing theoretical truth into a transcendent, self-sufficient value. The neutrality postulate itself is rooted in a variety of the humanistic worldview which, in line with the Kantian humanistic personality ideal, does not want to sacrifice the personality ideal to the science ideal. Both this personality ideal and the science ideal are determined by an apostate religious a priori.

This line of argument cannot be refuted by the humanistic conception of science, for every attempt in this direction unmasks the humanistic cosmonomic idea as the immense bias in its view of science.

Rickert certainly is correct in his claim that theoretical truth cannot rule over religion without falling prey to the basic mistake of rationalism. Conversely, however, one's religious orientation instead rules over one's concept of truth, just as certainly as theoretical truth does not exist "in itself" since it is only a refraction of the absolute religious truth regarding the relationship between Creator and creation.

*　　　*　　　*

Thus it turns out, *negatively*, that the possibility of a Calvinistic science of law cannot be denied on the basis of the neutrality postulate. *Positively*, the possibility turns out to be dependent on the question whether or not Calvinism, qua worldview, disposes over a defined conception of the pre-positive foundations of positive law.

In order to answer this question we first have to give an account of the cosmonomic idea that determines the structure of this worldview.

117

The Calvinistic cosmonomic idea shows that our entire temporal cosmos is an organic coherence of sphere-sovereign law-functions and subject-functions which are – from the numerical function up to the most complicated spiritual function, the function of faith – a refraction of cosmic time in the imperishable religious root of humanity transcending all temporality in subjection to the eternal religious meaning of the law: the service of God.

In terms of this view of our cosmos, the *logos* is one law-sphere among others, equally grounded in the same religious root as all other law-spheres. Within each law-sphere a meaningful subject-function of organic reality is subject to a meaningful whole of functional laws.

Since all law-spheres together are a refraction of the perduring, eternal religious meaning of the law to which the root of creation is subjected, they possess at the same time, in their functional meaning, sphere-sovereignty, such that no single one can be understood apart from the cosmic coherence of the law-spheres and in independence of the religious root.

This provides a view of our cosmos which is totally antithetic to every philosophy rooted in the immanence standpoint with its sovereignty of reason or the sovereignty of functional consciousness.

On a Christian, Calvinistic standpoint there is no room for "isms" in the sense of absolutizations of specific functions of our temporal cosmos. There is room neither for naturalism, as the absolutization of natural functions, nor for "idealism," as the absolutization of specific functions, nor yet for logicism, psychologism, moralism, aestheticism, or whatever *isms* the history of philosophy may still suggest. The same applies to a dualistic separation within our cosmos between idea and natural reality, between an abstract realm of "ought to be" and an abstract realm of "natural being." All these isms are rooted in a humanistic cosmonomic idea that does not take its Archimedean point in the *transcendent-religious root of creation*, but chooses its orientation in what are *immanent, temporal*, and therefore *relative, reason functions*. In their reifying attitude they are all apostate, idolatrous – irreconcilable with the absolute truth of the Christian religion. Any compromise with such a pagan philosophy saddles Christian thinkers with an internally contradictory synthesis.

Humanistic philosophy in every one of its variations implies an enormous impoverishment of meaning, or rather a *deprivation of the meaning* of temporal reality, because the humanistic cosmonomic idea is irreconcilable with the acceptance of the religious fullness of meaning regarding the cosmic organic coherence as it is revealed in the Christian religion. The humanistic cosmonomic idea necessarily breaks apart this coherence through its reifying and absolutizing attitude, or through sacrificing the immensely rich diversity in the cosmos to the absolutized functions of reality.

The religious organic orientation of the Calvinistic cosmonomic idea primarily reveals itself in the acceptance of a cosmic order of law-spheres, by virtue of which the law-spheres, according to the lesser or greater complexity of their general structure, serve as a foundation for each other in cosmic time. Symbolically expressed, cosmic time is the prism through which the enduring supra-temporal *religious meaning* acquires its refraction in the functions of the sphere-sovereign law-spheres.

We may call the foundational law-spheres the *substrate* spheres of the cosmically later spheres.[1] Eliminating any one of these substrate spheres will result in all later spheres losing their sovereign meaning.

The general sovereign structure of each law-sphere, both as to its law-side and factual side, reflects the organic coherence with the sovereign meaning of all the other law-spheres. This guarantees that no single law-sphere can exist apart from its organic coherence with the others.

Consequently, the general meaning of each law-sphere itself reveals a cosmic-organic structure whose *nucleus* guarantees its sphere-sovereignty. The *analogies* qualified by this nucleus are those elements within its structure that refer back to the meaning of the substrate spheres, while the *anticipations* are those ele-

---

1 [Dooyeweerd's philosophy of time apparently emerged during 1929. Its first elaborate treatment is found in his work of 1931, *The Crisis in Humanist Political Theory*. A few years later, in 1936, he published the first of four articles in the new journal *Philosophia Reformata*. These articles appear as Chapter I in the present volume.]

ments that point forward to the meaning of the later law-spheres.

Anticipations deepen the meaning of a law-sphere by approximating the meaning of a later law-sphere in terms of its own meaning. For example, the anticipatory function of the infinitely small number, by approximating the meaning of the spatial, deepens the meaning of the numerical law-sphere. Similarly, the anticipatory function of differentials deepens the meaning of the numerical law-sphere by approximating the meaning of movement. Again, the anticipatory function of good faith, good mores, and so on, deepens the meaning of retribution in law by approximating the meaning of morality.

In this way the sphere-sovereignty, in its religiously grounded organic structure, finds its mirror image in the *sphere-universality* of each aspect according to its meaning. The structure of every law-sphere reflects the totality of our cosmos. This is revealed to us only in the enduring religious meaning of the creation, as it finds its completion and fulfillment of meaning in Christ as the head of redeemed humanity.

5.   The method dispute within the science of law

This cosmological insight provides the method of legal science with a totally independent orientation. The *"Methodenstreit"* in the science of law oscillates roughly between two poles: the *naturalistic* and the *logicistic-normative* method. The former attempts to understand law in its vital cosmic context, but due to its naturalistic orientation it accomplishes a reduction to nature and therefore an elimination of the normative meaning of the jural. The latter wants to maintain the normative meaning of law but can only achieve this through a dualistic separation between norm and reality, where "reality" is identified with natural reality. In this way law is transformed into an abstract thought-form. In doing this it is logicized and robbed of its sovereign meaning.

New methods have presented themselves with the pretension of avoiding these polar extremes: the *cultural-scientific* and the so-called *phenomenological* methods. The former views law as a subjective connection of natural reality to the jural value. The latter attempts to discover the timeless essential laws of the jural according to the "eidetic-descriptive" method, resulting in laws that are themselves a-normative because they are absolutized in a way that completely divorces them from any connection with human subjectivity.

The first method, that of cultural science, entangles itself in insoluble antinomies by understanding the concept of law as a transcendental-logical relation between two (by definition mutually exclusive) domains of thought, namely *natural reality* and *value*.

The phenomenological method attempts to derive the essential laws in the jural sphere from the noetic-noematic givens of consciousness. However, eliminated in the process by the phenomenological *epochè* is the cosmic meaning of law itself, as it said to belong to the natural attitude of the evaluative and practical functions of consciousness.

That this method, too, is anchored in the humanistic cosmonomic idea can best be seen in Husserl's absolutization of being in its immanence to consciousness.[1] The being of consciousness in the sense of the Cartesian *cogito* is the absolute residue of the methodical "elimination of the world" (*Weltvernichtung*).[2] Thus far, this method, combined by various adherents in an internally contradictory way with Kelsen's "*Normlogik*," has nowhere succeeded in offering any uniform guidelines. Husserl's method of "intuiting essences" is dependent upon the subjective views of those adhering to it and leads to the most divergent results.[3]

6. Grounding a method for a Calvinistic science of law in a Calvinistic cosmology

The method which a Calvinistic science of law has to pursue is strictly based upon a cosmology, and its orientation is entirely directed by the structure of the Calvinistic cosmonomic idea. This orientation makes possible a method capable of specifying the mode of operation of the science of law as a systematic interpretation of law both according to its (mutually correlated) sub-

---

1 Husserl, *Ideen zu einer reinen Phänomenologie und phänomenologischen Philosophie*, 2nd impr. (Halle an der Saale, 1922), 1:92: "Immanent being (viz., of consciousness) is therefore undoubtedly absolute being, such that it is in principle *nulla re indiget ad existendum*."

2 Op. cit., § 49: "Absolute consciousness as the residue of *Weltvernichtung*."

3 An extensive critical discussion of these different humanistic methods is found in my inaugural oration, *De Beteekenis der wetsidee voor rechtsweten-schap en rechtsphilosophie* [The significance of the cosmonomic idea for legal science and legal philosophy] (Kampen: Kok, 1926).

ject-side and its law-side. Applying this interpretation, the legal scholar, while strictly maintaining the sphere-sovereignty of the jural, at one and the same time holds on to the cosmic coherence of the jural aspect with the organism of the [modal] law-spheres.

The jural is thus appreciated as a law-sphere anchored in the divine sovereignty, qualified by a sovereign meaning with its own law-side and subject-side. The law-side of the jural reveals a typical *normative* structure. All norm-spheres are cosmically grounded in the *logos* as the law-sphere of reflective analytical thinking.

In distinction from the laws obtaining within the pre-logical spheres, all functional norms are given only in the form of divine *principles*. Through the activity of human subjects these principles have to be formed (given shape, *positivized*) into concerete norms.

7. The element of "positivity" in the structure of the post-historical norm-spheres

The formation or positivization of normative principles finds its cosmic foundation in the historical law-sphere which in the cosmic order immediately succeeds the logical sphere.[1] *Positivity* is an analogical moment within all post-historical norm-spheres, referring back to the historical structure of cultural development. Thus the general structure of all the post-historical law-spheres already contains the element of positivity.

This insight cancels the humanistic distinction between "absolute" and "empirical" or "contingent" norms.[1]

Those norms considered to be *absolute*, namely those of the *logos*, the aesthetical and the moral, are no more absolute in the sense of existing outside the temporal cosmic coherence than the norms of human social interaction like the economical, lingual and jural norms.

Every post-logical norm inherently displays this element of positivity. Yet, human positivization is never an arbitrary creation, since it merely gives form to divine principles. The question now is whether or not within these post-historical

---

1   See e.g. Felix Somló, *Juristische Grundlehre* (Leipzig, 1917), p. 59; and W. Windelband, *Präludien; Aufsätze und Reden zur Einleitung in die Philosophie*, 3rd enl. ed. (Tübingen, 1907), pp. 292–293.

law-spheres, to which also the jural sphere belongs, the divine principles themselves are independent of historical development, or whether they display a dynamic character on the basis of the substrate of historical development.

8. The rationalistic character of theories of natural law

In the light of our cosmonomic idea we have now specified the question posed earlier: "How does Calvinistic science of law assess natural law?"

"Natural law" is a complex of widely diverging views of law, covering a period of more than two thousand years. The character and meaning of any theory of natural law is completely dependent upon the cosmonomic idea underlying it. The Aristotelian-Thomist view of natural law is structured differently than the nominalistic natural law of the late medieval period. And the humanistic, rationalistic natural law since Grotius displays a totally different method and worldview than ancient and medieval natural law.

In spite of the many differences between them, up to the emergence of the Historical School the theories of natural law obtaining in legal science were mostly rooted in a cosmonomic idea that chose its starting-point in the sovereignty of reason. This had important consequences for the understanding of the character of natural law.

Natural law turned into a rigid whole of logical principles which as such had nothing to do with historical development.

Thus arose the fatal and internally contradictory dualism of an immutable natural law founded on reason, and a contingent, arbitrary, and constantly variable positive law.

Since the rise of humanism, natural law has played the role of a self-sufficient, independent system of norms, acquiring a positive shape through logical deduction. Positive law, by contrast, was not given a foundation in truly *meaningful jural principles* but rather in the abstract maxim *pacta sunt servanda*: contracts must be kept. That served as a *delegating norm* legitimizing every form of arbitrariness. In practical terms natural law thus developed into an *external* boundary for the arbitrariness of those who form law.

In Aristotelian-Thomist natural law, at least the *naturalis ratio* is conceived as *objective logos* valid within a cosmic coherence and embodied in the teleological organic conception of the *lex naturalis,* which in turn is grounded in the *lex aeterna.* For the same reason this particular theory of natural law is sensitive to the structural difference between an organized legal community and a legal partnership, as is clearly evident in the important distinction it makes between *iustitia distributiva* and *legalis* on the one hand, and *iustitia communitativa* on the other.

9. The analytical character of the ethical and natural-law basic principles in Thomist-Aristotelian natural law

Natural law in the Thomist-Aristotelian tradition, however, has an objective logicistic character. This comes to expression in a deductive method that traces all principles of natural law back to the essentially analytical judgment that one ought to do what is good and refrain from doing what is evil.

The same analytical character is present in the famous basic rule of natural law, *To each his own.* All legal rules of natural law essentially are logical objectifications of actual a-logical jural principles. Only in their coherence with those jural principles is it possible that these objectifications can acquire a material synthetical meaning; but in their general logical character *as such,* that is to say, apart from this coherence, they merely contain endless tautologies.

We now understand why also the Aristotelian-Thomist natural law displays a rigid character, disconnected from any link with the historical law-sphere.

10. Rationalistic humanistic natural law

The situation is much more serious with *humanistic* natural law, because after Kant it transformed itself into an abstract reason-law (*Vernunftrecht*), understood in a normative sense.

This natural law in itself displays many nuances, from naturalism to idealism, but essentially it is constructed according to the abstract mathematical method. It is no longer the objective universal Logos,[1] This natural law in itself displays many nuances, from naturalism to idealism, but essentially it is constructed according to the abstract mathematical method. It is no

1 [See H. Dooyeweerd, "Kuyper's wetenschapsleer," *Phil. Ref.* 4 (1939): 193-232. Eng. trans.: "Kuyper's Philosophy of Science," in S. Bishop and J. H. Kok, eds., *On Kuyper: A Collection of Readings on the Life, Work and Legacy of Abraham Kuyper* (Sioux Center, Iowa: Dordt College Press), pp. 153-178.]

longer the objective universal Logos, but rather the subjective logical function which since Descartes has guided the subjectivistic turn in philosophy. It led to the construction of a legal system of natural law, positivized down to the smallest detail by mathematical thinking. Natural law itself became a positive reason-law operating with the pretension of having timeless validity. Cosmic reality was mentally broken down in order to build up a logicistic cosmos created by mathematical thought.

In this way the structure of the jural sphere was logically broken down as well, such that a legal world of one's own making was constructed *more geometrico* from the mathematical *element* of the *individual*. In this process the distinction, so important in the structure of law, between coordinational and communal relationships – between a partnership and an organized community – was lost for scientific thought. This distinction is grounded in the social law-sphere by virtue of the cosmic coherence. Having been lost, it recently had to be "discovered" again.

We may here leave aside the fact that all humanist natural law, as to its *material contents*, was derived from Roman law as *"ratio scripta."* Methodologically it was oriented to the humanistic natural-science ideal which had to blur all boundaries in order to bring to light the uninterrupted continuity of mathematical thought. But this kind of natural law once for all disappeared from the scene after the rise of the Historical School. Ever since the emergence of the disciplines of history and sociology no one thinks of defending it anymore.

11. The altered character of natural law since the revival of the idea of natural law in the modern era

A different kind of natural law has been in the ascendant since the end of the 19th century. It is a natural law that bears a totally irrational imprint, such as is found in the "free law movement." It appeals exclusively to a judge's sense of justice, which results in giving him *carte blanche* for making fair and just decisions in concrete cases, if need be even *contra legem* – against existing law.

Alternatively, it turns into a formalistic, logicistic natural law "with variable content" in the sense of Stammler's "social ideal," which once again lapses into the old fruitless analytical practice and whose logical principles are merely meant to express the formal-logical idea of *Richtigkeit* (correctness), although the *Grundsätze* (basic propositions) derived from this idea of law unexpectedly receive material content from the humanistic personality ideal (the human personality as an autonomous "*Selbstzweck*" – an end in itself).

What predominates, however, is the quest for a material natural law in the sense of concrete norms of justice that transcend the analytical fruitlessness of the formalist school. A variety of avenues have been explored to find an orientation for law: using a comprehensive philosophy of culture; providing the idea of law with content by situating it in relation to the worldviews of political parties or by relating it to a phenomenology of values; and so on.

12. The changed attitude of jurisprudence in respect of positive law

What is particularly striking is the changed attitude of jurisprudence with respect to positive law. Logical "conceptual jurisprudence" (*Begriffsjurisprudenz*) has had its day and is being replaced by a materially directed "jurisprudence of interests" (*Interessenjurisprudenz*). The formalistic conception of law is visibly losing ground. Just recall how the material concept of torts won out over the former, formalistic view in the decision of the *Hooge Raad* (Supreme Court) regarding Article 1401 ff. of the Dutch Civil Code. And think of the theory of the abuse of right (*abus de droit*) that has already penetrated deeply into the practice of law; or consider the theory of liability that is already widely accepted outside the law.

A more liberal view regarding the law is gaining ground across the board. No one seriously believes anymore that a legal system of laws is seamless. And this better insight is accompanied by a revival of interest in the pre-positive principles of justice.

Jurisprudence demonstrates the dynamics and flexibility of a considerable portion of jural principles in their connection with historical development. However, the modern humanistic theorists of natural law are incapable of conceiving these jural principles in their organic structure. They grope and search, they construct clever theories, but they too suffer from the basic defect of humanism's cosmonomic idea. Value-idealism, historicism, psychologism, logicism, etc., are rampant. Within these theories justice cannot be done to the structure of jural principles, for the *sine qua non* for a sound theory of these principles is the acceptance of the religious organic principle of sphere-sovereignty.

13. Jural principles are inherent to positive law

All positive law originates through positivization by competent organs of organized legal communities or coordinated legal spheres of divine material jural principles that are given only in a cosmic coherence. As we shall argue later on, the very competence of the organized legal communities (including that of the state) and of the coordinated legal spheres has its pre-positive foundation in the structural principles of these organized communities (*verbanden*) and coordinated legal spheres (*maatschapskringen*). Across the board the jural principles *inhere* in all forms of genuine positive law.

It is not superfluous to note that the jural principles are not *created* but *discovered* by the functions of subjective reason, and that they have no transcendent but only immanent validity *within the cosmic coherence.*

A twofold misunderstanding is thus precluded:

1) The misunderstanding of those who demand that true principles have an eternal value, elevated above time.
2) The mistaken view of those who think, in line with positivism, that whatever enters into the subjective *form* of a source of law (a legal stipulation, a contract, etc. etc.) is on that ground alone stamped as positive law.

14. Legal principles have no transcendent, timeless validity

The first misunderstanding is widespread also in Christian circles. It is therefore appropriate to point out emphatically that such a "metaphysical" conception of legal principles does not have a Christian but rather a pagan and humanistic origin.

It is the fruit of the *idealistic* metaphysics of all time, which is grounded in the immanence standpoint that looks for the "*Jenseits*" in the "*Diesseits*," for the eternal within time. The reason ideas are abstracted from their temporal cosmic coherence and at once absolutized to eternal values.

127

But reason ideas are not absolute. Every attempt to understand their meaning exhibits their relativity, their appeal to the temporal organism of law-spheres, from the numerical to the sphere of faith.

By way of illustration, compare Kant's idea of the jural in the well-known definition as the "sum-total of conditions under which the arbitrariness of one person can co-exist with the arbitrariness of another, subject to a universal law of freedom."

Even apart from the fact that we here have a logical-analytical concept (receiving its material meaning solely from the humanistic personality ideal of freedom), the logical-analytical meaning of the concept can be grasped only within the temporal cosmic coherence of the law-spheres.

This humanistic jural principle appeals to the numerical sphere, the spatial sphere, the mechanical, the biotical, the psychical, the logical, the historical, the social, the lingual sphere, the economical, the aesthetic, the moral and the faith sphere.

Just consider that law aims at regulating human behaviour in a functional way. And human behaviour is a cosmic complex of functions which operates in all law-spheres.

A *purely* jural action is a perfectly meaningless construction, and it is also not possible to grasp it in a concept, because the concept of a legal act presupposes a cosmic – i.e., temporal, organic, relative – connection between the jural sphere and the logical law-sphere.

The gravest danger that the objectionable metaphysical view of jural principles entails for the view of law is this: even as people pay homage to eternal principles "that do not enter time," they think they can approach temporal legal life without any principles and assume a utilitarian attitude towards the formation of law. For that matter, the concept "supra-temporal jural principle" is internally contradictory; "principle" (*beginsel*) means "beginning," and all beginning is within time.

No principle is supra-temporal, but only the eternal, religious meaning of law. And all normative principles, also those of a logical, historical, social, lingual, aesthetic, economic, moral and pistical nature are temporal refractions of the eternal meaning of the law, as has been revealed to us by Christ. Sin in its supra-temporal religious sense is not the violation of a functional

norm, but touches the *heart*, the root of the human race: it signifies a rejection of the eternal meaning of the law, the service of
God. But sin manifests itself *within time* in an attitude of revolt
against the functional ordinances as they were set by God the
Lord for every law-sphere.

Sin also affects the natural functions. In humankind nature
too fell, because it does not have existence in itself. Nature as
such, however, is not subject to norms.

15. Positivism: the absolutization of the element of positivity within the structure of the jural

The second misunderstanding stems from positivism and believes that positive law as such is independent of divine jural
principles. This view absolutizes the structurally dependent element of positivity within the meaning of law. In this way the
meaning of law is lost, because the entire law-side of the jural
sphere is subjectivized. The only law-conformity (*wetmatigheid*)
under which the positivistic science of law subsumes this mean-
ing-less subjective arbitrariness is that of the logical. But the legal norm is not a logical proposition but a law-type with its own
sovereign meaning, totally different from the logical.

The entire critique launched by Kelsen against the idea of natural law rests on a fundamental failure to appreciate the structure of every norm. His critique reaches its culmination in the
argument that natural law and positive law are two totally distinct norm systems, each proceeding from its own logical basic
or original norm, and that by virtue of the logical principle of
contradiction these two systems can never be valid simultaneously.[1] Yet this argument collapses once the structure of positive jural principles is subjected to a proper analysis. "Natural
law" in the sense of "jural principles" is not an independent
norm system, just as little as positivity is an independent concept. Every norm system exhibits its own sovereign structure in
an inextricable intertwinement of divine principle and human
positivization.

1 Hans Kelsen, *Die philosophischen Grundlagen der Naturrechtslehre und des
Rechtspositivismus* (Charlottenburg, 1928). Kelsen's critique in a radical
sense applies only to "metaphysical" and dualistic natural law. See in this
connection Fritz Sander, "Staat und Recht," *Wiener staatswissenschaftliche
Studien*, new ser., 1 (1922): 5 ff., and Alf Ross, *Theorie der Rechtsquellen*
(Vienna, 1929), pp. 56 ff.

Thus the Calvinistic view of law in principle overcomes the age-old dualism between natural law and positive law which essentially derives from an idealistic metaphysical source.

* * *

Truly material jural principles cannot be derived from an abstract principle through logical deduction. Rather they are exceedingly diverse, in keeping with the very structure of the jural, and therefore they can only be discovered in the connections of the jural sphere with life itself.

16. Fundamental structural differences between diverse hural principles

The legal order is not simply uniform in a logical sense, since, to start with, it is differentiated in numerous organized communal and coordinational relationships. The distinction between an (organized) jural community and a jural partnership relation is founded in the social law-sphere of sociation, regulated by norms of propriety, courtesy, sociality, tact, fashion, play etc. etc. An (organized) community integrates legal subjects into a new supra-individual unit. What is inherent in an organized community is the *function of authority* and the *solidarity* of its members.[1]

The jural partnership (*maatschap*), by contrast, leaves the individual legal subjects standing side by side as fellow equals. It does not resolve them into a supra-individual unit and therefore it also does not assign authority of one legal subject over another.

Organized jural communities and coordinated jural relationships do not exist in isolation from each other, for they are intimately intertwined in the cosmic structure of the jural sphere. An organized community participates in *sociational* interaction, and the members of coordinational relationships also have collective functions within the diverse organized communities.

---

1 See Johannes Althusius, *Politica methodice digesta, atque exemplis sacris et profanis illustrata*, 2nd enl. ed. (Groningen, 1610), chap. 1: "Communis et perpetua lex est, ut in quavis consociatione et symbiosis specie sint quidam imperantes, praepositi, praefecti seu superiores: quidam vero obsequentes, seu inferiors." (Common law, which is unchanging, indicates that in every association and type of symbiosis some persons are rulers, commanders, prefects, or superiors, others are subjects or inferiors).

Similarly, the members of an organized community also continue to stand in mutual coordinational relationships. Private-legal organized work communities, for example, certainly exhibit a *communal* character in their inner structure. But this is established by means of a contract from which both employees and employers derive common coordinational rights, even as the independent structure of the internal law of organized communities is fully maintained.

17. A structural analysis of the principle of indemnification in private law and of the modern principle of penal law: punishment according to guilt

A brief analysis of the modern principle of criminal law, namely punishment according to guilt, and of the principle of compensation in private law, namely indemnification according to the yardstick of horizontal legal interaction, already shows that jural principles display a different structure depending upon what they are: jural principles for coordinational relations, or jural principles for organized communities.

The principle of indemnification is a principle of jural coordinational relations. It bears the stamp of the horizontal norm and it typically rests on the substrate of economic equivalence. The retributive claim of private law, coming to expression in this principle, merely requires compensation for any damage inflicted by a tort (i.e., a wrongful act, according to the modern conception, in a *material* sense) caused by a legal partner to an adjacent person with equal rights. It determines the extent of the compensation in terms of the requirements of coordinational jural interactions that are horizontal in nature.

Punishment in a jural sense, on the other hand, can only be imposed by an organized jural community by virtue of its supra-individual function of authority. But this punishment cannot derive its retributive measure from the harm inflicted in a juridical sense to the victim of the wrongful act as a member of a coordinational relationship. Rather, it ought to be guided by an organized communal measure in its supra-individual nature.

Against this one may not appeal to the stipulations of the *leges barbarorum* in respect of *weregeld*.[1] Binding has shown in his trea-

---

1 [In old Germanic law, *weregeld* (also called "blood fine") was the value set upon the life of a slain man in accordance with his rank and paid out as compensation to his surviving relatives.]

tise on the "origin of public punishment in old Germanic law"[1] that *weregeld* did not exhibit the trait of punishment but rather of compensation, in order to prevent the blood-revenge of the organized sib communities. The meaning of punishment there was not compensation for the harm inflicted by a partnership member to another member with equal rights, but first of all an *authority's* reaction to those who harmed the foundations of the sib as an organized community.

The guilt principle of penal law is based upon weighing the seriousness of a wrongful act from the perspective of the ideal [non-material] harm understood in a deepened sense approximating the meaning of morality, a harmful act inflicted on the organized jural community in its authority structure.

Thus it is conceivable that in terms of the criminal retribution of the *state* (of course the state does not have a monopoly on each and every form of jural punishment!), justice demands a light punishment for a specific crime, while the same crime from the perspective of indemnification of private law may provide grounds for a sizable claim for damage by virtue of Article 1401 of our Civil Code. The reverse is also possible.

18. Interpreting the meaning of the different concepts of tort employed by the *Hooge Raad* in respect of wrongful private actions and wrongful government actions. The jurisprudence of the French *Conseil d'Etat*

In its interpretation of Article 1401 and following regarding torts in private law, the *Hooge Raad*, since its famous decision of 1919, employs a *material* concept of tort. Nevertheless, even after 1924 our Supreme Court has continued to apply a *formal* concept of tort in the case of wrongful acts on the part of the government.

Without any doubt, jural principles have guided the Court in its decisions. But our highest judicial college realized intuitively that private law does not have any principles applicable to the public-legal structure of the state as an organized community. It also understood that the positivization of the dynamic public-legal principles postulated in the modern public-legal idea of the just state (*rechtsstaat*) – to be distinguished from the pri-

---

1 Karl Binding, *Die Entstehung der öffentlichen Strafe im germanisch-deutschen Recht* (Leipzig, 1909).

vate-legal idea of the just state[1] – can fall only to the domain of the administrative judge.[2] – can fall only to the domain of the administrative judge.[2] The administrative judge does not have to adjudicate disputes between the state as a party in coordinated interaction with another party; it adjudicates disputes between *government and subject*. This explains the *formal* nature of the concept of tort which jurisprudence, for that matter, applies not only in respect of government acts but also in all cases of acts that take place within an organized community.[3]

Now it is worthwhile to analyze the jurisprudence of the French *Conseil d'Etat* on this point, since in its administrative jurisprudence regarding wrongful acts by the government it has positivized an independent principle of public law that is quite different from the principle of indemnification as found in Articles 1382–1386 of the French *Code Civil* (the equivalent of Articles 1401–1405 in the Dutch Civil Code). In his book on the authority of public power, Paul Duez remarks: "Whether it concerns responsibility for torts or for risk, the Court is not inspired

1   The private-legal idea of the just state requires only that the state, in its *external* private-legal conduct, subject itself to the horizontal jural norms for coordinational relationships.

2   This entails that the distinction between questions of equity and questions of utility, aimed at establishing the boundaries for the competence of the administrative judge, fails to appreciate the core meaning of administrative jurisprudence. If this distinction, with its odd terminology, is to have any juridical meaning at all, it must have no other aim than to prevent the administrative judge from applying a *material* concept of wrongfulness – in other words, to assign him the same role as the one played by the *Hooge Raad* since its decision of 1924. Fortunately, in the incidental arrangement of various categories of administrative jurisprudence, this view of the assessment of wrongful government actions, which is essentially a view belonging to private law, did not find general acceptance. See e.g. the Law on Crisis Jurisprudence of 26 July 1918, Sec. 494, and Art. 58 of the Civil Servants Act of 1929.

3   A very important decision in this connection is that of the German *Reichsgericht* of 20 Dec. 1923, in which its established jurisprudence, requiring that the judge has to consider solely the *formal* side of an annulment of a trade union because investigating the *material* grounds would come into conflict with the autonomy of the internal law of an association, was changed to this extent that testing also the *material* organized communities where the individual member is forced to join if he does not want to lose his job. This decision does not detract from the general principle, but simply draws the consequence from the partially *public-legal* position acquired by labor organizations in Germany since 1918.

133

by civil law; the theories included in its decisions are autonomous theories reflecting ideas of public law."[1]

What is this principle of public law? It is the principle of the proportional equality of public obligations and the rights of the citizens within the state as an organized community.

This is once again a principle for an organized community – to be exact, a principle for the internal structure of the state as an organized community within the jural sphere.

The modern theory of the sovereignty of law, in the form in which it was defended by Krabbe and Duguit where it undoubtedly had a material *natural-law* meaning, ignores, by reason of its starting-point, the cosmic structural difference between an organized jural community and a jural partnership. In consequence it cannot but result, on principle, in a rejection of the difference between public law and private law.

But such a theory in principle entails a negation of the (sphere-)sovereignty of law. For how can law reign with sovereignty if one starts by eliminating the inner structure of organized communities and coordinational spheres? Rejecting the distinction between public and private law implies a denial of the structural difference between the principle for organized communities and for coordinational law. This is done in the theories of Krabbe and Duguit, for they essentially continue the individualistic tradition of rationalistic humanistic natural law.

19. The structural difference between the principle of Article 68 of the Criminal Code and the principles applicable to church discipline

One final example may be added to those mentioned above.

The procedure of discipline followed in the Reformed Churches in the Netherlands does not recognize the principle *ne bis in idem* ["not twice in the same cause"] of Article 68 of the Criminal Code. Nothing is easier, but also more superficial, than to accuse church law on this point of being primitive or behind the times, or even in conflict with the "idea of law."

The truth is that an abstract "idea of law," such as found in Stammler, completely lacks any jural sense, for at most it displays a logical analytical meaning. Rightly understood, the idea

1 Paul Duez, *La responsabilité de la puissance publique* (Paris, 1927), pp. 60–61.

134

of law displays itself only in dynamic material jural principles. In these principles the meaning of the jural aspect is deepened in an anticipatory way by being focused upon the highly differentiated cosmic structures within the jural sphere.

What the science of law has to do is to interpret the *meaning* of the difference that exists between the procedure of church discipline and the penal law of the state and its accompanying criminal procedure.

Clarifying this difference is possible only if the science of law orients itself to the Calvinistic cosmology which we still have to explain in some of its basic outlines. In our brief exposition thus far we have discussed only the *structure of the law-spheres* in their *functional meaning*.

20. The structural reality of a real thing or entity

Cosmic reality is only given to us in the structure of individual "things" or "entities." The latter in no way are simply "phenomena" in the sense of a mere synthesis of logical categories, psychical forms, of intuition and psychical "matter." Rather they have real meaningful functions in all law-spheres. These reality functions are distinguished in *subject*-functions and *object*-functions.

A tree as an (individual) thing has *subject-functions* in the numerical sphere, the spatial sphere, the physical and the biotical law-sphere. By contrast, it has *object*-functions in the later law-spheres (the psychical, the logical, the historical, the lingual, the economic, the aesthetic, the jural, the moral and the pistical law-sphere). The object-functions of a thing, which are just as real as its subject-functions, exist only in correlation to subject-functions which the thing does not have. For example, as an object of perception the tree has an object-function within the psychical law-sphere. In this sense the psychical object-function exists only in correlation to the animal or human subject-function in the psychical law-sphere, but in no way is it a subjective creation of human consciousness.

Each thing, insofar as it is an individual unity of subject-functions, is qualified [led or guided] by its most complicated subject-function in cosmic reality which at the same time entails a delimitation of its subjective activity and which we call its *leading function*. The "leading function" of an entity unlocks or dis-

135

closes the anticipatory spheres of the meaning of its earlier sub-ject-functions in the direction towards itself and through this it *deepens* the meaning of these subject-functions. Thus in the internal structure of the tree, the numerical, spatial, kinematic and energy functions are *guided* by the organic function of life (the biotic function), although this takes place with full retention of the sphere-sovereignty of each function with its own law-con-formity (*wetmatigheid*).

There are *natural* and *spiritual* things. Just as reality is given only in the unbreakable organism of all functions of reality, so both natural things and spiritual things have reality functions in *all* law-spheres. Only their individual structures in their sub-jectand object-functions are totally different.

21. The organized communities display a cosmic entity structure with a distinct leading function

Among the spiritual, subjective entitary structures (*dingstruc-turen*)[1] one finds, for example, the state, which is qualified in a public-legal sense by the jural function of government; the so-called "visible" church, qualified by the function of faith; the organized business community, which has its guiding function in the economic sphere; and also all other organized communi-ties of human society.

Since all these organized communities also function within the jural aspect they necessarily have an internal structural jural sphere that is fully guided by their respective qualifying func-tion.

For example, internal business law is completely focused on the economic destination of this organized community; internal

---

1 In its fight against the concept of an entity, modern functionalism equates thing and substance (in the sense of a reifying metaphysics). However, the meaning attached by us to the cosmic thing structure has nothing to do with the metaphysical concept of substance, since it dispenses with the typ-ical metaphysical and reifying characteristic of supra-temporality and im-mutability.

Functionalism lacks a cosmological foundation and reduces the thing structure to functions. The effect is that all structural differences are elimi-nated as well. This lack of a cosmological foundation has caused a veritable crisis in the various disciplines. For the science of law, see Siegfried Marck, *Substanzund Funktionsbegriff in der Rechtsphilosophie* (Tübingen, 1925); and for the entire functionalistic school, see Ernst Cassirer, *Substanzbegriff und Funktionsbegriff* (Berlin, 1910).

ecclesiastical law is focused on the qualifying faith function; the internal law of a social association is focused on the qualifying social function of social intercourse, etc.

22. Elucidating the structural difference between the principles underlying process law within the state and the church

Since the cosmic structure of the internal law of the state and that of the church are totally different, it should not be surprising that the jural principles that obtain for them display a fundamental difference in their structure as well. The criminal procedure of the state, for example, has no other destination or purpose than the legal security of its citizens, whereas the disciplinary procedure of the church is guided by the leading function of the church as an organized community in which the purity of confession must be upheld. Similarly, the jural principle of legal security does not exhibit the same disclosure as that which governs church discipline. It provides an inner *delimitation* to the deepening of the meaning of law as based on the internal structure of the state. In the church, by contrast, the material idea of justice unfolds itself, right down to process law, in approximating the meaning of faith and revelation.

23. Are there constant jural principles?

It is only at this point, now that the structure of jural principles have been clarified in a cosmological sense, that we can attempt to answer the question phrased earlier, namely whether all jural principles bear a *dynamic* character by virtue of their foundation in historical development, or whether there are also *constant*, static jural principles?

What is certain at this point is that insofar as the existence of such constant, static jural principles can be demonstrated, it can only refer to *temporal principles*, principles that are given within the cosmic coherence. There are no supra-temporal, "purely formal" jural principles, such as those which Stammler's neo-Kantian theory of natural law believes one can deduce from the "idea of law."

137

24. Concept of law [law-concept] and idea of law [law-idea] (*rechtsbegrip* and *rechtsidee*)

Before we can answer the formulated question we have to pause for a moment in order to focus on the relationship between the *law-concept* and the *law-idea*[1] – a distinction that has dominated legal philosophy since Stammler.

According to Stammler, *Rechtsbegriff* (concept of law) merely refers to a logical method of ordering the contents of human consciousness, a purely formal *a priori* condition to which all positive law, however objectionable its contents may be, must conform if one is to speak of "law" at all. *Rechtsidee* (idea of law),[2] on the other hand, orders our legal experience according to the yardstick of justice in keeping with the "logical method" of "correctness" (*Richtigkeit*). With the aid of the formal idea of law (or law-idea) we thus arrive at an assessment of positive law as being "just" or "unjust."

This formalistic view does not understand law according to its material structure but as an abstract-logical category. In a Kantian sense it is supposed to provide the synthetical *form* to a socio-economic matter which in itself is totally formless. It does not conquer positivism in the *concept of law*, for it is irreconcilable with the acceptance of an intrinsic meaningful divine lawfulness of positive law *qua talis*. It cannot be reconciled with the acceptance of material legal principles of which all positive law is but a human positivization.

In the light of the Calvinistic cosmonomic idea, the *concept* of law is the result of a synthesis, performed by a religiously conditioned cosmological self-consciousness, between the logical-analytical meaning and the general material jural meaning of law in its "restrictive function," by which we understand the meaning of law [the *jural* meaning] whose structure is not yet deepened by an anticipation of a cosmically later structure.

In the *idea* of law, by contrast, the above-intended synthesis takes the general structure of the jural sphere in its "expansive" or "deepened" function, that is, in its anticipation of the meaning of the moral sphere and the sphere of faith. Here "idea of law" or "law-idea" is taken as "justice."

1 [Law-idea, or: idea of law. Not to be confused with "*wetsidee*": here translated as "cosmonomic idea."]

2 [In later years, Dooyeweerd in these word combinations would write "idea" with a capital, thus: the Idea of law.]

25. The law-idea is directed towards the totality [of meaning] and thus points to the religious fullness of meaning transcending the cosmic boundary of time

The above distinction between "concept" and "idea" is found whenever the meaning of any law-sphere is understood through synthesis. Thus we can distinguish between the *concept* and the *idea* of number,[1] of space, motion, organic life, psychical-sensitive consciousness, the logical, historical, social, lingual, aesthetic meaning, the economic, jural, moral and pistical meaning. The idea is always directed towards the totality and thus points beyond temporal reality to the supra-temporal religious fullness of meaning.

The "concept of law" presupposes a distinctive and normative lawfulness of the jural sphere, just as the number concept presupposes the internal law-conformity of numbers, the space concept the peculiar law-conformity of spatial configurations, the motion concept the particular law-conformity of functions of movement.

For that reason every variety of positivism, also modern "critical positivism," entails a distortion of the meaning of the concept of the jural, because it denies the original lawful meaning of positive law by accepting only an abstract *logical* law-conformity. In spite of being mistaken regarding the structural meaning of jural principles, it remains the enduring merit of the material natural-law theory of all times that it realized that the possibility of practicing the science of law is dependent upon the validity of a material law-conformity of the jural, elevated above all arbitrariness of the legislator.

26. General and individual structure

The concept of the jural displays a generality, which means that the structures of the jural sphere in its "unified" general structure is conceived in a coherence qualified by the general jural meaning transcending all differentiations of individual meanings.

Yet the concept of law presupposes the *individuality* of juridical structure within the jural sphere: the general structure of the jural sphere is the universal structure of the individual jural structures.

The general or universal structure of the jural sphere according to its law-side and subject-side is conceived as *retributive norm* and as *retributive subjectivity*. "Retribution" is "proportionality" and the meaning of this "proportionality" can only be conceived in its coherence with the general structure of al the substrate functions of the jural. The universal meaning of the jural contains analogies of all earlier structures.

27. Analysis of the general structure of the jural in its restrictive meaning

In the light of the Calvinistic cosmonomic idea, the general cosmological structure of the jural can be analyzed as follows.

Nucleus: *retribution in the cosmic time-order* where the latter has its *functional jural* meaning within *retributive time*.

A. Analogies on the law-side

(a) Numerical analogy:
The retributive norm combines a *multiplicity* of legal subjects in jural relations.

(b) Spatial analogy:
Every retributive norm is valid within a legal order encompassing a certain (territorial or personal) jural domain.

(c) Kinematical analogy:
Every retributive norm connects dynamical legal consequences to a legal ground.

(d) Biotic analogy:
Every jural norm demands form-giving (positivization) by a competent *organ* presupposing a living bearer.

(e) Psychical analogy:
The positivization as such is the juridical *will* (upon the substrate of the contents of the sensitive consciousness) of the competent organ.

(f) Logical analogy:
The legal rule is a norm that holds rational action accountable and which ought to be fitted in the legal system according to the analogy of the analytical *principium contradictionis*.

(g) Historical analogy:
Positivization as human form-giving to material jural principles on the substrate of historical development.

(h) Lingual analogy:
The legal norm implies a *symbolical expression*, containing a

certain meaning that has to be established through interpretation.
(i) Social analogy:
The legal norm is a partnership norm or communal norm on the social substrate of social intercourse.
(j) Economic analogy:
The retributive norm establishes a balance in *legal interests*, and when the latter are infringed upon compensation is required.
(k) Aesthetic analogy:
The retributive norm balances out any injustice by means of harmony in law. (The so-called aesthetic theories of penal law absolutize this aesthetic analogy.)

B. Analogies on the subject-side
(a) Numerical analogy:
The legal subject is fitted in a multiplicity of legal relationships.
(b) Spatial analogy:
Legal subjectivity has a determined domain of validity.
(c) Kinematical analogy:
Legal subjectivity is realized by legal actions (in the case of those who lack legal capacity by a representative or an organ) affecting legal life in a causal way. The normative juridical meaning of this causality is primarily seen in the *causa omissiones*.
(d) Biotic analogy:
Legal subjectivity requires a living *bearer* or *organ*.
(e) Psychical analogy:
In its juridical will (upon the substrate of the normal sensitive function of consciousness) the legal subject serves as the point held accountable for legal actions.
(f) Logical analogy:
The legal subject is the rational subject of normative accountability; its will cannot contradict itself in a logical sense.
(g) Historical analogy:
The positive meaning of subjective legal actions rests on the general substrate of historical development.
(h) Lingual analogy:
The subjective juridical will requires *symbolical expression*

which has a certain meaning that needs interpretation in order to be established.

(i) Social analogy:
Coordinated partnership relationships or organized communities function as legal subjects on the basis of social intercourse.

(j) Economic analogy:
The subjective legal relationship contains a jural good as its *legal object*, which, on the substrate of economic evaluative functions, is assessed according to a retributive yardstick.

(k) Aesthetic analogy:
The subjective legal relationships can exist only by restoring the subjective injustice in the harmony of law (on the substrate of the aesthetic function which resolves what is aesthetically dissonant into beautiful harmony).

General remark: No single analogical element can be understood in isolation. Its meaning is embedded in the total general structure of the jural sphere in the unbreakable coherence of law-side and subject-side and in the unbreakable cosmic coherence with the structure of all its substrate spheres. Patently clear is the fundamental difference between the concept of law analyzed in its cosmic structure and Stammler's law-concept with it logicistic, formal categories of law.

A closer analysis of the analogical elements can produce a detailed group of categories.

The social analogy, for example, contains on its law-side the element of juridical *authority* and juridical *subordination* (not to be confused with being a subject within a state), and alternatively the juridical element of being an [equal] partner. Related to this is the element of material competence inherent in the concept of *source of law*.

Similarly, the logical analogy contains the ingredient of lawfulness and unlawfulness; the historical analogy contains that of juridical validity; and so on. Furthermore, the legal concept of fault is not, as Stammler mistakenly holds, a juridical category present within the law-concept. Jural fault (guilt) in fact is an anticipatory element of the meaning of law that falls within the domain of the law-idea. It is indeed absent in a primitive legal order. Juridical time is not itself an analogical element, but, as we have remarked, it is the juridical function of the cosmic time-order that has a function in every law-sphere.

The general structure yields an endless differentiation in the individuality of jural structures. As a legal institution marriage contains a juridical individuality, just as is contained in a mortgage, in property, in the state, etc. etc.

In the normative law-spheres this functional individuality possesses, qua individuality, a typical substrate whereby it is cosmologically grounded.

For example, marriage as a legal institution has its typical substrate in the biotical bond of the sexes; a mortgage has its substrate in the historically grounded *economic credit*; the state has it in the historical concentration of power in the sense of establishing governmental authority over subjects; and so on.

28. There exists a pre-positive, constant natural law given in the form of principles

Once we have understood this cosmic structure of juridical individualities, it will be clear that within the jural sphere one can indeed in the full sense of the term speak of a *natural law*, namely in the sense of pre-historical jural principles (not dependent on historical development as such) grounded in a (natural) lawfulness that displays a static, constant character. But this natural law embraces only part of the jural principles, namely those that are *constant*. In this study we shall confine ourselves to an examination of the natural-law principles for marriage.

As a *legal* institution, marriage is the jural side of the cosmic, sexual bond between husband and wife. Its guiding function is found in the moral law-sphere of the bond of love (*verbandsliefde*).

The marriage bond is therefore a cosmic *community* having its typical substrate in the biotic gender functions and finding its "guiding function" in the moral law-sphere.

For the functional legal structure of marriage this cosmic structure contains static jural principles. The latter are not given with natural necessity since they have the character of normative, retributive principles.

29. Constant principles of marital law

In the first place, as a legal institution marriage is never to be treated as a partnership. Marriage is a natural jural bond[1] in the full sense of the word, in which jural authority ought to rule. This static principle entails:

1. the bond of marriage as the only possible jural bond of sexual relationships;
2. the juridical authority of the nuclear family as principle;
3. a common sphere of property right; and
4. the *durability* of the marriage relationship, resisting every arbitrary termination of this bond on grounds not justified by the nature of this jural bond.

The positivization of these static principles of natural law is cosmically grounded in its entirety by historical development and is subject to the *dynamic* jural principles which in turn are grounded in what is culturally dominant in a typical historical sense. It is only in this dynamic positivization that the function of the law-idea (*rechtsidee*) comes into play.

30. The dynamic function of the law-idea in its coherence with what is culturally dominant in a historical sense

In modern historical development one can discern a developmental norm – a cultural dominant – in the requirement that within the organizational boundaries of the cultural bond the independent cultural worth of every individual ought to be maintained.

This historical norm did not obtain during the Middle Ages, when the individual was still completely hidden behind the structure of the organized communities. Nor did it obtain during the individualistic Age of Enlightenment, when the idea of organized communities completely retreated behind the eman-

---

1 In the modern era the distinction between natural and voluntary organized communities has been elaborated particularly by Tönnies in his *Gemeinschaft und Gesellschaft* (6th and 7th ed., 1926, vol. 2), although it was known with full clarity to the Calvinistic jurist, Johannes Althusius, Politica methodice digesta chap. 2 (p. 12): "Species privatae et simplicis hujus consociationis sunt duae. Est enim alia naturalis, alia vero civilis." (The private and simple types of association are twofold: some are natural, others civil.)

cipated individual. It is, rather, an achievement of a late stage of the modern era.

Founded upon the substrate of this cultural dominant is the legal principle of preventing an abuse of right. This principle was mainly positivized in jurisprudence and found fertile soil in the Germanic view that all [individual] rights are linked to the duties of organized communities. Similarly, the meaning of the static jural principle of authority in the nuclear family within the marital bond, grounded in historical development, has acquired a deepening of its meaning whereby it comes under influence of the idea of law which as such has the important dynamic function of unfolding and deepening positive law. *The historical law-sphere*, with its sovereign meaning of cultural development, serves as *the nodal point of the entire spiritual dynamics within the cosmos.*

It is not difficult to see how this conception resolves the impossible dualism between law-concept and law-idea without allowing the law-concept to be exhausted by the law-idea. At the same time the law-idea receives, through its orientation to the dynamic jural principles, the material fulfillment that was completely lost in the logical formalism of Stammler's theory of natural law.

31. The apparent setting aside of the constant jural principles in positive law

The question remaining is: Are legal orderings that set aside the static principles for marriage at this point no longer positive law?

Unfortunately this question has a typically antinomic formulation and is therefore formulated incorrectly. Indeed there is no form of positive law that is not a positivization of divine "jural principles." Any other conception renders a meaningful "law-concept" impossible.

The free will of the framers of law concerns only the *manner* in which jural principles are positivized, thus providing a large scope for many possibilities. Absolutizing the element of positivity leads to *positivism*, just as an absolutization of jural principles leads to a rationalistic natural law.

Let us take an actual case. In the *Code for Marriages* of 1926 of the Soviet Union no mention is made of marital authority (matrimonial power), of adultery, or of grounds for divorce. A registered and a factually existing marriage are equal before the law. According to Article 18 the bond of marriage can be dissolved on the basis of mutual consent of both spouses or the unilateral wish of one spouse, i.e., without having to provide any legal grounds for divorce.

The question is: Does this regulation indeed constitute a positive marriage law for Russia?

Let us recall our earlier analysis of the difference in principle between the various organized communities and the corresponding differences in the internal structures of these organized communities. Very well, the internal law of marriage does not belong to the public-legal structure of the state as an organized community, nor is the state legislator the *natural* organ for translating the jural principles for marriage into positive law, any more than that the state legislator is the *natural* framer of coordinational law or internal law for the other non-state organized communities.

32. Increasing integrating tendencies in the social and jural law-spheres

The internal concern of the modern legislator with private law is intimately connected with the analogous development (on a historical basis) of law in the substrate sphere of the social (the law-sphere of social intercourse). Here we see a constant diminishing of the significance of the natural communities (namely those "grounded" in nature) for positivizing social principles into concrete norms of social interaction, in favor of the artificial social functions of organized communities. This development in the social law-sphere tends toward an increase in integration of the function of social interaction.

Primitive societies are made up of natural communities of sibs and clans, tribes and ethnic communities, set apart from each other by distinctive morals and customs that rule out any peaceful interaction between them. Accordingly, at this primitive cultural level there is no integrating law that transcends the boundaries of the natural organized communities (the foreigner is like a *hostis* without any rights whatsoever).

Modern society has greatly reduced the significance of the natural organized communities for positivizing social principles of propriety, courtesy, tact, etc. What is still alive in Western society as family, tribal, national or local customs are currently already viewed as gradually antiquating remnants. Superseding all boundaries of the natural organized communities, modern social life has positivized a codex of social norms whose wide diversity is no longer governed by natural organized communities but by the particular structures of the artificial organized communities. Think of the norms of modern fashion, of games and sport, of greeting and etiquette, etc. Current social norms are predominantly international in character.

The original opposition of natural organized communities is revived in full force whenever the Westerner comes into contact with the social norms of a primitive folk community or of a national organized community which until now was sealed off from Western influences.

33. The integrating function of the state in modern legal life

Legal life has unfolded upon the substrate of this social development. In this process the state, by virtue of its typical structure (the state finds its guiding function in the jural sphere), is the obvious body equipped for the positivization of integrating norms that are to maintain, among and above the organized communities, a comprehensive legal partnership and legal community of private law. Similarly, on the historical basis of a growing position of power the state has elaborated its internal public-legal organization into an ever more comprehensive legal community of public law.

In this way the state has established its integrating involvement in private coordinational law while respecting the internal autonomy of the coordinational spheres. It has imposed *ius cogens* (coercive law) only where a deviation would have constituted a slap in the face of the modern law-idea of private law.

In the same vein the modern state has also posited a coercive integrating law of marriage, again while respecting the internal individual communal law of marriage. As formerly, the natural framers of law remain competent to positivize marriage law.

For the material limits of competence of all state legislation is given in the internal structure of the non-political organized communities and coordinational spheres.[1]

1 This was already clearly seen by Johannes Althusius when he wrote in his *Politica methodice digesta*, chap. 1: "Propriae leges cujusque consociationis

147

34. The material limits of the competence of the state as former of law in the light of the cosmic structure of organized communities

The state as such cannot positivize law that is directed by a function different from the qualifying function of the state as an organized community.

As little as the state legislator can prescribe to legal subjects in their coordinational interactions the contents of their *internal* contracts in keeping with the particular *destination* of these coordinational spheres – since it can bind contracts only to *external* integrating state norms – just as little can the state *as such* form *internal* ecclesiastical law, associational law, or business law. It can bind these instances of internal law of organized communities solely to an *external* integrating law for organized communities. For the state is bound to its own cosmic structure and cannot change it at will.

This also explains why the jurisprudence for the assessment of unlawful actions applies a *formal* criterion of unlawfulness within the law of non-state organized communities. Just think of determining the legitimacy of decisions to expel or disbar, etc.).

It will therefore never be possible for state legislation fully to contain the law of marriage, since it can only embrace the modern integrating norms of the state for marriage. Through interpretation these norms must be explicated in such a way that they indeed reveal their *meaning* as integrating norms for the law of marriage and this interpretation can never be dependent upon the subjective "intention" of the legislator, but can only rely on the objective jural meaning of its norms in their cosmic coherence. That jurisprudence indeed interprets the legal norms of the state in this way can no longer be in question in our modern era.

peculiares, quibus illa regitur. Atque hae in singulis speciebus conscia-tionis aliae atque diversae sunt, *prout natura cujusque postulat*" (ital. mine, HD). ["Peculiar to each type of association are distinct laws by which each is governed, and these laws differ and diverge from association to association according to the nature of each."]

35. An interpretation of the meaning of the revolutionary Russian law of marriage

Coming back to the example of revolutionary Russia's marriage law, we first have to point out – as Freund remarks in his well-known commentary on this legislation[1] – that the Russian and White-Russian soviet republics, unlike the practice in the Ukraine, have cut all ties between the institution of marriage and church and state alike. Here the state has largely given up its integrating involvement in regulating marriage, particularly with respect to solemnizing or dissolving it. This is similar to what the state intended to accomplish by removing the church from involvement with marriage. The civil solemnization of marriage is unknown; and what happens in the church is of no concern to the state. There is an option to officially register a marriage, subject to certain requirements, but it is purely *declarative*, not *constitutive* (as it is in The Netherlands). What is found next to each other with equal rank are common-law marriages, which differ from "free love" by no more than certain features of a communal bond, and registered marriages. Registration has significance only as evidence.

All of this should be kept in mind when interpreting marriage law in revolutionary Russia. The "revolutionary theory" of the framers of law does not make law. It is historically interesting as a subjective cultural phenomenon, but as positive law it has neither validity nor meaning. When a state, partially or totally, abandons its integrating involvement with marriage law, then – if indeed a positive marriage law is to be created at all – its task must be taken over by the natural (in any event non-state) framers of law.

The stipulation that a marriage can be terminated simply on the basis of the mutual consent of husband and wife, or that it can even be terminated in consequence of the unilateral wish of one of the two marriage partners, simply lacks every possible meaning as positive marriage law. Its juridical meaning can only be that of a stipulation directed at magistrates not to bother about grounds for divorce.

Freund, too, understands these stipulations in this sense and he adds the remark that liberating the termination of marriage presupposes a high sense of responsibility among the marriage partners that is lacking at present. For that reason the conse-

1 H. A. Freund, *Das Zivilrecht in der Sowjetunion* (Leipzig, 1927), p. 17 ff., 80.

149

quences of this letting go of an important piece of integrating law of marriage can be quite serious when the natural formers of law, for example, fail to understand their task and take the completely negative prescription of the state to entail a carte blanche to act completely arbitrarily.

Freund points out that the relatively short period of time that this revolutionary divorce paragraph has been in force has already caused real chaos in sexual relations in the industrial cities, and that the government has been forced to introduce constraining measures. Because the natural framers of law have failed to regulate marriage in response to the state's stepping back, no law at all has been created to regulate the termination of marital life, and instead of positive law chaos reigns.

36. More refined consequences for the methodology of the science of law

Insight into the structure of the jural sphere and of its principles therefore has this additional significance for the method of the science of law in that it breaks in principle with the logicistic method which is in search of a purely *horizontal* legal system aided by the logical principle of delegation. A movement in this direction is found in the so-called normative school of law of Kelsen. Here the entire legal order is viewed as a logical hierarchy of higher and lower regulation, in which the higher is seen as the *delegating* and the lower as the *delegated* norm. Kelsen starts from a hypothetical original norm and from there proceeds to the legal layers of constitution, law, ordinance, private-law contract, sentence, and execution.

It is a consequence of this same logicistic methodology that has led various adherents of the norm-logical view of law (Verdross, Kunz and others, initially also Sander) to posit that primacy ought to be given to *international law*. Underneath a positivistic garb this methodology conceals a strong *politically charged* view of law that aims at the construction of the juridical *omnipotence* of a *particular* organized jural community – something that can never be based in positive law but only in "natural law" (in the humanistic meaning of the term). On the way toward achieving this goal the structural difference between the organized legal communities is eliminated while the structure of an organized community is resolved into *logical functions* of

150

the "legal rule" (*Rechtssatz*) either of the state or of international law. Hand-in-hand with this comes a formalistic theory of the sources of law, a theory that I have investigated extensively elsewhere.[1]

Those with insight into the highly differentiated structure of law will support, in the sharpest possible opposition to the logicistic methodology, a science-based legal system that is differentiated according to the dimensions of the jural sphere itself.

The systematic science of law is in principle already contained in the concept of law. The concept of the state can never assume the function of a system category for legal science – as one would suppose if the concept of law coincided with the concept of "*Rechtssatz*" of the state.

All instances of synthetical concept formation display a *cosmological character*, and the same holds for the law-concept insofar as it is indeed a *jural concept* – that is to say, insofar as it embraces the general cosmic structure of law in a synthetical way. Accordingly, the systematic study of law must likewise have a cosmological foundation.

This entails that the systematic treatment of law attempts to embrace the postulated many-sided *horizontal* relations between the *vertical* structural differences within the jural sphere, as postulated by one's concept of law. These vertical structural differences are, as we have seen, susceptible to a cosmological explanation only in terms of the structure of the organized communities and coordinational spheres. This insight indeed endows the idea of system with *general philosophical* significance that penetrates legal science in its entirety. Separate systems for constitutional law, international law, civil law, penal law, ecclesiastical law, and so on, contradict the very idea of *system*. The cosmological character of a system fits all functional structures of a specific law-sphere into a universal, in principle all-encompassing, coherence *while respecting their internal independence*.

The synthetical law-concept and law-idea, as we conceive of them, guarantee the possibility of such a systematic approach, an approach that constantly has to take into account the *historical* foundation of the process of integration of organized communities and coordinational relationships within the jural

---

1   See my more detailed study, "De Bronnen van het stellig recht in het licht der Wetsidee" [The sources of positive law in the light of the cosmonomic idea], *Anti-Revolutionaire Staatkunde* (quarterly) 4 (1930).

151

sphere. At a deepened cultural level the intertwinement between the vertical legal structures increases in intensity and complexity.

What can protect us against the obvious leveling of the vertical structures resulting from the logicistic method aided by a so-called formal-juridical concept of validity is a cosmological foundation of juridical systematics. The latter can only employ a *material* concept of *source of law* which delimits the sphere-sovereignty of the jural organized communities and jural coordinational spheres according to *material* boundaries of competence anchored in their respective cosmic structures. It also entails a *material theory* of *juridical validity*. I have elaborated this idea in more detail in my study, *The Sources of Positive Law in the Light of the Cosmonomic Idea*.[1]

37. What is a revolutionary view of law?

Finally, an apparently obvious objection against our view of the relation of jural principles to positive law ought to be considered.

Is it not *our* theory that is revolutionary in nature, since it takes the liberty to test the validity of statute law as positive law against "principles" that are absolutely not accepted by everyone?

We can face this objection with equanimity, since it is really directed at a straw man.

The revolutionary subjectivism of the humanistic theory of natural law consists in (a) its failure to analyze the principles of natural law on the basis of the objective cosmic coherence (the "nature of the matter," as Roman jurists called it), and (b) its deliberate attempt instead to deduce natural law, *more geometrico*, from its subjective ideas of reason by embarking on a methodical breakdown of the structure of the jural sphere.

In essence, what is revolutionary is the conception of law present in positivism and political absolutism, because in its aim to set aside the divine structural ordering of jural life it is forced to pass off revolutionary *chaos* as "law." The essence of the revolutionary conception of law consists in its rejection of divine ordinances for jural life.

---

1 See previous note.

By contrast, our conception rests upon the most solid basis that a theory can have: the cosmic structure itself, as ordained by God's sovereign creational will.

It does not "construe" according to arbitrary premises, but interprets all human formation of law in accordance with its cosmic jural meaning.

No lawmaker – not even one who radically denies the existence of God – can withdraw from the divine law-conforming structure of the jural sphere; for whenever he tramples upon the divine ordinances for the formation of law no law is formed, but only chaos – *in a way that is plain for all to see and is convincing to the lawmaker himself.*

It is not the legislator that determines subjectively what is marriage, what is property, what is a mortgage, and so forth; for all these institutions have a law-conforming foundation transcending human subjectivity in the cosmic order set by God for our temporal world.

If this were not so, if law in its richly differentiated structure is a creation of human arbitrariness, no science of law would be possible. Then the requisitory of Kirchmann would apply: "Three amendments by the legislators, and whole libraries turn into scrap."[1]

38. Who is competent to evaluate?

That we refuse to call chaos a "legal order" must have the assent of all for whom the concept of "positive law" has not lost all meaning and who can still distinguish between the commands of a band of robbers and the norms of justice![2]

Judging whether or not human stipulations are indeed positive law is not dependent upon the subjective discretion of the individual human understanding (that would be the consequence of humanism's individualistic natural law as well as of "critical positivism"!). That judgment lies with the supreme

---

1 "Drei berichtigende Worte des Gesetzgebers und Bibliotheken werden Makulatur." [Julius von Kirchmann (1808-84) was a legal philosopher of the Historical School who distrusted jurists and deemed legal science of no value.]

2 [Allusion to Augustine, *The City of God* 4.4: "Without justice, what are kingdoms but great robberies?"]

judge of all drab theory: namely, legal life in its cosmic law-conforming structure and its materially competent organs.[1]

No human society can exist without a true legal order. It is not possible to erect such a legal order by setting aside the divine jural principles in their cosmic-organic structure. "Arbitrary revolutionary legislation" – as witness the historical development of law – has never succeeded in forming [true] law. Any time it lacks the momentary support of brute force it turns out to be a paper construction. The scornful laughter of divine *nemesis* will ring over such "law" whenever human pride claims to form law other than based upon the jural principles ordained by God. And the sharp point of the bayonet that does not serve the cause of justice can form law as little as the paw of the lion that crushes its victim. As Althusius put it: "There is no civil law, nor can there be any, if it does not contain something of immutable equity natural and divine. If it departs altogether from the meaning of natural and divine law [*ius*] it is not to be called law [*lex*] but is actually unworthy of the name."[2]

---

1   This idea leads to the definitive rejection of the so-called theory of a *competence over a competence* in respect of the state legislator. Wherever sphere-sovereignty obtains in an internal structural law, there the legitimate organs to whom legal authority in that sphere is due (thus not just any individuals) have to safeguard their sphere-sovereignty as much as they have the means to do so. Both the Reformed churches and the church of Rome have understood their relationship to the state in this sense. The practical juridical significance of this view is seen, for example, in connection with the question regarding the relation of collective labor contracts to their being declared binding by the law of December 24, 1927. On my view it follows that declaring such contracts to be binding depends upon a collective agreement that contains a piece of internal business law, and not vice versa. In other words, declaring it binding no longer has any effect the moment a company's internal organs themselves change the internals law of the firm (cf. Meissner and in part Oertman, versus the so-called *Gesetzestheorie* of Kaskel and his school). [Otto Meissner (1880-1953) was state secretary in the Weimar Republic. Paul Oertman (1865-1938) was an influential author on contract law. Walter Kaskel (1882-1928) was a specialist in labor law.]

2   Johannes Althusius, *Politica Methodice Digesta*, ch. 9, p. 122: "Nulla enim est, nec esse potest lex civilis, quae non aliquid naturalis et divinae aequitatis immutabilis habeat admissum. Nam si haec prorsus discedit a sen²tentia juris naturalis et divini, non lex dicenda est, sed nomine hoc prorsus indigna."]

III

Presuppositions of Our Thought about Law and Society in the Crisis of Modern Historicism[1]

1. Introduction: The background of the modern understanding of state and law

IN 1931, WHEN I had published my work *De Crisis in de Humanistische staatsleer*,[2] an older colleague, himself a distinguished historian of law, told me that in his opinion there was no reason at all to speak of a general crisis, since there might be at most a crisis among a few German scholars. In the meantime the First World War has been succeeded by the Second, and today no well-informed person will deny that the humanist way of thinking about law and society and about society in general, which was dominant in an earlier period, currently finds itself in a fundamental state of crisis, which in turn is a manifestation of a crisis in the very foundations of our entire Western culture.

In the nature of the case, when certainties that used to be considered sound and firm enter the twilight zone, some serious reflection is called for. In the eyes of many today, the theoretical dogmatism of former days appears strange and surreal. Theoretical thought is rooted in a central layer of human consciousness, whence it receives its presuppositions and ultimate convictions that transcend theoretical thought itself. These presuppositions and certainties bear a supra-theoretical character and are governed by a religious ground-motive which sustains a spiritual community between all those who proceed, consciously or unconsciously, from the same ground-motive. As a *central* spiritual driving force the ground-motive not only determines our theoretical view of reality but also our practical orientation in life.

1   Review article of H. W. Scheltema, *Beschouwingen over de vooronderstellingen van ons denken over Recht en Staat* (diss. Leiden; Groningen: Wolters, 1948). In *Rechtsgeleerd Magazijn Themis* 68 (1949): 193-248.
2   [Eng. trans., *The Crisis in Humanist Political Theory* (Grand Rapids: Paideia, 2010).]

2. Ultimate presuppositions presented as theoretical axioms

In periods when one particular ground-motive exerted a dominant influence and overpowered all other ground-motives in Western culture, our culture had a spiritual foundation and a united purpose. Theoretical thought in the West felt "at home" in a society and culture that was shaped by the intellectual-spiritual impregnation of its distinctive ground-motive. This explains the self-confidence that concealed its supra-theoretical source in the dogmatic proclamation of the "autonomy of science." The ground-motive of theoretical thought had dressed itself in the garb of a *theoretical axiom*.

Such a dominant theoretical dogmatism experienced no need to account in a radical, self-critical way for the true nature of its presuppositions. Nor were its foundations subjected to the critical doubt that manifested itself in its intellectual framework whenever the ground-motive revealed dialectical tensions that drove thought from the one pole to the other. So long as the thought behind this critical self-reflection remained firmly rooted in its ground-motive, the critical doubt was never truly fundamental.

Kant's *Critique of Pure Reason* undoubtedly broke with the dogmatic self-confidence of an Enlightenment philosophy which allowed only the humanist ground-motive of nature and freedom to dominate in one of its opposing tendencies: either in the cult of human autonomy through the scientific control of nature, or in that other tendency, the motive of a person's ethical freedom and autonomy that arises naturally as a consequence of the self-liberation of science. Yet the Kantian critique of knowledge itself remained so much rooted in this polar ground-motive that Kant did not raise the question regarding the presuppositions of his own epistemology. Positing the autonomy of theoretical thought in its specific humanist sense continued to characterize the dogmatic inclination of his "critical" line of thought. It was possible to maintain this theoretical dogmatism precisely because the hidden ground-motive of his thought at this stage dominated the Western thought community almost in an uncontested way.

156

The crisis in the thought of the 20th century, however, is much deeper than the one to which Kant gave expression in his critique of knowledge. At least in its most prominent and representative manifestations, the twentieth-century crisis reveals the unmistakable features of a process of spiritual uprooting that affect the deepest foundations and presuppositions of science itself. The critical doubt thus generated is, for those who experience it, borne from the spiritual anxiety of a person who is drowning after seeing his ship break apart and finding himself tossed on the turbulent ocean of world events.

This anxiety bears an *existential* character in the fullest sense of the word. The surrounding social reality of a thinker caught up in this doubt increasingly appears "alien" to him the more it loses the spiritual impregnation of its former ground-motive. Such a thinker has the experience – to use Martin Heidegger's terminology – of being "thrown" into a brute and meaningless reality. Driven by the urge towards self-preservation, people begin to look for support in the inner possibilities of their existence, of their "Dasein." But this "existence" is no longer firmly anchored in a supra-temporal certainty. Ontological reflection on human "Dasein" is now only found in the "historical consciousness" which elevates the human being above the brute natural reality, above the blind "being-there." This historical consciousness, embedded in the flow of "historical time," teaches one that human existence is a "Sein zum Tode" ("Being unto Death") that one has to accept in full "consciousness of guilt."

Ever since the Renaissance, modern humanism has been driven by the proud *freedom motive* aimed at a new society, dialectically accompanied by the modern *nature motive* – i.e., the tendency to gain autonomous control of reality by means of modern science. Today, however, the humanist *freedom motive* has lost its vital power. Modern man, uprooted, finds his "autonomous freedom" only in the existential possibility to plan his future in a mood of "concern," aware that this future ends ontologically in a "nothing," in "death." At the same time, the classical humanist *science ideal* as well, with its aim to establish the ideal realm of autonomous freedom through the "control of nature," has lost its spiritual foundation. For the spiritually uprooted descendants of the humanist pioneers the once highly valued "objective science" now has the significance of a mere artificial aid in an ultimately hopeless struggle for existence.

3. Modern historicism

Such is the philosophical self-reflection of modern historicism, which may well be designated as a full-blown revelation of the deadly disease of our Western culture. One finds it in Spengler's *The Decline of the West*, in Heidegger's *Being and Time*, and in Sartre's *Being and Nothingness* – three representative works that follow the course of this self-reflection from the prelude to World War I to the spiritual climate after World War II.

Whoever makes ready to diagnose this disease without restricting himself to the surface phenomena but penetrating to the root, must have the courage to puncture the mask of the dogmatic self-assuredness of the dominating thought in times past in order to lay bare its true character. For the process of spiritual uprooting evident in modern historicism and its self-reflection in the most recent philosophy cannot be understood apart from the entire dialectical path of development which the dominating humanist basic motive of the West has experienced since the Renaissance.

Modern uprooted historicism, which is no longer capable of rising above the historical time-aspect and which has lost its faith in an eternal destiny of humankind, is but a degenerate descendent of the "historical mode of thought" as it was born amid the still vibrant religious ground-motive of humanism during the late 18th and early 19th century as a polar reaction to the classical science ideal of the "Enlightenment" with its natural-scientific mode of thought.

At that stage the historicist mode of thought was still firmly rooted in the humanist freedom motive, which since Rousseau and Kant had pitted its own deeper claims against the overestimation of the natural-scientific mode of thought. The only thing that changed was that this freedom motive, and the personality ideal governed by it, acquired a new irrationalist turn. Through this process the *rationalistic* and *individualistic* view of human society, still dominant in the thought of Rousseau and Kant, was transposed into a universalist one, taking as its starting-point the *community*, while the rationalist search for a universally valid law was replaced with the concept of *individuality* flowing from the unique nature of a "folk-spirit" as the irreducible national source of a culture, a concept attained through a *"geisteswissenschaftliche"* understanding based on the method [not of the natural sciences but] of the humanities.

Romanticism and post-Kantian freedom idealism broke with the critical division posited by Kant between "nature" and "freedom." Whereas Kant was concerned only to safeguard the faith in the autonomous freedom of humankind over against the deterministic consequences of classical natural-scientific thought, post-Kantian idealism aimed at discovering within "natural reality" itself a hidden trace of "creative freedom." "Natural necessity" and "freedom" were to be united in dialectical thought, and this dialectical synthesis between the two opposite tendencies of the humanist ground-motive was carried through in the new historical mode of thought. Savigny, the founder of the Historical School, expressed this in his well-known introductory article about "the aims of this journal" which appeared in 1815 in the first issue of the *Zeitschrift für geschichtliche Rechtswissenschaft* (Journal for historical science of law): "Every historical period must therefore acknowledge something as given, *which is nonetheless necessary and free at the same time* [emph. mine]: necessary insofar as it is not dependent upon the particular will of the present; free, while it has proceeded just as little from an alien will (such as the command of a Master to his Slave), and is brought forth, rather, by the higher culture of a folk as an always changing and developing whole."

In Schelling's nature philosophy this new historicist mode of thought had also turned to natural reality (the proper field of the classical deterministic science ideal), to meet it head-on. "Nature" too, viewed as "History," was said to exhibit in its developmental potentialities the poles of "natural necessity" and "freedom." In the lowest potency (brute "matter") necessity dominated; in the highest potency (the "living organism") creative freedom prevailed. In this way the whole of reality had come to be viewed as intrinsically *historical*. A new science ideal, borne from the irrationalist turn of the freedom motive, had thus replaced the old science ideal and designed a reality after its own image.

But this historicist view of reality at this time remained bound to a firm faith in an eternal – whether or not Christianized – idea of humanity which in the process of historical development

159

merely finds its empirical expression in a wealth of individual cultural configurations. Although positive law, the empirical state and empirical society were seen, on this view, as intrinsically *historical* phenomena, they continued to be grounded in eternal ideas of reason that granted them *meaning* and *value* to begin with.

4. The subsequent influence of historicism

This is what Hegel meant with his (frequently misunderstood) statement: "What is real, is rational."[1] When at the beginning of the 19th century sociology emerged as an independent discipline, its founders, Saint-Simon and Comte, explicitly intended to reconcile the natural-scientific mode of thought of the Enlightenment – the putative crowning discipline of the encyclopedic system of human knowledge with the new historical mode of thought of Romanticism and freedom idealism. In this way sociology, from its very beginning, took over the historicist view of reality, which nonetheless, in line with the classical science ideal, had to be united with the natural-scientific method of thought.

Although Comte still acknowledged that the solidarity of the social organism finally rested upon ideas of community, these ideas in principle lost their supra-temporal significance in his positivist system. The historicist mode of thought had already started to separate itself from its idealistic presuppositions by viewing them merely as products of a historical process of development of humanity's spiritual life.

Comte's famous law of three stages was one of the first attempts to historicize the guiding ideas of Western culture that owe their contents to religious ground-motives as central driving forces. In this train of thought, the natural-law ideas of the previous era were viewed as an expression of the *metaphysical* stage, which denied the laws of social reality and accorded a leading role to speculative humanist jurists. This process had to come to an end in the chaos of the French Revolution. Similar to the earlier *theological* stage, the metaphysical era had passed for good. In future, *positive* ideas would govern the final phase of the history of humanity, submitting human society to the classi-

---

1 "Was wirklich ist, das ist vernünftig."

cal science ideal that had been worked out by Galileo and Newton for the natural sciences.

To be sure, the start of this process of historicizing the deepest presuppositions of thought about law and society was not consistently followed through in Comte. His thought was still in the grip of Enlightenment belief in an ideal final goal of world history, in the course of which, under the guidance of positivist ideas, the ideal of true Humanity would be fulfilled. That these ideas, too, would eventually lose their grip on society did not occur to Comte's rigid mind. The positivist stage meant for him the eschatological terminus. He still held to the belief in progress.

The same can be said of evolutionism, which after Comte commenced its triumphal march in Western culture and took command of its thought about law and society. It stripped classical humanism of its metaphysical pretensions about a "free rational human nature" by reducing human spiritual life to a secondary function of the organic development of a conglomeration of cells. None the less, evolutionism remains firmly rooted in the classical humanist science ideal which in turn is driven by the humanist ground-motive of the autonomous freedom of humankind.

Even historical materialism, with its historico-economistic view of social reality and its eschatological, utopian hope, in the final analysis remained rooted in the same ground-motive. Marx's future differed widely from Spencer's, yet Spencer, the evolutionistic preacher of the survival of the fittest and the one who praised the free play of societal forces, and Marx, the radical prophet of the decline of the capitalist system, shared a belief in a free and autonomous mankind as the final point of historical development. Anyone who believes in an ideal final goal for history always has a transcendent-religious basis for his scientific and practical pursuits.

The classic science ideal, as we have seen, oriented as it was to the natural-scientific mode of thought, remained in polar opposition to the classic freedom motive in its personality ideal. Similarly, the historicist mode of thought, elevated to a new science ideal, turned out to be a polar counterpart to the new, universalist and irrationalist conception of humanism's freedom motive.

161

After the collapse of German idealism during the second half of the 19th century, faith in the absolute value of the human being was temporarily able to take shelter in "objective science." Science had now also brought the historical reality of society within its purview and would, in its steady progress, lead mankind to ever higher levels of freedom and happiness.

Yet the historicist mode of thought harbors radical consequences in its theoretical view of reality which will assert themselves as soon as it starts to loosen its tie with its religious root and commences to view its humanist presuppositions themselves as historically determined products of the mind.

At this point in time, thought about law and society became entangled in a process of spiritual uprooting in which either a mood of decline or a blind pursuit of power dominated. This process announced itself long before World War I, although the prevailing optimistic faith in the future of mankind precluded an explicit acknowledgment of it. As early as the the final phase of Nietzsche's thought it broke through in frightening, almost pathological form. According to him, man is "the animal whose nature has not yet been fixed" and who has no existential possibility outside nature and history. Nature has stamped man as an animal, but as an historical being man has an advantage in comparison with the other members of the animal world which are still rigidly bound to their instincts and their environment. The development of the human being is not *fixed* because man disposes over his own future. But the historical aspect of reality provides us, stripped of all ideologies of humanity and moral autonomy, with the development of *power* tendencies only. Thus historical development offers only one real possibility for the future: an unbridled striving towards an increase of power, not hampered by a single traditional norm.

The realm of the super-human *Herrenmensch* must be erected upon the ruins of Christian and Humanist ideologies, upon the "transvaluation of all values." In this demonic religion of power the control motive of the classic science ideal is utterly divorced from its spiritual root: namely, the Religion of Humanity as the absolute value of the human personality. In the pathological division of the humanist personality ideal which has lost its religious core, it took on an anti-humane character. Combined with the irrationalist doctrine of the *folk-spirit*, this uprooted power religion led to the ideal of the *Herrenvolk* (the Master Race), eventually presented in the myth of Blood and Soil or in the myth of Eternal Rome.

Historicism, uprooted and delivered over to the demonic power religion, has lost all faith in eternal ideas that give direction to historical development. In a neurotic attempt to yet find an inspiring motive for working for a future, a myth – if need be in the form of primitive notions extracted from the historical past – is used in mythological garb to serve as an incentive for the *folk* instincts.

This historicism no longer has any yardstick for differentiating between what is historically progressive and historically reactionary. The Historical Law School had already leveled the difference in principle between primitive undifferentiated *folk*-law and civil private law (which arose only as the result of a process of societal differentiation) by proclaiming *jurist law* (which had initiated the development of civil private law) to be "folk-law on a technical level."

What prevented Savigny and Puchta from drawing these radical consequences from the historicist view of law was the powerful influence still exerted by the Christian idea of humanity as well as by the classical tradition of the *ius naturale et gentium*. The classical Roman *ius gentium* as prototype of modern civil law remained for them, just as for the humanist theorists of natural law (whom they combated as a matter of principle) as well as for the classical Roman jurists, the expression of the *naturalis ratio* (natural reason). It remained for them the *ratio scripta*.

The perilous consequences of historicism surfaced in a much more dangerous form in the Germanist wing of the Historical School. This wing promoted the idea of the folk-spirit, and against *jurist law* it posited the undifferentiated "social" conception of the Germanic folk-spirit as the ideal, in opposition to the reception of the "individualistic" Roman law. But even Gierke in good time saw the danger of this Germanist onslaught and in the interest of keeping the idea of humanity within law he reached a compromise with the classical idea of natural law. The basic principle of civil private law, the acknowledgment of *human rights* as such, independent of membership in any particu-

163

lar societal collectivity such as *folk*, gender, social status, church or race, was not to be sacrificed in a one-sided glorification of the undifferentiated – and for that reason totalitarian – community idea of Germanic law as it existed prior to the reception of Roman law.

Taking the historicist conception of the Germanic *folk-spirit* to its extreme reactionary consequences was reserved for national socialism. Historicism, uprooted from the humanist ground-motive, revived the primitive phenomenon of *trustis*[1] in old Germanic law in order to create a power center aided by the myth of a *Führer* and his following. In this movement, destroying an individual's personhood and annihilating conquered peoples' national consciousness went hand in hand with worshiping primitive *folk* customs and practices and repudiating the classic foundations of civil private law. Even in cases where this uprooted historicism did not lead to such a pathological cult of power, it operated like a process of subversion, undermining the foundations of the modern differentiated legal order.

4.1   Typical legal spheres

The modern differentiated legal order with its rich diversity of typical legal spheres presupposes the grand process of differentiation in modern society. In an undifferentiated primitive community one encounters no civil private law, no constitutional and administrative law as *ius publicum*, no internal business law, no internal ecclesiastical law, etc. etc., but only an undifferentiated *folk*-law. Here the spheres of competence are not yet delimited according to the *inner nature* of these societal spheres because the primitive forms of such organized communities encompass *the entire life* of all their members.

Truly differentiated spheres of life, by contrast, exhibit a distinctive inner nature and a typical inner structure, which express themselves in all modal aspects of reality, the jural included. They are not merely variable *historical* phenomena but are based in the constant order of reality. The two legal branches of civil private law and public law, which classic legal science incorrectly viewed as *exhausting* the whole of legal life, do not emerge until a differentiated state is established. By its inner

---

1   Name of a group of free warriors who formed a king's bodyguard and were personally bound to him by an oath of unquestioned loyalty.

164

structure such a state is characterized as a public-legal territorial community of government and subjects on the basis of a monopolistic organization of the sword power. Thus it differs in principle from an undifferentiated *regnum* as the private property of a powerful lord.

It remains the enduring merit of classic legal theory that from the beginning it appreciated the constant inner structure of civil private law and public law. When the Roman jurists grounded the private *ius gentium*, the classical model of a genuine civil private law, in the *naturalis ratio* and understood it in sharp contrast to the *ius civile* as the initially most primitive and undifferentiated *folk-law* of the Romans, then this did not result from philosophical speculation (these legal theorists were far too sober and too oriented to concrete life for that). Rather, it was the fruit of their keen insight into the inner nature of this type of law for the praetorial office. The *ius naturale*, as the pre-positive foundation of the *ius gentium*, brings to expression a *juridical freedom and equality of people as such* in their societal interaction. It turns into a foreign metaphysical construction only when this principle is applied outside the limits of civil private law.

Civil private law presupposes a genuine *ius publicum* (public law), the internal law of the organized state community as a *res publica* (a public concern), and according to its inner nature it encompasses only a relatively small sector of private legal life. It is a *ius commune* and remains strictly *distinct* from all those legal spheres that are qualified by an extra-jural destinational function. Civil private law by definition cannot be bound to a typical qualifying function, such as the economic, the social, the pistical or other functions, for then it would cease to exist as that typical integrating law of the state in respect of all possible *specific* forms of private law. It would also mean that civil private law could not continue to function as that legal sphere within which the human person functions as a legal subject as such, independently of membership in particular communities, estates or classes. Its nature is such that it does not function as law for any communal relationship in which the members are bound into a whole, since it serves the private-civil sector of *coordinational* relationships within society, where individuals or organized com-

165

munities are coordinates and function *alongside* each other, be it through collaboration or through conflict.

Humanist natural law, directed by the religious ground-motive of nature and freedom, articulated this classical conception of the *ius naturale et gentium* during the Enlightenment era. Since its inception (in Grotius and his followers) it struggled against the prevailing undifferentiated legal institutions of the medieval period. In Locke, natural-law theories tried to permeate the *ius gentium*, which with the Romans still acknowledged the institution of slavery, with their formulation of the theories of natural human rights. It aimed at a new legal order in which no other kind of law would be acknowledged except civil private law based on the natural-law theory of human rights and the public law of the state. This constituted the basic error of rationalistic humanism. Through this overestimation of the typical spheres of legal life of the state it degenerated into an abstract individualistic conception that found its counterpole in an absolutistic conception of state law. In these natural-law theories the sovereign will of the individual and the sovereignty of the government are dialectical opposites. Natural-law theory, lacking insight into the rich structural diversity present in a differentiated society and into the social interconnections between the distinct societal spheres of life, is incapable of arriving at a harmonious perspective on the legal order that recognizes internal boundaries for the various spheres of competency.

It is therefore understandable that the first half of the 19th century, when the rationalistic natural-law theory and the new historical mode of thought that permeated the Restoration movement joined each other in shaping post-revolutionary society, people took recourse to an external division between the restored state, based upon the legitimacy principle, and the free society with its private civil legal order.

From the beginning the greatest threat to the classic conception of civil private law was that it might be linked – in line with the newly emerging science of economics – to the view of a "free society" understood as a typical *economically* qualified sphere in which individuals are liberated from all the restrictive bonds of guilds and capable of making their natural human rights serviceable to the pursuit of their economic self-interest. In this

166

way the foundation was laid for the typical nineteenth-century conception of the "private citizen," that offspring of the "third estate" that came to ascendancy during the French Revolution – the bourgeois citizen as independent entrepreneur and merchant who through his private property could actually be the only proper subject of civil private rights.

The Civil Code seemed to have been written for these individuals and for them alone. Those who did not own anything and those who were socially dependent had to find other ways to work themselves up to the status of "citizen." In this way a particular class in society was elevated as the model of a civil legal subject. This resulted in a fundamental denial of the inner nature of civil private law. Lost was any insight into the boundaries of the inner competency of civil private law as distinct from the typically economically qualified business law. Though the latter is enkaptically bound in the former and in that sense is subject to civil legal norms, its *specific inner nature* cannot be covered by civil law.

The historical developments that took place beginning with the second part of the 19th century thoroughly shook the humanist theories of law and state that were fixated on the old liberal conception of society and the view of the state correlated with it. In this historical process the individualistic formation of "society" underwent a fundamental change through the rise in the differentiating economy of powerful interest groups that pushed the "individual" to the background. At the same time the pressure of contemporary political trends forced the state to discard its outmoded form that dated back to the Restoration, in order to acquire more and more the form of parliamentary democracy. On top of that, the state started to interfere in the free society through legislation.

It turned out that the external division between "state" and "society" – and with it the earlier conception regarding the relationship between "public" and "private law" as the two sole, separate spheres of legal life – could no longer be maintained. And the historicist view of social reality was able to use this situation in support of its belief that neither society, nor legal life as society's jural aspect, exhibited any constant structural differences and boundaries to competencies that were rooted in the inner nature of the various spheres of life.

5. Breaking down the division between state and "society"

Soon after its inception the new science of sociology started to break down the artificially constructed walls of division between state and "society." It demoted the state to a dependent instrument of societal forces and completely set aside the natural-law theories regarding the *salus publica* and the freedom and equality of people within the domain of civil law, rejecting them as metaphysical speculations utterly foreign to real life.

Attention was increasingly focused on the economically qualified sphere of society in which the central forces must be found which in the final analysis determine the structure of society and consequently also legal life. Under the influence of the natural-scientific mode of thought, and before long of neo-Kantianism (Rickert and Weber) with its historically oriented method of the "cultural sciences," the new focus led to a growing misunderstanding of the nature of the state. Closely connected to this error one also finds an increasing lack of insight into the inner nature of civil private law and public law and of the place of these two legal spheres of the state within the complex system of the modern legal order.

Leon Duguit, who was influenced by the sociology of Durkheim, insisted on a transformation in principle of civil private law and the order of the state. In his case, the classic ideas were written off as antiquated metaphysics. The theory of the socio-economic function of law started to infiltrate classic legal science after the latter, under the powerful influence of Jhering's "*Interessenjurisprudenz*," began to view the legal order as a form of the vital interests of society.

The neo-Kantian legal theories – a genuine transitional phenomenon on the road of the spiritual uprooting of humanist thought – was not really able to put up a defense against the flood of historicist positivism. They were themselves already too much infected by historicism to credit a belief in constant structural principles that were supposed to lie at the foundation of the modern differentiated societal spheres. After all, the empty logical forms of neo-Kantian thought, which were conceived of as the epistemological prerequisite for every possible

168

positive law, were without any juridical *content*. Stammler viewed law merely as a logical *ordering form* of historico-economic matters, and he was therefore co-responsible for the theoretical leveling of the boundaries between civil private law and economically qualified commercial law.

Insofar as neo-Kantianism clung to a "natural law with changing content" (Stammler), this variant functioned merely as a *formal guideline* that was totally dependent upon faith in the autonomous human personality as an end-in-itself. After World War I the role of this legal theory was over. For a while the neo-Hegelian philosophy of law entered the scene of the 20th century (Binder, Schönfeld, Larenz and others), but it was infected to such an extent by relativistic historicism that it was soon transformed into a willing instrument of the National Socialist cult of power.

Eventually, as our own century sweeps aside what is left of the individualistic view of society, and as the state intervenes more and more in the economic life of society and after two world wars embarks on a state-run welfare system, humanist thought about law and state no longer finds a firm basis to stand on. One could no longer recognize the familiar humanist ground-motive as the hidden driving force beneath the catastrophic unfolding of the 20th century. Instead, social reality seems to be dominated by strange demonic powers. Given the growing inner uncertainty of the heirs of the humanist thinkers about law and the state, they try in vain to find a firm point of orientation in "historical consciousness." Freedom and necessity are no longer susceptible of being embraced in a dialectical synthesis, as had been possible in the days of Savigny. Social reality seems to have become a mirror image of the uprooted historicist *Zeitgeist* before which all structural boundaries are blurred and every idea of the value of the human person and of community as a higher incarnation of the humanist personality motive is relativized. For many, the former slogans of freedom and equality, democracy and social justice have so thoroughly lost their earlier classic meaning[1] that the vacillating thinker listens to them with the doubt of a Faust hearing the resurrection song: "I

1   Think also of the influence of Vilfredo Pareto (1848–1923) and his sociological critique of "ideologies." Pareto was the teacher of Mussolini.

do hear the message, but my faith is wanting." This doubt truly affected not just the superficial spirits. Rather, one can say that humanistically oriented theorists about law and state, who pretend to know nothing about the deeply felt uncertainties of this day and age, are withdrawing into the technical details of their field, understood in a positivist sense. They are in the grip of an escapist mood that makes them close their eyes to the fundamental crisis of the humanist theory of state and law in the 20th century.

6. Critical evaluation of Scheltema's dissertation

This rather long introduction was necessary to situate Scheltema's dissertation, which he entitled "Reflections on the presuppositions of our thought about law and state" and which earned him the LL.D. degree *cum laude* at the University of Leiden. For unless one understands the intellectual-spiritual background of this work of 456 pages, one cannot possibly do justice to it.

Unfortunately, the author himself does not attempt to elucidate this background. When he speaks of "the presuppositions of our thought about law and state" he does not, by means of a genuine transcendental critique, penetrate to the hidden ground-motives of the latter, but rather – in the spirit of historicism – introduces them as purely *historical* premises of contemporary thought. Thus in § 7 of his *Introduction* he remarks:

As follows from what has been said thus far, the reflections on law and the state to be discussed below are not examined in their absolute significance for thought, which then proceeds at once to study and assimilate it. Rather, they are viewed by thought against the background of its development as moments of itself.

Thought then views itself as the result of this development, as the outcome of all the forces that exerted their influence on it. It is difficult to determine how thought reflecting on its own history relates to that thought which pursues its goal with a spontaneous and apriorist self-confidence, either derived from axioms or from empirical facts. Both forms may be viewed, as it were, as facets of a single subject. In periods during which this subject prevails in an unchallenged position or disposes over a restored self-confidence, its thinking will move straight towards its goal. Yet whenever it starts to doubt itself it will view its own thoughts as the accidental product of its own history. In order to trace the causes of its lost self-confidence and certainty,

170

it will start rooting in its past, in its personal presuppositions. Thought turned inward upon itself, still busy reflecting, with no results as yet to show the outside world, cannot view itself as a self-contained process perfectly following the laws of logic. . . . It cannot base its justification on absolute or objective results. The only way it can defend itself against doubt about its own right of existence is through the certainty that it is an intrinsic duty of humankind, associated with its inclination toward self-preservation and self-defense, to harness itself and maintain itself against his self-doubt and the uncertainty that envelops him.

7.   Humanist presuppositions

Nowhere does the author state explicitly that he is talking about *humanist* presuppositions, as I have identified them in my introductory remarks. The reader has to infer this from the fact that when in passing he refers to any positive Christian notions they are for all intents and purpose eliminated from the intellectual maze that he explores. For example, he attempts to explain what he calls the "theocratic" political theory entirely in terms of the dominant *Zeitgeist* of the Restoration period. In the context of his study this is partially justified, because during the period chosen by him as his starting-point, namely the early part of the 19th century, neither the Roman Catholic ground-motive of *nature and grace* nor the scriptural reformational ground-motive of creation, fall and redemption exercised a dominant influence upon the cultural development of the West. Insofar as these ground-motives asserted themselves in opposition to the *Zeitgeist* in legal and political theories and in politics, they largely took on a form in which dependence upon the dominant humanist ground-motive is clearly present. It was not until the late 19th century that the emancipation of Christian legal and political theory emerged in its two major schools, assisted by the onset of the process of decay within the humanist ground-motive that had been dominant up to that point and had therefore pressed its stamp also on the leading thinkers about law and society. If it were not for the fact that this revival of Christian motifs is practically ignored by the author, he might have considered options for the future other than those which he is able to discern in his critical doubts regarding former certainties.

171

By introducing the fiction of a "general thinking subject" he hides the true nature of the presuppositions he has in mind:

> We proceed from the assumption that a certain supply of ideas and opinions about state and law lies – at all times and therefore also now – at the basis of the thinking of every individual, and that this thought-world develops in a way comparable to the growth of an individual. We view this general thinking as the subject which in our chaotic times has lost its self-confidence and peace of mind and which must try and acquire greater clarity about its situation through an analysis of its own presuppositions (p. 11).

But surely, given the present crisis, such a "general thinking subject" is a very problematic construction. The author is aware of this and therefore invites the reader to accept this construction as a working hypothesis, to evaluate its correctness and usefulness once the investigation is completed. He defends this general thinking subject with an appeal to Hegel's *Vernunft* (Reason) and Bergson's *évolution créatrice*. It is not clear what the relevance of Bergson's "creative evolution" is in this context, but it is certain that Hegel's *Vernunft* had quite a different meaning and hardly fits the author's method of research.

Scheltema's "thinking subject" turns out in the course of his investigation to be simply an "ideal-type" of the citizen and his thoughtworld, understood in the sense of the sociology of Max Weber. Such a sociological ideal-type has nothing to do with Hegel's metaphysical idea of the dialectical self-unfolding of Reason as "thought directed towards Being," and just as little with Kant's "epistemological subject." It is nothing but a fictitious construction consonant with the way in which Weber envisaged it as an interpretive tool for an "historical understanding of the subjective meaning of social action." Such an ideal-type is not helpful for a genuinely critical introspection by humanist thought fraught with self-doubt. What this requires is the courage to penetrate behind the purely theoretical fictions of historicist thinking into the real spiritual background of the mode of thought that one intends to investigate. Hence my introduction.

Meanwhile, the work of Scheltema has undoubtedly turned out to be an interesting experiment in investigating, within the field of sociology of knowledge, the development of the intellectual milieu of the "citizen" of the 19th and 20th centuries and of his "social milieu" – and its reflection in the scientific theories of the time. This thought-world, understood in the ideal-type mode, and the social reality shaped by this thought-world, are then "the presuppositions of our thinking about law and state" that Scheltema subjects to a critical analysis.

The fact that this kind of "sociology of knowledge" basically goes back to Karl Marx and has been worked out most recently by Franz Jerusalem, Karl Mannheim and Max Scheler, and that it is in turn rooted in deeper presuppositions which reveal – at least in its extreme, relativistic application – the process of spiritual uprooting, has not, I think, entirely escaped Scheltema. Nonetheless, his analysis of the presuppositions about state and society in the period investigated by him is encumbered with a hefty dogmatism, in the sense that he does not understand them for what they were – at least not in his view of "social reality." In his description of the development of law, state and society since the Restoration, he uncritically employs historicist thought which in spite of itself presents its assumptions as scientific axioms. I shall highlight this state of affairs in more detail when I give an overview of the contents of his dissertation.

Scheltema's view of the development of the "thought-world of the bourgeois citizen" since the beginning of the 19th century is typically historicist, strongly reminiscent in a formal sense of Spengler's morphology of world cultures. The development of the bourgeois thought-world is viewed as a succession of periods of growth, blossoming, decay and collapse, caused by the fact that thought was not able to keep up with the grand expansion taking place in reality. However, he gives this formal concept of historical development a distinct content and peculiar twist that look almost Hegelian (though entirely bereft of the actual meaning of Hegel's profound thought grounded in the dialectics of German idealism). Scheltema's formal concept of historical development helps him to view the multiplicity of legal and state institutions as the result of developmental processes; this concept also governs the entire plan and subdivisions of his dissertation.

173

Briefly, it boils down to this. The "growth period" during the Restoration period, which more or less terminated with the February Revolution [of 1848], should be seen as the rise of the modern bourgeoisie. The thought-world of "the citizen" of this period consisted on the one hand of the ideas that were new in the preceding era, and on the other of Restoration ideas: namely, an appreciation of the old institutions, and doubt regarding the constructive capacity of the revolutionary political ideas.

The kind of thinking which earlier embarked recklessly upon destruction, in this period came to its senses and deepened itself: it established a kind of synthesis between the revolutionary ideas and what was passed on by tradition. This was followed by a period which the author characterizes as the development of (social) reality on the basis of and in keeping with these mature ideas of "the ideal citizen": after a period mainly turned inwards there followed another period with a growth that was much more outward. During the Restoration era the bourgeois citizen accepted the restored institutions as they were, although they remained foreign to him. He made up for it by withdrawing into "society," which was still strictly separate from the state. The bourgeoisie established the basis of their wealth in complete freedom. This enabled them during the next period to take over the state in order to transform it according to their ideas.

Social reality, now completely permeated by bourgeois ideas, was a society in which the bourgeoisie felt totally "at home" and which they made their primary concern. This was a materialistic period in which thought completely objectified itself and was almost completely identified with reality. Thanks to the results of "objective, materialistic science," reality experienced steady progress, and new groups steadily acquired citizenship.

The third era, finally, which according to the author dates more or less from World War I, was characterized by a social reality that outgrew its old forms and saw the old progress in wealth replaced by economic chaos. Because the bourgeois thought-world tried to hold on to the old social order, it proved no match for the new economic challenges. Whereas ideas were prominent during the first period, and a unity between bour-

174

geois thought and the social milieu emerged during the second, ideas now lagged behind developments in reality. Thought was detached from social reality and lost its unity of direction. The thought-world itself, with its impact on the social order, survived, but it formed a rudiment rather than a vital constituent of new developments. "As a result, both reality and thought changed their meaning, or rather, in the long run they became completely meaningless as components of a divided and vanishing whole." This was therefore the era of decline and spiritual upheaval, in which citizens had to find their way through introspection by subjecting their intellectual-spiritual traditions to a careful analysis in order to evaluate the correct meaning of their thoughts and norms in the face of fresh circumstances.

Each of the three periods is now treated in a separate chapter. In each case, after a short introduction, the following issues are addressed: 1) a characterization of the citizen as a thinking and acting element of society; 2) a characterization of the society in which the citizen lives and work; 3) a view of law; 4) a view of the state; and 5) a characterization of the legal and political theory of the period. In addition to this, and without stating it explicitly, the author employs a method borrowed from the sociology of knowledge, in which he apparently proceeds on the basis of the standpoint of Auguste Comte, namely that in the final analysis it is ideas (understood in their relativized historicist sense) that occupy the guiding and integrating role in society.

The reader gains the impression that Scheltema himself does not have a clear understanding of the true character of this method. At least, he nowhere refers to the sociology of knowledge as one of the most recent branches of the discipline of sociology. In addition, when he tries to define the relationship between his investigation and historical research proper he arrives at statements that cannot pass muster. In order to explain that his study does not bear a historical character, he remarks: "In many instances we are not concerned whether or not a particular development took place 30 or 40 years earlier or later, and we constantly focus on something in the past that has significance for us today, quite apart from the question what it meant to a bygone era. We proceed as if a specific concept with which we are concerned today, may be applied without objection to a point in time chosen by us in the past" (p. 7). Surely, this is not the way a sociologist of knowledge is allowed to handle his material.

When the author allows the marginal utility theory to play a dominant role in the economic thought of the Restoration period, and contrasts it as the "old doctrine" with the "new" value theory of Marx (p. 119), then this cannot be defended on the basis of the statement quoted above. These are scholarly mistakes *per se*. A responsible study within the domain of the sociology of knowledge can never proceed in an *un*-historical fashion. It ought to rest on a proper *factual* knowledge, where the word factual ought to be understood in the widest possible sense, including those theories that were actually defended at the time.

This requirement also applies to the general philosophical trends and the schools of legal philosophy of which the author provides brief summaries, mostly without mentioning authors and sources. Apparently he is not sufficiently at home in this material and often provides characterizations that create an entirely wrong impression. On page 3, for example, he says that the "phenomenological school" (one might ask: *which one?*) "advises scholars calmly to proceed as they penetrate their material and master and order it by means of logical thought . . . while eliminating consciousness, that is to say, eliminating all the contents of consciousness that can hinder scholarly investigation – think for example of serving specific interests, satisfying ambition, clinging to tradition." Evidently, the author is thinking here of Husserl's "phenomenological reduction of consciousness," but he has not grasped the true meaning of this method and in fact allows the phenomenological method to slide into that of the sociology of knowledge. Yet the latter, according to phenomenology, still belongs to the "natural attitude towards reality" which needs to be eliminated!

In another place (p. 70) he states that the different schools of neo-Kantianism maintain "the fundamental separation between thought and reality," yet the separation "is now no longer so much a symbol of the separation of citizen and the world he inhabits as it is a tool in the systematic construction of the sciences." In spite of some fundamental differences between the schools of Marburg and Baden, this certainly misrepresents the view held in common by all neo-Kantians, who agree with Kant's epistemological conception, namely that empirical reality does not acquire its construction except through the categories of logical thought!

Even in the case of the legal and political philosophy of Hegel, which he treats, by way of exception, in somewhat greater detail (pp. 59–63), a number of mistakes are inexcusable. For example, the author holds that Hegel took the judicial power to be the crowning peak of Montesquieu's *trias politica* that belonged not to the state but to civil society. A reading of Hegel's *Grundlinien der Philosophie des Rechts*, § 287, would have convinced him of the opposite view, even though Hegel in his treatment of civil society paid a great deal of attention to the function of the judiciary (and of the police). Yet separating one of the powers from the all-encompassing might of the state would flatly contradict Hegel's idea of the state. The extremely complicated relationship between civil society and state in the thought of Hegel can never be understood as a *separation*. Here the state is not the antithesis of society, but rather the synthesis of the objective spirit which resolves *into a unity* the antithesis manifest in society between the self-interest of the individual and the general interest, two elements that still need to arrive at an *inner* synthesis.

I could go on and adduce further examples to show that the author has not sufficiently mastered the material involved in the various subdivisions of the grandiose design of his dissertation. But I have no desire to do so, frankly. Whoever wants to write off his book on this ground in a certain sense engages in a bombardment of an open city. Apparently the author is quite aware of his shortcomings and disarms possible criticism in advance by frequently pointing out that he merely provides superficial overviews.

Despite all these shortcomings this work is a synthesis of considerable merit rarely found in a dissertation. The mere fact that I do not dismiss it with a perfunctory review but devote an entire article to it should assure the author that I do indeed consider it to be an important work fully deserving of an honest critical analysis. I shall therefore now proceed to present a more detailed discussion of the way in which he developed his conception in the three main parts of the work, while naturally restricting myself to the main themes.

8. The citizen within society

The first chapter provides a description of the citizen in respect of his thought-world and his position within society.

The citizen is characterized by a search for ultimate certainty in science, i.e., in theoretical thought. Apparently the author has in mind what I have called in my introduction the classic humanist science ideal, deeply rooted as it is in the modern motive of freedom and autonomy. During this period, thought as the citizen's ground of certainty is still inhibited by Restoration tendencies. Scheltema sees the Restoration as the symbol of the citizen's anxiety about any immediate projection of thought onto reality. According to him, the birth of critical doubt concerning what has been handed over from the past is intimately connected with the growth of citizenship. This generated the main problem of this era: what is the relation between *aprioristic* thought pursuing its aim in a spontaneous and self-assured manner, and *empirical* thought directed towards testing its own ideas against observed facts. This main problem finds its philosophical expression in German idealism and particularly in Kant's critiques.

Undoubtedly this is an ingenious idea of the author, for it serves as the foundation of his whole characterization of the era in terms of sociology of knowledge. The essentially natural-law ideas of the preceding period now had to be realized in empirical reality, and for that purpose the aid of the historical method of investigation was needed. The experience gained in the French Revolution made it clear that without empirical knowledge of history one cannot erect any reliable new order in society.

However, I must note at once that already at this point the author's method of the sociology of knowledge fails. For the critical doubt about which he speaks arose during the preceding period – long before the French Revolution started to experiment with its aprioristic ideas. It began with Descartes' *Discours de la méthode*, turned into an empiricistic psychologistic direction

178

with Locke's critique of human knowledge, intensified in the thought of Hume, and found its conclusion in Kant's *Critique of Pure Reason*. Now, Descartes' *Discours* appeared in 1637 and Locke's *Essay concerning Human Understanding* in 1690! It is difficult therefore to try to explain all of this in terms of the growth of citizenship during the Restoration. We are here confronted, rather, with an inner dialectic of the humanist ground-motive itself, which also had an impact in the domain of state and society but which cannot be understood in terms of the sociology of knowledge. In addition, it is certainly not correct to state, as the author does on page 23, that Kant's critical philosophy is the most representative trend of the Restoration era. Much rather it is the complex Romantic, post-Kantian and historico-sociological mode of thought (the latter being completely foreign to the thought of Kant) that governs this period – in polar opposition to the natural-scientific ideal of the preceding era. Kant exerted a decisive influence only on the codification movement in Austria. But in this period his moral philosophy with its categorical imperative came in for severe criticism with the rise of a strong universalist and irrationalist mode of thought. And French sociology of the Restoration period, which joined the Historical School in its attack on the aprioristic speculations of natural law, was by no means inspired by critical idealism. It indeed had an unlimited trust in science.

But let us return to Scheltema's analysis of the thought-world and social milieu of the citizen. The citizen of this period was forced to restore the old political order, though not without experiencing the infiltration of the new ideas of the preceding period: constitutions guaranteeing fundamental rights, and the separation of powers. The citizen himself withdrew into "society," which the author interprets, in accordance with the dominant view of the time, as the individualistic sphere in which every person pursued his own economic interests, protected by the Napoleonic codification. At this point Scheltema immediately gets trapped in the mistaken view of the civil private law of this era, an error I point out in my introduction. He views it – similarly, for that matter, as the view current today – as a typically *economically qualified* law. According to him, the *Code civil* contained law suited to merchants and entrepreneurs but not to

179

farmers and the nobility. The ideal citizen envisaged by everyone was the entrepreneur or merchant. What suited them was a sharply defined concept of property and contractual obligations in commercial trade relations. "The legal subjects are primarily seen as individuals who are sovereign within their own sphere." Here the author again blithely follows the historicist mode of thought of the prevailing schools of sociology which have no insight into the structural principles of a differentiated society and the complicated interlacement of structures in the "social forms." As a consequence he does not realize, for example, how the juridical form of a contract served to weave civil and non-civil private law together, even as their respective inner nature was preserved.

In addition to civil private law the author also subjects penal law and process law of this period to a brief analysis. Here too he discerns the same expression of the new conception of the citizen. The restored state as the guardian of order indeed overarched, in legitimist forms, an expanding bourgeois society. It harbored, as the author assumes with the French founders of sociology, the driving forces that would in the next period transform the state itself in the spirit of citizenship.

I consider the author's interpretation of the state during this period – however brief it is – as the best part of this chapter. His remarks about the ambiguous character of this political arrangement testify to a keen analytical ability.

It indeed transpired that during this period many states fell into an irreconcilable split between the legitimistic monarchical principle and the new element of citizenship, a split that also showed up in a vague relationship between "legislative" and "executive" power. However, the strong national awareness permeating the various states of this era cannot be explained in terms of the rationalist bourgeois thought-world of the time, but must be understood from the historico-idealistic mode of thought and the reaction called forth from the subjugated peoples by the Napoleonic imperialism. The author does not fully succeed in keeping these two trends of thought apart.

His brief characterization of the legal and political theory of this period suffers from this as well. His sociological method seduces him to view the scientific and philosophical theories entirely as a reflection of the thought-world of the ideal-type citizen. This signals an overestimation of the significance of citizenship in society – something a critical sociology of knowledge should not be guilty of. With regard to legal theory he does not consider the conflict between natural-law thinking and historicism as all that important against the background of the big debate for or against codification. Both sides, according to him, desired "norms that were appropriate for the citizen and his society, norms that could evolve with the citizen" (p. 54).

As a result, the author does not realize that the rise of the Germanist wing of the historical mode of thought, in alliance with the newly developing discipline of sociology, paved the way for the transformation of the foundations of civil private law in a socio-economic sense that was in direct opposition to the classic civil law tradition.

9.   The thought-world of the citizen

The second chapter once again begins with a characterization of the thought-world of the citizen. The author here finds sufficient material to make his thesis plausible that bourgeois thought in this second era turned outwards and allowed itself to be absorbed by a reality permeated by this thought. During the second half of the 19th century critical reflection for quite some time receded entirely to the background while the direction shown by positivist "objective science" moved more and more into materialistic pathways.

Nevertheless, it remains a dangerous and forced undertaking to view the prevailing climate of thought of this period as a projection of ideal-type bourgeois thought! Then Marxism too – with its historical materialism and its anti-state view of human society – ought ultimately to be squeezed into this fictitious scheme as well. When socialism opted to go the "bourgeois" route it actually paid the price of violating the basic theses of Marxism which led to a gradual move away from the materialistic view of history.

The author continues to see the capitalist "society" of this period, with its class struggle, in terms of evolving citizenship.

> The externally oriented conception of citizenship saw the separation [between the classes] as a conflict of interests, a clash of classes occupying different positions in society. Such an opposi-

tion between groups with diverging interests completely fitted the prevailing ideas of the time: each class had to take optimum care of its own interests. . . . What belongs to this externalization of ideas and norms is – we would prefer to say – a differentiation of what previously was inseparably bound together (p. 83).

In this way the class struggle turns into a normal phenomenon of civil, bourgeois society, a condition of its prosperity and progress by helping the proletariat acquire *genuine* citizenship, which for Scheltema always means: an economic position of power in society as the basis of constitutional rights and civil liberties. This is perhaps a typically "bourgeois" view of the class struggle. However, the actual goal of the class struggle was simply not to acquire "citizenship" but to destroy the state as an instrument of the domination of capital and with it to eliminate the entire *bourgeois* legal order. For a historicistic, economistic view of social reality is just not reconcilable with the classic idea of the state and the classic idea of civil private law. The thesis that the improvement in the position of the working classes in society was owed to the class struggle is hardly tenable in light of the facts. Orthodox Marxism certainly will not appreciate it if this improvement is deemed as belonging to its credit side.

The conclusion to which the author comes after a fairly extensive confrontation with the Marxist theory of value sounds more like the "personalistic socialism" after the Second World War than authentic Marxism:

Here the deeper foundation of the logic of socialist ideas clearly comes to light. The bourgeoisie's mode of thought was bound to a given order in which it felt at home and which it knew incorporated its principles. The socialists, however, saw through this order and its natural coherence, and demonstrated that the bourgeois principles were not, or not sufficiently, realized (p. 131).

This of course completely fits the line of thought of his earlier statement: "We proceed as if a specific concept with which we are concerned today, may be applied without objection to a point in time chosen by us in the past."

It once again becomes apparent how dangerous it is for the discipline of sociology to operate with the ideal-type of a citizen, for such an ideal-type is construed on the basis of a view of the relationship between the state and civil society which does not account for the inner structures of social reality and which elim-

182

inates in historicist fashion the boundaries between the truly *economically qualified* social relationships and those that are *not economically qualified*. The same is done by Marxism in its construction of the bourgeois man as a *type*.

When Scheltema starts to work out this historico-economistic thought-world in his ideal-type of the "citizen" in his outward orientation, then it comes as no surprise that he concludes (p. 111) that historical materialism as a pattern of thinking and acting actually suits this citizen. However, a truly critical sociology of knowledge should instead come to the insight that a person's mode of thinking, insofar as it is indeed determined by temporal societal relationships, will vary widely depending upon *the inner nature* of the distinctive spheres of life in which that person functions. The mode of thought of an entrepreneur in commercial life is *typically* different from that of a citizen of the state, the head of a family, or a member of a church, and all of these are different again from the *type* of thinking of an academic.

If the aim is to penetrate to the *deepest presuppositions* and most *basic motives* of the thought-world of a particular period, then it is no longer appropriate to operate with the conception of a citizen as a type which is modeled after a specific economic theory and a historicist sociology. What is required is that one comes to understand the *central* spiritual motive powers of human life. Modern, spiritually uprooted historicism is no longer capable of accomplishing this and so fails to arrive at genuine self-criticism. The ideal-type method vis-à-vis the fundamental doubt of the author about the basic theses of traditional humanism is a form of escapism.

What now, according to Scheltema, is the nature of political and legal life during this period? Here again, law in his eyes is the law of a growing and flourishing society – not merely in the thought-world of the citizen, but in *actual fact*.

> What once again obtained here, as had surfaced repeatedly in an earlier period, is that the citizen, pursuant to his new attitude towards the outer world, also projected law into the outer world, into true reality. In the era of our previous chapter, people were preoccupied with the construction of their order by employing law as its material: then their plans were not separable from the norms they drew up and applied. The categorical imperative, the basis upon which morality and law rested, was

183

a form of bourgeois thought: in consequence, law immediately belonged to their thought-world – to what was familiar in a strange world. Yet when this sphere was lost, law lost its former position. It was no longer familiar material in the process of construction; it had meaning, it existed, only to the extent that it was ready to hand in reality. Law was now researched and studied as an element of reality. The given order met the insights of the bourgeois citizen; the norms were no longer something posited for reality – they were rather found within this reality (p. 157).

Since I have already elaborated my principled objections to this historicist sociological view of law, accompanied by its narrowed and absolutized view of differentiated legal life, I need not repeat them here. What is relevant in this context is to focus our attention on the significant way in which the author applies his view. According to Scheltema,

this new way of thinking now results in viewing law as part of reality. It is observed in the first place to the extent that it operates within reality as the cause of effects. And the real effects are now: immediate, tangible or observable events. With the norms that form an order come actions that conform to these norms, that observe these norms – actions by those who, as members of this community, are subject to the order obtaining for this community. But this unity in the thought-life of the members of the community, and the rules which on this basis are elevated to law, are overlooked. In the first place, indeed, this thought-world is ignored insofar as it does not as yet, as an objective science, constitute a (for the time being incomplete) mirror of the genuine, true reality. In addition, the moral will, as a similarly inner ingredient, is denied any true reality. In opposition to the true motives or aims of the will, the will itself becomes a shell of inferior status: a point of accountability, a form whose contents is determined by the outer reality. And those who do not want to view the will as solely determined by external causes will still immediately separate, in a person's action, causes and effects. The view that emphasized the continuity of the will and its conformity with prevailing insights and norms is rejected as unreal and lacking any objective scientific status (p. 158).

In the eyes of materialism, norms too do not become real until they are violated:

For then, independently of the will of the person who acts, the applicable sanctions take effect: one can then observe the operation of these sanctions as the effect of the validity of the norm. At this point people begin to distinguish between the sanction and the validity of the norm. Violating the norm is now accepted as
184

normal: precisely through its sanction the norm acquires reality (p. 158).

In connection with this view the author also draws a sharp distinction between moral norms and legal norms. As *categorical* norms moral norms cannot truly be the subject of a modern empirical science. In a *hypothetical* sense only legal norms can be such a subject (p. 158).

This general characterization of the "law" of this period, which is rather a characterization of its "legal thought," illustrates Scheltema's approach. In the absence of referring to any particular juridical theories and authors, he evokes a whole complex of associations among those who are trained in nineteenth-century legal science: the evisceration of the will theory of Savigny in the "pandect" literature after 1850, its formalization in Jhering's *Interessen-Jurisprudenz*, in Binding's theory of norms and Thon's theory of subjective rights based upon it, in Kelsen's logicizing of the will into the logical point of accountability in his theory of legal rules as hypothetical, aimless logical judgments of the form *When A is . . . then B ought . . .* And so on.

Indeed, here the ideal-type method also exhibits its obverse. It comes loaded with implications and calls forth a whole universe of thought that cannot possibly be treated in detail within a limited context. Once again the question is: What is the scope of this characterization? And: Does it really relate to the *law* of this period *itself*, and if so, to what extent?

The author assigns to it an all-encompassing significance for law. The freedom of the citizen changed from an internal into an external one: his primary interest is directed towards the real basis of freedom, a person's own (economic) power. Law turned from being the protector of freedom into its intruder. This was true in particular of the new form of legal rights called into being by the class struggle, namely social legislation. The latter to a large extent did not acquire intrinsic authority for the citizens, but it did acquire a place next to the old civil codes. According to Scheltema, this new form of law notably bore a hypothetical character. It was constituted by norms that were followed in each concrete case after weighing the pros and cons, including the sanctions attached to non-compliance. The author is of the opinion that this was really true of the bourgeois attitude to-

185

wards *all* forms of law in this period. What was lost during this period was the intrinsic connection between the citizen and his rights: it now had to be discovered and described from reality. And in this more or less materialistic *modus operandi* he considers the distinction between norm and sanction to be of fundamental significance. Repelled during this period, he writes, was the historical interpretation of law, which looked for the legislator's intention in the *sources* he drew on. The reason for this shift was that it no longer fitted the view of law as a component of objective reality. It was then that the dogmatic-constructive method gained the upper hand. Curiously, however, he views in the same light the method that opposed the dogmatic-constructive method, namely the teleological method that was bent on interpreting the law on the basis of legally protected *interests*. The latter method of interpretation, according to him, was an expression of the same materialistic way of thinking as the constructive-dogmatic method.

Obviously, the sociological method of explanation employed by the author once again fails. For whoever explains two diametrically opposite conceptions of law with the same ideal-type mode of thought explains neither of the two. In addition I should note that the constructive-dogmatic method is not in the least typical of this period. It goes back to the post-glossator school! It was revived in Puchta's *Begriffsjurisprudenz*, which initially was supported by Jhering himself. In the third volume of Jhering's work of 1858, *The Spirit of Roman Law*,[1] he even designed a whole methodology for it. All of this was hardly a mode of thought with a materialistic basis focused on empirical facts. Much later, when the school of Gerber and Laband introduced this method in constitutional law, it was done with the explicit intention to elevate this branch of legal science to the level of civil law. Quite apart from its value in general, the method did not represent the externalization of juridical thought, since it followed simply from the positivist turn it was given in the school of Gerber and Laband. Gierke already issued a serious warning against this positivist turn in his book on the basic concepts of constitutional law.[2]

---

1   Rudolf von Jhering, *Geist des römischen Rechts* (Leipzig, 1858).
2   Otto von Gierke, *Die Grundbegriffe des Staatsrechts* (Tübingen, 1915).

The fusion between social reality and the outwardly turned thought of the bourgeois citizen is viewed by the author as an expression of the gradual growth of new law outside legislated law and the accompanying loss of the monopolistic position of codified law and the increasing significance of jurisprudential law. The more formalistic character of law during the preceding period was replaced by greater influence for the principles of good faith and equity. (Surely this is not an expression of a more or less materialistic mode of thought!) No sooner did judges begin to look behind the wording of the law for the interests protected and balanced therein, than they began to apply the legal stipulations largely in a sense they deemed just. The courts also began to take on a leading role in the gradual transformation of the make-up of society and the rising importance of interest organizations.

If Scheltema had indeed applied the critical sociological method here, he would have found a most promising field for analyzing the increasing interweaving of the sphere of non-civil private law with the spheres of civil law and public law. But of course, in his historicist view of reality this does not happen. Nowhere does the author show any sign that he recognized this fundamentally important state of affairs. In the context of this view which blurs the boundaries, civil private law encompasses the *entire* domain of private law. As a result, the constant structural principles of this domain, too, fade into nothing. For the period under discussion he actually believes that the very *foundations* of the domain of private law were altered. The ideal-type of the "citizen turned outward" in its historistically leveled sense is once again his key for gaining insight into the development of legal life in its entirety and of the whole juridical manner of thought in this period.

This is clear from what he says about the "revival of natural law" during the latter part of the 19th and the beginning of the 20th century. The legal theory of interests proved inadequate as soon as opposing interests or interest groups began to clamor for recognition and protection – as soon as the working classes or powerful trusts began to press their wishes against the resistance of the other citizens. For that reason it became necessary to have a revival of natural law in order to provide for this short-coming:

> The heyday of objective science, as we have said, imparted the same self-confidence to thought as it had during the period of scholasticism or during the reign of natural reason with the humanists. Thus it stands to reason that now natural law surfaced once again and that a system was built on the basis of a given or assumed nature (p. 171).

This characterization of *"la renaissance du droit naturel,"* as the French call it, is very misleading. After all, it is a richly varied phenomenon springing from very different schools of thought. But nowhere is it, *pace* the author, an expression of self-confidence in natural reason leading to the construction of "grand systems" such as those once found in the aprioristic natural-law theories of Grotius, Pufendorf or Wolff. The current renaissance is far too deeply impregnated with the historicist mode of thought. It centers on "variable natural law," grounded in a changing sense of right or at most in a formally conceived idea of law. In the "free law movement," with its emphasis on value judgments and arbitrary decisions, natural law takes on an *irrationalist* character. It is mainly oriented to a historico-sociological way of thought that hardly shows any understanding of the classic *ius naturale* as a foundation for civil private law. Scheltema portrays the revival of natural law as reflecting the divide between society's bourgeois and socialist segments:

> Regarding the nature of law the first consideration was the old bourgeois conception of law. In this sense it clashed with nature not to hold a person bound to his word or to restrict more than was necessary a person's right to enter into contracts as he wished. What belonged to the essence of law, in the bourgeois view, was Kant's categorical imperative ... To this sphere belonged the equality of citizens before the law and the idea that the same law applies to all, that the law bound all equally. This conception is worked out in the spirit that was absorbed in the outside world. The distributive nature of law is now placed in the foreground, requiring that a certain equality or proportionality be observed, be it in the assessment of burdens or the distribution of benefits, in the possibilities of the future or opportunities open to all. Those who, in the spirit of socialism or communism, want to allocate to everyone a more or less equal position in society and allot a proportional share in what is collectively produced in accordance with each person's needs and

188

each person's ability – they too take the nature of law as the basis for their proposal . . . In line with our analysis, one can say that the initial natural unity of the legal order now falls apart in two natural essences, each conforming to a component part of the substance or the reality currently serving as the foundation (p. 172).

This is once again conceived of in a typically historicist fashion. Classical natural law, as Grotius already realized in his *De iure belli ac pacis*, does not belong to the sphere of the *iustitia distributiva*, but exclusively to the *iustitia commutativa*. This is essentially the same for Kant, even though he uses the first term when he means *commutative law* to refer to the rights allocated to individuals by the civil judge.

However, the distributive justice in the sense intended by the author belongs rather to the domain of public social law. When he simply allows the classic civil-law interpretation of natural law "in the spirit that is absorbed in the outer world" to work itself out in a kind of distributive justice, and basically continues to view it as the old civil-law conception, then it is clear that for him the boundaries between civil private law and social public law are completely arbitrary.

Particularly forced is the leap he makes immediately afterwards towards the positivist legal theories which are hostile to natural law. He explains these theories in similar fashion from the outwardly directed thought-world of the citizen as . . . revived natural law! This does not detract from the fact that the author, from his sociological angle, frequently offers a very original perspective on these theories. For example, I was struck by the fact that he attributes the abandonment of the concept of subjective right to a conscious flight from the contradictory thought-world of middle class and working-class citizens.[1]

> People no longer wanted to hear about subjective rights, but only about objective law. Only in this way could the wrangling be relativized by the leaders of certain groups and movements who acted on behalf of their interests and who intended to push them through against the wishes of others.

In his summary conclusion regarding the development of civil law during this period, the author once again interprets this development as an expression of a similar process in society. Both

---

1 Scheltema does not mention any authors and uses the impersonal term "people," but it is clear that he has Duguit and Kelsen in mind.

started to grow "outside the framework of their former character," but the bourgeois citizen with his outwardly directed thinking did not inwardly keep up with this growth. With the rise of large-size organizations, intended for individuals, the unity of civil private law began to disappear. The power politics of these organizations was bent on barring the judge from their sphere. Contracts reached through arbitration and similar practices began to exclude the courts on a broad scale. Increasingly a large part of law in society came to be formed and determined by those who were to some extent dependent on the new bearers of power. In this way, next to the codified legal order, many small legal orders came into being without a unitary focus of accountability. According to Scheltema, this group-law was purely a question of the power-formation of groups within society. If I have understood him correctly, he sees this solely as a process in which civil law disintegrates. He does not have a positive appreciation for the inner nature of this group-law.

The most successful part of this chapter is once again the characterization of the state during this period. Surely this flows from the nature of the subject, for the author can now concentrate entirely on describing the liquidation of the Restoration elements of the previous period and the penetration of the entire state by the thought-world of the bourgeoisie; and he can do this without suffering to the same degree from what we have criticized as the effects of the ideal-type method followed by him when he ventured to apply it to a characterization of the thought-world as a whole and to the legal system with its complicated intertwinement of typical structures.

He describes in this chapter how the bourgeois citizen gradually conquered the state. "Now that the citizen was united with his outer world and everything conceivable had become an object of thought, in particular of objective science," the former separation between state and society, which also hampered the citizen from entering "the sacred domain of the state, inaccessible to ordinary thought" was no longer tenable. Similar to the way in which those who were at first excluded from genuine private citizenship in society eventually managed to acquire it, now the old liberal opposition within the domain of the state between active and passive citizenship (Kant, Guizot) also fades. Suffrage developed along these lines in the direction of democracy, while the emancipation of women should not be forgotten either. Gradually everyone, no matter what position he held in society, became an active citizen of the state with the right to vote.

Thus the Dutch parliament increasingly became representative of "the people" in the new sense of the word. The earlier separation of citizen and government started to fade to the extent in which the government itself took on a bourgeois character. Similarly, the wall of separation was taken down between the old ruling class, which was concerned to maintain the restored part of the old state institutions, and the other citizens. What the author has in mind here is what Hauriou describes as the process of incorporating the institutional idea of the state in the people. The introduction of ministerial responsibility to the popular representatives certainly was the most important element of the constitutional revision that marked this victory of the bourgeoisie. It laid the groundwork for the coming of the parliamentary system, a development that also brought the government's administrative policy into the public sphere. The author here actually describes the same process that Guetzewitch has called the "rationalization of power,"[1] and he does so completely in line with his characterization of this period.

Interesting, though not entirely satisfying, is the way in which Scheltema locates the material concept of law within this intellectual framework. Although the government, according to the old constitution, had spared the protected interests of the citizens, it was to be expected – since they now placed themselves in the foreground of the political sphere – that they would demand an important share in the task of the political organ to which they felt themselves most closely linked: the legislator. In future, the function of the legislator will be determined by the nature of the matter to be regulated not just in a limited domain but across the board. Consequently, the government will no longer be entitled to enact prescriptions on its own within the sphere of material law. The functions of legislation and administration are now separated as sharply as possible. Naturally this division is made on the basis of the thought-world of the bourgeosie:

---

1   B. Mirkine-Guetzewitch, *Les nouvelles tendances du droit constitutionnel* (Paris, 1931).

191

In contrast to the old era, when they were most affected by a ruler's granting their requests, the bourgeoisie realized that what primarily affected them now were those arrangements that infringed upon their private domain. . . . The criterion was not so much the absolute importance of the decision: for example, the legislator was not directly involved in declarations of war or generally in foreign relations, except when treaties touched on "stipulations or alterations affecting legal rights" – i.e., in general those elements that infringed on the spheres of the citizens (pp. 191–192).

Undoubtedly there is a kernel of truth in this reading, although it does not quite fit into the sociological-historicist way of thinking. The material concept of law certainly was not – as our author assumes (p. 196) – first discovered by Laband. It is deeply rooted in the intellectual climate of natural law found in the 18th century. Rousseau provided the first sharp formulation of it in his fundamental distinction between, on the one hand, the *law* that is an expression of the general will, grounded in the principles of *freedom* and *equality*, and, on the other, the *decree* that is an administrative act of the magistrate, applicable only to particular cases and always subject to the law.

The *trias politica* theory was a second factor capable of leading to a material understanding of the law.[1] In the Restoration period the law concept in its natural-law sense was only carried through in the codification article of the Constitution. This affected indeed the civil legal sphere of the citizens. The theory defended by Laband and Buys canceled the natural-law foundation of the material concept of law. Consistent with their positivist, formal juridical method – of which Kelsen merely drew the consequences – this theory merely provided a *formal* criterion: law in a material sense was the positive legal rule (*Rechtssatz*) binding every citizen. This fitted perfectly into the second phase of the modern idea of the formal "just state" (*Rechtsstaat*). Here it was no longer a question of defining a materially delineated legal sphere of the citizens (such as civil private law). Initially, as we know, Laband had a particular intention with his new theory. In his work on Budget Law he wanted

1 Cf. the well-known verdict of the Dutch Supreme Court of 13 Jan. 1879 [namely, that the right of Parliament to enact laws overrides the authority of the Crown to take administrative measures not specified in the Constitution or in statute law].

to demonstrate on the basis of his understanding of sovereignty that since budget law is not a law in a material sense, the King is entitled to authorize expenditures not covered in the budget.

Viewed in this light it is not clear what Scheltema has in mind with the "private domain of the citizens" that this new material concept of law was meant to protect. Since 1887 the constitutional criterion in the Netherlands is simply: "regulations maintained through sanctions" (*not*: co-maintained by *police force*, as the author incorrectly holds). It is difficult to find here a "private domain" for the citizens. Yet Scheltema's ideal-type citizen by definition carried with it a distinctive domain of his own, and therefore he concludes:

> In a certain sense the old separation of state and society was still maintained. The legislator did not have to consider it. Yet through the material concept of law the executive was forced to consider the given social order and particularly to spare the fenced-off spheres of the citizens – it was allowed to interfere here only after taking laws or court decisions into account (p. 192).

The material concept of law employed by Laband indeed formally also encompassed codified law. But the new material concept of law was not needed to provide this guarantee. It harked back to conceptions of natural law and was already taken up in the Constitution during the previous period.

Later on in his exposition Scheltema implicitly takes back his construction of the private domain of the citizens that was supposed to be entailed in the material concept of law, and he replaces it with the special domain of the legislator:

> The citizen was no longer protected by a balance of power [i.e., between the three powers], but by the material concept of law – by the delineation of the domain of the legislator. But in respect of that part of the legislative organ which the citizen saw as his representative, no protection was any longer required. . . . The old state powers thus evolved from an isolated position into a unity. The spheres of the citizens were now no longer protected against but within the state order (p. 195).

The way in which this point is elaborated in § 142 once again makes clear to what extent civil law and state in Scheltema's method of research are mere historical phenomena without a constant structure:

193

When state and society were no longer strictly separated thanks to citizens' awakened interest and political influence, civil law too lost its aura of sanctity and its inviolability before the state... . The role of the legislator had changed. Its foremost concern was no longer to formulate the principles of citizenship for social life, because the very policy of the state was now determined by the legislator. Society with its laws no longer came first for the legislator: he remained deeply concerned about society but he was no longer forbidden to alter its structure or mandated to regulate what was already tacitly accepted in society – what was entailed in the natural order (p. 222).

Since law was now viewed as sanctioned interest and since the capitalists and the working classes had opposing interests, the legislator had to make choices and arbitrarily lay down rules. In other words, for the author, civil private law changed its structure in tandem with society. This view completely fits the historico-economic conception of civil law as the economically qualified law of society.

In this line of reasoning, the same applies to the state. Political theory now conceived of the state as the consolidation of specific social forces, and the author views this as a necessary consequence of the sociological legal theory of Jhering which predominated during this period (he means the final stage of Jhering's theory).

If law is an interest recognized by the state, then similarly these recognized interests – including those who bear these interests – conversely determine the state (p. 223).

Liberal political theory viewed the state as responsible for the general welfare, the common weal. But in the conflict of interests between capital and labor "the common interest" became an empty phrase. The general interest of the state was now equivalent to the particular interest of a segment – namely the dominant layer of society (p. 223). If the sociological view is correct that the state is merely an instrument of class dominance in society, then the principle of the *salus publica*, rooted in the normative structural principle of the state institution, becomes meaningless. Scheltema once again follows this historicist-sociological conception without any criticism. As a result, he also interprets the political theory of this period as nothing but an expression of the structural changes to which both state and society were subjected.

194

Just as was the case in regard to the general welfare, so the general concept of the state distanced itself from the concrete order the moment it became the subject of intense social and political conflict. Capitalist society had turned into a political slogan: thus, only politicians still acknowledged an intrinsic connection of society to the essence of the state, but this could no longer be done by objective scientific scholars. The power to determine and maintain a social order now became a basic feature of the state (p. 224).

Thus, according to Scheltema, the theory of *state sovereignty* – the state as a bearer of power endowed with an original governing authority binding together the inhabitants of that state into a unity – became the theory best suited to this era and one that was also most generally accepted. In its realistic biological elaboration it led to the theory of the state as a "life-form," as Kelsen would teach (Scheltema once again does not mention any authors). To this theory belongs the view that the entire legal order is deducible from the will of the state in a positivist juridical sense.

Yet this theory did not succeed in bringing to expression the fullness of the thought-world of the citizens. According to Scheltema the theory had only a limited meaning: it saw the state "of a piece," opposite the conflicting interests of the individual or of societal groups, or opposite still other spheres, and the theory then accorded supreme power to the will of the state. Yet the state during this period could not deny what bound individuals and groups alike, namely the given legal order. This side of the issue was now primarily brought to the fore by the theory of the *sovereignty of law*. This theory, writes Scheltema, ensured a sheet anchor for bourgeois principles and socialist ideals independent of the state. He explicitly shows his preference for the theory of state sovereignty as intended by Jellinek, and he defends this theory against the view of Krabbe (p. 232).

The schematic characterization of these opposing theories presented by Scheltema does not take into account the fundamental differences present in the thought of those who defended these theories. There is a real difference, for example, between the views of Gierke and Jellinek regarding state sovereignty. Gierke defended the autonomy of corporative organized communities vis-à-vis the state, but he did not intend to derive

195

all positive law from the power of the state. And it is equally un-founded to claim that Kelsen, who defended the theory of legal sovereignty in a logicistic sense, intended to provide a firm foundation for civil and socialist principles. In pursuing the line of reasoning introduced by Laband, Kelsen rather wanted to eliminate from his pure theory of law all ethical-political postu-lates.

In the divergence of theories about state and law during this period the author recognizes a symptom of an awakening feel-ing of helplessness on the part of the citizen as an individual in the shadow of a state that constantly grew more powerful. As long as prosperity lasted this feeling could be latent, but in the subsequent period it would grow into the citizen's inner alien-ation with respect to his social milieu. And Scheltema sees the same phenomenon in the divergence of philosophical theories of law during this period.

10. The dramatic climax in Scheltema's exposition

In the third chapter – by far the most extensive one – Schel-tema's exposition reaches a dramatic climax. Despite the unnec-essary repetition of arguments already presented earlier, this certainly is the most gripping part of his book.

The author remarks that his view of the war of 1914, which marks the beginning of the third period, flows naturally from the sketch given in the second chapter:

> The grand structure of capitalist society in full bloom, with the imperialistic states pursuing colonial policies bent on acquiring the raw materials indispensable for their free societies, man-aged to overshadow internal tensions like the class struggle; but through its own momentum and for lack of brakes it could eas-ily derail.... In their international interaction the states were not bound to laws comparable to their domestic rules. . . . Since the stakes involved were so high that all capitalist states had an in-terest in maintaining the peace, it looked at first sight as if no further guarantee was necessary. What is remarkable, neverthe-less, is that while social developments and in particular also specific, economically extremely powerful groups pushed the leaders of the imperialist states in a direction where sources of conflict were plentiful, those states themselves had no brakes or rudder to avoid these conflicts. *Fate, their very structure, seemed to doom them to destruction, to war* (pp. 251–252; ital. mine, HD).

196

The catastrophe overpowered the citizens who were totally absorbed in the external world and the optimistic belief in progress; it fell totally outside their plans and calculations. The external world suddenly turned into a foreign world, a world governed by inescapable demonic forces. They were not able to see that the push toward a general war was intimately connected with the citizen and his state.

But while the individual citizens did not, at the first misfortune, give up their trust in the society in which they had grown up, those who had to give guidance to the newly developed capitalist society began to waver.

> Once the old, reliable truths of the citizen were left behind, every step led to more doubt and uncertainty. Every new idea revealed society's dependence upon new circumstances: as the complicated nature of the relationships became clearer, the relationships themselves became unclear.

Scheltema now gives an ample description of how doubt and uncertainty permeated society, coupled with a deep loss of trust in earlier ideals. Whether people liked it or not, in the long run they had to give up their former attitude towards reality. Reality pushed citizens away, as it were, forcing them to fresh self-assessment. As he analyzes this fundamental crisis the author arrives at his own view of the split in bourgeois consciousness, a view that bears a close resemblance to what I designated in my introduction as the pathological splitting up of the humanist personality ideal as a result of the spiritual uprooting of this ideal. For the author, however, this was no more than a historico-sociological process. He points out that the mounting conflict in the bourgeois thought-world was of an entirely different nature than the earlier one, such as the class struggle. The class struggle, presumably, fitted perfectly within the bourgeois thought-world and could therefore easily be absorbed into the civil order. The new conflict, by contrast, could not be bridged within the context of the civil order. This conflict was based in the nature of thought and its reactions to becoming uncertain, and it could therefore not be accommodated through the structure of a society, through an external order.

The sociologically necessary process of decay of the subject which was so intertwined with its reality – the giving up of all the trusted ideas and of all the familiar ways of thinking and act-

197

ing – now proceeded along the lines of the only option left, namely that of splitting up bourgeois consciousness into two extreme trends which were no longer capable of understanding each other. The author calls them the radical or revolutionary current (national socialism and fascism) and the conservative current. They were mutually exclusive, although they had sprouted from the same ideology of citizenship.

To sketch the uniqueness of this conflict the author uses the clinical picture of schizophrenia:

A schizophrenic does not malfunction because of the inadequacy of one of his two personalities, but because of the co-existence of the two. Similarly, we do not have to ascribe this development to one of these currents. It should instead be blamed on the bourgeois state which turned out to be incapable of absorbing them in a higher unity (p. 263).

It is striking that the author does not tell us among which of the currents within the schizophrenic civil order he would want to classify Bolshevism. One strongly gets the impression that he considers it to be the conservative one, for during the third period he calls "conservative" every approach that still hopes to establish a better order through the class struggle. Here I think he misapprehends the spiritual identity of this anti-humanist offspring of Marxism, just as he did with Nietzsche's philosophy of the Superman which he simply classified among Spencer's evolutionistic theory of the survival of the fittest (p. 275)! This shortsightedness, to my mind, is the result of the absence of a *radically* critical analysis of the presuppositions of thought about state and society, something that is most regrettable now that our culture is approaching the final contest between the Western and the Bolshevist spiritual powers!

The author views the conservative attitude of thought as the normal one and the revolutionary attitude, which arose first and foremost among the peoples that were conquered during World War I, as the despairing one. But the revolutionaries, who just like the conservatives have the bourgeois goal "to restore former prosperity," deliberately demolish the whole bourgeois system of ideas in order to enlarge the freedom of the subject. The author calls this "the contribution that the revolutionaries made to bourgeois society."

198

By driving shallow conservatism into a decisive conflict and so to a deeper self-reflection, they constitute an indispensable and intrinsically necessary element of the history of the bourgeois world. They will make the conservative aware of his anxiety, his narrow-mindedness, his backward outlook. Despite appearances, it is the revolutionaries who understood the enormous task of the subject who once again ought to be marching at the head of the movement, and the revolutionaries were the ones who took hold of every available means to reinforce the willing subject and remove whatever might stand in its way (p. 291).

In line with the dogmatic and quasi natural-scientific, sociological mode of thought of the 19th century, the author believes that the decline in economic development automatically brought forth the conservative and the revolutionary standpoints (p. 299). But when he engages in a more serious analysis of this process of disintegration, the reader is often struck by subtle characterizations rich in content, once again witnessing to the author's broad talents and his keen ability to penetrate his material psychologically. All of this cannot suitably be summarized because for that purpose the author's expositions are too varied and diverse, often linked in kaleidoscopic fashion. I can only recommend reading this work.

The author views this process of disintegration as commencing in will and action and continuing in the thought of both camps. After the Second World War the final result, presumably, was the liberation of conservative thought from the yoke of old ideas and the emergence of the possibility that the unity between citizen and reality might be restored (p. 328).

What follows is an extensive treatment of this disintegration process in society. The "harmonie économique" envisaged by classic economic theory rested on an individualistic order that served the "common interest" even as everyone pursued, within bourgeois norms, his self-interest.

The powerful formation of groups in the second period and the accompanying intervention by the powerful state disrupted the presuppositions of this natural order. The enormous unemployment and successive economic crises could no longer be seen as symptoms of a disease that would soon be conquered. In modern economic theory, the earlier assumption turned into a hypothetical limiting case, a mere possibility.

Through incidental governmental intervention the conservatives after World War I attempted to maintain the old individualistic social order as well as possible, without realizing that its foundation had been eroded. The revolutionaries, by contrast, deliberately constructed their totalitarian system which transformed individuals and groups into dependent instruments of a centrally guided state economy.

Gradually, however, the conservative countries too were forced – by the repercussions of the totalitarian regimes – to resort to more far-reaching acts of government intervention. And during World War II the conservative gave up his dreams, overcame his anxiety, and did what was necessary for his self-preservation. The entire society was put in the service of a single aim: victory.

As soon as the conservative has demonstrated the strength to break with his inhibitions, the division between the conservative and the revolutionary worlds lose their meaning. The revolutionary now turns into an adventurer.

The conservative is now also in a position to follow his example. However, he does so only insofar as is required for the survival of his bourgeois order. The revolutionary, by contrast, symbolizes the small group that wants to build its own power at whatever cost by elevating his own sphere to the sole and absolute value. As he does so, the revolutionary fails to see the whole of which he is a part (pp. 370–371).

It should be realized, notes the author, that a strict centrally guided economy cannot fit the bourgeois thought-world, because it disregards the *personality*, the individual's own intellectual-spiritual activity which constitutes the real foundation of citizenship. Growing sociological insight has helped us to see, so he remarks, that the abstract opposition between the self-sufficient individual and the member's absorption into collectivism clashed with reality, and that the individual and the collective group are necessarily involved in mutual interaction.

Possibly, Scheltema here has in mind the phenomenological exposition of Theodor Litt in respect of the social delimitation of individual consciousness and his conception that in the final analysis individuals are the sole bearers of social relationships. What is absent in Scheltema's exposition, however, is a treatment of *individualism* and *universalism* (see for example his views about individual and community in § 222 and § 226). It is a theme that continues to divide sociology. Absent above all is a consideration of the real structural problem of a differentiated society. This is a theme about which reformational Christian philosophy during the past twenty-five years has developed new insights that are of fundamental importance for the problem the author has in view. Particularly in his last chapter these insights ought not to have been ignored, because it treats a period in which the Christian world of thought started to free itself again from humanism and began to assert itself also in the reconstruction of the Netherlands after the Second World War.

What Scheltema explains in this context regarding a growing appreciation for group life in society and for the community idea in general, next to a recognition of the worth of the individual, opens up few prospects for overcoming the fundamental crisis of our society. For in the post-war climate, with the general overestimation of the community idea and the unabated cancer of the historicist mode of thought, there is no understanding of the inner structural differences in kind of societal spheres and the significance of their mutual interwovenness.

Litt too remained a *sociological* universalist and therefore construed society in terms of the scheme of a whole and its parts, even though he rejected *ontological* universalism which elevates the collectivity to the level of an independent essence, a substance.

Universalism and individualism are both incompatible with the structural order of actual society – also the most recent society.

As for universalism, it does not realize that spheres of life with a radically different structure and nature cannot be understood in terms of the whole-parts relation. What is needed is the figure of the enkaptic binding and interweaving of social spheres that leaves intact the original sphere of competence of spheres that are enkaptically bound. Municipalities and provinces are proper *parts* of the *state as a whole* because their nature is determined by the state. These parts may display autonomy within the whole, and the boundaries of this autonomy are dependent upon the interests of the whole. By contrast, the nuclear family, the business firm, the church, and so on, are radically different in nature from the state and therefore can only be bound to the state in so-called *territorial enkapsis*. Within this interlacement they maintain an essential sphere-sovereignty, and the limits of this sphere-sovereignty are never determined by the interest of the state but by the inner nature of each of them.

As for individualism, it is equally not susceptible to being reconciled with the structural order of a real society, because it does not allow for genuine *communal* relationships. It does not distinguish the various social spheres of life according to their internal structure but only in terms of the external purposes and aims of those individuals that are bound by them.

In the third volume of my *Wijsbegeerte der* Wetsidee I have demonstrated extensively that humanism never really succeeded in rising above the dilemma between universalism and individualism.[1] As we have remarked repeatedly, Scheltema, by adhering to a historicist view of society that eliminates the inner structures of social life-forms, understandably can only discern a chaotic disintegration of the old bourgeois legal order taking place in the legal development of the most recent period. According to him, everything taking place in the domain of law in recent times results from a threefold driving force.

> In the legal system, which lost its inner coherence through its externalization, subjectivity caused the growth of those subdivisions that were no longer hemmed in. This expansion of law resulted largely from the assertion of everything that surfaced as a negation of the former general principles. Next to this, the conservative attempted to hold on to everything related to wealth, while the revolutionary demolished law in order to create a power machine, also of human beings. The anxiety of citizens of either orientation about the possible collapse of society entirely dominated thought in this area and it led to two antagonistic attitudes. Law, exposed as it was to these three forces – the centrifugal, the conservative, and the revolutionary – lost its internal anchor and grew apart. It experienced thoughtless growth because the schizophrenia caused only certain one-sided tendencies to be operative (p. 391).

According to Scheltema, the same process, though in still more complicated forms, took place in political life. In the circum-

1   [*WdW*, 3:131–199 (*NC*, 3:157–261).]

stances portrayed, the state organism simply proved inadequate. Parliament was perfectly suited to register and coordinate acknowledged bourgeois interests, but it was totally incapable of giving guidance to any new developments that could not be viewed as flowing from these interests. Parliament had changed into an aggregate of group interests. With its regulating power considerably expanded during this period, at the expense of the legislative branch (the common practice of tabling framework bills that reserved a great deal of regulatory competence to the Crown), the government saw itself constantly thwarted by criticism from parliament.

Although the center of gravity once again shifted from popular representation to the government, the latter too was incapable of assessing the process taking place in society and finding a general solution for the problems. With a degree of myopia, only patchwork was accomplished. Regulatory ideas and plans regarding the organization of industrial life are viewed by the author in the same light. And even if government and parliament had had clear insight into the demands of the moment, then, according to him, they would not have been able to accomplish anything, owing to the dominant misunderstanding of the citizens. For "the fabric of the given society" consisted in

> the communal and like-minded ideas of the bourgeoisie regarding their social order and the place occupied within it by the individual. This community aimed at encompassing the person of the citizen with all his impulses and wishes, needs and energies, thoughts and beliefs [!], and to offer him, within its limits, the greatest possible freedom and latitude (p. 418).

At this point in time, however, the social fabric was ailing and subjected to a process of division and disintegration. In these circumstances, every individual and every group followed a pattern of thought that worked disruptively and thus contributed to the chaos.

No words can express more clearly the author's universalist view of society. It is fully in line with historicism and rooted in the historicized humanist bourgeois worldview. And now that society is beginning to lose the features of this view of life and the world, our author sees only phenomena of decay and disintegration. Using these spectacles indeed calls up this image. But is the first requirement of critical self-reflection not that one should be critical about the lenses through which observations are made? One should not identify the fundamental crisis of humanist thought on law, state and society with the disintegration of Western society as such!

On the basis of this brief explanation Scheltema once again describes the "schizophrenic division" of the state leading to two mutually exclusive types of states, the conservative and the revolutionary. Both types, including the ideas that accompanied them, perished in World War II. At the same time a measure of demolition and chaos arose that only the bourgeoisie could bring about. The gap between present-day conditions and its former prosperity is bigger than ever. But here too, Scheltema sees a glimpse of hope for the future: "As a result, there is a chance that thought, driven out of its one-sidedness, may once again assume a guiding role, such that the bourgeois world is no longer followed on its path of decline and ruin" (p. 440).

The dissertation concludes with a brief overview of the legal and political theory of this period and a summarizing conclusion for the present. Understandably, the author found it difficult to adduce theories that are supposed to be characteristic of the period since 1914. The Norm-logic of Kelsen, and Smend's work on "The State as Integration," both of which he specifically mentions, belong entirely to the previous period that he constructed. He does not discuss the theories of national socialism and fascism. Moreover, the fundamental crisis in the (humanist) legal and political theory was apparent already in the theories of Kelsen and Smend. But then, this crisis started much earlier than Scheltema believes.

In a short epilogue Scheltema draws the following conclusions. The existing order, or (as he explicitly adds) the *character* of this order, is in need of a radical alteration because it corresponds to a reality that no longer exists and which does not take the current predicament into account. He is of the opinion that it is the task of scholarship to raise our consciousness of it. According to him, science can also render another contribution. It can clearly determine the choice as to what should be discarded and what can be maintained *in a recreated form*. The individual and his sphere of freedom has been identified as a foundation of the old order, along with the substantial basis left to him: a construction, optimally utilizing the talents and energy of individuals for the benefit of the community, has turned out to reinforce mightily the strength and cohesion of the whole. To Scheltema it is clear that in the altered relationships the former position of the individual, which was already lost, is no longer tenable. But another question, he writes, is whether one should not attempt, in the gradual and careful construction of a new order, "to assign a place to the individual that will be good for the whole" (p. 456).

The author does have an eye for the multicolored tissue of social groupings, but he looks at it with the typical view of the modern historicist who does not accept constant structural principles and original spheres of competence rooted in these constant principles.

> What is accepted in advance is the tangle of groups, states, entities based on blood or soil, shared spaces, a corresponding education and training, occupation or trade, or similar inclinations to sport or play, social intercourse or isolation evolved from or based on economic, social, political or religious factors – not to speak of those not mentioned here. And for those who in the night of objectivity look on from a distance, all groups are the same [!]: they are all "states" . . . they are all elements of equal value in a reality that one knows before one investigates them (pp. 447–448).

Compared to the initial individualistic mode of thought, this leveling conception of groups is seen as a big improvement by Scheltema. Yet he does not think this sociological conception steers citizens in the direction they ought to pursue because it still belongs to the traditional and outmoded presuppositions of bourgeois thought and the attendant reality that is already gone. It is not at all the case today, he cautions, that all groups, all communities, are of equal value.

> Above all it is now the state that has to be proclaimed as the state: not at arm's length, by way of exception, but from within, by those who will attempt to form the state (and all the groups it embraces or helps shelter) into a new order (p. 448).

The state that no longer acknowledges the old dividing walls of "spheres of life" is indeed the only sheet-anchor for many who have been uprooted from their spiritual grounding through the crisis of modern historicism. While briefly referring to the renewed significance of Christian schools of thought and practical action in the current crisis (p. 452), Scheltema does not expect any positive effect from this side for the task of reconstruction. For that purpose, he suggests, they are too much intertwined with what is generally accepted, while Roman Catholicism in particular is inclined to pursue a regression to the medieval ideal. In terms of the standpoint of Scheltema this assessment is understandable, but it is based on far too superficial impressions to absolve him from the duty to penetrate more deeply into the significance of emancipated and rejuvenated Christian thought.

With that I conclude my critical reflection on this remarkable dissertation. I hope it will convince the author that I have attempted to do justice to his work. For all the criticisms that I have not spared him, I have also wanted to pay him my salute. For however much I consider the implication of this dissertation to be disastrous, and however much I object to the method employed, it still remains a work of great stature and a most representative expression of the modern historicist spirit of the age.

IV

A New Study of Aristotle's Concept of Justice[1]

1. The thought of Plato and Aristotle in the light of the genetic method of investigation

EVER SINCE THE GROUND-BREAKING investigations of Werner Jaeger, carried forward in the Netherlands particularly by Nuyens and Vollenhoven, our understanding of the major works of Aristotle in the areas of physics, metaphysics, biology, psychology, logic, ethics and political theory, has been altered in a fundamental way. These works used to be pored over in an attempt to derive a closed system of "the mature" Aristotle, but it turned out that they do not at all display an inner conceptual unity. Rather, they often contain views and conceptions that belong to different phases in the philosophical development of this eminent Greek thinker. A fruitful study of his works is therefore only possible through applying the genetic method of investigation and in that way establish to which period of development the mutually contradictory parts belong.

In all of this one has to proceed, of course, from the early writings of Aristotle when he still mainly followed his teacher Plato. But now a new complication arises. In all the works of Plato available to us, his thought exhibits an even less closed system than that of his famous pupil. In particular his doctrine of ideas (which according to the earlier generally accepted view is relatively easy to distinguish from Aristotle's mature theory of the immanent essential forms) underwent a process of development that displayed widely diverging conceptions. One simply cannot view the first comprehensive articulation of this theory – as presented in the dialogue *Phaedo*, where Plato almost entirely turned his back on the temporal experiential world – as characteristic of *the* Platonic doctrine of ideas and then proceed by con-

1 ["Een nieuwe studie over het Aristotelisch begrip der gerechtigheid," *Rechtsgeleerd Magazijn Themis* 77 (1958): 3-61. Translated by D. F. M. Strauss, who has also supplied subheadings. Edited by Harry Van Dyke and Deon Van Zyl, a former professor of Roman Law and a judge in South Africa.]

trasting it with the Aristotelian mode of thinking which, after its "emancipation" from the Platonic, is to be qualified as "empirical."

In fact, after the *eleatic dialogues* one can discern in Plato an increasing interest in empirical phenomena, particularly with regard to the area of politics and law. In one of the first of these dialogues, *Parmenides*, the initial sharp separation (*choorismos*) between the world of ideas and the empirical world appears to be radically altered, causing a crisis in the doctrine of ideas. The criticism that Aristotle would eventually level against Plato's doctrine of ideas employed arguments that were largely formulated by Plato himself during the later phase of his thought. The metaphysical theory of being, which Aristotle developed later in opposition to his teacher's doctrine of ideas, appears to a high degree to have been dependent upon the dialectical concept of being which Plato introduced in this critical phase of his thought. Apart from the different ways in which it was worked out, Aristotle's teleological conception of the relationship between matter and form likewise unmistakably found a point of contact in a development found in the dialogue *Philebus* where Plato, after resolving the crisis in the doctrine of ideas, saw the *essence* of the material genetic process as a *genesis eis ousian*, that is, as a "becoming" that was directed towards a limiting ontic form and which therefore implied a final cause.

2. The religious background of the form-matter motive

More fundamental than the genetic method of investigation for a proper understanding of the relation between the Platonic and the Aristotelian way of thinking is insight into the *religious* background[1] of the form-matter motive that governed Greek thought since its inception, although it was Aristotle who captured it with this fixed designation. As I have attempted to demonstrate

---

1 [It should be kept in mind that Dooyeweerd attaches a distinct meaning to the term "religion." Whereas matters of faith and belief appear within the certitudinal (fiduciary) facet of our experiential world, on a par with moral, jural, aesthetic, social and epistemic phenomena, religion for Dooyeweerd transcends all these dimensions of life – it refers to the root of life whence all these issues of our existence receive their central and all-encompassing *direction*.]

in Volume I of my work *Reformation and Scholasticism in Philoso-phy*,[1] on the basis of an extensive investigation of the sources, the entire dialectical development of Greek thinking since the Ionian nature philosophy is only comprehensible in terms of the inner tension which this religious ground-motive harbours within itself. Looking at the dialectically opposite representations of the deity as they derive from assigning religious priority to the matter principle as the principle of the eternal flowing stream of life, or to the form principle of the culture religion, one can hardly deny that this central motive originated in the conflict between the older Greek religions[2] of nature and life and the younger culture religion of the Olympian gods. Just compare the representations of what the old Ionian philosophers of nature (e.g., Heraclitus) considered to be divine with those of Anaxagoras, Plato or Aristotle.

This inner religious antithesis between the form principle and the matter principle turns out to be of cardinal importance also for understanding Greek conceptions of justice and Greek views of the significance of the state for the formation of law.

The Athenian *polis* turned into a proper [city-]state only after the patrician clans were stripped of all power. This process started with the political reformations of Solon and was completed by the statesman Cleisthenes. The other Ionian cities experienced a similar development. Prior to this, society was undifferentiated, with no room for the idea of the state as a *res publica*, an institution serving the public interest. The Greek city-state gradually became the true bearer of the Olympic culture religion, which was elevated to the religion of the state. The older religions of nature and life, in which the theme of life and death had a central place, were pushed back to the private sphere of the house religion, the clan religion, and the mystery communities. However, in the critical transitional phase of Greek culture, between the Mycenaean archaic period and the Persian Wars, the religion of life pushed itself to the foreground in the ecstatic Dionysian movement, whose excesses prompted action by the legis-

1 [Herman Dooyeweerd, *Reformation and Scholasticism in Philosophy*. Vol. I: *The Greek Prelude* (Grand Rapids: Paideia, 2012).]
2 [Here the term "religion" is used in the differentiated sense of faith and not in the central ground-motive meaning of the term.]

lator. In addition, the Orphic religious movement that exerted such an enormous influence upon many Greek thinkers, particularly also on Plato, had a Dionysian basis.

It is generally known that the Ionian philosophers of nature, as well as Parmenides, Heraclitus and the Pythagoreans (in particular Hippodamus), adhered to a conception of justice in that it was understood in close connection with the *Anangkē* that functioned in the old religion of life as the avenging fate to which all those beings are subject that separate themselves from the eternally flowing divine stream of life by attempting to take on a firm individual form and shape. The divine principle of life cannot be captured in a specific form; it is not limited by any form. The nature philosopher Anaximander therefore calls it the *apeiron*, i.e., the unlimited and formless. The things that separate themselves in a limited form commit an injustice (*adikia*) toward one another because they can maintain this form only temporarily at the expense of the other. Therefore there is a natural order in time forcing them to "pay back" their individual bodily form-existence to death. "Natural justice" reveals itself as an *avenging* justice, in which a steadfast proportionality between coming into being and passing away is maintained.

This has nothing to do with the modern natural-scientific conception of the law of causality in physico-chemical processes. Rather, this requires thinking about an order of natural law that governs all of nature (*phusis*). The juridical relations between the clans of primitive Greek society were viewed merely as a particular application of this order. There is also another feature of this archaic conception of retributive justice that deserves special attention. This justice also ensures that nothing transgresses the boundaries of its competence as fixed by the natural order. Heraclitus says that the sun will not leave its path lest it be found by the Erinyes, the avenging virgins of *Anangkē*.

Parmenides even gives this idea a metaphysical twist in his statement that through *Dikē* (retributive justice) and *Anangkē*, eternal being is confined to a fixed spherical form (of the firmament [*ouranios*]), and that these avenging powers do not allow overstepping the set boundaries in order to indulge in the treacherous process of coming into being and passing away. Once again it is the same order of natural law which in the relation be-
210

tween the primitive clans forbids any interference of one collective bond into the sphere of competence of another.

The first pregnant conception of justice is found in the archaic phase of Greek thought, in which the Aristotelian method for determining the concepts of law and justice (by subsuming them under a higher species through the addition of specific features) was not yet known. We shall see that the application of this method in particular led to a leveling of the irreducible nucleus of the jural aspect of society because it was not designed to grasp the irreducible modal aspects of temporal human experience.

Furthermore, in this archaic phase of Greek thought primacy was not yet assigned to the form motive and the *polis* still lacked the character of a real state. Political power resided completely in the primitive, undifferentiated clans. As soon as the latter lost their central significance within Greek society a fundamental change occurred in the Greek conception of law and justice. A form of resistance arose against the view of an order of natural law oriented to the old religion of life. The conception of law now attached itself to the legislative activity of the Ionian city-state, which had established itself in the governmental form of a direct democracy. In the 5th century B.C. the form motive of the Olympic culture religion, of which the city-state was the exclusive bearer, clearly gained the upper hand in Greek thought. This process concurrently led to a depreciation of the matter principle as it revealed itself in the view of the formless stream of life as the divine origin of all coming into being and passing away of things.

The new conception of law in Greek philosophy appeared for the very first time in the thought of Protagoras, the founder of the school of Sophism. It appeared in the distinction drawn by him between *phusis* (nature) and *nomos* (legislation). According to him, nature does not know any law; all law arises exclusively from the *nomos* of the state. It must be remembered that Protagoras, according to reports by Plato and other Greek thinkers, saw *nature* as being absorbed in the constant flow and change of en-souled matter (*hulē*). Unlike the older Ionian nature philosophers and unlike Heraclitus, Protagoras did not acknowledge in this flow and change a constant divine ordering of measure and proportionality. In other words, *nature* in his thought is depreci-

211

ated and stripped of its divine character. As a "natural being" the human person is hardly more than an animal. The only capacity elevating the human being above the animal is his talent for culture, his technique. But this can only come to fulfillment within the Greek city-state. It is the state that provides human *nature* a truly human form. For this reason those who live outside the Greek city-state, the *barbaroi*, are viewed as not fully human. This view became characteristic for the entire classical theory of state and law. It was not definitively overcome until the rise of Stoic philosophy, in part under the influence of the Cynics.

Under the primacy of the form-matter motive of the culture religion Greek thought could not return to a notion of an order of natural law before the form motive began to exert its influence also in its view of nature. The first move in the direction of this altered view of nature was made by Anaxagoras (5th century B.C.). He proceeded from a chaotic initial state of matter in which the origin of all things were still mixed in a disorderly way. According to him the form-giving movement that transformed this chaos into an ordered cosmos originated in the divine *nous*, the thinking spirit, which as *ruler* of matter could not itself be mixed with any matter whatsoever. Thought out consistently, this view led to the idea of a divine architect who ignited a movement in the eternally present matter that is directed towards this form-delimitation as its *goal*. What is truly divine in nature is no longer sought in a formless, material vital principle, but rather in its formative principles which are traced back to a rational design of the divine form-giver, similar to human cultural works that are generated according to a free rational design.

Mainly under the influence of Diogenes of Apollonia, this technical teleological view of *phusis* governed the Ionian nature philosophy of the 5th century B.C. Thus it paved the way for a new conception of natural law which was oriented to the form motive of the culture religion and which could provide a natural-law foundation to the state and its legislation. In the meantime it was precisely this Greek conception of the state, governed as it was by the form motive, which typically bore a totalitarian character. From its inception it excluded every idea regarding a principled delimitation of the competence of the legislative power of the *polis* in respect of the private spheres of life, even though the state was supposed to serve the perfection of the individual. If the human being can acquire its rational-moral essential form only in the state, then the state has to be the perfect and total community and it cannot leave any room for the sphere-sovereignty of those other societal relationships which have an internal sphere of competence and a destination that is in principle independent of the state. As the exclusive center of the culture religion the state assumed an absolute position within classical Greek society. Thus the idea of justice directed towards this conception of the state necessarily lacked an element that had been essential in the archaic understanding of law: the delimitation of the spheres of competence of distinct spheres of life, a delimitation that was believed to be inherent in the retributive nature of the natural legal order.

Since Socrates, this idea of justice assumed instead an ethical and aesthetical character as an expression of the divine idea of the good and the beautiful (*kalokagathon*), according to which everything in the temporal world is driven to its form-perfection. In the thought of Plato the idea of justice is the sum total of virtue proceeding from a constant disposition of the will as directed to a rational-moral harmony within the human soul and the state. The state is necessary for educating the citizens to this virtue of justice because the sensual inclination of the human being, in which the matter principle reveals itself, does not of itself follow the guidance of reason. In opposition to the radical wing of the Sophists, who regarded laws merely as artificial means of the weak to rein in the strong, the moral task of the state was strongly defended by Socrates as well as by Plato and Aristotle. It also explains why Aristotle later on, in a most comprehensive sense, identified justice with the justice of statutory law, for he assumed that the laws of the *polis* ought to be obeyed for the sake of the moral end of the state: the perfection of the life of its citizens into a good and beautiful life.

3. Discussion of the work of Peter Trude

This introduction is intended to precede my discussion of the book of Peter Trude, *Der Begriff der Gerechtigkeit in der aristotelischen Rechts- und Staatsphilosophie* [The concept of justice in the Aristotelian legal and political philosophy]. This book began as a dissertation prepared under the supervision of E. von Hippel and was published in 1955 in the series *Neue Kölner Rechtswissenschaftliche Abhandlungen*. In his *Preface* the author remarks that the earlier investigations of the Aristotelian concept of justice were largely restricted to a short and frequently incorrect account of Aristotle's exposition in Book V of the *Nicomachean Ethics*. German scholarship till now has seen only two works devoted to the Aristotelian concept of justice: a dissertation by H. A. Fechner defended in 1855 at Breslau with the title *Über den Gerechtigkeitsbegriff des Aristoteles* [On the Aristotelian concept of justice], and a monograph by Max Salomon, *Der Begriff der Gerechtigkeit bei Aristoteles* [The concept of justice in the thought of Aristotle] (Leiden, 1937). The author holds it against both these studies that they essentially took into account only the *Nicomachean Ethics*, while leaving aside the earlier *Eudemian Ethics* and the *Magna Moralia*. The authenticity of the latter two works has been scientifically established beyond doubt by Von Arnim. The effect of this is that the ongoing development that took place in Aristotle's concept of justice was overlooked. In particular the author raises various factual objections to Salomon's exposition, specifically regarding his denial of a genuine natural law in Aristotle's theory of law and justice.

It is therefore proper that Trude has opted for the genetic method. However, he appears not to understand the critical demands that the application of this method makes on the scholar. For example, he speaks in general about *the* Platonic phase in the philosophical development of Aristotle without in the least ascertaining *which* phase in Plato's thought is of importance as a starting-point for Aristotle's early writings on justice. In other words, Trude treats Plato's philosophy as a static system, in particular the doctrine of ideas, the conception of the soul and the treatment of virtues. Furthermore, the author has made a fairly arbitrary selection from the relevant early writings of Aristotle. He has consulted only the three oldest books of the *Topica* (one of the logical works) and the text *Virtues and Vices* (which he regards as authentic). Writings that are of fundamental significance for the genetic method of research, such as *On Justice*, the *Eudemos*, the *Protreptikos* and the fragments of the lost book *Politikos* are passed over in silence. Although Jaeger's groundbreaking work *Aristoteles* is mentioned in a Bibliography, Trude

214

nowhere makes use of the results of this investigation. As a result, an important insight into the real *process of development* in the early writings of Aristotle passes him by. For example, the distance between *Eudemos*, the writing *On Justice* and the *Protreptikos* is just as great as that between Plato's *Phaedo*, his *Politeia* and his *Philebus*. Trude's scheme of the development in the ethical views of Aristotle is completely based on Von Arnim's investigations into the chronological sequence of the three "ethical writings" as well as the studies of P. Gohlke about the genesis of the Aristotelian ethics, political theory and rhetoric (1944 and 1948).

Whereas Jaeger still assumed that the "Great Ethics" (*Magna Moralia*) could be left aside in the search after the original ethical conceptions of Aristotle, since this work is supposed to contain only a selection from the *Eudemian* and *Nicomachean Ethics*, Von Arnim attempted to show that this work, just like the two other works of Aristotle, contains the text of lectures Aristotle presented to his students and that it precedes chronologically the *Eudemian Ethics*, which in turn originated earlier than the *Nicomachean Ethics*. These results are confirmed by the closer investigations of P. Gohlke, who believed as well that he could prove the authenticity of *Virtues and Vices*, a work that Aristotle wrote during his Platonic period. The oldest writings on logic, particularly Books III–VI of the *Topica* that were of significance for his earliest ethical conceptions, were completed *before* Aristotle established his own school. Only after the founding of this school did the second definitive text of the *Magna Moralia* come about. Then came the *Eudemian Ethics*, followed finally (borrowing from Books IV–VI of the latter) by the *Nicomachean Ethics*. Certainly all of this is of crucial importance for an investigation into the development of Aristotle's concept of justice (although we will see that in the succession here assumed between the three ethics, there are still unresolved problems). Nevertheless it is hardly sufficient as a foundation for a genetic analysis. Apart from the other early writings on ethics, Trude should also have incorporated the *Politics* and the *Metaphysics* in his genetic investigation, as was done by Jaeger. Even though various objections could be raised against Jaeger's conclusions, he did lay the foundation for the insight that the development of Aristotle's ethical

215

insights was intimately connected with his metaphysics and political theory. Trude does refer more than once to the *Politics*, but he nowhere distinguishes between earlier and later versions of this work.

What has escaped Trude entirely is the religious background of the form-matter motive. This shows its negative effect, in the first place, in the brief sketch which he gives of the historical development of the Greek concept of justice. He exclusively employs the well-known studies of Hirzel but he appears unfamiliar with the later writings of Cornford, Guèrin, Kelsen and other relevant authors. The fact that Greek thought had an idea of natural law long before Aristotle, oriented to the matter motive of the archaic religion of life, is not known to him – at least not against this religious background. But the very revolutionary character of the denial of any form of natural law by Protagoras should have kept Trude from asserting that Aristotle was the philosophical founder of natural law. Later on, guided by Hirzel's studies, he nonetheless mentions different older Greek thinkers among the adherents of the idea of an unwritten natural law (*agraphos nomos*), but he does so without once considering the question what they actually understood by natural law and *nature*.

Apparently the only form of a "philosophical" theory of natural law acceptable to Trude is a natural law founded upon the rational nature of the human being viewed as an "immanent, real law-idea" inherent in man's rational nature (p. 170). But the idea of natural law found among the old Ionian nature philosophers and Heraclitus was not any less philosophically based on their conception of *nature*. And they likewise believed that this natural law is accessible to human philosophical reflection. The fact that they did not restrict natural law to human societal relationships – indeed, they viewed it as being embodied in a divine order for whatever is subject to coming into being and passing away – is no reason to call their conception of natural law "unphilosophical."

In the second place, Trude's lack of insight into the religious background of the form-matter motive exacts its price when he asserts that Aristotle's views of ethics and law, after their emancipation from the Platonic doctrine of ideas, involve a turn from theonomous to autonomous scientific knowledge. It is clear from his whole argument that he has in mind the autonomy of theoretical thought in the modern sense of its presumed emancipation from all religious presuppositions. This, however, is a fundamental misconception of the Greek view of autonomous *theoria*. Although Greek philosophical thought emancipated itself to a greater or lesser degree from the mythological representations of popular beliefs, it remained deeply rooted in the dialectical religious ground-motive that emerged from the meeting of the older religions of nature and the Olympic culture religion. But this motive differed radically both from the scholastic Christian motive of nature and grace that governs the Thomist view of the relative autonomy of natural reason, and the modern humanist ground-motive of nature and freedom which forms the religious background of Kant's critical philosophy. When Trude argues (p. 172, n. 148) that Kant was not the first to distinguish sharply between nature and freedom, then he merely demonstrates that he does not understand the difference in principle between the Aristotelian form-matter motive and the Kantian motive of nature and freedom. For the Kantian freedom motive grew out of the religious cult of the autonomous human personality since the Renaissance. It at once developed a religious conception of nature that was radically different from the Greek and the medieval view (*Deus sive natura – God or nature*). Since the development of the modern science ideal, directed as it is towards the mathematical control of nature, this ideal got entangled in a dialectical tension with the freedom motive. Such a dialectical tension between nature and freedom is not found in Aristotle: in his thought the words nature and freedom have a fundamentally different meaning than in Kant.

4. Did Greek thought increasingly liberate itself from religion?

I have now summarized the main objections I have against Trude's work, but it would not be right to leave it at that. This new study on the Aristotelian concept of justice certainly has many good qualities and deserves to be recognized as a positive contribution to legal philosophy.

Moreover, as to my second objection, it would not be fair to blame this study in particular for its lack of insight into the religious background of the Greek form-matter theme. Trude shares the common assumption that Greek thought at first was strongly influenced by mythological ideas but increasingly liberated itself from religion by placing itself squarely on the basis of reason and experience. This misinterpretation is still found in a stark formulation in Husserl's last work with the title *The Crisis of European Sciences and Transcendental Phenomenology*.[1] So I would now like to highlight the positive aspects of Trude's study, even though I will frequently have to insert my principled objections to his starting-point as well as criticize some other points.

According to Trude the early Aristotelian concept of justice was still conceived of in an idealistic way, similar to the Platonic concept. Like the latter it was essentially viewed as the intrinsically harmonious ordering of the three parts which according to Plato make up the human soul: the appetitive (*epithumētikon*), the spirited (*thumoēides*) and the rational part (*logistikon*). In Aristotle, as in Plato, each one of these parts of the soul was correlated with a special virtue, namely temperance, courage, and wisdom. Even though the *Topica* does not *explicitly* speak of courage as a virtue of the *thumoēides*, this is the case in the work *Virtues and Vices*. Here wisdom (*phronēsis*) is still primarily conceived in the Platonic sense of *epistēmē* (knowledge) – the wisdom that is based on an immediate theoretical intuition of the metaphysical ideas and is thus a form of immediate theoretical knowledge of good and evil that is not in need of logical proof.

Justice is then not viewed as a special virtue, but as the general all-encompassing virtue that effects the hierarchical ordering of the three parts of the soul as well as their corresponding virtues. Already in the *Topica* we do find Aristotle's later conception of virtue as the soul's active disposition (*hexis*); but the characteristic criterion of virtue as found later in the *Nicomachean Ethics* – observing the *proper mean* between *too little* and *too much* (e.g., courage as the mean between rashness and cowardice) – is still entirely absent. Absent above all is the later application of justice to fellow humans and the community, while not a trace is found of the later distinction between *general* and *particular* justice.

1 Edmund Husserl, *Die Krisis der europäischen Wissenschaften und die Transzendentale Phänomenologie* (Belgrade, 1936).

Here the first question that arises is whether or not it is correct to believe that Plato saw justice as an inner virtue apart from any connection with fellow humans and society. Apparently Trude bases this interpretation exclusively on Plato's prominent dialogue on the ideal state, the *Republic*. Yet also in this dialogue the idea of justice is definitely not solely related to the harmonious ordering of the three parts of the soul inside the human individual. Trude himself has to acknowledge that justice is even predominantly related to the inner ordering (*taxis*) of the political community as well as to the order in the macro-cosmos (the universe). Both Plato and Aristotle (also the later Aristotle) relate the concept *koinoonia* (community) to everything that is a unity within a multiplicity of parts, and here the ordering of the parts is persistently viewed according to what is ruling or guiding and what is subordinate as essential for the unity of the whole.

In Plato's ideal state, the ordering of the three estates according to the principle of justice called *to heautou prattein* (i.e., that each estate acts in conformity with its own task, in order to ensure the harmonious cooperation within the whole) cannot possibly be seen purely as an inner virtue conceived apart from any external action or any relation to the community. It is a truly *social* justice, concentrated on the community of the *polis* and aimed at a proper division of tasks, in particular of public functions. Accordingly, Trude's statement that in his later conception of justice Aristotle was the founder of social ethics which played no role in Plato's thought is untenable. One can only say that in his later development Aristotle applied his concept of justice *exclusively* to human societal relationships, whereas Plato continued to see justice as a particular manifestation of the general idea of justice which is related to the entire ordering of the sensible world and to the harmonious ordering within the human soul.

Insofar as Plato's idea of justice continued the memory of the archaic view of *dikē* as an order governing all nature – to which undoubtedly the element of demarcation among the three estates also points – it deserves notice that this metaphysical idea had severed every connection with the central motive of the older religion of life. In both Plato and Aristotle the concept of *taxis* (ordering) was exclusively oriented to the form motive of the Olympic religion. In his *Topica* Aristotle explicitly called *taxis* the *eidos* or *ontic form* of the state. And the unmistakably universalist and totalitarian view of the *polis* present in the thought of both Plato and Aristotle – albeit elaborated in different ways (less radical in the case of Aristotle) – also explains why neither applied the element of delimited competency to the state itself.

Accordingly, their idea of social justice left no room for individuals and non-political organized communities to enjoy a freedom under the law *over against* the polis.

5. Justice and proportionality

Of special importance is Trude's investigation into the meaning of the Aristotelian concept of equality or proportionality in his initial conception of justice as worked out in the oldest portion of the *Topica*. As we know, in the later view of Aristotle, equality (*to ison*) is, next to the social relation to fellow human beings, the special hall-mark of particular justice. *General* justice in the *Nicomachean Ethics* is no longer related to this equality. In the *Topica*, where it is said in a fully general sense that justice brings about equality, this distinction is not drawn. Trude holds that the early conception of justice is intrinsically Platonic, for it is still totally related to the inner harmony of the parts of the soul. But in view of the fact that in the *Topica* equality is related to the *distribution* of assets and liabilities,[1] this statement runs into difficulties, for justice is not related to the inner order of the soul only, but also to external actions. In this context the author has to concede that Plato too knew this distributive justice.

Following Von Arnim, Trude nonetheless believes that he can maintain the thesis that in the *Topica* Aristotle's own concept of justice is understood only as a virtue "directed towards what is internal." According to him equality, which is contained in the truly philosophical definition of the virtue of justice, must be understood exclusively in the sense of being directed to the inner balance between the three parts of the soul. The equality that has an external direction towards the distribution of assets and liabilities in the *Topica* would not have been meant as a feature contained in the philosophical definition, but only as a meaning for the word justice already present in Greek linguistic practice. According to the author this view is confirmed by Aristotle's early

1 *Topica* 143a15, 145b35.

work *Virtues and Vices*. There too the threefold conception of the soul still dominates, alongside the Platonic view of *phronēsis* as primarily a purely theoretical wisdom which in a secondary sense also encompasses the practical wisdom that is directed towards moral actions. Once again justice, in a fully Platonic sense, is related to the *entire* soul.

But here it acquires the closer definition of a virtue giving each person his due according to the yardstick of a certain value (*dianemētikē tou katāxian*). Nothing is said here about *equality* in distributive justice. But even though it cannot be doubted that here already the later Aristotelian concept of distributive justice (*iustitia distributiva*) is designated, according to Trude it is only to be understood as one of the meanings of the word justice in ordinary usage at the time. After all, this work also celebrates justice as honoring the customs and mores of the fatherland, submitting to the written laws, speaking the truth, keeping one's word, and so on. In other words, we find here, according to Trude, only an enumeration of the various meanings that the word justice can have in ordinary usage. The list includes, as the first and truly philosophical meaning, the Platonic one, which is related to the inner harmony of the soul. Independently of the earlier linguistic practice, this early-Aristotelian view of justice is developed from the Platonic theory of the soul, which was also related to the theory of virtues. The *philosophical concept* of justice is therefore not here derived from language usage and rooted in experience; it is developed, rather, in an aprioristic manner from the concept of man, that is to say, from "pure reason." And according to Trude it is therefore still completely *idealistic* and does not have – as in the later theory of Aristotle – an *empiricistic* foundation.

This argument is not very convincing, particularly as regards the work on virtues and vices. What might perhaps be defended in respect of the *Topica*, namely that Aristotle is there interested in usage, cannot be assumed about a purely ethical work without providing support for this hypothesis in the text. Trude provides not a shred of evidence for his interpretation. His premise that the Platonic conception of justice exclusively relates to the inner harmonious ordering of the soul is untenable, and so is his attempt at interpreting "the early-Aristotelian conception" (which one – we
221

might ask). Nonetheless his investigation of the view of justice as it is developed in the *Topica* and the work on virtues is a welcome supplement to the genetic investigation of Jaeger regarding Aristotle's ethics.

The same can be said of Trude's examination of the concept of justice in the *Magna Moralia*. Trude takes this concept, along with the one developed in the *Eudemian Ethics*, to belong to the "transitional period" of Aristotle's thought. But this reading is once again much too simplistic.

In the *Magna Moralia* the Platonic tripartite soul makes room for a bifurcation (a rational and a non-rational part), although Book I in one place still alludes to a threefold division.[1] This is merely a transition to the later view that abandoned the separate parts of the soul by replacing them with the different capacities of the soul. In this connection a drastic alteration takes place within the theory of virtues – under the influence, according to Trude, of Aristotle's growing interest in the data of experience. The most important feature of this alteration, so Trude claims, is that *phronēsis* is now merely the virtue directed towards action and therefore functions as the practical virtue of the rational part of the soul. It is sharply separated from the theoretical virtue of wisdom (*sophia*), which belongs exclusively to thought directed toward what is eternal and divine. With this corresponds a subdivision of the rational part of the soul into a *deliberating* (*bouletikon*) and a *knowing* (*epistēmonikon*) part. Justice is now assigned to the non-rational part of the soul – together with temperance and courage. It thus loses its earlier Platonic meaning of an objective hierarchical value-ordering that obtains in the human soul, the state and the cosmos – although the rational part of the soul continues to have a higher value than the non-rational part. This leads to the introduction for the first time of a criterion for virtue found in the concept of the mean between too much and too little. And justice, although it still functions as the comprehensive practical virtue, acquires a totally different meaning. It is now related to obedience to the law (*nomos*) and this statutory justice (to the extent that law in general commands the exercise of all virtues) is the *perfect* virtue. However, human action that is in keeping with this general justice is not yet tied to the criterion, as

1 *Magna Moralia* I.4.1185a21.

222

it would be formulated in the *Nicomachean Ethics,* of being related to one's fellow-man (*pros heteron*).

The latter criterion is reserved for a second concept of justice, namely for *distributive* justice, which is already developed alongside the primary concept of justice in the *Topica* and in Plato, where it is linked to *equality.* This equality in the distribution of assets and liabilities presupposes a relation between persons involved in legal transactions. In Book I of the *Magna Moralia* it is characterized as a virtue focused on striving towards gain (*pleonexia*). This was also the definition in the early-Aristotelian work *Virtues and Vices.* In striving towards gain this virtue then consists in taking into account the proper mean between too much and too little of assets and liabilities that one claims for oneself. This form of justice is also related to a proper balance in the levy of taxes within the political community. The later distinction between *justitia communitativa* (exchange justice) and *justitia distributiva* (distributive justice) is not yet found in the *Magna Moralia.* In general the yardstick of equality is here determined according to the relationship between the actual value of goods that ought to be taken into consideration in economic transactions. Those who are poor and those who are rich ought not to pay an equal amount of taxes but different amounts in proportion to their property. In the exchange of shoes against a house the *value* of the exchanged goods ought to be equal, not the *quantity* of goods.

What is also absent in the *Magna Moralia* is the form of distributive justice developed in the *Nicomachean Ethics.* In allotting offices and honors the standard of proportionality is applied to the *personal* qualities of those concerned. As a specimen of distributive justice the *Magna Moralia* finally mentions retributive justice (*to antipeponthos*). It too has to be applied according to the equality yardstick of factual proportionality. The *Magna Moralia* restricts this retribution to the domain of penal law. It does not recognize anything like the retributive nature of the jural aspect of society as such. When Trude therefore believes that the *Magna Moralia* does not yet distinguish special kinds of justice, he does not appear to be entirely correct.

Retributive justice is unquestionably posited here as a particular specimen of distributive justice in contrast to the non-retributive kind.

6. The development of Aristotle's ethics

All too cursory is Trude's treatment of the *Eudemian Ethics*, a work that is actually of fundamental importance for tracing the genesis of Aristotle's ethical conceptions. Trude holds that this work merely provides some further clarification of the standpoint already found in the *Magna Moralia*. Not just Jaeger, but also Greenwood and Kapp before him, came to the conclusion that the *Eudemian Ethics* assigns a meaning to *phronēsis* which differs in principle from that of the *Nicomachean Ethics* and which still corresponds completely to the late Platonic conception in the *Protreptikos*, namely that the theoretical intuition of the godhead as the highest good becomes the absolute norm (*horos*) for ethical behavior. On this view, the *Eudemian Ethics* still maintains the standpoint of a theonomic ethics.[1]

Although the Platonic doctrine of ideas is already left behind and the empirical method of research is accepted, the idea of the divine *Nous* as unmoved Mover here still plays the role of the Platonic transcendent idea of the good. If this interpretation is correct, the chronological succession between the *Magna Moralia* and the *Eudemian Ethics* as construed by Trude, following Von Arnim and Gohlke, cannot be maintained. Trude should certainly have discussed the well-documented conception of Jaeger. He merely makes the apodictic statement, "The reduction of *phronēsis* to an activity merely directed to practical reason, which could already have been established in the *Magna Moralia*, is also found in the *Eudemian Ethics*." To which he merely adds in a footnote: "as was recently shown by Von Arnim in discussing Jaeger."

But the issue here is not just the role of *phronēsis*. Jaeger bases his opinion *inter alia* on the role played by the "first friendship." All kinds of friendships are derived from this highest or perfect one. The concept *prootē philia*, as Jaeger has shown, derives directly from Plato's dialogue *Lysis*, where it denotes the highest metaphysical value (the good itself), of which all earthly forms of

1   Particularly *Eudemian Ethics* VII.14.1248a26 provides a strong argument for this reading.

friendship are shadow images. With the abandoning of a transcendent world of ideas the good now becomes, in the *Eudemian Ethics*, an immanent value, enclosed within the rational ontic form of human nature; yet it remains directly grounded in the metaphysical idea of god which according to Jaeger was the real theme of the original metaphysics developed by Aristotle. In the *Nicomachean Ethics* the term *prootē philia* (first friendship) is gone and replaced by the term *teleia philia* (perfect friendship). Jaeger's views are too important to pass over in silence if we want to gain insight into the development of Aristotle's ethics.

7. Trude's analysis of the ripened views of Aristotle

While the investigation of the development of Aristotle's earlier ethical views occupies only twenty-four pages in Trude's book, the entire content of the rest of his work consists of a truly worthwhile systematic analysis of the concept of justice as it is developed in the *Nicomachean Ethics* and supplemented in the third book of the *Politica*. The most important differences with the conception of justice of the other ethical writings are to be found [i] in the acceptance of the general criterion that justice should be focused on one's fellow man; [ii] in the clear distinction between a particular justice with its yardstick of equality in distributive justice, and an exchange justice with a distinction between an arithmetical and a geometrical equality; and [iii] in the recognition of equity as a special kind of justice related to all spheres of law. Equity has to correct the shortcomings in general legal stipulations and is related to a specific cognitive ability.

In his analysis of the concept of general justice Trude introduces fresh viewpoints that undoubtedly deserve close attention. For example, he is of the opinion that once Aristotle identifies general justice with *legal* virtue (the virtue that is focused on compliance with the law) he does not just have in mind law in the strict sense of what is explicitly promulgated by the legislator, but he means every legal norm regulating communal life, thus including legal customs and mores. Trude holds this opinion in opposition to the dominant view. In support of his interpretation he could have drawn a strong argument from Aristotle's early work on virtues and vices where this broad conception is indeed found. However, although he could not find support for his view in the *Nicomachean Ethics*, in this context he does not appeal to the

225

work on virtues and vices. Equally important is his argument that the meaning of *pros heteron* (being related to the other) as a general conceptual characteristic of general justice in the *Nicomachean Ethics* must be different from what is held in the *Magna Moralia* where it is accepted for particular justice only. Since general justice encompasses the practice of all virtues, for example also courage and temperance, the "being related to the other" here cannot mean that it must be practised towards other persons, such as in exchange relations which presuppose the presence of at least two persons for the possibility of an act of exchange to take place. The only possible meaning is that the other virtues are subsumed under justice insofar as they are in general practised *with a view to the community* and also insofar as they do not appear in actions that presuppose a partner. In other words, general justice became the perfect virtue, encompassing all others to the extent that whoever observes it practises this virtue not merely as related to oneself as an individual, but as a member of the community and on the basis of community interest.

The author interprets this as a socio-ethical revolution in respect of the concept of general justice still occurring in *Magna Moralia*. We have already seen that Trude is mistaken in his view that this socio-ethical conception of justice is not found in Plato. For Plato, justice in its relation to the state is indeed the all-encompassing social justice that aims at the well-being of the community. The fact that in the *Nicomachean Ethics* general justice is ethically grounded in the well-being of the state, as elaborated in Aristotle's *Politica*, is therefore fundamentally in conformity with Plato rather than being an original idea of the author of the *Nicomachean Ethics*. The real deviation from his tutor is found earlier in the *restriction* of the general concept of justice to the relationships of human society, while in the thought of Plato it *additionally* had a cosmological and psychological meaning, a meaning ultimately grounded in the divine idea of the good, an idea that the *Nicomachean Ethics* argues against in an extensive polemic.

In the *Nicomachean Ethics* the content of general justice remains what is commanded by the laws (*nomoi*). This introduces a formalistic element into the concept of general justice, for laws could be both good and bad and as such fail to provide any warranty that they indeed command what is virtuous. According to Trude this is a consequence of sacrificing the early Aristotelian-Platonic transcendent idea of justice in its relation to the divine idea of the good. That idea of justice embodied the ethical value hierarchy. It lacked the formalistic relation to what is commanded by law, since it already contained an intrinsic material ethical value. Trude here observes a shortcoming in Aristotle in his later concept of justice vis-à-vis the Platonic one and holds that the former can only reveal the *full* contents of justice in conjunction with the latter. On the other hand he holds that the concept of justice as it is developed in the *Nicomachean Ethics* cannot be called purely formalistic, since the virtue and general well-being of the state (the social *eudaimonia*) is elevated by Aristotle to a normative criterion for the justice embodied in laws. The laws of the state *ought* to be directed towards the well-being and virtue of the citizens.

Moreover, in the late-Aristotelian concept of justice Trude believes that in many respects one can see valuable progress over the Platonic concept. In the first place, based upon the principle of social well-being, Aristotle added social ethics to individual ethics, thus providing an ethical foundation for law. In the second place, progress is made by introducing a specific feature of law, namely the social relationship with fellow human beings – and in the third place by combining law and justice with friendship (*philia*). The latter is not just portrayed as the most perfect basis of justice, but in its perfect form it is also acknowledged as the "highest law." Thus statutory law is practically viewed as a mere ordering of *imperfect* human nature. *Philia*, by contrast, as the "highest law," is appreciated as an ordering of the *perfect* human nature. According to Trude this shows how close Aristotle already approximated Christianity, for *philia*, "so to speak," was here already being acknowledged as a "supernatural" virtue closely connected to the supernatural virtue of Christian love. In this way Aristotle prepared the transition from ancient philosophy to Christian philosophy. Conceiving *philia* as perfect justice marked a break in principle with the morality that still prevailed during the Homeric Age, centered on courage as the highest virtue.

227

It is clear what the intention of our author is. Apparently, Christian philosophy is for him Thomist scholasticism. Thomas accepted the Aristotelian views of ethics and the state as the natural substrate for the supernatural Christian ethics and church doctrine, and in his natural ethics he adopted the late-Aristotelian conception of general justice as *justitia legalis*. But once again it is a sign of lack of insight into the central significance of the religious ground-motives in Western philosophy when Trude foists upon Aristotle the typical scholastic distinction between "a natural and a supernatural" virtue, similarly to the way we saw him assume, in another context, that the Kantian distinction between "nature" and "freedom" is also found already in Aristotle. This merely shows to what extent the lack of a transcendental critique of Western thought, which reveals the diverse religious ground-motives as the ultimate hidden *starting-points*, leads the interpretation of Greek conceptions into scholarly aberrations. But in the thought of Trude this typical scholastic tendency toward accommodation, which itself starts from the synthesis motive of nature and grace, assumes a most questionable form when he attempts to show that the Bible already contains – in the apostle Paul, at Rom. 6:18 and Col. 3:14, and in Eccles. 12:13 – a conception of general justice and its connection with love that is related to the Aristotelian view. By ascribing to the biblical conception of love and justice, in their radical religious sense, an association with the Aristotelian conception of friendship and general justice, the biblical view is utterly denatured and in fact interpreted in terms of the Greek motive of form and matter. When biblical conceptions are viewed in isolation from the radical ground-motive of creation, fall and redemption, one gets lost in a superficial play on words which completely eliminates the radical appeal of the Word-revelation to man's *heart*, the *root* of human existence. In contemporary theology, both in Protestantism and in the Roman Catholic *théologie nouvelle*, the insight that there is a deep gulf between the biblical thought-world of the Old and New Testament and that of Greek philosophy is more and more gaining ground. Interpretations of Scripture in a Platonic or Aristotelian sense, as was done in the spirit of earlier scholasticism, are now emphatically rejected. But one cannot say that this kind of biblical exegesis is definitely a thing of the past – as is evident from the above criticism of Trude's line of reasoning.

It is only by acknowledging Trude's starting-point in scholasticism that we can also understand why he thinks he can find the full contents of justice by combining the late-Aristotelian concept of general or legal justice with the metaphysical idea of justice as developed by Plato in his dialogue concerning the ideal state. But one wonders if he was mindful of the import of such a combination. He remarks that in the *Nicomachean Ethics* Aristotle did realize that his formalistic concept of justice was in need of a supplement and that he therefore in no way rejected the Platonic value hierarchy. Indeed, unlike his rejection of the Platonic doctrine of ideas, Aristotle continued to accept this hierarchy of values, as is clearly evident in his *Politica*, where the household – which he defined as limited to the satisfaction of the lower needs of life (as demanded by the "matter" in human nature) – is seen as being a lower part subordinated to the perfect total community of the state and serviceable to the higher rational-moral needs of man. Only in this way does man acquire a good and beautiful life.

In his exposition Trude openly expresses admiration for the Platonic idea of justice. He writes on pp. 86-87:

> It goes without saying that justice in a Platonic sense, which posits contemplative wisdom – the cognizance of the ideas, i.e., of the spiritual realities – as the highest value, to which feeling, and then spirit, are subordinated – that this justice in its application to human society in the form of laws makes for a healthy and good state, morally speaking. Laws in this sense lay down a qualitative ordering which corresponds to the spiritual ordering of values for the entire universe. Such a philosophical conception of law is opposed not only to a merely utilitarian and liberalistic view of the state, but even more to those anti-moral views of the state that aim at a reversal of all values, an aim that commenced with the Sophists and has continued right up to modern materialism. In that light it is obvious that the late-Aristotelian conception of justice suffered a serious loss when it gave up on the Platonic and the early-Aristotelian conceptual contents of justice, and that this gave the late-Aristotelian conception its most essential negative criterion.

But the claim that the Platonic idea of justice in its application to human society in the form of law would be capable of erecting a morally sound state is a statement that can hardly pass the test of criticism. Does the author really consider the Platonic design of the ideal state that is fully oriented to the idea of justice in a moral sense a wholesome design for the state? The unbridled state absolutism evident in state-regulated sexual communism for the two highest political estates, the elimination of private property and of a private marital and family life for these estates, the assignment to the state of children born from their sexual relationships, including a detailed system of education regulating the life of these children, and the total stripping of all political rights from the lower third estate of peasants and artisans – do they indeed, according to Trude, meet the requirement of a morally sound order for the state? Yet all this derives from the hierarchical value-ordering entailed in the Platonic theory of justice. Aristotle undoubtedly rejected these communistic ideas of Plato, while Plato himself, in his later dialogue on the *Laws*, abandoned these ideas since they did not fit empirical human nature with its imperfections. But that Plato's subsequent project of the "State with Laws" as well as Aristotle's own project for the best form of government essentially does not, on principle, know a single limitation of the jural power of the polis is immediately clear once attention is paid to these two views. That Trude does not realize that here we find the original defect in the Platonic and Aristotelian conception of justice is amply seen from the praise contained in his statement quoted above.

Trude does acknowledge that "Aristotle appears to see in the state not only the highest of all human communities, [but] he also allows the state to penetrate deep into the sphere of private individuals" (p. 69). Trude also concedes that this occurs in a way totally different from what happens in modern states:

> In contrast to liberalism's restriction of the state to what is most necessary in terms of utilitarian considerations and public actions, leaving the private sphere of the individual intact, and furthermore, *in total contrast to the emphasis in practice on individual rights, which is so characteristic of the modern state* (emph. added), the best Aristotelian state not only embraces the ethical perfection of the individual but also takes this as its primary goal, which is then seen as the state's primary duty.

Unfortunately, Trude fails to follow up this remark with any principled critique of Aristotle's concept of justice and his idea of the state. To the contrary, he emphatically points out that for Aristotle the final moral goal is not the *state*, as it is for Hegel, but

230

the *good and blissful life of the individual*. This is certainly correct, but it does not take away from the fact that Aristotle views the state as the *perfect* community in which all other communities can have the role of service components only – all parts of lower value. The classical Greek view of the different societal spheres does not look at their inner nature, their internal structural principle that is anchored in the divine order of creation, but at the goal they serve, as defined by Greek thought. Therefore their mutual relations are conceived in terms of the means-end scheme in which a value hierarchy is assumed that clashes fundamentally with the creation order. Hence it fails to acknowledge any limits to the competence of the state, grounded in the inner nature and structural principles of the spheres of society. Thomas's acceptance of the Aristotelian view of the state as the "perfect community" therefore entailed a fundamental denaturing of the biblical ground-motive of creation, fall and redemption, even though he naturally attempted, in line with scholasticism, to *accommodate* the Greek form-matter motive to the biblical idea of creation.

It always needs to be remembered that Thomism's philosophy of law and politics managed to restrict the absolutistic consequences of the Platonic and Aristotelian concept of justice by withdrawing the "supernatural" domain of society from the competence of the state and by subordinating the State to the Church. Thus, parents could be granted the unassailable natural right to educate their own children, because education transcends the order of the state as the perfect natural community: education falls within the supernatural sphere, where children are to be brought up to become good sons and daughters of the Church. But this delimitation of the jural power of the state was certainly not contained in the Greek concept of justice in its orientation to the form motive of the culture religion.

8.   Justice and social ethics

According to Trude the social-ethical side of the late-Aristotelian concept of general justice is of special significance for our time. He believes that precisely this viewpoint, namely that one should obey the laws of society for the sake of the general good, has to a large extent become something foreign and that the blame for this undoubtedly lies for the most part with the laws and practices of the modern state.

And indeed, particularly in the intermediate period of the two world wars, a flood of literature has emerged about the crisis of the state and its legislation, emphasizing in particular the fact that the private interests of well-organized groups have increasingly managed to exert their influence on administration and legislation. This has undermined people's sense of the state as an institution for the common good and has caused a diminishing respect for the law.

However, when these phenomena of crisis are pointed out, one should avoid generalizing and exaggerating them. In the days of Plato and Aristotle the Greek *polis* found itself in a state of inner decay, and complaints about the dominance of group interests and the erosion of respect for the law were probably better founded then, than in contemporary Western democracies. But the conceptions of justice and state propagated by these Greek thinkers certainly cannot be recommended as remedies, as Trude wishes to do. Moreover, their accepted value hierarchy cannot be reconciled with an intrinsically biblical view of temporal society.

A strange impression is also left by the application of the Aristotelian conception of general justice to the trials of war criminals since 1945. If, so Trude argues, a person for the sake of the state community obeyed laws promulgated with an evil or criminal purpose, under the mistaken but exculpatory supposition that they were good, then such a person not only did not commit a crime but even acted in a virtuous way insofar as he practised general justice. He remarks:

> Consequently, this distinction flowing from the Aristotelian concept of general justice is throughout justified and fruitful and is of notable significance and great topical interest for reversing the values that state-forms and state-laws aim toward, particularly also for the ethical and jural treatment of the post-war trials regarding the problems that emerged, for example, in connection with the wartime behavior of soldiers between 1939 and 1945 (p. 88, n. 409).

This is a highly questionable line of reasoning. It could excuse multiple war crimes and even make them praiseworthy insofar as they were committed by convinced national socialist soldiers for whom the command of the Führer after all was always good and unassailable and in accordance with the well-being of the Third Reich! That views like these are still defended in all seriousness at a German university is undoubtedly remarkable and does not contribute to our peace of mind.

9. General justice and particular justice

In his analysis of the late-Aristotelian concept of particular justice as developed in the *Nicomachean Ethics* and in Book III of the *Politica*, Trude proceeds from the assumption that the general foundation of this justice remained the same as in the *Magna Moralia*. It is therefore also here a virtue *alongside* other virtues, representing the mean between too much and too little in the sensory drive (*pathos*) for gain. Thanks to its "specific standard" of obligatory relatedness to the other, and thanks to its criterion of equality, Trude considers particular justice to be the "juridical virtue" *par excellence* because its object is the juridical, which is distinguished from other similar norms thanks to these specific hall-marks. However, just as in the *Magna Moralia*, the criterion "relatedness to the other" then has a meaning that is different in principle from general justice as defined in the *Nicomachean Ethics*. Whereas it still implies, according to Trude, as we have seen, that it is exercised with a view to the whole state community, yet the virtue of particular justice is not *based upon* this communal motif, for it presupposes only a majority of persons who form a necessary condition for the actions in which alone this virtue can be practised. This would in turn imply that particular justice is not restricted to the human relationships *within* the Greek polis, since, for example, it can also express itself in trade relations between a Greek and a Persian. According to Trude this is a common element between particular justice and the Aristotelian concept of *philia* (friendship) which is equally capable of appearing between Greeks and foreigners.[1] I shall presently return to this highly questionable view of the author, but at this juncture I would like to state that Trude's very extensive analysis that follows of the different kinds of particular justice and the related

---

1   *Nicomachean Ethics* 8.1.1155a21.

analysis of the role of equity in the late-Aristotelian conception of law to my mind belongs to the best part of his study and contributes in many respects to a keener and richer understanding of the ripened conception of Aristotle.

In his treatment of distributive justice (*dikaiosune dianemetike*) the author correctly points out that in the *Nicomachean Ethics* and the third book of the *Politica* this justice is no longer applied, as it still was in the *Magna Moralia*, to both public-legal and private-legal relationships, but that it is restricted to the domain of political philosophy and constitutional and administrative law. Aristotle here takes the standard of equality in the sense of a geometric proportionality, which is to say that in the distribution of goods or burdens among citizens the qualitative differences between them ought to be taken into consideration. The value (*axia*) of the goods or burdens assigned to persons should be in proportion to their qualities and circumstances. However, one has to know which differences in personal qualities are to be taken into consideration when applying this norm of proportionality, since not all arbitrary differences (such as in skin color, size and prosperity) are necessarily relevant here.

Aristotle locates the criterion for the relevant differences in the concrete goal that is contemplated when assigning the assets and liabilities in question. The goal is dictated each time by the nature of the case. In the third book of the *Politica* he illustrates this with the example of distributing flutes among flute players. The goal of this distribution – namely, to attain the best possible flute ensemble – suggests the following principles for a just distribution of instruments:

1) Those who have mastered the art of playing the flute obtain the better flutes; and
2) those who play the flute equally well receive equally good flutes.

Trude captures this example in the following juridical formulation: The above-mentioned qualitative relationship between persons forming the first element of the equation (A : B) could be taken as the "facts of the case" and the legal ground in the applicable jural norm for the distribution, whereas the second element of the equation, constituting the relationship between the goods to be assigned (a : b) functions as the *legal effect*. Thus, the system of Aristotelian ethics is not only governed *in its foundation* by teleology (goal-directedness), but the teleological viewpoint also plays an essential role in finding the *contents* of distributive justice. Trude here brings to light a very important element in Aristotle's method of applying standards of equality – one that is often neglected in legal philosophy. Some authors deem the geometrical standard useless because Aristotle does not provide a material criterion for determining which differences between people in the distribution of assets and liabilities are relevant. But the whole teleological foundation of late-Aristotelian ethics indeed implies that our Greek philosopher had no choice but to look for this material criterion in the immanent goal of the social relationship in which the standard of equality is to be applied. Whether or not this teleological method indeed provides any certainty is an entirely different question. Trude is convinced that it does, and in support of this assessment he gives a number of examples from modern criminal and civil German jurisprudence (the latter is not really to the point). According to him, one can already find in the thought of Aristotle the basic idea of modern *Interessenjurisprudenz* (interest jurisprudence). The latter turned against the method of *Begriffsjurisprudenz* (conceptual jurisprudence) which still dominated in the 19th century. In it, the overestimation of abstract juristic logic ignored the social interests which a law aims to serve.

However, the difficulty I see about the teleological method of Aristotle in the application of distributive justice is that it overlooks the fact that the element of *harmonization* of interests inherently belongs to the modal structure of the jural aspect, whereas the social goal aimed at by a public juridical ordering can never as such determine the material *manner* in which this goal ought to be pursued within the jural aspect of society. The societal *goal* of a public-legal norm – and only norms such as these fall under distributive justice – is located outside the boundaries of the law and so cannot provide a concrete criterion for the application of the intrinsically *jural* principle of proportionality.

235

Allow me to explain this with reference to the only concrete example Aristotle gives in Book III of his *Politica* regarding the application of his teleological method of distributive justice within the domain of constitutional law, namely in the distribution of offices in the state. As personal criteria for the application of the geometrical yardstick of equality he exclusively mentions the *virtue* and the *competence* of candidates for these offices. If, by analogy, we apply the logic followed in the example of flute playing,[1] then the set aim for Aristotle is the distribution of offices for obtaining the best possible fulfillment of public functions, which in his line of thinking ought to be directed to the well-being of the state as a perfect society. But this public social goal of filling the offices is not a simple matter, particularly not when it concerns the highest state functions, which Aristotle no doubt had in mind first of all. The best possible appointments to these government offices are dependent upon an extremely complicated set of factors, subject to a variety of points of view. In addition, one's appreciation of this goal will also in part depend on the political view of the adjudicator. In a modern democratic state, appointments to the higher administrative offices cannot just take into account the morality and competence of candidates, but also needs to consider the historical weight of the different political and religious convictions of the population.

---

1 Regarding the example of flute playing it should be noted that also here the *goal* – namely of achieving the best flute ensemble – does not really provide a material *jural* criterion for the distribution of the available flutes. After all, this goal does not necessarily imply that the bad flute players too ought to receive an instrument. In the example from the *Magna Moralia* regarding the distribution of taxes according to a citizen's financial capacity no goal at all is specified against which the applicable yardstick could be tested. If it were argued that the goal of raising taxes is to provide the state with the necessary financial means to fulfill its task, and that therefore in the distribution of burdens only income and property ought to be considered, the conclusion would not be justified in a logical sense. For it is very well possible that distributive justice requires taking into account other factors. One need only think of family size. During the medieval period, knights were exempted from taxes; as long as they were obliged to serve as chevaliers in the army this exemption was justified, because they had to bear particular burdens not applicable to peasants and town-dwellers.

All these criteria, each considered in isolation, can lead to contrasting outcomes because the interests they are to take into account are inevitably diverse. However, the jural principle of proportionality entailed in public justice requires a *jural harmonization* of these interests with the public interest (*salus publica*) according to its qualifying jural aspect. But the material content of this jural principle of proportionality can never be deduced from the ideal goal of the state as it was conceived by Aristotle (namely, the formation of citizens to a good and perfect life). This is so because the latter lacks an intrinsic *jural* meaning. To be sure, *general* or *legal* justice, as the perfect virtue focused upon the state community, does require, according to the Greek thinker, the rule of law in the state to which also distributive justice ought to be serviceable when distributing public offices. But this law itself is in turn conceived as that system of laws that has as its aim the perfection of the citizens, and so it refers once again to Aristotle's conception of the goal of the state. And the latter turned out to lack any jural meaning. Why? If for no other reason than that it was oriented to an intrinsically totalitarian idea of the state which denied both the inner structural principle of the state and the intrinsic modal structure of the jural aspect.

Distributive justice, which certainly is of fundamental significance for public-legal relationships within the state as an organized community, can therefore never derive its intrinsic *jural* criteria from a teleological viewpoint. And the fact that the Aristotelian conception of justice had to appeal to such an a-juridical teleological point of view for providing material content only proves that Aristotle's idea of law – the nature of his jural conception – misconstrued the intrinsic nature of the jural aspect. The same remark is applicable to commutative or exchange justice which, according to the late-Aristotelian conception, is a second kind of particular *justitia* sharply to be distinguished from distributive justice. The standard of equality of this second kind of justice consists of an arithmetical relationship which exclusively takes into account the proportional value of the goods to be allotted or the losses to be assigned, while the parties concerned are treated as perfectly equal. Trude holds that also here the teleological method must be used in order to decide to which cases this standard of equality ought to be applied. He holds, moreover, that Aristotle applies commutative justice to the entire sphere of private-legal interaction between citizens, both contractual and the private-legal relations originating in crimes. But also here an impartial teleological yardstick is needed for determining in which cases the differences in qualities of those concerned can be disregarded. For example, a person's age or degree of accountability must definitely be considered in establishing whether or not that person is of legal capacity. Trude thinks that only the goal of the legal rule under consideration can supply a criterion. But this teleological criterion in the context of civil law becomes even more problematic, if possible, in the case of public law, since the former, according to its nature as *jus commune*, cannot bind the legal rule to a specific extra-legal goal. In the domain of civil law Trude has not found a single explicit point of contact for his teleological conception in Aristotle's writings.

The examples mentioned by the Greek thinker in the *Nicomachean Ethics* regarding the applicability of commutative justice concern contracts such as a sale, lease, pledge, and so on, as well as delicts against a specific person. But it is known that Aristotle had many reservations about trade and the money market because he considered them unnatural methods of enrichment and because they were not directed in the first place towards providing reciprocal and equal services to the community. Therefore he also rejected the charging of interest on the familiar ground (also accepted by the medieval Church) that money cannot generate money. But the deepest ground for his lack of appreciating trade, as well as industrial and manual work, is found in his view that the free Greek citizen should above all dedicate himself to the well-being of the state. Both the pursuit of wealth and working for wages impede men in their dedication to this most noble task. According to his conservative view, the private economy of the citizen ought to consist in running a farm, where he is master of the household and organizes the labor of his slaves economically. From this source the citizen is to generate enough wealth to allow for leisure time to be devoted to the affairs of the state. Once again the classical Greek order of values regarding the spheres of life comes to expression here, manifesting itself in the conception of the state as the "perfect community," while even child-rearing is made totally subservient to the formation of good citizens of the state.

From this it is clear that Aristotle's view of "exchange justice," insofar as it related to commercial activity, was directed against trade as an independent source of income. The arithmetical yardstick that he applied here indeed aimed at maintaining the monetary equivalence of performance and counter-performance while condemning commercial profit. It is true that he did not consider it a breach of commutative justice if the difference in economic value of a transaction of sale or loan was voluntarily accepted by the "injured" party. The basis for this was the maxim *"volenti non fit iniuria"* (to a willing person no wrong is done).[1] But this does not detract at all from his ethical condemnation of taking profit in commercial transactions as such. His whole conception of exchange justice in voluntary economic interaction was indeed founded in the teleological system of his ethics – though not as construed by Trude, namely that for Aristotle the answer to the question of when the arithmetical standard of equality must be applied can be inferred from the specific goal of private-legal norms and social relationships. Apparently Trude has not perceived the real background of Aristotle's view of exchange justice in voluntary economic interaction. If he had, he would not have called this conception useful for modern legal relationships on the condition that they be applied within the framework of a teleological interpretation of the law.

In this context I return to the earlier mentioned opinion of Trude, namely that according to Aristotle exchange justice is not limited to human relationships within the Greek *polis* but also applies to trade between Greeks and barbarians (for example Persians). The author does not provide any reference for his opinion, and given the background of the teleological ethical system of our Greek thinker it seems to me highly improbable that Aristotle indeed could have meant this. After all, in Aristotle particular justice can never reach further than general justice as the *perfect total virtue* which encompasses all particular virtues. And we have seen that the latter is explicitly related to

1 *Nicomachean Ethics* V.9.1136b14 [see also V.6.1134b11].

the polis as the perfect community. It is therefore the perfect civic virtue which can apply only to those social relationships that can be considered parts of the Greek state as a whole. What is not found anywhere in the writings of Aristotle is civil private law in the sense of the Roman *ius gentium* which recognized as subjects with equal rights all free men regardless of their nationality and apart from Roman citizenship. Not until the Stoics did a concept arise of a natural law that could be used by the classical Roman jurists as the philosophical foundation of this *ius gentium*.

It is therefore much more likely that Aristotle, when applying his concept of commutative justice to economic trade, only thought about transactions between Greek citizens of the polis. Trude himself notes this repeatedly, apparently unaware that it is in conflict with his earlier supposition. It is only in respect of relationships of friendship that Aristotle in his later ethics broke through the boundaries of the polis. But this *philia* (love) actually does not fit within the framework of Aristotle's general justice as perfect *aretē* (virtue) embracing all particular virtues. In Book I of the *Politica*, where Aristotle discusses the friendship between husband and wife and father and children, he still completely treats it as a virtue that can only achieve its completion and perfection within the communal relationships among citizens of the state. It is not impossible that he arrived at the more expanded conception later, on the basis of experiences with friendship relations between Greeks and barbarians, similar to the way he broke with the prejudice that all barbarians are naturally doomed to slavery and all Greeks are naturally destined to rule.

10. Commutative and retributive justice

It remains difficult to make out in the *Nicomachean Ethics* what the relationship is between exchange justice (commutative justice) and retributive justice. Apparently Trude did not notice this difficulty. It is occasioned by the fact that retribution here acquires a much broader domain of application than in the *Magna Moralia*, where it was still restricted to penal law. In the *Nicomachean Ethics* its domain is extended to include private law and the entire sphere of public law; for, as Aristotle remarks, "it is retribution according to proportionality that provides the state with endurance."[1]

The difficulty now is that this gives rise to a certain contradiction with what Aristotle remarked about exchange justice which, together with distributive justice, the *Nicomachean Ethics* distinguishes on principle from retributive justice. For while in the case of contracts of purchase, exchange or lease, exchange justice appears to entail the application of an *arithmetical* standard of equality which here cannot be anything but the equivalence between the purchased or leased goods and the money payment, Aristotle now argues that retributive justice is to be applied here, operating according to a *geometrical* standard. As example he chooses the instance already mentioned in the *Magna Moralia* about the exchange of shoes for a house – and links this to an explanation of the function of money in trade. Trude calls the latter of no importance, thus all the more showing that he fails to notice the difficulty in question. In truth, in his treatment of retributive justice Aristotle maintains the conception of geometrical equality as developed in the *Magna Moralia*, which differs in principle from the late-Aristotelian conception developed in the exposition of distributive justice, which coincides at least in part with the arithmetical equality of exchange justice. For in the retributive value determination of the number of shoes that equal the value of a house, all differences in personal qualities between the parties involved in the exchange transaction are eliminated; the value relationship remains exclusively focused on the goods exchanged. In the *Magna Moralia* this did not create a problem, for there the distinction between exchange justice and distributive justice turned out to be absent. After the introduction of this distinction, however, it is incomprehensible how there can be any fundamental difference between the arithmetical justice which Aristotle reserves for the exchange justice in its application to sale and lease, and the geometrical equality which he assumes in the application of retributive justice to an exchange contract. Trude attempts to camouflage this anomaly by assuming that the latter instance, too, calls for an equation with four terms,

---

1   *Nicomachean Ethics*, V.5.1132b33.

just as in distributive justice. He writes: "The manner in which the values of the goods to be exchanged relate to each other is the way the persons relate to each other who are involved in respect of the goods and money payments resulting from the exchange" (p. 103). But in reality the personal differences between the contracting parties are not relevant. In Aristotle's line of reasoning the only relevant difference in their performances exclusively concerns the exchanged *goods*.

Naturally, every contract gives rise to a legal relationship between parties, involving mutual obligations that are distinct in a *legal* sense. But one cannot allow these obligations to function as the personal correlate of the value relationship of the exchanged goods without depriving the arithmetical equality standard of exchange justice of any meaning that is distinct from the geometrical proportionality of retribution. Also in cases of "compensation for loss" in private law, mentioned by Trude as one of the examples of a purely arithmetical standard of equality, a value relationship has to be established between the inflicted loss and the monetary compensation to be paid, a relationship which of course again corresponds with the relationship between the right of the person suffering damage and the obligation of the person causing the damage.

But in what respect then does retributive justice still differ from exchange justice, hence geometrical from arithmetical equality? Only in the case of contractual interaction where the object both of performance and counter-performance (for example, in the case of holding property in deposit) is exactly identical, with money playing no role, would it still be possible to speak of an arithmetical equality, insofar as one at least waives the possibility of a negotiated safe-keeping fee and the duty of the custodian to compensate in the case of loss or damage to the goods through fault. However, the examples mentioned by Aristotle regarding the application of this standard provide not a single point of contact for this narrow interpretation.

This whole problem is ultimately generated by the fact that the Aristotelian concepts of arithmetical and geometrical equality are here not understood in a *jural* sense, since they merely focus on the *numerical quantity* and *economic value* of goods. We have demonstrated above that this lack of jural meaning cannot be made good through a teleological method of interpreting law, with the aid of which one could determine in which cases the arithmetical equality standard of exchange justice is to be applied and in which cases the geometrical standard of retributive justice or distributive justice has to be used.

11. Particular justice as the jural virtue par excellence

With this we automatically arrive at that part of Trude's exposition where he attempts to show that *particular justice* in its late-Aristotelian sense is the "specific jural virtue" which has to derive its content predominantly from a teleological method of jurisprudence (pp. 104 ff.). He writes:

> With his particular justice [Aristotle] created a concept of justice of which the characteristic feature – namely, to carry out the demand to relate to the other (*pros heteron, ad alterum*) – corresponds with the concept of law as mostly understood today.... In this sense Aristotle's particular justice may be viewed as the elaboration of the specific virtue of law, since for the equality of comparison the law requires a relationship between at least two people, a characteristic of law without which law would be inconceivable. Aristotle must be given the credit for working out this conceptual element of law and justice in its fundamental significance.

This statement is further explained by the (no doubt important) remark that the late-Aristotelian conception of particular justice acquired a considerable expansion in meaning as compared to what is found in the *Magna Moralia*. Whereas in the *Magna Moralia* particular justice, as the virtue regulating the desire for gain, was still restricted to the personal striving of the acting person, in the late-Aristotelian conception it is also related to the allocation to others of legal goods and liabilities by a third party. That is to say, it is also related to the task of judges and administrative organs. The result is an expansion also of the conception of virtue as observing the just mean between too much and too little in emotional desires, since it is now not only related to inner psychical drives but also to the action itself. (Precisely this feature was taken by Von Arnim as an important clue that the *Magna Moralia* predates the *Nicomachean Ethics*.) Trude thinks this expansion made particular justice applicable over the entire domain of law, while at the same time grasping law in its essential conceptual hallmarks.

What are we to make of this explanation? Earlier we argued that the standard of equality considered by Aristotle to be characteristic of particular justice does not in itself contain a jural meaning. That this is also not the case with the "hallmark" of relatedness to one's fellow man must be clear if one bears in mind that this applies to all societal relationships, irrespective of whether they are observed according to their jural or any other aspect.

Also the feature that "particular justice" relates to the "desire for gain" in the broad sense taken in the *Nicomachean Ethics*, namely in the allocation of gains and losses "in the broadest sense possible," as Trude puts it, cannot delineate the jural aspect from the other modal aspects of human society. The terms "gain" and "benefit" and "loss" in and of themselves are without any precise meaning. In addition to a jural meaning they can equally well be understood in an economic, moral or religious sense. Apparently Trude realizes this, and so he adds a qualification not found in the exposition of Aristotle, namely that it concerns *legal* gains and *legal* losses, an interpretation which of course does not square with his phrase "in the broadest sense possible." His qualification reads: "Whatever can simply appear in one way or another as a legal advantage or a legal disadvantage forms the object of particular justice." With this qualification Trude merely acknowledges that it is not gains and losses that are characteristic of legal relationships, but that it is the other way around: only when this connection is understood in a *jural sense* will it be *legally* relevant. It cannot be stated more clearly that this *hallmark* too does not in itself contribute anything to the meaning of law.

Furthermore, Trude hardly strengthens his case when he goes to some length citing definitions of law found with contemporary German jurists whose views, he believes, agree with the link Aristotle makes between particular justice and the pursuit of advantages and disadvantages. For example, he invokes Lehmann who holds that both public and private law are focused upon re-lationships of power – which purportedly correspond with the Aristotelian concept of "benefit." Lehmann defines private law as "the law of self-interested power relationships" – which Trude again thinks is identical to the Aristotelian element of pursuit of advantages and disadvantages. But power relationships are cer-tainly not to be interpreted as "legal advantages," unless the con-cept of power is meant in a *jural* sense, namely as *jural* power. Yet this is not the case in the thought of Lehmann, whose definition links up with the thought of Savigny, who conceived of power in the historical sense of cultural will-power while assigning to law merely the role of delimiting the private power spheres.[1]

Aristotle did not at all understand his particular justice in a jural sense, since he intended it as a "moral virtue." He tried to distinguish this virtue from the other "moral virtues" by adding to the general concept "moral virtue," as the next higher genus (*genus proximum*), specific features (*differentia specifica*). But this method of concept formation can never serve the purpose of de-lineating the irreducible modal meaning of the jural from the other aspects of society (such as the moral aspect, the social as-pect, the aesthetic or the faith aspect). One cannot, as Aristotle did, conceive law in its irreducible modal peculiarity as *object* of the virtue of particular justice and then proceed to define this ob-ject by assigning specific hallmarks to this virtue. Modern ethics gives the concept "virtue" a *moral* meaning only. If one wants to speak of a specific *jural* virtue, then why not also of a specific *aes*-

---

1 The concept *legal power* is a basic jural concept that differs intrinsically from the concept of power as understood by Savigny, the founder of the Histori-cal School of Law. Cultural power over a person or thing as such does not have any jural sense. It can be exercised without the requirement that such a person disposes over legal power. Such a power cannot be "delineated" by law because it resides outside the jural sphere. Law can only delimit jural competencies and jural duties. Thus it makes no sense to call "cultural power" a *legal advantage*, as Trude intends, because law cannot assign or take away such power. Yet the concept of historical power, which is a-jural in meaning, has played an important role in legal and political theory. Georg Jellinek, for example, viewed legal power as a "jurally delimited" historical power. This led him, in his discussion of the problem regarding the relationship of state and law, to the internally contradictory view that the state, as a sovereign historical power organization, restricts itself through its legal norms.

245

thetic virtue, a specific *logical* virtue, and so on? Actually, in addition to moral virtues Aristotle also speaks of "dianoethic" virtues, which are present when our theoretical function of thought is properly directed and which are classified in higher and lower virtues depending on whether they are directed towards the eternal and necessary truths, or towards actions that result in beautiful art, i.e., towards that which is subject to change owing to our intervention.

This shows that the Greek concept of *aretē* (virtue), as it was understood since Socrates, did not have any modal (i.e., oriented to the fundamental *aspects* or *modes* of our experience) meaning-delimitation. How could it then serve as a basis for the definition of the jural according to its irreducible modal nature? The method of searching for the *genus proximum* and the *differentia specifica* can never lead to satisfactory results when defining a modal aspect, since it presupposes that that which has to be defined can be reduced to a specimen of a more encompassing genus. The *jural* aspect of our temporal experiential horizon is not a *species* of a more encompassing genus but an *ultimate* and therefore *irreducible* mode functioning alongside the other modal aspects[1] in an unbreakable coherence, a coherence that comes to expression in a distinctive way within the modal structure of each one of them.

Thus, within the jural aspect as well, this coherence with the other modal aspects comes to light in that it contains "analogies." It contains, on the one hand, moments that refer back to all aspects arranged as earlier aspects and, on the other, moments that point forward to all the later aspects. This explains why, within the structure of the jural aspect, one also finds numerical and spatial analogies, such as are found in the criteria for equality (arithmetical and geometrical) introduced by Aristotle. Yet none of these so-called "analogical" or "corresponding" moments can be viewed as "specific features" of the jural, because they are also found in the non-jural experiential aspects.[2] In the jural aspect they can only assume a *jural* meaning, for here they are *qualified* or *determined* in their modal meaning by the irreduc-

---

1 Such as the moral, the aesthetic, the economic, the lingual, the social, the cultural-historical, the logical and the pre-logical aspects.
2 Think, for example, of economic, aesthetic or lingual proportionality.

ible nucleus of this aspect. If they are understood *apart from* this nucleus, they become multivocal – that is, they become *indeterminate* in their meaning. This is clearly evident, for instance, in the way Aristotle employs the concepts equality and proportionality. In his conception of particular justice they are sometimes used in an original arithmetical sense (the number of things that can be the object of human actions), and sometimes they are used in the sense of an economic value relationship between these things, and finally (as in the case of distributive justice) in the sense of a relation between ethical and economic values. And this in turn explains why these concepts by themselves do not contain *jural* standards of proportionality and why they cannot simply be used in a juridical sense.

If the irreducible meaning of the jural aspect can only be comprehended in the unbreakable coherence with *all* other modes of experience, then a satisfactory theoretical analysis of the structure of this aspect does not allow that just one or two analogical moments (such as equality or proportionality) are abstracted from its structure, for *all* analogies must be shown in their mutual unbreakable coherence and order of arrangement. This includes the moment of a harmonization of interests as well as the harmonization of original spheres of jural power, to which I have referred above. This moment, too, when taken by itself, is strictly multivocal, since it refers back to the aesthetic aspect whose nucleus is beautiful harmony. No, if it is to attain a genuinely jural meaning it has to be understood in terms of the core meaning of the jural aspect.

I am still of the opinion that the jural nucleus is found in the *retributive way* of harmonizing interests. We have seen how this core moment of all law was intuitively grasped by the pre-Socratic concept of natural law in close connection with the moment of delimiting competence or legal power. To this we can add that it is also found in ancient Egyptian, Indian and Chinese conceptions of law. The fact that Aristotle accepted it merely as a specimen of particular justice demonstrates that in his thought retribution had lost its basic core meaning, partly as the result of a method of concept formation which simply cannot be applied to the irreducible aspects of our experience. *It is therefore all the more remarkable that the moment of retribution nonetheless surfaced so*

247

strongly in the late-Aristotelian view of justice which for all practical purposes was applied to all legal relationships.

When commutative justice and distributive justice are not conceived as qualified by the jural nucleus of a *retributive* harmonization of interests, they turn into multivocal, undefined concepts which no longer contain any legal standards.

The same lack of delineation is also present in Aristotle's general concept of moral virtue as a constant inclination of man's will, acquired through exercise and habit (*ethos*), which subjects the emotional desires to the rule of reason by maintaining the proper mean between too much and too little in these desires and among those actions that are directed towards the satisfaction of these desires. In vain do we look in this definition for the irreducible nucleus that demarcates the moral aspect from the other aspects. The Aristotelian concept of ethical virtue is completely governed by the Greek form-matter motive.

In his dialogue *Philebus* Plato tried to capture in a concept the flowing stream of sensory desires and pleasurable feelings bound to the material body that might be brought into a dialectical connection with the principle of delimiting form. To that end he proceeded from the Pythagorean conception of matter and form as the *apeiron* (the unlimited) and the *peras* (the measure or limit). Everything still taken up in flowing sensory life, not yet delimited by a rational form, allowed for degrees of more or less, stronger or weaker. It was the form principle, the *peras*, which delimited this process. In connecting the flowing matter principle with the delimiting form principle, the process of sensory desires was understood as a process of becoming directed towards the goal of reaching an ontic form (*genesis eis ousian*). This conception served Aristotle as a point of departure for his concept of virtue – albeit worked out in an independent way.

Observing the proper mean in pursuing the sensory desires limits the latter to a rational form, a measure, and aims at reaching man's highest good: bliss (*eudaimonia*). The principle of equality of particular justice is also seen as a mean (*mesotes*) between what is too much and too little.

To understand this whole conception is only possible against the religious backdrop of the Greek form-matter motive explained earlier. The Greek form principle, as it emerged from the

248

culture religion of the Olympic gods, was a *cultural* principle with a strong aesthetic tenor, rather than a *moral* principle. It rested on a deification of the cultural aspect of our experiential horizon, just as the matter motive of the older religion of life originated from a deification of the aspect of organic life. The cultural mode of giving form to a material distinguishes itself on principle from animal formations through the control or power over the material, such that the form-giving proceeds according to a free and variable rational design and not according to a rigid instinctive and invariable pattern.

The ethical rule of reason over sensory desires was likewise conceived as a free, controlled shaping of matter that lacked all limits. The notion of a virtue thus formed had a cultural rather than a *moral* meaning. This also explains why Socrates could speak of the virtue (*aretē*) of a sofa-bed if it was produced in a "virtuous" way by a competent craftsman. It explains as well why Aristotle established such a close connection between his ethics and the cultural education task of the state.

The fact that the late-Aristotelian doctrine of virtues was taken over by Thomist scholasticism in its natural ethics as a substructure for its "supernatural" ethics of grace of the Christian virtues, once again demonstrates the deviation from the biblical ground-motive of creation, fall and redemption.

12. The role of equity in particular justice

Trude concludes his analysis of the various forms of particular justice in the late-Aristotelian ethics with an investigation of the role of equity.

Just as the principle of *aequitas* first came into force in Rome in *praetorian* law, as a correction to the rigidity of primitive Roman folk-law, so the Greek city-states saw the rise of equity law in the jurisprudence of the praetor, a process that was part of the later, differentiated legal development. The exaggeration of the equity principle at the expense of statutory stipulations gave rise to a sharp controversy about the value of this principle. While the supporters of the equity principle praised it as better law, bringing to expression *true* justice as compared to the rigid stipulations of statutory law, many Greek thinkers, among them Plato, rejected it on the ground of deeming it a violation of legal stipulations – an inconsistency that could only be detrimental to true justice.

Now then, Trude shows how Aristotle, in his earlier period, accepted the Platonic conception of equity as a restriction of law also in its negative assessment. But Aristotle arrived at a positive evaluation already in the *Magna Moralia*. The Platonic definition of *aequitas*, provided in the *Topica* as an infringement of a right, is now only applied to *statutory law* – which is sharply distinguished from *natural law*. This infringement is accepted as a requirement of justice when the legislator, through the general formulation of the stipulation, did not foresee all particular cases in which the legal rule would have led to unjust consequences. In such an instance equity requires that the person who formally would have derived a right from law, surrenders it by choosing the solution which the legislator would have chosen had he regulated this specific case. In the meantime equity here remains a mere *guideline for the party concerned* in his relation to others.

In the *Nicomachean Ethics* equity also becomes a guideline for jurisprudence and the decisions of administrative organs. This late-Aristotelian conception of equity is based on a view about the inevitable imperfection of human standards of justice and law. This imperfection is a result of the fact that human nature is composed of form and matter, and although the ethical norms for action in themselves are rooted in the rational-ethical ontic form of human nature, in their realization they participate in the matter principle, the principle of moveable being. It is only on account of this subjection to the principle of eternal flow that Aristotle says that in the practical domain of ethics, the domain of action and efficiency, nothing is firm and immovable.[1] And he also relates this to the variability of human conceptions of justice, a trait that had induced some people to draw the conclusion that ethical standards rest only on statutory law and custom and are not grounded in nature.

To my mind Trude is quite correct in pointing out, *contra* Salomon, that Aristotle held on to natural law and that he did not defend relativistic or subjectivistic ethics, but ethics based upon objective and absolute principles.

1 *Nicomachean Ethics* II.2.1104a31

To be sure, in contrast to his earlier Platonic conception defended in the *Proteptikos*, the late Aristotle did oppose the view of ethics as an *a priori* exact science. Precisely through its connection with the material side of human nature the scientific statements of ethics lack the certainty which Aristotle attributes to an *a priori* science directed towards unchangeable *being*. Ethical norms never possess a universal validity that allows of no exceptions. Rather, the acting agent always has to take into consideration the peculiar circumstances of each case, as is also required in medical practice and navigation.[1]

This applies particularly to justice and to law, which are related to changeable practical life more strongly than the other "virtues." Accordingly the norms of justice can never be captured in a general formula that is just without exception. Equity must therefore be seen as a form of particular justice for improving statutory law in cases where it would lead to unjust consequences.

Equity is a virtue which is directed to the natural true law, and to this extent, according Aristotle, it does not stand in opposition to law as such – as Plato (and also Kant in the modern era) believed. It is opposed only to imperfect law embodied in positive statutory rules.

As early as the *Magna Moralia*, equity was linked to a special cognitive capacity, designated as "well-meaning insight" (*eugnomosunē*). This element of goodwill when deliberating about a judgment still implied a certain dualistic view of the relation between equity and justice, as if the former transcends the demands of justice. In the *Nicomachean Ethics* the last trace of this dualism was gone and equity was acknowledged as a full-blown form of particular justice. In this connection the particular cognitive capacity was designated by the neutral term *gnomē* (or *sungnomē*), which Aristotle explains as the "correct distinction or assessment of what is equitable." This *gnomē* is no longer linked to the goodwill of the one who does the assessing, but is related to the *truth*. The person who assesses according to equity is the one who assesses in terms of truth, i.e., according to true, natural law as it applies in connection with the peculiar circumstances of the case. In this way Aristotle attempted to reconcile the two contrasting opinions mentioned earlier regarding the value of equity.

---

1 *Nicomachean Ethics* II.2.1104a8.

Trude believes he was completely successful in the attempt. He particularly emphasizes the significance of the late-Aristotelian views about equity for juridical methodology. According to him Aristotle, thanks to his discovery of a peculiar cognitive capacity for the law of equity, must be regarded as the founder of juridical logic. Trude believes he finds confirmation of this in the fact that *gnomē* is explicitly related to the acquisition of *truth*. As basic principles for juridical thinking he thinks the following guidelines are found in the thought of the Greek philosopher.

1. One can never be perfectly precise in determining general legal rules.
2. One must proceed from a pre-existing objective idea of law – the idea of natural law as a norm for legislature and executive.
3. One must accept a normative method in juridical thought, whereby the idea of law is related to the world in which we live and whereby that world is subjected to value judgments.

This method is served by two additional means: (i) the teleological direction of the legal norm to the ethical end, namely the *eudaimonia*, the well-being of the individual; and (ii) the careful discrimination between individual cases to which the legal norm has to be applied in order to determine where equity overrides the general rule.

It can be conceded that these methodological guidelines can be inferred from late-Aristotelian ethics. But I am not eager to subscribe to the claim that Aristotle had a solution for a problem that has retained its topical interest to the present day, namely *the place of equity within law*. This problem is intimately connected with the boundaries between law and morality. Equity is a legal principle that unlocks and deepens the meaning of the jural by pointing to the meaning of morality. Thus we can discern in equity a moral anticipation within the structure of the jural aspect.

But its *jural* character cannot be maintained without a connection with the principle of a retributive harmonization of legal interests. Even in a primitive legal order this principle serves as the necessary foundation for its (still rigid) ordering function in society. The principle of the juridical harmonization of interests requires that the application of equity does not prejudice the principle of legal certainty. The same applies to a closely related principle, that of *bona fides* or good faith.

It is essentially on these grounds that the Supreme Court of The Netherlands has steadily refused to accept an appeal to equity or good faith against the explicitly agreed upon terms of a contract, although its verdicts have cited only the formal argument of the wording of the law. For although Art. 1375 of our Civil Code expressly refers to equity and Art. 1374 explicitly states that agreements ought to be executed in good faith, the application of these two principles is not allowed to prejudice the main rule of Art. 1374: "All legitimate agreements have the force of law for those who entered into them." One may be of the opinion that the Supreme Court has given too rigid an interpretation of this principle when compared to the official answer to Question 21 regarding the New Civil Code, which states that in any given case the possibility should be left open for supplementing this rule or setting it aside. But the latter cannot be done without a suitable criterion for upholding the main principle, which puts limits on equity jurisprudence. If judges and administrative organs were to acquire the competence to deviate from the statutory rule whenever a concrete case would lead to unforeseen and unfair consequences, all legal security would be undermined and any genuine jural harmonization of interests would be undone.

The above-mentioned main principle of our contract law contains one of the least contested principles of so-called natural law. Therefore it cannot, on the basis of natural law, be set aside in favor of an equity jurisprudence that oversteps its bounds.

Although Aristotle, as we have seen, emphatically relates his equity principle to natural law, his methodological guideline for the application of this principle does not in any way guarantee a harmonization of this principle with legal certainty. For natural law, on which the equity principle is made to rest, is clearly directed by Aristotle to the individual case. It embodies justice *in casu*; it does not embody the [general] ordering principle embodied in the maxim *"pacta legitima sunt servanda"*: lawful agreements ought to be complied with.

Thus the late-Aristotelian concept of equity suffers from the same shortcoming as does his view of general and particular justice, namely a lack of an intrinsically jural demarcation of its meaning. Whereas the view developed in the *Magna Moralia* factually restricted the significance of equity to the *moral* sphere by having it serve only as a guideline for the person unfairly benefiting from the application of a legal stipulation, in the *Nicomachean Ethics* the boundaries between law and morality are factually erased by conceiving the elevating moral yardstick for the unfairly benefiting person into a general juridical guideline, also for jurisprudence and administrative practice. Only when a sharp distinction is drawn between the jural and the moral aspects of equity (while fully acknowledging the internal link between the two) will it be possible to bring the long-standing dispute regarding the function of equity in law to a satisfactory solution.

13. Unwritten law, natural law and positive law

Significant, finally, is Trude's investigation into the relation of unwritten law, natural law and positive law in the legal philosophy of the mature Aristotle.

According to Aristotle, law that obtains for human beings falls within the field of ethics, which belongs to "being" that is caught up in motion or change since its form principle can only be realized in conjunction with the matter principle of human life. The starting-point of ethics is justice as *virtue, not* the complex of *legal norms*. Legal norms are discussed only secondarily and incidentally as the object of virtue.

Aristotle also refers to a divine law in the sense of a law among the gods, but it falls outside the field of ethics since it belongs to immutable *being*, i.e., the domain of pure divine form, where being is completely separate from matter.

Because late-Aristotelian ethics considered man-made law only from the primary viewpoint of justice, Trude submits that through this approach the question regarding the *essence* and *ground of validity* of this law once again took center stage. This in turn implied the question regarding the existence of a law that obtains independently of human positive formation, i.e., a so-called natural law.

How did Aristotle envisage the "flexible" character of man-made law in its relatedness to the matter principle of the cosmos? Proceeding from the older investigations of Hirzel,[1] Trude states that Aristotle in the first place could have established this variability empirically in Greek legal conceptions, which were

1   [Cf. Rudolf Hirzel, *Themis, Dike und Verwandte; ein Beitrag zur Geschichte der Rechtsidee bei den Griechen* (Leipzig, 1906).]

based on the concept of unwritten law (*agraphos nomos*). An appeal was made to this unwritten law whenever positive law was seen as unjust or interpreted in very different senses. But as to the different senses of the *agraphos nomos*, Trude repeatedly makes the mistake of identifying it with higher law, at least insofar as a divine law or an understanding of natural law was still maintained and insofar as the concept of "unwritten law" had not already acquired the superficial meaning of the private customs and *mores* obtaining among different nations.

But Trude should have been warned that this interpretation is mistaken by his own explication of the concept of "unwritten law" in the *Rhetorica*, where different conceptions also come to expression, but where a clear distinction is drawn within *agraphos nomos* between customs and *mores* on the one hand and equity on the other. This distinction came to expression in a compelling way among the classical Roman jurists, who subsumed unwritten law together with written law under *ius civile*, which was placed in sharp contrast to *ius naturale* and *ius gentium*. This did not in any way entail a weakening of the concept of "unwritten law," for it rather indicated a sharpening of the concept of "natural law" by liberating it from the multivocality of the Greek term "*agraphos nomos*."

Trude claims, without offering any evidence, that a change can be observed in the Greek conception of law. Originally law was viewed as divine, but in the course of time it changed into natural and finally into mere private *mores* and customs:

> a change which corresponds to a turn from a straightforward divine mediation to a form of conceptual scientific knowledge and which displays an intrinsic connection with it (p. 147).

This modern conception, which is strongly reminiscent of Comte's law of the three stages, does not fit the real unfolding of Greek thought. As long as Greek thought did not assign primacy to the form principle of the Olympic religion of culture, no contrast was entertained between divine and natural law, for in this phase both nature and its order were conceived of as divine. Following Hirzel, Trude himself has to concede that, for example in Anaximenes, the commandment to honour one's parents was still acknowledged as a universally valid divine law or a law of nature. And in a later phase of Greek thought the acceptance of natural law combined well with the reduction of legal stipula-

255

tions, formerly viewed as divine or natural, to the private laws, mores or customs of a people.

The last mentioned change may have been a natural result of the process of disclosure taking place within Greek culture. Through this process the rigid traditions of the undifferentiated clans lost their claim to being an immutable, divine order. But this process cannot be interpreted as a development which, in accordance with the turn to a scientific view of law, marked the next phase in the transition from a natural-law view to a positivistic conception.

Given his position on natural law, Trude of course could not persist in this view. Besides, his historical sketch of the development of Greek conceptions of the *agraphos nomos* refutes his thesis (defended in an earlier context) that Aristotle should be seen as the founder of the authentic idea of natural law.

Following in the footsteps of Hirzel, Trude also mentions other examples of changes in the Greek conception of law. In opposition to the general rules of state-law (*nomos*), which slowly developed into the *tyrant* of Greek democracy, in the course of time the wish arose to take the particular case and the individual human being and make them the starting-point for the making of laws. Aristotle himself brings out the significance of the individual in judicial construction where he says that a person who is without equal in surpassing others in virtue and skill ought not to be subjected to the law that holds for those other people, for such a person is a law unto himself.[1]

Connected with this appreciation for individuality is the question raised by Aristotle whether it is better to be governed by a single person or by laws. Eventually, equity jurisprudence directed against the rigid rule of law contributed to a more dynamic conception of law.

Thus Aristotle everywhere finds an empirical point of contact for his thesis that human law belongs to "mutable being." In the *Nicomachean Ethics* he next distinguishes different "species" of human law. There is first of all the law of the household community (*dikaion oikonomikon*), which subdivides into law between master and slave (*dikaion despotikon*) and law between father and

1 *Politica* III.13.1284a13.

256

son (*dikaion patrikon*). However, this is but "imperfect law" which remains fully subservient to the law of that perfect community the state (*dikaion politikon*), which in turn subdivides into *natural law* (*phusikon dikaion*) and statutory law (*nomikon dikaion*). He defines both natural and statutory law as particular law (*idion dikaion*), which functions within the various states as *positive* or *truly valid law*. However, they are distinguished through the fact that natural law is in force independent of human determination and is based on the law-idea that is immanent in rational human nature. Statutory law, by contrast, has no validity prior to its determination and is relatively arbitrary in content because it is not determined by the law-idea. As examples of such a purely statutory law Aristotle mentions a law that stipulates levels of ransom payments, a law regarding the number and content of sacrifices to be brought to the gods, and so on.

Natural law *qua form* belongs to " immutable being." Its mutability is exclusively found when man applies it to mutable circumstances and cases. Unlike statutory law, natural law is not just directed towards what is useful (*sumpheron*), but towards what is morally good. It can be known clearly (*dēlon*) through its rational character without the need for positive human determination. Statutory law, by contrast, has a conventional character and rests on agreement (*sunthēkē*). Natural law can be taken up in statutory law, but that does not turn it into statutory law in the above-intended sense.

This opposition between a natural law and a purely conventional law reveals an intrinsic dualism in the Aristotelian conception of law. In the final analysis it is rooted in the irreconcilable dualism in the Greek ground-motive of form and matter.

This was not noticed by Trude, for otherwise he would not have praised Aristotle for his sharp distinction between natural law and statutory law. He writes: "The univocal and fundamental opposition of two non-overlapping species of law in legal philosophy is first found in this clearly articulated view, and it is far more fruitful than many modern subdivisions of the legal system" (p. 163). Presumably, he finds in this opposition another argument for his statement that Aristotle should be seen as the founder of genuine natural law.

257

However, so long as one subscribes to the normative meaning of positive legal stipulations – as Trude clearly does – it is internally contradictory to accept a kind of statutory law that rests purely on convention. Not one positive legal norm can maintain its supra-arbitrary character as legal rule if it does not give positive shape to a normative jural principle transcending all human arbitrariness.

If all the jural principles entailed in the modal structure of the jural aspect as to its norm-side, as well as their typical individualization in the structures of human societal spheres, are together designated as *natural law* – which I consider to be confusing, as will be explained below – then it must be remembered that this "natural law" by its very nature is always in need of human form-giving by competent legal organs if it is to become *positive* law.

On the other hand, this form-giving can never arbitrarily *create* a single positive legal norm, because it presupposes a supra-arbitrary jural principle that needs to be given positive form.

Jural principles and positive form-giving belong together; in other words, they are inextricably united in the structure of every genuine jural norm. The opposition between purely conventional legal norms and jural norms of natural law point to a dualistic breaking apart of this essential structure, and it can therefore never become "fruitful" for legal philosophy and legal science. It betrays an internally contradictory absolutization of the two structural elements contained in the nature of every truly positive legal norm. It also explains the unsolvable struggle in the course of centuries between the so-called doctrine of absolute natural law and legal positivism.

It was the very separation already advocated in Aristotle's theory of natural law – namely, between on the one hand natural law and on the other statutory law supposedly completely based on human arbitrariness – that made it relatively easy for modern legal positivists to argue that natural law and positive law are, logically speaking, mutually exclusive.

The examples from modern German law that Trude provides in order to demonstrate the "fruitfulness" of the Aristotelian opposition are capable of convincing the short-sighted only. That the legal stipulation for traffic could prescribe driving on the left-hand side as well as on the right-hand side does not prove that this legal rule rests purely on human arbitrariness. It simply gives (an undoubtedly variable) form to a supra-arbitrary jural principle that participants in traffic may not endanger the safety of others. And the jural principle of legal certainty requires that a choice must then be made whether to keep to the left or to the right. Similarly a statute of limitation undoubtedly has a supra-arbitrary basis in the principle of legal security. But the legal stipulation of the *period* of superannuation is part of the variable form-giving of this principle which always leaves room for differing arrangements in different jurisdictions. The same applies to due process in civil and public law.

What is designated by Aristotle as statutory law, in opposition to natural law, does not receive a supra-arbitrary foundation in his thought. However, his concept of general justice implies that also the "ethically neutral" statutory law, inspired by the ethical motive of the general welfare of the state, ought to be obeyed. With Trude one may conclude that this implication at the same time imposes the ethical norm on the legislator to enact only such laws as are ordered to this ethical end of the state.

Yet we have seen that in the thought of Aristotle the concept of the "general welfare" does not have any delimitation of its meaning as a jural principle. In particular it lacks any delimitation of the competency of the legislator. When Aristotle does distinguish between state law and the law of the household it certainly does not mean that he assigns to the household a legal sphere that is intrinsically independent of state law. The mere fact that he restricts the validity of natural law to the sphere of the state proves that he does not in any sense acknowledge an inviolable natural right for family, marriage or business enterprise.

Deserving of special attention in this context is what Trude remarks about Aristotelian natural law in regard to "human rights." Salomon, in support of his view that the Aristotelian concept *phusikon dikaion* does not denote natural law in the normal sense, had argued that Aristotle simply did not know inviolable human rights (which surely form an essential ingredient of what is taken to be natural law, historically speaking). In my opinion Trude is right in not accepting Salomon's argument as valid. But his rebuttal clearly shows that he did not see through the import of Aristotle's classifying natural law under state law (*politikon dikaion*), a fact from which Salomon derived a second argument for his conception.

For what is the case? The natural-law conception of human rights could only emerge after the disintegration of the classical Greek idea of the state, which viewed the *polis* as the perfect society. The theory of human rights proceeds from an original freedom and equality of all men and assigns to them inviolable human rights *independent of their belonging to a political community.* For that reason theorists began to draw a sharp distinction between natural law and state law. Human rights were irreconcilable with the Aristotelian view that natural law constitutes a mere subdivision of state law. The theory was never able to justify slavery with the Aristotelian argument that *by nature* some men are destined to rule and others to serve.

By contrast, Trude tries to show that the acceptance of natural human rights does fit into the Aristotelian conception of natural law. On page 170 (note 141) he commences by conceding that in the time of Aristotle the problem of human rights could not be posed as sharply as at a much later time – when it "emerged as the historical antithesis to the thesis of absolutism." For that reason alone it is understandable, he writes, that a thinker with such a strong empirical orientation as Aristotle did not talk about human rights, particularly not because he nowhere gave a further exposition of the contents of natural law and confined himself to defining its essence, and above all because he treated natural law, not in terms of a set of objective norms, but only in terms of the ethical question: How must I behave in order to achieve happiness and attain to my natural perfection?

Nonetheless, Trude is of the opinion that Aristotle's concept of natural law – if not in so many words, then in its essence – does include human rights, if for no other reason than that they are implicit in the basic rule of particular justice, namely that every person has to receive what is due to him. To be sure, from this basic rule of the Aristotelian virtue of particular justice Thomas Aquinas derived subjective, natural human rights. But Thomas was acquainted with the Stoic-Christian tradition of natural law and therefore attempted, in the fashion of scholasticism, to ac-

260

commodate the Aristotelian doctrine to it. This was possible because in terms of the scholastic religious ground-motive of nature and grace the state could no longer have the absolute meaning of being the perfect society as it had in the thought of Aristotle. But it is certainly not warranted scientifically to interpret the natural-law conception of Aristotle on the basis of Thomist accommodation.

14. Jural principles and natural law

I want to close this review article with a critical remark about the classical idea of natural law as such, particularly because an attempt has been made (in a dissertation recently defended at the University of Utrecht[1]) to position my conception regarding the relationship between jural principles and the formation of law within the context of natural law. The classical theory of natural law, to which Aristotle's theory belongs in spite of its minimal articulation, is based on a conception that is intrinsically unacceptable from a biblical point of view. Whether inspired by the Greek religious ground-motive of form and matter or by the humanist ground-motive of nature and freedom, it always rests on a reification or absolutization of what has been called the "natural" standards of law and morality. Because of a loss of insight into the religious root-unity of human existence and that of the central love command, the insight was also lost that the meaning of the jural aspect of the temporal world-order can only reveal itself in its unbreakable coherence with all other aspects and in its central relation to the religious root-unity of all temporal aspects.

In other words, classical natural law did not take into account the relativity of all temporal legal principles. Natural law was viewed as an "absolute law" of unchangeable content which at most could assume a flexible element through human appli-

---

1 O. J. L. Albers, *Het Natuurrecht volgens de Wijsbegeerte der Wetsidee; een kritische beschouwing* [Natural law according to the philosophy of the law-idea: a critical appraisal] (Nymegen: Janssen, 1955).

cation.[1] Such an absolutization of jural principles necessarily eliminates their jural *meaning* which is only given in a many-sided coherence between the jural aspect and all the other aspects of our temporal experiential horizon. In particular, what could no longer be understood was the intrinsic meaning-connection between the jural and the cultural-historical norm-principles, which presupposes their mutual irreducibility. In consequence, at the beginning of the 19th century it led to a fruitless struggle between the modes of thought of natural law and historicism. This struggle was fruitless because historicism, in turn, proceeded from an absolutization of the cultural-historical mode of experience, and hence tried to reduce the jural point of view to a modality of the historical.

Supra-arbitrary jural principles by their very nature require a variable human form-giving because in the temporal world-order the jural aspect is founded on the cultural-historical aspect. For that reason they can never be conceived apart from cultural-historical standards. Legal principles themselves exhibit a flexible meaning that is connected to their historical foundation and the gradual meaning disclosure of the jural aspect of experience. The maxim of natural law, *pacta sunt servanda*, (agreements must be complied with), does not have any juridical meaning apart from a more precise specification, which necessarily relativizes its validity. In fact, the absolutization of this rule of natural law would exclude the possibility of a legal order. After all, one can also agree to join in theft, to commit a murder, to disturb the public order, and so on. As soon as the stipulation is added that agreements ought to be *legal* and ought to have a permissible content, a condition is introduced that may assume a different meaning in different times, in accordance with the historical-cultural level of a society. A primitive legal order in general displays a strong formalistic character. In such a legal order

---

1 The view of a "natural law of variable content," introduced by the neo-Kantian legal philosopher Rudolf Stammler, certainly does not belong to the classical tradition of natural law. The term "natural law" can only cause confusion when it is employed in this [variable] sense, because the idea of a variable natural law does not at all acknowledge a law that would, independently of human determination, have real validity by virtue of rational human nature or an immutable "natural order."

legal principles do not yet exhibit a disclosure of their meaning which requires first of all that the cultural-historical principle of the society in question has to be opened up. Such a legal order, if not yet opened up, has no room for acknowledging the legal status of the individual person independent of his belonging to the folk community. The entire legal position of the individual was dependent upon membership in a sib or folk community. Foreigners had no rights, just like the people who were expelled from the folk community.

Here there is also no room for the typical legal principles which are expressed through the process of societal differentiation accompanied by a process of differentiation of legal life. In an undifferentiated society the basic principle of civil law – namely, the freedom and equality of human beings in their private-legal, inter-individual relationships, insofar as they fall within the state's sphere of competence in civil law – has no meaning, owing to the absence of the social foundation of genuine civil private law. For the same reason an undifferentiated society does not have any room for the distinction between on the one hand the principles of civil law regarding loss and compensation that prescribe the legal consequences of a delict or breach of contract in private law, and on the other the principles of public criminal law.

It serves no purpose to subsume all these principles under an absolute natural law. But neither can they be reduced to cultural-historical principles. As jural principles they continue to display a supra-arbitrary nature, despite their relativity, because they are grounded in an encompassing dynamic world-order which is ordered to a disclosure of the coherence of the temporal world-order which owes its origin to divine creation.

Aristotle, who in general was fully alive to the flexibility of human law, which he traced back to the matter principle, nonetheless assigned to his "natural law" an absolute and immutable character because he assumed that it was based on the immutable rational ontic form of human nature, just like the state community to which it was necessarily related. Whoever understands the religious background of the Greek form-matter motive that gave birth to Aristotle's separation of natural law and statutory law, can no longer hold the opinion that this conception of natural law can be taken over by an intrinsically Christian view of law.

V

The Debate about the Concept of Sovereignty[1]

1. Introduction

IN THE EVOLUTION of the Science of Law and Political Science in the second half of the 19th century many dogmas that used to be taken for unassailable truths were cast into the crucible of criticism. Among these dogmas none was of such signal importance as the concept of sovereignty. Particularly since the two world wars the idea that the dogma of sovereignty ought to be consigned to the scrap heap, from both a scientific and a practical point of view, has increasingly taken hold in democratic countries.

Undeniably, the attack has now shifted to the consequences of this dogma for the area of international law, because international relations have more and more become the center of interest. For although the 1948 Charter of the United Nations accepts as a principle the sovereignty of member states (in art. 2, sub 1 and 7), since 1919 a strong trend among scholars of international law had been moving in the opposite direction.[2] The rapid development of international relations today appears to favour this trend – one may consider the Schuman Plan and the decision of the Consultative Council of Europe recommending the

---

1 [Rectorial address, delivered on the occasion of the 70th anniversary of the Free University on 20 Oct. 1950. This oration – considerably enlarged – was published as *De Strijd om het souvereiniteitsbegrip in de moderne rechts- en staatsleer* (The debate about the concept of sovereignty in modern legal and political science) (Amsterdam, 1950). A shortened version appeared in the *Free University Quarterly* 1 (1951): 85–106 and was published in a carefully edited version in *Essays in Legal, Social, and Political Philosophy* (Lewiston, NY, 1997), pp. 101–120. The text here presented is a translation of the enlarged 62-page study. Certain sections partially overlap with the translation of 1997, from which some alternative formulations have also been adopted in the interest of clarity.]

2 Cf. the literature cited in Hermann Heller, *Die Souveränität* (Berlin, 1927), in Francis W. Coker, *Recent Political Thought* (New York, 1934), chap. III, and in Jacques Maritain, "The Concept of Sovereignty," *The American Political Science Review* 44.2 (1950): 343.

formation of a Western European defense force within the context of the Atlantic Pact.

But in constitutional law and general political theory, resistance to this dogma had already reared its head in the second half of the last century. As early as 1888 the German constitutional lawyer Hugo Preuss stated his belief that the elimination of the concept of sovereignty from the dogmas of constitutional law would be but "a small step forward" on the road this discipline had in fact long since taken.[1]

Since then, sociology of law has asserted itself as a participant in the controversy, and several of its prominent exponents have pointed out that the important metamorphosis of the socio-economic structure of Western society has increasingly ousted the state from its central position, which formerly seemed to be the basis of the doctrine of sovereign power.[2]

Finally, one of the more prominent proponents of neo-Scholastic philosophy, Jacques Maritain, has also made his stand against this dogma. In a recent article, entitled "The Concept of Sovereignty," he declared: "The two concepts of sovereignty and absolutism have been forged together on the same anvil. They must be scrapped together."[3]

That in spite of these combined attacks the concept of sovereignty had by no means been eliminated from legal and political science became evident in 1927 in the forcible plea made by Hermann Heller for its complete rehabilitation, a plea that became a fierce indictment of the tendencies aimed at undermining this fundamental concept. Also, the Viennese professor Alfred von Verdross, once an adherent of Kelsen's *Reine Rechtslehre* (pure doctrine of law) and a fierce opponent of the traditional conception of the authoritative sovereign state, accepted this con-

---

1 Hugo Preuss, *Gemeinde, Staat, Reich als Gebietskörperschaften* (Berlin, 1889), p. 135.
2 We shall enter into a more extensive analysis when discussing the variant of the theory of the sovereignty of law as used in the sociology of law.
3 *The American Political Science Review* 44.2 (1950): 343.

ception in his book of 1937 on international law as the necessary foundation of international law.[1]

On the whole it may be said that in the systematic science of law the doctrine of sovereignty still predominates, even though there is a tendency to avoid its extreme consequences in international relations.

Before the tribunal of science one would certainly not be justified in taking a stand in the current debate before considering the many roles the traditional concept of sovereignty has played in legal and political science since the 16th century, and before taking into account the problems that would arise if it were eliminated.

Moreover, it is an undeniable duty of both science and politics to inquire whether the currents that claim to be opposed to the doctrine of sovereignty have indeed disengaged themselves from it, or only want to impose it again on science and practice in some other form. As so often happens in debates about normative concepts, terminological misunderstandings and obscurities can cloud scientific discussion.

Finally, for those of us who in the pursuit of science take their stand on the basis of the fundamental principles of our University, it is of paramount importance to ponder whether they can accept the way the problem is framed in the modern debate about the traditional concept of sovereignty, or whether those who start from the principles of the Reformation must follow essentially different lines of thought.

It does not seem out of place on this 70th anniversary of our University to draw your attention to these fundamental questions. In doing so I shall first of all review the original content and the further evolution of the dogma of sovereignty since the

1 Alfred von Verdross, *Völkerrecht* (Berlin, 1937), pp. 44 ff. In earlier writings
– *Grundlagen und Grundlegung der Völkerrechts*, vol. 29 in Niemeyers *Zeitschrift für internationales Recht* (1921),
– *Die Einheit des rechtlichen Weltbildes auf die Grundlage der Völkerrechtsverfassung* (Tübingen, 1923), and
– *Die Verfassung der Völkerrechtsgemeinschaft* (Vienna, 1926)
Verdross still adhered to the "reine Rechtslehre," albeit with the rejection of its positivistic basis. Cf. also G. A. Walz, *Völkerrecht und Staatliches Recht* (Stuttgart, 1933), pp. 104 ff.

16th century, when it made its entry into legal and political science.

2. The History of the Dogma

2.1 Bodin's concept of sovereignty and the humanistic doctrine of natural law

Five years after the massacre of St. Bartholomew, when Jean Bodin published his famous work *Six livres de la République* in which he based his view of the s t a t e on the concept of sovereignty, this concept was to have a revolutionary impact both on political science and positive law.

Although Bodin made use of the Romanized train of thought of early and late mediaeval legists, and although in the further elaboration of his concept of sovereignty he had an immediate precursor in the counsellor of Emperor Frederick III, Aeneas Silvius, none before him had declared sovereignty to be the essential characteristic of every state.[1] The central idea of this concept of sovereignty was not contained in its definition in the Latin edition of Bodin's book: *summa in cives ac subditos legibusque soluta potestas*, "supreme power over the citizens and subjects which is not bound by state law." Its central idea came in the way it was elaborated. The formula is often misunderstood on account of insufficient study of Bodin's theory in the original source. Bodin by no means maintained that the sovereign head of state was above all laws. He considered the sovereign, in explicit contradiction of Macchiavelli, to be subject to *ius naturale* and *ius divinum*. He considered him, like any of his subjects, to be bound by treaties (contracts), which he, in contrast to the medieval Germanic conception, distinguished sharply from laws as

---

1 See the statements in his short tract *De ortu et autoritate Imperii Romani*; in Melchior Goldast, ed., *Monarchiae Sancti Romani Imperii* (Hanover and Frankfurt, 1611–1614), 2:1558 ff. I have summarized it in my series of articles entitled "In den strijd om een christelijke staatkunde," *Antirevolutionaire Staatkunde* 2 (1926): 63–84 [Eng. trans., *The Struggle for a Christian Politics* (Grand Rapids: Paideia, 2008), pp. 196 f.]

authoritative ordinances. Finally, Bodin considered the sovereign to be bound to the basic principles of the *ius gentium*.[1]

And although in his day there could not yet be a truly positive law of nations since the concept of state had hardly dawned, it was certainly not in accordance with Bodin's doctrine of sovereignty to deny that the state was bound to treaties it had entered into. The only thing that was incompatible with the concept of state, according to him, was subjection to a *higher government*. Bodin did not even mean to elevate the sovereign head of the state above the so-called *lois fondamentales* of absolute monarchy. According to him the French king was subject to these fundamental laws insofar as they inhered in the possession of the crown, notably to the Salic law of succession.[2]

The adage *Princeps legibus solutus est* (the Prince is above the law) was, as we all know, derived from the commentary on the *Lex Julia et Papia* (1.iii.31) by the Roman legist Ulpianus and was in Late Imperial times explained in terms of absolutism. It was commonly accepted in the post-glossarist school and in the rising humanist legal school of Alciat, Budé and Zasius. And, in opposition to the extreme absolutist conception, we find it defended, for example, in the law school of Toulouse during the reign of Francis I. It was Zasius who started the (qualified) ethical conception, as it was afterwards defended by Bodin.[3] John Calvin, too, educated as he was in the humanistic law school, clung to the juridical validity of the principle of Roman law as interpreted by Zasius – as has been convincingly demonstrated by Bohatec in opposition to Beyerhaus.[4] This is true not only of Calvin's youthful work, the Seneca Commentary, but also of his

---

1 [Dooyeweerd warns against the widespread misunderstanding that the *ius gentium* ought to be understood as the starting point of international law, whereas in fact it forms the point of departure of civil law. He writes: "The *ius gentium* was the first realization of a truly *civil law* in the Roman Empire." *Essays in Legal, Social, and Political Philosophy*, (Lewiston, NY: Mellen Press, 1997), p. 93.]

2 The sources related to all these points are given in my series of articles cited in an earlier note [cf. *The Struggle for a Christian Politics*, pp. 200-212.]

3 See the sources listed in Josef Bohatec, *Calvins Lehre von Staat und Kirche mit besonderer Berücksichtigung des Organismusgedankens* (Breslau, 1937), pp. 47 ff.

4 Bohatec, ibid., pp. 36 ff.

later writings, especially his homily on the first book of Samuel, even though he increasingly emphasized the moral duty of the prince to obey his own positive laws. So in this respect Bodin's concept of sovereignty was nothing new.

On the other hand, the way in which Bodin elaborated the concept of "supreme power" was epoch-making. According to him the unity and indivisibility of sovereignty did not allow for any restriction of its mandate, either in power or duty or time. The Emperor of the Holy Roman Empire, whose sovereign power was very much curtailed by the well-known *Wahlkapitulationen*, was therefore – much to the chagrin of the German legists – denied the title of sovereign and consequently that of supreme head of state. The French king was subordinate neither to him nor to the Pope. Mixed forms of government were inexorably rejected as being incompatible with the concept of sovereignty. But above all, sovereignty implied, according to Bodin, the *absolute and sole original competence for the formation of law within the territory of the state*. Legislative power, the first and most important consequence of sovereignty, did not allow for any other original authority for the formation of law.[1] The validity of custom was made absolutely dependent on direct or indirect recognition by statute law, and the same holds, by implication, for all instances of a direct formation of law within the different spheres of life that are present within the territory of the state. The monopoly in the domain of the formation of law, which the Roman Emperors had not claimed prior to absolutist Byzantine times, is here proclaimed to be, as the natural outcome of sovereignty, the essential characteristic of any state whatsoever and identified with the government.

Apparently the later absolutist theory of Roman law in this regard was already propagated via the *Corpus Juris* by the founder

---

1 Compare the parallel Bodin draws between the sovereignty of God and that of the prince: "Now just as this great sovereign God cannot make a god that is his equal, since he is infinite and logically cannot make two infinites, so we can say that the Prince, whom we have presented as the image of God, cannot make a subject equal to himself lest his power come to naught."

of the Glossarist school, Irnerius.[1] But this had been of little significance because it was solely applied to the Emperor of the Holy Roman Empire, whose position of power was quite at odds with this theory. Moreover, it served merely as a fictional construction.

In its general application to the formative process of the absolute national state, however, Bodin's theory managed to become a practical program and dominate the whole concept of positive law for the next few centuries. Science was pressed into the service of politics, which aimed at complete demolition of medieval society.

Upon the collapse of the Carolingian state, society in the Germanic countries had relapsed into a fragmented, undifferentiated condition in which only the hierarchy of the organized church could bring about any unity and coordination. Society presented a secular infrastructure and an ecclesiastical superstructure, whose relation to each other corresponded to the fundamental religious motive of Roman Catholicism (the predominating cultural power down to the 14th century): the *nature-grace motive*.

The Holy Roman Empire and the Church together embraced all of Christendom. The emperor was considered the worldly head and the pope the spiritual head. Until the 14th century, however, the emperor's authority for a good deal rested on that of the Church.

The secular infrastructure presented a motley collection of social corporations which were cut on two patterns: the guild pattern and the pattern of the *mundium* relation, with many crossovers in between.

The guild pattern was an artificial imitation of the ancient primitive Germanic sib, while the *mundium* relation was a somewhat weakened imitation of ancient Germanic absolute domestic power: the *mund*.[2]

---

1 *Summa Codicis* h.t. § 2. See also Siegfried Brie, *Die Lehre vom Gewohnheitsrech*, I (Breslau, 1899), p. 114.

2 The word *mund* (*mundium*), similar to the Roman word *manus*, here refers to the armed hand as symbol of domestic power.

The first pattern evolved in the medieval towns with their craft and merchant guilds, and in the country in the free hamlets and commons. The second took effect, in stronger or weaker forms, in all medieval relations and gradations of authority, i.e., in the higher, medial and lower fiefs (*seigniories*), feudal relations, manors, etc.

Governmental power could be traded: it was a *res in commercio*, not a public office in the service of a *res publica*. The lords could freely dispose of it. Once in the hands of private persons or corporations it became their inviolable right. Hence medieval autonomy always implied the exercise of governmental power on one's own authority, which did not change even with the rise of political estates. In this undifferentiated condition of society, in which the guilds covered all spheres of human life, a genuine state could not evolve. The idea of the *res publica* lived on only in the theory of the legists versed in Roman law and Aristotelian-Thomistic philosophy. It had no roots in contemporary social reality.

Medieval legal life as it appeared before the reception of Roman law and before the emergence of the modern idea of the state displayed fully the features of the society to which it belonged. No point of contact was to be found for the distinction between the differentiated spheres of public law and civil private law in their intrinsic connection to the structure of the state. The attempts by modern historians such as Below and Mitteis to find this distinction in medieval society are not fruitful because they do not take into account the undifferentiated structure of medieval society. Of course this does not mean that a purely private-legal understanding fits medieval relations of authority, because it too ignores their undifferentiated character.

In this state of affairs it is understandable that Bodin, in his concept of sovereignty, claimed exclusive control of the formation of law for the sovereign head of state. Medieval autonomy in the formation of law was indeed incompatible with the concept of a state, for the very reason that it was undifferentiated. In this situation every autonomous domain of law that claimed an original sphere of competence did at the same time claim governmental power of its own, which turned against the idea of the *res publica* as it did not recognize any limitation imposed by the public interest.

But Bodin's doctrine of sovereignty, which pandered to absolute monarchy's policy of bureaucratic centralization, overshot its own objective, namely the monopolization of governmental power. No sooner did society's ongoing process of differentiation enable the state to monopolize all governmental power, than it turned out that at the same time the evolution of law was passing through a process of differentiation of its own, one that could not possibly be confined to the framework of the law-sphere of the state. The doctrine that all positive law finds its legal source in the will of the sovereign law-giver then proved to be a political dogma in the fullest sense of the word, a dogma that was at complete variance both with the modal meaning of the jural aspect and with the rich structural variety of society.

It is to the everlasting credit of the Calvinist jurist Johannes Althusius that at a time which was scientifically quite ripe for this absolutist conception of state-law, he expounded a theory of the structure of society based on the recognition of a divine world-order and the intrinsic character of societal spheres. He pointed out that each societal sphere has its *lex propria* and its own sphere of law which cannot be derived from any other.[1]

It may be true that this "doctrine of symbiosis" lacked the scientific apparatus for a deeper analysis of these societal structures: its legal construal of every form of consociation from some sort of contract followed the uniform schematic methods of natural law and was still not free of the hierarchical-universalist views

---

1 *Politica methodice digesta*, c. 1, 20: "Propriae leges sunt cujusque consociationis peculiares, quibus illa regitur. Atque hae in singulis speciebus consociationis aliae atque diversae sunt, prout natura cujusque postulat" ["Peculiar to each type of association are distinct laws by which each is governed, and these laws differ and diverge from association to association according to the nature of each."] See in connection with the significance of Althusius's theory of symbiosis my study, "De bronnen van het stellig recht in het licht der Wetsidee; een bijdrage tot opklaring van het probleem inzake de verhouding van rechtsbeginsel en positief recht [The sources of positive law in the light of the law-idea; a contribution to clarifying the relationship between jural principle and positive law]," *Antirevolutionaire Staatkunde* (quarterly) 4 (1930): 253-63.

of medieval theories. But in any event it had emancipated itself from the Aristotelian-Scholastic theory which bestowed the autonomous competency for the formation of law only on the so-called *societates perfectae*, namely the state and the church, and which therefore could offer no real defense against Bodin's doctrine of sovereignty in the domain of secular law.[1]

For the time being, however, the future was Bodin's. Science – including legal and political theory – was increasingly affected by modern humanism's philosophy with its religious ground-motive of *nature* and *freedom*: the domination of the realities of nature by science, and the absolute autonomy of the free human personality in the domains of science, morals and religion.

The domination motive gave rise to the science ideal of classic humanism, which proclaimed the methods of mathematics and natural science – the latter having been founded by Galileo and Newton – to be the universal mode of thought according to which a new world-picture was conceived that left no room for structural and intrinsic differences grounded in the order of creation. It was called into existence by the new motive of freedom but if carried through consistently was bound to collide with it. The construal of reality modeled on the concepts of natural science left no room for autonomy and freedom of the human personality.

Even in Bodin's political philosophy this scientific ideal – not yet consolidated in his day – began to make its influence felt. Science was pressed into the service of a cause that wished to erect a state as a rational institution for the purpose of domination, after demolishing the undifferentiated feudal society of the Middle Ages.

This being the objective, Bodin, in his political theory, wanted to develop the means to this end in a rigorously methodical, mathematical way.

Bodin started with a definition: "The state is the lawful governance with sovereign power over several households and what they have in common." He then declared: "We premise this def-

1 In his book *Völkerrecht*, p. 40, Verdross accepts Bodin's concept of sovereignty on the very basis of this scholastic idea of the state.

inition, because in all things one must first discover the principal object and only afterwards the means to attain it. Now, a definition is nothing but the object of the matter under discussion; and if it is not well founded everything that is built on it will collapse soon after."

But his definition was by no means the result of a conscientious inquiry into the inner nature and structure of the state as an organized community[1] and of the other societal spheres of life. It was dictated by a political objective that ignored the divine world-order from which Althusius started, and aimed only at the complete domination of society by the instrument of the state.

Within the framework that had thus been determined by his political objective, Bodin's concept of sovereignty performed the following variety of functions that we must bear in mind in order to assess their relative merit:

1. drawing the boundary lines between the state and all other political and non-political social spheres of life;
2. guaranteeing the unity and indivisibility of the state concept through the unity and indivisibility of sovereign governmental authority;
3. defining the concept of positive law as the certified or implicit will of the sovereign legislator;
4. defining the relation between the different spheres of competence in the formation of law, all of which are to be dependent on the only original competence, i.e., the competence of the sovereign head of state by virtue of his law-making power.

The humanist doctrine of natural law founded by Grotius adopted Bodin's concept of sovereignty. It was also pressed into the service of the policy of demolition and renovation. By means of analyzing society as it presents itself into its elements, i.e., the individuals, and by means of a synthetic construction of the desired new society out of these social elements with the help of a juridical social contract, it wanted to build up a new social and legal order *more geometrico*. In order to make Bodin's concept of sovereignty acceptable to the humanistic ideas of freedom and

1 [Because the Dutch term *verband* does not have a direct equivalent in English, we follow the practice established in *A New Critique* where it is translated as *"organized community."*]

275

autonomy, the humanistic doctrine of natural law construed the state in terms of a social contract between naturally free and equal individuals, usually complemented by a contract of authority and submission (except in the case of Hobbes and Rousseau),[1] and in Pufendorf even by a third contract specifying the form of government. As a *societas inaequalis*, after all, the sovereign state could not be construed as a free and egalitarian association. The concept of sovereignty received its most consistently absolutist elaboration in Hobbes's *Leviathan* and Rousseau's so-called infallible and all-powerful *volonté générale*.

In addition to Bodin's concept of sovereignty, the humanists also accepted his conception of the relation between legislation and custom.[2] Tested against the classical Roman tradition of the *ius naturale et gentium*, they deemed indigenous customary law a *ius iniquum*, a bulwark of feudal society, doomed to collapse.

In the new order, no other law was permitted besides civil law and the *ius publicum*, designed according to the classic Roman model. In other words, only typical *state-law* was permitted. In the footsteps of the Spanish scholars Vitoria and Suarez, Grotius complemented this state-law with a law of nations. However, the most extreme natural-law defenders of the concept of sovereignty, such as Hobbes, Spinoza and Pufendorf, did not accept this law of nations as genuine positive law.

What would soon take place in different countries, namely the process of codification, was aimed at the goal of absorbing all formation of law on the territory of the sovereign state into its legislation. In his famous work *On the Law of War and Peace*, Grotius mentions in passing that in addition to international law and the

1 See however J. P. A. Mekkes, *Proeve eener critische beschouwing van de ontwikkeling der humanistische rechtsstaatstheorien* (Utrecht, 1940), p. 278 where he believes he can discern a camouflaged second *contrat social* in addition to the first one.
2 See Grotius, *De jure belli ac pacis* 2.4.5/2. The same does not apply to the Romanists of the 16th and 17th centuries who stood outside the school of Humanistic natural law, including in particular the great French Calvinistic jurists Hugo Donellus (*Commentarii De iure civili* 1.10.1.6) and Franciscus Duarenus (*Opera, Commentarius in Tit. De legibus*, cap. 11), and in the Netherlands Johannes Voetius (*Commentarius ad Pandectas* 1.3.27 and 28, all of whom acknowledged the termination of a law through customary law (cf. the theory of the classical Roman jurists.

civil law brought into existence by the state there is still another type of law, one that holds for smaller groups (*ius arctius patens*), in which connection he is particularly thinking, among other things, of towns, hamlets and guilds. However, this recognition does not play any role in his system of natural law, for understandable reasons. For Grotius it is natural to assume that the sovereign legislator alone possesses the *original* competence to the formation of law on the territory of the state.[1]

Not until the British philosopher John Locke do natural-law theories, inspired by the humanistic personality ideal, begin to show a reaction to the absolutistic concept of sovereignty.

Factually the purely formal construction of the social contract did not succeed in safeguarding human freedom *vis-à-vis* the sovereign government. For that reason Locke sought a guarantee for the freedom of the individual in his innate human rights, which led to a very limited aim for the state community created by the contract. According to Locke, the individuals give up only so much of their natural freedom as is required for the organized protection of their innate human rights. It boils down to nothing more than that the state has the task to maintain through sanctions the civil private rights of its subjects. This classic liberal idea of the *just state*, denying the state the unilateral competence to intervene at will in socio-economic life, led to a sharp distinction between the state and the autonomous civil society, a distinction that acquired extra weight with the rise of the discipline of economics which declared government legislation subordinate to the economic laws of civil society (the physiocratic and classical schools of economics).[2] On the one hand this development nullified the foundation of the legislator's sovereignty in the domain

---

1 *De iure belli ac pacis* 1.1.14. However, he does say there that the *ius arctius patens* does not derive "*ab ea potestate civili.*" But he immediately adds: "*quamquam ei subditum.*" Thus it does not have any validity independent of the legislator. This shows Gurvitch's misunderstanding that Grotius defended a juridical pluralism in respect of social spheres of law equivalent to state-law. In connection with Gurvitch's Grotius interpretation, see my study "De 'Théorie de l'institution' en de staatsleer van Maurice Hauriou I," *Antirevolutionaire Staatkunde* (quarterly) 14 (1940): 301-347.

2 Look at the statements of the physiocratic teachers Dupont de Nemours and Quesnay regarding the subjection of state-laws to the laws of society, in Gurvitch, *Sociology of Law* (London, 1947), pp. 66-67.

of law formation; on the other hand it also denied the unity and indivisibility of sovereign state authority.

Although Locke in a formal sense proceeded from the concept of sovereignty, his theory regarding the separation of powers had to lead with inner necessity to a disintegration of the concept. As Ernst Klimkowski has shown,[1] the theory of separation found its historical basis in the political history of England, particularly in the Puritan Revolution of Cromwell, and soon acquired its definitive form in the *trias politica* theory of Montesquieu.

In the thought of Locke there is nothing left of governmental sovereignty, although he does retain the view that the legislative power, assigned to King and Parliament, is the first and supreme consequence of sovereignty.[2] The conception of popular sovereignty, current among the legists prior to Bodin and revived by Locke, does not in the least meet the requirements that Bodin has set for the supreme legislative competency of government: *summa in cives ac subditos legibusque soluta potestas*, i.e., the supreme power that stands over citizens and subjects and above the laws.

It is also notable that the legal theory of Leibniz and the school of Wolff, under the influence of Locke, increasingly paid more attention to non-state law, particularly to the economically qualified business law, for which an original sphere of competence is demanded that is not derived from the legislator.[3]

By contrast, the concept of sovereignty acquired a new meaning in the radically democratic turn given to it in Rousseau's the-

1 Ernst W. Klimowski, *Die englische Gewaltenteilungslehre bis zu Montesquieu* (Berlin, 1927).
2 *Two Treatises of Government*, Book II, Ch. XI, p. 299. [This citation could not be traced, but see Bk II, Ch. XVI, § 167.]
3 Notably Leibniz, in his *De tribus juris gradibus* (Mollat ed., pp. 12 ff.). Christian von Nettelbladt (1696-1775), one of the most influential theorists of natural law from the school of Leibniz and Wolff, strongly under the influence of Locke, made a clear distinction between the (economically qualified) society and the state – between the *regimen societatis* (a system of economic interest groups) and the *regimen civitatis*: "Thus a double government arises, the civil or public, and the private, where the latter exists in the social power of autonomous groups that are entirely independent of the power of the state (quoted in Gurvitch, *Sociology of Law*, p. 66).

ory of the *volonté générale*, transforming Bodin's theory regarding governmental sovereignty into absolute and direct popular sovereignty. The apostle of liberty also turned against the contract theory of his predecessors in a desire to give back to each individual the natural freedom, surrendered through the *contrat social*, in the higher form of "inalienable civil rights." Rousseau's definition of legislative sovereignty, concentrated in the *volonté générale* which presumably is directed purely towards the general welfare, acquires absolute juridical power, to such an extent that there is not even room for any legal delegation of law-making to non-political organized communities. On principle, private corporations, because they withdraw the individual from the general welfare, are not acceptable in Rousseau's view of the state.[1]

2.2 The historical interpretation of the concept of sovereignty and the doctrine of state-sovereignty

At the time of the Restoration, the doctrine of sovereignty took quite a new turn, because it now joined up with the principle of legitimacy and the so-called monarchical principle and fundamentally rejected every contract theory as propounded by the doctrine of natural law.[2]

Whereas in the preceding period the problem of sovereign power had been addressed from the viewpoint of natural law, quite detached from the historical past, and whereas only a formulation in accordance with that point of view had been applied to the absolutist or to the more liberal-constitutional tendencies of the time, the Restoration period, with its conservative historical mode of thought, put all the emphasis on the real or imaginary historical rights of the dynasties that had been dethroned by the revolution.

1 The *Social Contract*, Part II, Chapter 3: "It is therefore essential, if the general will is to be able to express itself, that there should be no partial society within the state."

2 Cf. Erich Kaufmann, *Studien zur Staatslehre des monarchischen Prinzips* (diss. Halle; Leipzig, 1906) and Heinrich Otto Meisner, *Die Lehre vom monarchischen Prinzip* (Breslau, 1913).

The pre-revolutionary position of the Bourbons in France served as a model.[1] The preamble to the Charter of Louis XVIII, drafted by Beugnot, provided the standard formula for the monarchical principle of legitimacy[2] that passed into the constitutions of several German states and was proclaimed the unassailable dogmatic starting-point for determining the constitutional status of the princes in art. 57 of the Final Act of the Congress of Vienna. Here we read:

> Because the German Federation, with the exception of the free cities, consists of sovereign monarchs, the basic concept flowing from this must concentrate the total power of the state in the head of state and through a constitution based upon the estates of the country the sovereign can only be limited by the estates in respect of specific rights.

That the sovereignty assigned earlier to the German territorial princes had an indisputable foundation in the German imperial law of the *ancien régime* was silently passed over by the Viennese diplomats. Thus the theory of legitimacy, emerging from the historical mode of thinking, collapsed into the *Begriffsjurisprudenz* which deduced from the pre-revolutionary constitutional status of the French kings a universally valid concept of sovereignty.

In this formulation the sovereignty of the king was not based on the constitution, but inversely the constitution was granted as a charter by the sovereign prince by virtue of his supposed plenitude of power, which was considered to be founded on historical rights. And the required cooperation of the estates or the parlia-

---

1   Meisner, op. cit., pp. 5 ff., nonetheless believes that in Germany the theory of the monarchical principle developed independently of French influence. In Germany it presumably can be traced back to a paper by Karl August von Wangenheim, *Die Ideen der Staatsverfassung* (1815). G. Jellinek, *Allgemeine Staatslehre*, 3rd ed. (1919), p. 471, thinks that it may not be impossible to confirm Meisner's claim through further research, but he points at Beugnot's formulation as the source of these ideas.

2   In this formula it is stated that the King, "after a long absence," responding to the desire of his subjects, grants to his people a constitution by the free exercise of his sovereign power. The King retains his royal status, according to which all the authority of France resides in the person of the King, although the people participate in its exercise. For the French text, see Duguit et Monnier, *Les constitutions et les principales lois publiques de la France depuis 1789*, 2nd ed. (Paris, 1908), pp. 183 ff.

ment for the exercise of legislative power rested on the voluntary self-restriction of sovereign power.[1]

This theory, with or without Christian assumptions about the divine right of kings, received an explicitly counter-revolutionary twist when it turned itself against the idea of the state as a *res publica* and – as in the case of Haller and Maurenbrecher – proclaimed sovereign governmental authority to belong to the private rights of a monarch.[2]

On the one hand the concept of sovereignty[3] – in accordance, incidentally, with Hobbes's and Rousseau's conceptions – was thus tightened up when compared to Bodin's conception which still considered royal sovereignty legally bound to the realm's *lois fondamentales* that were independent of that sovereignty. On the other hand, however, the historical views of the Restoration period struck the first blow to the principle of Bodin's doctrine as regards the monopoly of the sovereign law-giver in the domain of he formation of law. This came about under the influence of an irrationalist and universalist turn in the humanistic freedom motive as elaborated in post-Kantian idealism (notably in Schelling's transcendental idealism).

The humanistic theory of natural law stood under the influence of the *rationalistic* and *individualistic* mode of thought oriented to the classical mathematical science ideal, although since Locke it undoubtedly took into consideration empirical historical data. Even Kant's practical idea of freedom, sharply separated from nature, still showed its orientation to the thought pattern of the science ideal, since he conceived the application of the categorical imperative according to the general scheme of a

1 This was of course totally different from the view defended in the Netherlands by the anti-revolutionaries that in 1813 sovereignty was explicitly assigned to the Prince of Orange in the name of the Dutch people and was accepted by him on condition of a wise constitution. On this view, King William I possessed a sovereign authority that did not derive from the constitution of 1814 but was only *acknowledged* by it. As we know, the "monarchical principle," which was defended among others by Stahl, was rejected by Groen van Prinsterer.

2 Carl Ludwig von Haller, *Restauration der Staats-Wissenschaft*, 2 vols. (Winterthur, 1817), 2:64–69. Cf. Romeo Maurenbrecher, *Die deutschen regierenden Fürsten und die Souveränität* (Frankfurt, 1839), p. 167: "the sovereignty of hereditary monarchy is pure private law of kings (their *property*, *patrimony*)"; quoted in Jellinek, op. cit., pp. 472-473.

3 Neither Hobbes nor Rousseau deemed the sovereign subject to a constitution; cf. Rousseau, *Du contrat social* 2.12.

natural law, without taking into account the individual potential and calling of the human person in his ethics. In Kant's conception of the autonomously free personality the ethical *autos* (the selfhood) of the human person is sought in the universal *nomos* (the moral *law*). Kant also did not arrive at a genuine *idea of community* because he clung to the individualistic mode of thought.

In the post-Kantian freedom idealism the boundary between nature and freedom posited by Kant was no longer acknowledged. The aim was to embrace these two antithetical motives which in a dialectical synthesis created a polar tension within humanism's religious ground-motive by discovering within nature itself a hidden trace of freedom and in freedom a hidden trace of nature. As a substitute for the rationalist mode of thought which attempts to dissolve all individuality into general laws, a new irrationalist thought pattern emerged which, conversely, aims to reduce the law to a dependent reflex of individual talent.

The autonomous freedom of the personality is now understood in such a way that the *nomos* (the law) had to originate from the individual *autos* (the individual talent of the personality). This conception no longer had any room for Kant's bourgeois morality. The irrationalist turn was accompanied by a universalist reaction to the individualism of the preceding period that did not have an eye for individuality.

Society was now viewed as an organic whole with its parts, and the individual personality of the human being was understood as belonging to an equally individual community endowed with a collective personality.

This new conception of the humanistic freedom motive also asserted itself in science. The standard mode of thought borrowed from the natural sciences was ousted everywhere by a new historical mode of thought which aimed at "understanding" the individual in its individual-historical connections instead of being focused on discovering universal laws. Over against the rationalist belief that one could construe political and legal order on an unalterable model which would be in accordance with the doctrine of natural law and be ready-made for all times and all peoples, independent of the historical past, all stress was now laid on the organic character of a culture's historical development that has its true source in the unique national character or

Volksgeist. Thus a new ideal of science arose, which, by making the historical aspect of society absolute, led to an exaggerated historicistic vision of reality. And this historical mode of thought was, of course, bound to turn against the traditional conception of positive law as a product of the sovereign will of the legislator.

The *Historical School of Law* founded by Friedrich Carl von Savigny, who proclaimed law to be a phenomenon of historical evolution that originates organically (i.e., without being intentionally created) from the individual spirit or conviction of a people, totally broke with the former rationalist conception of the relation between statute law and customary law. In his theory the state itself was pushed back into a secondary position. It was merely viewed as a superstructure above the infrastructure of the folk community, as a folk's political organization. Just as every folk community produces its own law from its unique nature as a people, so it also generates its own individual historical form of government. Over against the doctrine of natural law was placed that of folk-law in its historical evolution. That folk-law, the school held, does not spring from the will of the sovereign lawgiver but finds its basis of validity in a people's historical sense of justice. Folk-law at first reveals itself in practice as customary law, but when social relations become more complex it acquires a technical organ in a class of lawyers and a technical form in *Juristenrecht* (a species of "lawyers' law").[1] In relation to this, legislation has only a secondary though not unimportant task. It can only be overruled in times that are unfavorable for the formation of law through the convictions of the people, as happened in the Byzantine era of the Roman Empire.

A codification of law, however, is according to Savigny nothing but an illusion produced by the theory of natural law. As a historical phenomenon, law is constantly developing and therefore cannot be frozen in codes of law. Soon the practice and interpretation of jurists will spin around the legal texts an invisible and continuously changing web that withdraws itself from the control of the legislator.

1   Savigny, *Vom Beruf unserer Zeit für Gesetzgebung und Rechtswissenschaft* (1814).

If this train of thought were consistently carried through, the traditional concept of sovereignty, which since Bodin is focused on the state, would have to be discarded as an unnecessary element in the definition of positive law.

In the meantime, both leaders of the Romanist wing within the Historical School, Savigny and Puchta, had such a one-sided private law orientation that they were unable to make an explicit connection between their view of law and the traditional problem of sovereignty. Furthermore, at least Puchta was so heavily influenced by the classical Roman tradition (which only had an interest in the two legal domains related to the state, namely civil private law and public law) that he could not manage to free himself on principle from the one-sided view that restricted positive law to the state only. It is striking how Puchta once again in his *Gewohnheitsrecht* reconciled his theory of folk-law with this traditional conception. According to him, positive law had two sides that could not be separated without annihilating the concept of law. The first is given in the popular conviction about what law is, and the second is the *realization* and *sanctioning* of this conviction in making it *valid*. This is only possible through an organ of the general will, namely the state. The folk, after all, in a natural sense, as infrastructure of the state, is an *"incertum corpus"* that lacks the ability to act. The state is the sole jural bond of the folk totality. But although it is no maker of law, nevertheless there can be no positive law without the realization of the folk conviction by the state organs of jurisprudence and police.[1]

Since Puchta – in opposition to Savigny – held that genuine law-making can only proceed from the totality, he also rejected the view that autonomy can serve as a formal source of law, as was advocated by the Germanist wing.[2] He denied the possibility of making law through contractual means. Not the will of a party,

1 G. F. Puchta, *Das Gewohnheitsrecht*, 2 vols. (Erlangen, 1828-1837), 1:138-143. About this theory see my extensive analysis contained in "De bronnen van het stellig recht in het licht der Wetsidee I," *Antirevolutionaire Staatkunde* (quarterly) 4 (1930): 50-68.
2 *Gewohnheitsrecht*, 1:155 ff. This does not contradict what Puchta remarks in his *Cursus der Institutionen* (2nd ed., 1853, p. 54) about autonomy; see my "De bronnen van het stellig recht in het licht der Wetsidee II," *Antirevolutionaire Staatkunde* (quarterly) 4 (1930): 224-63, at 245.

but only the communal will of the folk totality as it is organized in the state, is capable of turning the legal conviction of the people into valid law.

And Puchta does not hesitate – once again in opposition to Savigny[1] – to draw negative conclusions for international law. According to him there cannot exist a *law* of nations, but only a *morality* of peoples. This consequence of the concept of sovereignty, which is also drawn by certain theorists of natural law such as Spinoza and Hobbes, was combined in the Hegelian school (Lasson and others) with the theory of *Weltgeschichte* (world history) as *Weltgericht* (world judgment).

In practical terms this once again assumed a sovereignty of the state in respect of the formation of law, albeit that this sovereignty here is twisted in an irrationalistic and universalistic sense. It is not the legislator but the judge who exercises the formal sovereignty in the formation of law. The judge is a technical state organ of the organically developed folk-law of which the science of law as well as law itself are merely particular expressions.[2] At least this is the case in respect of the domains of pri-

---

1 In his *System des heutigen römischen Rechts*, I, § 11, Savigny accepts international law as an essential, though insufficient law. It finds its source of origination in the shared legal consciousness of a spiritual community of peoples, in particular Christian Europe, a community that has its foundation partly in kinship, partly and especially in shared religious convictions. Naturally, what Savigny has in mind here is an unorganized community which in the text below will appear to us as a highly problematic universalistic construct.

2 *Gewohnheitsrecht*, 1:181: "Law acquires its true effect through the courts, which constitute a branch of the constitution; that is to say, through civil society [meant in the sense of the state] and that branch of the power of the state known as the department of justice." With the aid of an argument based on the nature of state power, this view is then once again reconciled with the doctrine of folk-law. Cf. op. cit., p. 182: "Yes, since it [the state] proceeds from the same source from which issues customary law, and since the constitution at once is the final formation of a people, it is impossible for the state to be hostile towards such activities as flow from its own source and from the substantial basis of its union and contents." This is indeed a strong position, since in an earlier context Puchta acknowledges that the authority of the state can limit and even entirely prohibit the practical effect of customary law. According to him, the doubt that arises in cases like these as to the validity of folk-law as customary law rests merely on "external grounds" and not on the "nature" of this law or on the "nature" of state power. Puchta here actually falls back into a natural-law mode of thinking that calls attention to its conflict with positive law.

vate law and penal law, because with regard to constitutional law Puchta considers the practice (*Übung*) of constitutional conventions sufficient.[1]

This in turn boils down once again to a view that identifies private law with its civil-law sector, that is to say, with the Roman *ius gentium* (adapted to German legal life, this was in force in Germany until 1900, when the Code of Civil Law was introduced). For the classical tradition of Roman law was once again, in the old natural-law manner elevated, particularly by Puchta, to *ratio scripta*. With this process of canonizing Roman law, the *Begriffsjurisprudenz* (conceptual jurisprudence) that arose since the post-glossarist school was once more introduced into the Historical School. In spite of every effort to combat the theory of natural law, this tradition succeeded in continuing its influence within the dogmatic science of law of the Romanists.

However, it was not the *Romanist* but the *Germanist* wing of the Historical School, led by its two principal exponents, Georg Beseler and Otto von Gierke, which began to draw conclusions from the doctrine of folk-law that turned out to be fatal for the traditional concept of sovereignty. If all law, as Savigny taught, is a historical product of the individual folk nature, then the reception of Roman law in the Germanic countries must be considered a degeneration of a healthy development of German legal institutions. The spirit of Roman civil law, stigmatized as being individualistic, was, just as the absolutist concept of government of the Roman *imperium*, quite antagonistic to the social, corporative foundations of Germanic law. For that reason the supremacy of the classical tradition of Roman law must be broken both within civil private law and public law – and the Germanists did not hesitate to call upon the legislator for this purpose.

Beseler even meant that at least *part* of folk-law could maintain itself independent from the state, particularly when legal disputes of the civil judge are left out of consideration.[2]

The study of the Germanic corporate system led to a more sociological view of jurisprudence, and in diametrical opposition to the Romanist Puchta, the Germanists proclaimed the autonomy of corporations to be a formal original source of law. They

---

1 *Gewohnheitsrecht*, II, p. 234.
2 Georg Beseler, *System des gemeinen deutschen Privatrechts*, 3 vols. (Berlin, 1847-1855), I, 96 ff.

discovered internal collective law of organized communities as a kind of *Sozialrecht* unknown to the classical tradition.

At first, under the influence of the historical mode of thought, this Germanist assault threatened to undermine completely the foundations of civil law and the concept of a state. But Gierke saw the danger in time and arrived at a compromise with the idea of natural law. The doctrine of human rights (in the classical tradition of the *ius naturale et gentium* as the foundation of civil law) could not be sacrificed to the Germanic concept of folk-law which bound the whole legal status of the individual to the undifferentiated organized communities in society.[1] *Individualrecht* was to be maintained as an independent sphere of law alongside the newly discovered *Sozialrecht* of organized communities. Neither could the classical concept of the state as a sovereign *res publica* be allowed to succumb to the undifferentiated corporative principle of Germanic law.

However, Gierke wanted to replace the conception of the bureaucratic sovereign state, derived from the idea of the Roman Empire – a conception clearly manifest in Bodin's identification of the *res publica* with government – with an organic idea of the state in which government would be recognized as an essential organ of an organization of the state that comprised both the government and the people. This organized state, according to Gierke, like any other social corporate sphere, is a real spiritual organism with a personality of its own. But it is a differentiated community in which both the legal subjectivity of the individual citizens and that of the narrower collective social spheres, integrated into the whole of the state, remain unaffected.

In this way "*das Genossenschaftsprinzip*" – the Germanic principle of association – could have a wholesome influence on the modern idea of a constitutional state. Thus, sovereignty in the full sense of the word could not be assigned to the government or to the people, but only to the state as a whole. The government can only exercise sovereign power as an organ of the essentially corporate state. In 1874 Gierke wrote:

> For us, the communal being as such is the highest subject of public law. Government is but the most important branch and ruling organ of the state personality and in no way coincides with it. However, much of today's political theory, particularly

1 Gierke, *Naturrecht und deutsches Recht*; rectorial address (Frankfurt, 1883), p. 16.

the outdated concept of sovereignty, still contradicts this view. For as soon as one makes the state personality the starting-point of constitutional law, one can in the final analysis speak only of the sovereignty of the state itself, not of the sovereignty of a branch of the state. That notion is a remnant of an older view of the state, which we ought to put behind us.[1]

It was by no means Gierke's intention to deny the very special constitutional position of kingship in a monarchy: in a monarchy the king is indeed the head of state, in his own *right*. This constitutes a clear concession on his part to the legitimacy doctrine of the "monarchical principle."[2] He also did not object to the historically accepted custom to speak of royal sovereignty – on condition that what is meant is neither sovereign power over the state nor over statutory law, but only over the other parts of the state.[3]

The theory here defended of state sovereignty in some regard improved on the traditional concept dating back to Bodin and in many ways was superior to the conceptions of Gerber, Laband and Jellinek who are generally considered the typical representatives of this doctrine. The earlier humanist theories of sovereignty had no insight into the real nature of the state as an organized community or a juridical organ. The state was by turns identified with the government and then again with the people as an aggregate of individuals. The individualistic mode of thought of the humanist doctrine of natural law was in no way capable of arriving at a genuine idea of an organized community or of conceiving a genuine idea of community in the wider sense of the term.

To be sure, the Aristotelian-Thomistic tradition of scholasticism also had a conception of the state as an organic whole with parts. Here the state as an ordered unity (*unitas ordinis*) was sharply distinguished from an aggregate of individuals. As

1 Otto von Gierke, *Die Grundbegriffe des Staatsrechts und die neuesten Staatsrechtstheorien* (offprint of a treatise that appeared in vols. I and II (1874) of the *Zeitschrift für die gesamte Staatswissenschaft* (Tübingen, 1915), p. 27. See also idem, *Das deutsche Genossenschaftsrecht* (Berlin, 1873), 2:831.
2 That the doctrine of state sovereignty is incompatible with the view of monarchical authority as a king's private right is argued by Jellinek in his *Allgemeine Staatslehre*, 3rd ed. (Berlin, 1914), p. 473. Already earlier, Edmund Bernatzik had shown the inner contradiction in this combination; *Republik und Monarchie* (Freiburg im Breisgau, 1892), pp. 27 f.
3 Gierke, *Grundbegriffe des Staatsrechts*, p. 120.

early as the scholastic theories of the Spanish thinkers Molina and Suarez, this line of thought, once the modern concept of the state emerged, assigned sovereign power to the state as a *corpus*.[1]

However, this scholastic theory of an organized community in a universalist Greek sense conceived of the state as the whole of natural society, of which all lower communities as well as individuals could only be subordinate members, within the scope of the natural order.

By contrast, the theory of organized communities of Althusius meant a break with the scholastic universalist view of human society. It regarded neither the individuals nor the private corporations as parts of the state, but only the cities and provinces.[2] Althusius also assigned real sovereignty to the state as an organized community with its parts. When he equates this state bond with the *populus* we have to remember that he does not take the people as a collection of individuals but defines them, rather, in terms of membership in the state as an organized community.[3] The government as highest magistrate (*summus magistratus*) exercizes the power of the state not in its own name but in the name of the body politic, which itself derives its inalienable sovereignty from God.[4]

Gierke is quite mistaken in his attempt to find in the conception of Althusius a theory of popular sovereignty in the sense of the humanist doctrine of natural law. Moreover, the natural-law conception of a contract, of which Althusius availed himself for

1 Gierke, *Johannes Althusius und die Entwicklung der naturrechtlichen Staatstheorien*, 3rd ed. (Breslau, 1913), p. 162.

2 *Politica*, Ch. IX § 5: "Membra regni, seu symbioticae universalis consociationis voco, non singulos homines, neque familias, vel collegia, prout in private et publica particulari consociatione, sed civitates, provincial et regiones plures inter se de uno corpore ex conjunctione et communicatione mutua constituendo consentientes."

3 See *Politica, Praefatio*: "Jura haec (scl. majestatis) a populo seu membris regni et Reipublicae constituta sunt, ab illis inceperunt, atque non nisi in illis consistere possum et ab illis conservari."

4 *Ibid.*: "Concedo horum jurium principem seu summun magistratum esse dispensatorem, administratorem, vel procuratorem. Proprietatem vero illorum et usum fructum adeo jura ad regnum seu populum universum pertinere contendo, us hisce etiam si velit, se abdicare, atque in alium transferre et alienare nequaquam possit, non minus quam vitam quam quisque habet, alio communicare potest."

juridically constituting the state and the other organized communities, was a construct derived from traditional feudal law and estate law, rather than the methodological tool that the humanist theorists of natural law employed during the 17th century in the interest of a social policy of demolition and reconstruction.

The large influence of Althusius's theory of sovereignty became apparent in the distinction that began to be made between the *maiestas realis* ascribed to the state as a whole, and the *maiestatis personalis* asscribed to governments. This distinction for some time dominated the theory of the state, although only in a formal sense, without drawing from it any constitutional consequences. It was still alive in the theory of Grotius regarding the *subjectum commune* and the *subjectum proprium*, but since the middle of the 17th century it completely disappeared from the theory of the state.[1] It was practically revived in the distinction drawn by Gierke between the sovereignty of the state and the personal sovereignty of the King over the other members of the the state community.

Yet without any doubt Gierke's theory of state sovereignty springs from a different spirit. In assigning to the state and to the other organized communities a real communal personality, putting them on a par with the individual human personality and then, in a metaphysical way, constructing a distinctive body and soul for each one of these,[2] indeed places us within the intellectual climate of post-Kantian freedom idealism where the humanistic personality ideal and ·freedom motive acquire an irrationalist and universalist turn.

Meanwhile, the new doctrine of the sovereignty of the state, insofar as it was really in accordance with the thought of the Historical School, harbored all the seeds that were destined to completely undermine the traditional humanist concept of sovereignty. Since the theory of folk-law had led to the doctrine of the autonomous formation of law in the different organized communities, the concept of sovereignty could no longer have the characteristic quality of being the only original competency for the formation of positive law. And yet it was in that concept that Bodin believed he had found the key.

---

1 See Gierke, *Althusius*, pp. 164 ff.
2 Gierke, *Das Wesen der menschliche Verbände* (1902).

If, in principle, the concept of sovereignty can no longer play an essential role in the definition of positive law – Gierke explicitly rejects the view of positive law as the command of the sovereign – then the question was bound to arise regarding the role it could still play in the definition of the *state*.

Gierke himself still stuck to Bodin's conception that sovereignty was to be considered an essential quality of every state. The latter, in his opinion, is distinguished from all other organized communities as a sovereign organization of power, which is not to be taken in the sense of *Genossenschaft* (association), but of *Gebietskörperschaft* (territorial body or regional authority), because in his system the first concept applied only to the non-political bodies.[1] And what he understands by "sovereign power organization" is explained as follows: "The essence of the political community is found in the fact that it has as its content the powerful execution of the general will. Its substance is the general *will*, its manifestation is organized *power*, its task is the purposeful *deed*." According to Gierke, political life in this sense has always existed, already in the family, the ancient clan, and the tribe. Yet one does not begin to speak of a true state until an independent organism is formed for political life. Once this happens the functions of the state can be exercised through an entire hierarchy of narrower and wider political bodies (municipalities, provinces, federations, etc.). These all participate in the character of the state.

> Such a powerful body must display a specific character and a series of qualitative differences that distinguish it from all other political bodies whose power is not limited from above by a similar power and that stands above every lower power subordinate to it. For a highest power is differentiated from every other power through the specific characteristic that it is entirely and simply power. The will corresponding to such a power is different from every other will, for it is simply a general sovereign will determined only by itself. Therefore, among the political bodies, which all display the nature of a state, this highest bond of power alone is called the state.[2]

---

1 Gierke, *Deutsches Genossenschaftsrecht*, 2:866: "The concept *Genossenschaft* [corporative association] is the *genus* for all those German juristic bodies that differ from a state or municipality. In relation to the concept *Körperschaft*, however, it constitutes a *species*." Similarly, Heinrich Rosin, *Das Recht der öffentlichen Genossenschaft* (Freiburg im Breisgau, 1886), pp. 40f. Preuss opposes this distinction, *Gemeinde, Staat, Reich*, pp. 240 ff.

2 Gierke, *Grundbegriffe*, pp. 96 f.

Thus the concept of sovereignty was unmistakably transferred from the jural sphere to the political sphere of power – from a natural-law category to a historical category. For, as I have argued in my analysis of the general theory of law-spheres, power or control represents the core moment within the modal structure of the historical aspect of reality.[1]

Georg Jellinek too noted that in the new doctrine the concept of sovereignty could only be accepted as a historical category. From this he at once drew the conclusion, in contradistinction to Gierke and in the footsteps of Carl Friedrich von Gerber and Paul Laband, that sovereignty could no longer be considered an essential characteristic of every state but that the existence of non-sovereign states had to be acknowledged as well, such as the member states of a political federation and so-called vassal states.[2]

Following Gerber, Jellinek was willing to accept the concept of sovereignty only in a negative and formal sense, namely, as negating any subordination or restriction of the power of the state to another power. Sovereignty, according to him, does not predetermine anything about the positive content of state power and the special competencies that come with it. It is not state power itself, but only a certain property of it.[3]

However, as soon as the concept of sovereignty was transferred from the sphere of natural law to the historical sphere of power, a new problem arose for which the doctrine of state sovereignty could not offer a satisfactory solution, namely the question about the relation of the sovereign power of the state to law. Gierke, who believed his organic doctrine of the state had laid the foundation for a view of *ius publicum* as a fully adequate "Right" based on mutuality of rights and duties, and who had enthusiastically endorsed Bähr's plea for a constitutional state with a well-regulated system of administrative justice, got entangled in a problem so framed that no sound and scientifically acceptable resolution was possible. "State and Law," he wrote, "are two in-

1   See my *WdW*, 2:139-159 [NC, 2:192-217].
2   Jellinek, *Allgemeine Staatslehre*, p. 487.
3   This conception was first defended by Gerber in his *Grundzüge eines Systems des deutschen Staatsrechts*, 3rd ed. (1880), p. 22. *To him expressions such as monarchical sovereignty, popular sovereignty and "national sovereignty" are merely slogans of particular political trends. Kelsen too repeatedly alludes to the "political misuse of the concept of sovereignty."*

dependent and distinct sides of communal life. The State manifests itself in the effective execution of desired common goals and culminates in political *action*; the Law manifests itself in the demarcation of spheres of activity for the wills, for which it is binding, and culminates in the *acknowledgment* of law as right."[1]

This untenable juxtaposition of State and Law, which was in conflict with Gierke's own thesis that the state has an essential jural side, revealed the internal conflict between, on the one hand, the concept of sovereignty transposed into the sphere of power, and on the other the doctrine of folk convictions as the sole material source of validity of positive law. In my book of 1931, *De Crisis in de Humanistische Staatsleer*, I demonstrated that this conflict gave but a new form to the radical cleavage in humanism's religious ground-motive between nature and freedom.[2]

As long as the Historical School continued to dwell in the intellectual world of German freedom idealism, it tried to bridge the antithesis between power and right, nature and freedom, in a dialectical, so-called *geisteswissenschaftliche* mode of thought. Already in his famous introductory article of 1815 Savigny taught that a culture spawned by a folk-spirit is, in its totality, "necessary and at the same time free."[3]

In the same line of thought Gierke attempted to telescope dialectically, on the one hand, the sovereign power of the state as the expression of the ruler's will that recognizes no higher power above itself, and on the other the law as the free expression of a people's convictions:

> In order to attain the inner strength to carry out its cultural mission, the State needs to be supported by the notion of Right. Were it experienced purely as the acting power which, merely because it has the physical force, demands and receives obedience for every act of will deemed useful, then all political life would petrify into despotism. Thus a healthy State seeks to base its power at the same time on Right, so that a people's collective consciousness experiences the fact of a given ordinance at the same time as an instance of right, which automatically entails limits to a State's competence and a State's corresponding legal

---

1 Gierke, *Grundbegriffe*, p. 105.
2 [Cf. Herman Dooyeweerd, *The Crisis in Humanist Political Theory* (Grand Rapids: Paideia, 2010,) p. 65, *et passim*.]
3 Savigny, *Zeitschrift für geschichtliche Rechtswissenschaft* 1 (1815).

obligations. To realize its goal of an orderly human society, Right in turn needs the State's assistance in administering retribution. As the example of international law shows, without the support of state power Right cannot fully carry out its task and will remain, rather, a right that is unfinished. And so Right remains incomplete until the State makes its power available, delivers judgments for elucidating Right, and forcefully leads every individual will that conflicts with Right back to obedience to the norm.[1]

But this dialectical telescoping of right and sovereign power failed to answer the question on what basis it was possible. If state and right are indeed two diverse and independent aspects of society, then it is not clear how the sovereign will-power of the state could be subjected to right. Gierke's dialectical antithesis of sovereign state power and right reveals, as I said, the radical religious antithesis in the hidden starting point of his political philosophy: the irreconcilable conflict between the nature or domination motive and the freedom motive. A theoretical antithesis cannot be brought to a genuine synthesis unless the starting-point of theoretical thought supplies the deeper unity of the opposing poles. But the entire ground-motive controlling humanist political theory, namely that of nature and freedom, nowhere offered such a starting-point. Its further development, therefore, was bound to take Gierke's dialectical pseudo-synthesis between state power on the one hand and right on the other, and break it apart again into a polar antithesis.

Gierke's disciple, Hugo Preuss, who later drafted the Weimar Constitution, was the first to eliminate the concept of sovereignty, on principle, as a logical conclusion from Gierke's freedom-motivated theory of the organic personality of societal relationships.[2] The sovereignty concept, according to Preuss, is the necessary correlate of the individualistic concept of personality, both of which stem from Roman law. As a historical category the concept of sovereignty suited absolute government, which had no room for genuine public law. After all, law by definition sets limits to personal will-power, but sovereign – that is, absolute – power on principle falls outside the sphere of law. According to Preuss, in the state the sovereign personality, like the person in Roman private law, is an absolute individual. It leaves

1 Gierke, *Die Grundbegriffe des Staatsrechts*, pp. 105 f.

no room for an internal multiplicity of "persons" who as members are ordered in the political whole, and so no room either for any internal public-law relations between member persons and the "totality person." It absorbs all personality into the internal sphere of the state and thus leaves room only for private law.[1] The modern constitutional state, in contrast to the absolutist state, evolved out of the Germanic legal principle of the autonomous *Genossenschaft*. And the concept of sovereignty no longer fits this constitutional state. If the state, as Gierke has expounded, is an organic corporate person amid a whole series of organic corporate persons, which can in turn integrate themselves again as members into more comprehensive "persons" of this kind, then this solves the problem of the member states of the German federal state and of the integration of that state into the still wider community of nations on the basis of international law. If, however, sovereignty belongs to the essence of the state, then there is room neither for a federal state nor for an international legal community.

For this reason, says Preuss, the modern state must be conceived as a true *Genossenschaft*, a *Genossenschaft*, moreover, that is a type of community not based on arbitrary association but a natural one, grown organically, and evolved, thanks to its perfect organization, into a *Körperschaft*, a "corporate authority." The authority wielded by the state over its subjects differs in no way from authority in other relationships; the state is distinct from these solely in its territorial range, as a *Gebietskörperschaft* with *Gebietshoheit*. By *Gebietshoheit* Preuss understands that only a genuine state, in contrast to provinces and municipalities which also fall under the *Gebietskörperschaften*, can dispose of its territory independently, all on its own; and since this territory belongs to its essence as person, a state can also, if so desired, abolish itself on its own. The concept of *Gebietshoheit*, according to Preuss, was first developed in the medieval towns and had nothing to do with the Romanist concept of sovereignty.

In this way the elimination of the concept of sovereignty appeared helpful particularly for the theory of inter-state relations which, once the concept was retained, began to work with all kinds of forced constructions, such as the concepts of "*shared* or

1 H. Preuss, *Gemeinde, Staat, Reich*, pp. 100f.

half sovereignty" or *"internal* and *external* sovereignty." And to the extent that the theory accepted the legal concept of non-sovereign states, it also appeared to offer no sound criterion for distinguishing such states from municipalities and provinces.

But the concept of sovereignty was not so easily done away with. From the outset it had played a far more varied role than was apparent from Preuss's descriptions. Not only had it served to distinguish the state from every other societal sphere and to grant it the monopoly of governmental authority over all other powers within its territory, but it had also helped to define positive law and the mutual relations between spheres of competence in the formation of law.

To be sure, Gierke's impressively elaborated *Genossenschafts-theorie* had opened men's eyes to the autonomous formation of law within the great diversity of societal relationships, but it had not been able to indicate a material criterion for demarcating the original sphere of competency of the non-state relationships vis-à-vis the original sphere of competency of the state. Their autonomy, in the end, was placed as a formal, albeit original, source of law next to case law and state legislation. And even if one joined the Historical School and proclaimed the nation's sense of justice as the final source of validity for positive law, and even if one joined Beseler and Gierke – in opposition to Puchta – and accepted the possibility that both the national community and the other communal spheres can form customary law directly and independently of the state by activating its jural consciousness, one could not escape this question: Which law would have to give way in case of a conflict?

To that question the doctrine of sovereignty had at least given an unequivocal answer. And Gierke himself did not know how to replace it with a solution that was fundamentally different. "Of course," he remarked, "no sooner does a state exist than neither autonomous law nor customary law can insist on its validity without explicit or implicit acknowledgment by the state. But acknowledgment or tolerance is not the same as creation."[1] And in a review essay on Laband's *Staatsrecht* he even went so far as to acknowledge the formal omnipotence of the state legis-

---

1 Op. cit., p. 32.

lator.[1] Here, when all was said and done, the concept of sovereignty served once more to delineate the reciprocal relation of legal competency between the state and the other spheres. *The concept cannot be eliminated unless another solution is offered for the problem that presents itself here.* And the paramount question at stake is whether one considers this an intrinsic problem of *law* and *right*, or a historical question of *power* and *might*. The latter case immediately reveals the unresolved antinomy in Gierke's dialectical connecting of law and power. For then the original jural competency is ultimately dissolved in the sovereign power of the state, and law has lost the very independence Gierke claimed for it.

A sharp light was cast on this aspect of the problem by Georg Jellinek. He pointed out that the concept of sovereignty was always understood, even by the most absolutist-minded doctors of natural law, as a concept of *law*. But that was not difficult for them, because they could bind the state to natural law. Jellinek admits: "Our knowledge of law notwithstanding, which lets its existence depend on the existence of an organization that creates it, reveals that one of the thorniest issues in the whole theory of constitutional law is the question whether the organization that guarantees the law stands above the law or beneath it."[2] Bodin's conception of sovereignty, which placed the state (in the form of the government) above the positive laws, can then no longer be accepted without denaturing law to a *fiat*. Therefore the state itself must also be bound by the law. But how could this binding be construed in terms of Jellinek's doctrine of state sovereignty? Here Jellinek resorted to his familiar construct of a state's self-restriction as an organization of power. The state binds itself, and so also its organs of administration and justice, to existing law. In this act of binding itself the state continues to obey its own sovereign will and not a power above itself. The same holds, according to Jellinek, for the relation of the state to international law.

Jellinek tried to make this construct plausible in terms of both social psychology and jurisprudence.[3] We can let his socio-psychological exposition rest as not relevant in the present context.

1 In *Schmollers Jahrbuch für Gesetzgebung, Verwaltung und Volkswirtschaft* 7 (1883): 1189.
2 Jellinek, *Allgemeine Staatlehre*, 3rd ed. (1929), p. 476.
3 Ibid., pp. 477 ff.

In terms of jurisprudence Jellinek viewed his theory simply as the application of Kant's doctrine of the autonomous legislation of practical reason. Kant had taught, after all, that the purely moral will can follow only those norms which it has posed for itself in accordance with its own inner nature and not norms which stem from a power outside itself. The making of a contract, too, is viewed by Jellinek as an instance of legal self-obligation.

Meanwhile, both arguments skirted the problem Jellinek himself had raised. Kant's doctrine of autonomous morality, in which the humanist freedom motive received its pregnant application, could not as such be transferred to the field of law, and the contract theory with which the humanistic teachers of natural law, Kant included, had tried to justify the sovereignty of state authority could no longer serve the purpose after the rise of the Historical School.

The manner in which Jellinek framed the problem of the relation between state sovereignty and law flowed directly from his dualistic concept of the state which already in 1931 I analyzed as to its true background and worldview in my book entitled *De Crisis in de Humanistische Staatsleer*.[1]

Under the influence of neo-Kantianism, the dialectical "*geisteswissenschaftliche*" mode of thought, which had tried to combine nature and freedom in a single conception, had to make room again for a strict methodological dualism. The sociological view of the state, oriented to "physio-psychical reality," and the normative jural conception of the state parted ways. *Sein* and *Sollen* – the "is" and the "ought" – were once again sharply separated, a separation that also led to the abandonment of Gierke's conception of social communities as personal, real, spiritual organisms. Jellinek taught that the state as a social reality, as "a communal entity equipped with the original governing power of a sedentary people," must be understood apart from any normative criteria. And the same holds for law to the extent that it is viewed merely as existing social conduct, as "factual legal practice."

In opposition to this sociological concept of state and law a normative jural alternative is posited: namely, the state as territorial

1 [Cf. Herman Dooyeweerd, *The Crisis in Humanist Political Theory* (Grand Rapids: Paideia, 2010).]

body in the sense of a jural person with law as norm, as a kind of "ought to be." But when Jellinek, in violation of his own methodology, once again adopts in his jural concept of the state what he himself calls the "purely factual" sociological element of "original governing power," and when he then proceeds to define the state in a normative jural sense as "a territorial body equipped with original governing power," then this definition at once disintegrates again into its two mutually exclusive components.

The sovereign will of the state was conceived of in a merely socio-psychological sense, apart from any normative jural aspect. It is impossible for the state's will thus understood to bind itself autonomously to jural norms. It is only the normative function of the jural will that can be subject to jural norms. In his theory of the autonomous self-binding of the moral will Kant did not have the psychological, but the normative ethical will-function in mind. In this way Jellinek's conception of the self-binding of the will of the state to law dissolves itself in the inner antinomy of his dualistic conception of the state.

The same antinomy is revealed when Jellinek attempts to answer the question at the heart of the problem of sovereignty, namely the relation of sovereignty to material juridical competency. In line with his theory regarding the binding of the sovereign state's will to law, he denies that the sovereign power of the state is identical with absolute power of the state. He assures us that it is "jural power" and therefore "bound by law"; but immediately afterwards he says that the state "does not tolerate any *absolute* juridical limits." He holds that "the state can dispense with every self-imposed limit," although this can only be done "in the form of law and through the creation of new limitations." "What is enduring is not any specific limit, but the setting of limits." Thus it boils down to a situation where the state, albeit in the form of law, freely determines the boundaries of its own original competence, similar to the way in which the well-known German theorist of constitutional law, Haenel, elaborated it in his famous theory of a "competence over competence."[1] To be sure, Jellinek considers his definition of sover-

---

1 Albert Haenel, *Studien zum deutschen Staatsrechte*, 2 vols. (Leipzig, 1873–88), 1:149, and *Deutsches Staatsrecht* (Leipzig, 1892), 1:114 ff., 797.

eignty – the unrestricted jural power over its own competence – to be merely a methodological image in aid of "justifying the lawfulness of acts by the state to expand its competence." As well, he states that under all circumstances the sovereign power of the state over its own competence does find its boundary in the acknowledgment of the rights of the members of the state, be they individuals or groups. But this limit, dictated by the humanistic freedom motive, did not acquire a truly jural significance in Jellinek's theory of law. Had he himself not declared a moment earlier that the existence of law is dependent upon its actualization by an organization that always has to be a *power* organization? Therefore, when the state as a *sovereign* organization of power fails to actualize the alleged rights of its citizens, then these rights cannot possibly imply a *jural* limit but at most a *moral* limit to its competence. The juridical existence of these rights therefore remains at the mercy of the sovereign will of the state, which can at any time cancel every self-imposed limit.

In Jellinek's theory the sovereign "jural power" of the state is not truly a *jural* power; it does not intrinsically constitute a juridical competence. Rather, it is merely an *historical* will-power which falls outside the domain of law and which ought to bind itself to the limitations of law.

All of this once again clearly highlights the fact that every definition of positive law in which the sovereign power of the state is incorporated as an essential element, violates what I call the modal sphere-sovereignty of law. Also the construction of sovereignty in the theory of natural law simply served as a mask for the humanistic motive of *power* and *control*. The traditional concept of sovereignty could not but clash with the modal distinctiveness and the modal irreducibility of the jural aspect of society and so become a source of irresolvable antinomies between law and power.

2.3 *The doctrine of the sovereignty of law and its alleged victory over the traditional dogma of sovereignty*

The above clash seemed to be avoided by the doctrine of the *sovereignty of law*, which in three variants, namely the *psychological* one of Krabbe, the *norm-logical* one of Kelsen, and the *legal-sociological* one of Duguit and Gurvitch, turned against the traditional concept of sovereignty, no matter whether it presented itself in the form of the sovereignty of government, of the people, or of the state.

In reality, however, the doctrine of the sovereignty of law has not in any way overcome the internal contradictions of the traditional concept of sovereignty.[1] It wants us to believe that the problems would vanish into thin air if, instead of government or its highest officials, the impersonal legal order were declared sovereign. But the truth of the matter is that the legal order can only be the law-side or normative side of the jural aspect of human society. Moreover, the great structural diversity that characterizes our modern, highly differentiated society, as we observed before, necessarily comes to expression in its jural aspect as well. Thus the doctrine of the sovereignty of law nowhere escapes having to define the interrelationship between the state and the other spheres of society. Which of the variants of law can rightfully claim sovereignty? Will it be constitutional law, civil private law, international law, business law, church law, and so on? Whatever one's choice may be, it will invariably result in assigning an absolute competence to just one of the social spheres.

But an *absolute* competence can never be a truly *jural* power, and thus the doctrine of the sovereignty of law in turn clashed with the modal structure of law. And yet this doctrine arose in an attempt to save the independence of law from the theory of state sovereignty, a theory which at critical moments, even when the doctrine insisted on the fundamental independence of law from the power of the state, nevertheless derived from the sovereign state-power an absolute juridical competency in the domain of the formation of law.

Modern humanism's doctrine of the sovereignty of law derives from three totally different sources, which explains its significantly different elaborations.

The first is the *folk*-law theory of the Historical School which based law no longer on the sovereign will of the state legislator but on the people's convictions as these develop historically.

The second is the logicistic trend in the science of law which originated in *Begriffsjurisprudenz* and led to an overestimation of

1 In fact, the logicistic elaboration in Kelsen has only increased the confusion. Only the theory of Gurvitch, discussed below, is an exception, which makes it the most interesting of the theories of the sovereignty of law.

the logical unity and fixed nature of positive law as an "objective" system of legal propositions. After Gerber and Laband introduced this trend of thought in the discipline of constitutional law by defending a "purely juridical method" bereft of all non-juridical viewpoints (such as political, ethical and others), it was carried to its extreme consequences by Kelsen and his school. They treated it within the framework of neo-Kantian epistemology and dissolved the state and the other organized communities in society into a logical system of "legal propositions."

The third source of the doctrine of the sovereignty of law is modern sociology of law. It broke entirely with traditional legal science by viewing positive law no longer primarily within the context of the state and its organization, but as a general social phenomenon explicable in terms of social causes. The sociology of law was at first largely influenced by a positivist, natural-scientific mode of thinking, though to some extent it did retain a historical link with the theory of folk-law as defended by the Historical School. Under the influence of modern philosophy of life, folk-law theory acquired a new, irrationalist elaboration in the sociology of law of Georges Gurvitch, where positivist thought was supplanted by a dialectical method oriented to the humanities.

2.3.1   The view of Krabbe

The folk-law theory for all intents and purposes eliminates the problem of competency in the area of the formation of law. Its main thought is that law is not made but grows organically with and from people's convictions. Customary law is a direct deposit of people's convictions about justice. It manifests itself in the actual practice of members of the folk. As noted above, whenever this basically irrationalist, romantic conception of law was in any way consistently applied, it could only destroy any meaning that the concept of sovereignty might have for defining positive law. The only question was: Could it ever be applied consistently?

The Dutch jurist Krabbe linked up with this folk-law theory and gradually evolved it into a rationalist psychologistic conception. His doctrine of the sovereignty of law, on his own admission, was inspired by the humanist motive of freedom. He wrote about the doctrine that in opposing "the evil principle that might

302

precedes right" it deduces all power from the law, in the belief that it "catches sight of the principle of freedom by holding high this power of the law."[1]

Krabbe did not claim that sovereignty of the law obtained in all ages. Especially in a later work he argued extensively that the equation of the power of the state with the power of the law was an historical process that began with the struggle between the old authoritative state and the modern constitutional state, a process that was not completed until the advent of republican or parliamentary forms of government. Not until the idea of law triumphed completely over the idea of authority – the idea of the superiority of a government's will – did the modern state restore the original condition which is supposed to have existed before the rise of governments equipped with organized military power. What was then restored was the ancient sovereignty of folk-law, a law that the people formed in keeping with their convictions about justice.[2] That was the situation in the old Germanic tribes; that is again the situation in England where the impersonal "rule of law" holds sway (even though the doctrine may often relapse into the old view of a personal Sovereign or a sovereign State, as it did in John Austin's analytical school of law).

The critical point in Krabbe's doctrine was the elimination in principle of the problem of competency, though as he developed his theory it reasserted itself in its full weight the moment he had to account for the interrelations between the different social spheres within which law acquires positive form. Then we see Krabbe fall back on the German theory of the unrestricted competence of the state over all communities that "aim at a more restricted end (i.e., the satisfaction of pleasure)." This unrestricted competence, he writes, results from the fact that the communal goal embracing the whole human person, which occupies the highest rung in the hierarchy of social ends, has acquired a "communal personality" in the state.

Next we read in him that except for international law there is no independent validity of law over against the state. However, in case of conflict the law of the state has to yield to the more encompassing international legal order of the cultural community

---

1 Hugo Krabbe, *Die Lehre der Rechtssouveränität* (Groningen, 1906), p. 193.
2 Hugo Krabbe, *De moderne Staatsidee* (The Hague, 1915), pp. 2–36.

of the nations.[1] But then, what is the basis for the competence of this supreme and all-encompassing community? This cannot possibly be determined by the international legal order itself, since that legal order presupposes the competency of the community in question. And so we end up with the absolute sovereignty of the international community over all the other spheres of society – the absolutism of the *civitas maxima* which in the measure that its organization grows becomes a true "communal person" and eliminates the separate states as communal persons or else degrades them to mere instruments for carrying out the goals set by the international legal entity.[2]

In this way the doctrine of the sovereignty of law once again has sovereignty swallow up law. And the foundation of this doctrine – the theory of a folk's sense or consciousness of justice which Krabbe expressly posited over against the traditional concept of sovereignty – was later completely paralyzed by him and transposed into the traditional principle of democratic natural law: the rule of the majority principle. Since the sense of justice in a folk can vary from person to person, and since a consciousness of justice above all demands unity of norms in which the jural value prevails over the content of the norm, the individual's sense of justice must yield to that of the majority.[3] This once again transformed the irrationalist idea of folk-law of the Historical School into the rationalist natural-law theory of popular sovereignty.

2.3.2   Kelsen's theory of the sovereignty of law

The doctrine of the sovereignty of law as presented in Hans Kelsen's "pure law theory" moved in an entirely different climate of thought.

Proceeding from the "logic of origin" of the Marburg School of neo-Kantianism,[4] Kelsen accepted the concept of sovereignty

---

1   Ibid., p. 271; idem, *Die Lehre der Rechtssouveränität*, pp. 343 ff. According to Krabbe, international law does not address states but bears directly on individuals.
2   Krabbe, *Die Lehre der Rechtssouveränität*, pp. 243 ff.
3   Krabbe, *De moderne Staatsidee*, pp. 50 ff.
4   This no longer plays a role in his work *The General Theory of Law and the State* (Cambridge, MA, 1945).

only in a "norm-logical" sense, in which case it could only have the meaning of expressing the logical unity of a system of positive legal norms and its logical irreducibility over against every other system of norms. Given this meaning, the *sovereignty* and *positivity* of law become identical concepts since the sovereignty of law also excludes its deduction from a system of natural law.[1] From Kelsen's standpoint of legal positivism, natural law is not law. He firmly rejected Jellinek's dualistic concept of the state and held that the state, like every other societal sphere, can only be understood as a normative *juridical* unit, consisting of a logical system of "legal propositions" that is merely personified in the traditional concept of the state. To the positive legal norm itself he denied any imperative character; from a "norm-logical" viewpoint it is transformed into a hypothetical logical judgment of form. "When A occurs ... B must follow." That is to say, when a certain legal event takes place, sanctions or compensation ought to be imposed. This judgment is not directed at anyone in particular. The legal norm has no "address."

This logicistic conception alone seemed to sever all connection between a positive legal rule and an imperative sovereign will of the state. Positive law seemed to have been stripped of every subjective element. The entire subject-side of law – the legal subject, subjective right, a legal fact, etc. – is resolved into its law-side and is then logicized into a system of pure "objective" logical judgments.

As a logical and irreducible unity a system of legal norms can only be understood in a scientific way on the basis of a basic or original norm. This basic (original) norm cannot itself share in the nature of positive law, for as ultimate source of validity of the entire juridical process of positivization it must serve as the basis of this process if it is to be conceived as jural in nature. This original norm then requires a supreme organ with absolute competence to form law, while all other competencies ought to be seen as logically deduced from it.

On this basis, the legal system has to be created as a logical hierarchy of higher (i.e., more general) and lower (i.e., more spe-

1 Kelsen, *Das Problem der Souveränität und die Theorie des Völkerrechts* (Tübingen, J.C.B. Mohr, 1920), p. 86.

305

cific) norms. This will repeatedly require new legal organs to give shape to the higher principles. These organs will have *delegated* competency from immediately higher organs and *delegating* competencies to lower organs. At the lowest step of this process one finds the execution, which itself is no longer to be viewed as a legal norm, but merely as the last act in the positivization of legal norms. This is the famous theory of *Stufen* (levels) which Kelsen took over from his pupil Adolf Merkl.[1]

Viewed purely in a juridical-logical way, apart from all so-called ethical-political postulates, Kelsen's earlier conception recognized two options: either one accepts the sovereignty of the state as a system of logical norms, or one accepts the sovereignty of the legal order of international law. The one hypothesis excludes the other. With implacable logic, Kelsen drew the absolutistic consequences of both possibilities. If the state as a legal system is sovereign, then it is juridically omnipotent; then no other sphere of original competency may be acknowledged next to that of the state; then all law dissolves itself logically into constitutional law and all organs active in the formation of law are transformed into organs of the state. But if instead the legal order of international law is sovereign, then logically no room remains for sovereign states and all law-forming organs become organs of international law.

From the outset it was not doubtful which of the two hypotheses Kelsen would favor. The former, according to him, boils down to an absolutization, if not a deification, of the State. In the closing paragraphs of his work *The Problem of Sovereignty and the Theory of International Law*,[2] he arrived, from an ethical-political perspective, at a radical denial of the primacy of the legal order of the state and a veritable panegyric for the primacy of international law:

1 Kelsen, *Allgemeine Staatslehre* (Berlin, 1925), pp. 248–250. Adolf Merkl, *Die Lehre von der Rechtskraft entwickelt aus dem Rechtsbegriff* (Leipzig, 1923), pp. 203 ff. See in this connection my extensive analysis in *De Beteekenis der Wetsidee voor Rechtswetenschap en Rechtsphilosophie* (Amsterdam, 1926), pp. 26 ff. and 93.

2 Kelsen, *Das Problem der Souveränität und die Theorie des Völkerrechts* (Tübingen, 1920).

The unity in law for Humanity is only provisionally and by no means definitively divided over more or less arbitrarily structured States. Humanity's *civitas maxima* or global organization is the political heart of the juridical hypothesis of the primacy of international law. At the same time it is the basic thesis of pacifism which in the domain of international politics represents the opposite of imperialism. Just as for an objectivist worldview the ethical concept of being human is Humanity, so for an objectivist theory of law the concept of law is identical with international law, and precisely for that reason it is at once an ethical concept.[1]

In his work of 1934, *Pure Theory of Law*, it would appear that Kelsen even accepted the "logical unity of the juridical worldview" on the basis of the primacy assigned to international law as a consequence of the epistemological foundations of his "Normlogik":

> The theoretical unravelling of the dogma of sovereignty, the main instrument of the imperialistic ideology in its opposition to international law, is one of the most essential results of the pure theory of law. Although it did not quite triumph in a political sense, it may still have political effect … Establishing such a possible effect cannot detract anything from the purity of the theory. Unintentionally, the exact sciences, too, precisely because they aim at nothing but pure knowledge, make possible technological progress. In this sense one may say that the pure theory of law, insofar as it ensures the epistemic unity of all law by relativizing the concept of the State, creates a not insignificant organizational unity of a global, centralized legal order.[2]

However, Kelsen did not seem to realize that his elaboration of the theory of the sovereignty of international law entailed an absolutization, indeed a deification, of the *civitas maxima*. Here again the theory of the sovereignty of law swallowed up the idea of law into the idea of sovereignty. In his "norm-logic" the jural "ought" turned into an empty thought-form in which ultimately even brute force could be understood as law. And once again it was the motive of control of humanism's science ideal, this time in the form of the "logic of origin," that causes the concept of sov-

1 Op. cit., p. 319.
2 Kelsen, *Reine Rechtslehre; Einleitung in die rechtswissenschaftliche Problematik* (Leipzig, 1934), pp. 153–154. In his *General Theory of Law and State* (Cambridge, MA, 1945), p. 388, it appears that Kelsen returned to his initial standpoint.

ereignty to triumph over the idea of law, "nature" over "freedom."[1]

2.3.3   Duguit and Gurvitch – a sociological approach

Among the sociological variants of the theory of the sovereignty of law we find two contrasting approaches. The French sociologist of law and student of constitutional law, Léon Duguit, held a rationalist and naturalist view, whereas the Russian sociologist Georges Gurvitch opted for an irrationalist and dialectical approach oriented to the humanities.

The two founders of modern sociology as an independent discipline, Henri de Saint-Simon and Auguste Comte, had the intention of arriving at a synthesis between the natural-scientific mode of thought of the Enlightenment and the historicist movement of the Restoration inspired by humanism's freedom motive. From the latter it took over a universalist and historicist view of human society and a fundamental resistance to the apriorist and individualist construction of humanist natural law. On the other hand they were strongly influenced by the science of economics that arose during the second half of the 18th century. Proceeding from Locke's liberal natural-law theory, they drew a sharp distinction between the state and civil society. Society could be understood in terms of economic natural laws. The physiocrats had taught that state legislation is subordinate to the laws of society's economic order and that in a case of conflict it had to give way.

This young sociology focused all its attention on "civil society." The state was seen as a merely secondary product of the forces operative in "society" and of the clash between economic classes, both of which were to be conceived as governed by general static and dynamic laws in the natural-scientific sense of

1   [In his autobiography, the mathematician A. A. Fraenkel points out that the entire "logic of origin" of Hermann Cohen, the founder of the neo-Kantian Marburg school to which Kelsen belonged and which aimed at the generation of *being* through *thinking*, was based upon a misunderstanding of the difference between a limit and a *quotient* (the symbol of dx divided by dy) in calculus. While reifying dx to be the "absolute," Cohen consistently rejected the application of the limit concept at the basis of calculus. "It stands to reason that the mathematician has to reject this approach as false (or as meaningless)." A. A. Fraenkel, *Lebenskreise – Aus den Erinnerungen eines jüdischen Mathematikers* (Stuttgart, 1967), p. 92.]

308

positivism. In this way "society" on the one hand was viewed in a universalist sense as the organic whole of human society in which the increasing division of labor created an ever growing interdependence and solidarity among its component parts, while on the other hand "society" was considered an historically evolving system of forces that was to be investigated with the aid of a method of research that transformed the natural-scientific approach into a historical method.

As was to be expected, the combination of universalist sociology with natural-scientific thought became a source of inner antinomies. The universalist view of society included an idealistic motif of the historicist orientation of the Restoration period. For both Saint-Simon and Comte, the most important factor guaranteeing the cohesion and solidarity of the social organism was a community of *leading ideas* such as had been secured during the medieval era by means of theological guidance from the Church. But on the other hand the positivist method was to base itself exclusively on the *social facts* while eliminating all metaphysical concepts and proceeding without any normative points of view. In the subsequent development of sociology during the 19th century, the idealist motif was left behind in an increasingly radical way. Ideas were viewed merely as an ideological reflex of existing social relations developing in a strictly natural-scientific way.

Not until the beginning of the 20th century, under the influence of Max Weber and Heinrich Rickert, did a reaction emerge against the dominance of natural-scientific thinking and did a cultural methodology make headway in sociology.

Meanwhile, from the outset the new discipline's positivist orientation did not prevent it from putting its purported unprejudiced research in the service of a practical political program of reform that turned against the "sovereign authoritative state" of the preceding period. Saint-Simon had already predicted that the state as an "authority over persons" would give way to a "management of economic affairs." With the idea of the sovereign state as a *res publica* focused on the "general interest," the natural-law foundation of civil private law and the doctrine of human rights were likewise pushed aside as a metaphysical speculation of jurists.

309

It is clear that the influence of these political tendencies of positivist sociology within the science of law would combat the dogma of the sovereignty of the state in an even more radical way than it had undergone when it came into conflict with the theory of folk-law in the Historical School. Yet just as little as the folk-law theory led to a radical break with the dogma of state sovereignty did the sociological school bring this about – that is, so long as both moved within the domain of the science of law, for the concepts and methods of legal science are geared solely to state law.

The conclusive proof of this is found in the last phase of the thought of Rudolf von Jhering.[1] For although Jhering initially belonged to the Historical School, in his final years he developed a naturalistic sociological conception of law which viewed law as a necessary product of the vital interests of society. But by fitting this approach into the context of a normative science of law it led him to a view which fully returned to the traditional dogma of sovereignty. Law as an expression of the living conditions of a society requires for its positive realization the state as the monopolistic organization of social coercion. As a power organization the state then binds itself, just as in the case of Jellinek, to this law as "norm or policy of coercion." The state as the highest organization of power is sovereign *as such*, implying that the formation of any and all positive law once again turns out to be dependent upon the sovereign will of the state. Autonomy is derived from delegation on the part of the state. Finally the sovereign power of the state is again incorporated in Jhering's final definition of law: "Law is the sum-total of society's living conditions in the widest sense of the word, ensured by the external coercion of state power."[2]

This totally changed with the rise of the sociology of law proper. Breaking on principle with the science of law, it pursued the positivist way of thinking oriented to the natural sciences, which left room only for a "causal explanation" of law as a social phenomenon; it had no room for the juridical problem of competence which belonged to the normative orientation of the science of law, nor for the traditional concept of sovereignty. When

1 An extensive analysis of this development is found in my article "De bronnen van het stellig recht in het licht der Wetsidee III," *Antirevolutionaire Staatkunde* (quarterly) 4 (1930): 325-362.
2 Jhering, *Der Zweck im Recht* [Purpose in law], 8th ed. (Leipzig, 1923), p. 399.

Eugen Ehrlich, in his *Fundamental Principles of the Sociology of Law*, discussed the problem of the sources of law, he explicitly eliminated the juridical problem regarding the sources of law which, if correctly formulated, imply the sources of juridical competence. He was only concerned with the discovery of the factual causes resulting in the organization of human beings, on average, in social communities where certain rules are observed and where this practice translates itself socio-psychologically into the conviction: "that this is so is only *right*." In this way the sources of law are for him identical to the social "facts of law": namely, "custom," "possession," "authority," and a "declaration of will."[1]

One cannot speak of a doctrine of the sovereignty of law in Ehrlich. His sole aim is to demonstrate, without any ulterior political motives, that state law with its "legal propositions" merely fulfills the role of "norms for decision-making" and is completely secondary *vis-à-vis* the inner order of the different organized communities, since all law is essentially law of organized social communities. The problem of sovereignty is located entirely outside his a-political, naturalistic purview. He acknowledges that the science of law with its normative orientation has its value as "practical doctrine of law"; he merely denies that it is the proper *science* of legal life.[2]

A theory of the sovereignty of law could only arise in the sociology of law on either of two conditions: (a) if it joined Duguit in order to achieve the practical goal of fundamentally transforming the state and its legal order (as had been tried by the French founders of the discipline of sociology); or (b) if it joined Gurvitch and his theory of "normative facts" as original sources of law by reintroducing a normative juridical viewpoint (and implicitly the juridical problem of competence) into the study of "social facts."

For his views in the field of sociology of law, Léon Duguit was strongly influenced by the great French sociologist Emile Durkheim, although he largely simplified his teacher's extremely complicated intellectual framework and its ongoing evolution away from naturalistic positivism. Similarly to Durkheim, Duguit viewed law merely as the objective expression of social

1 Ehrlich, *Grundlegung der Soziologie des Rechts* (Munich, 1913), pp. 68 ff.
2 Op. cit., pp. 1 ff.

solidarity, which in primitive societies has the *mechanical* nature of "solidarity through similitude" and in differentiated societies the *organic* nature of "solidarity through division of labor." The objective legal rule is independent of any will. Initially he viewed social solidarity in terms of a consistent naturalistic positivism as a purely physical and vital necessity, as an "equilibrium of physiological needs and the resulting exchange of social services." And in line with this view he also interpreted objective legal rules as mere signs of this necessity, totally bereft of any normativity, hence also free of creating any obligations.

In his later period, however, Duguit saw himself compelled to assign to social law a certain normative meaning because he needed a foundation for his struggle against the classical idea of the state with its dogma of sovereignty, a struggle to which he had devoted his entire career. Nevertheless he rejected every idealistic or "metaphysical" view of social norms. In his eyes such norms were only valid as socio-psychological phenomena that come to expression in people's feelings of solidarity and justice. He did not want to accept as a source of law the "collective consciousness" of Durkheim or the folk-spirit of the Historical School.

In a rationalist and individualist fashion, Duguit also reduced all organized social communities to individuals. The state is nothing but a balance of power between stronger and weaker individuals where the former enforce their will upon the latter. Concepts such as subjective right and competence, legal person and legal organization, he dismissed as products of a metaphysical construction of natural law. Governments have no *right* to claim obedience and they have no competence whatever to create law. Rulers and subjects are equally bound to the norms of "objective law" that flow independently of their will from the factual solidarity of social life and individuals' sense of justice. Not even law itself can bring into existence a single legal norm. At most it can acknowledge an objective legal norm that already exists.

Thus the sovereignty of "social law" is proclaimed across the board, asserting itself in both the national and the international context. The juridical problem of competency seems to have vanished completely. Obviously, if law does not require human *formation* there is no need for competent organs charged with this task. Vanished as well is the problem which the traditional doctrine of sovereignty was meant to solve: the problem of the inter-relation between the various spheres of competence.

Yet it is a problem that just cannot be ignored. The very necessity of forming law through competent organs is already entailed in the modal structure of positive law. In his work on constitutional law Duguit saw himself compelled to reintroduce the formative factor in positive law by distinguishing between *normative* and *constructive* legal rules: "Positive law . . . does not create objective law, but it cannot be denied that it is a factor in its formation."[1] Thus the problem of the formation of law returned in all its force when Duguit articulates his political program for reforming civil private law and public law, indicating how it flowed from his conception of the sovereignty of "social law." He does this in the misleading form of a simple description of factual tendencies toward such reforms observable in legal developments since the second half of the 19th century.[2] Then it suddenly turns out that there did exist an individualist civil private law and a public law against which the sovereign "social law" had to struggle, even though the sociological theory implied that there is no law next to the *"droit social."* Then Duguit calls on collective agreements, common practices in business law, and membership contracts to prove that the private autonomy in civil contract law, from which the *Code civil* proceeds, is in the process of disappearing. Next he points to the syndicalist movement which leads everywhere to the organization of occupations and branches of industry, contributing powerfully to the socialization of law. Finally he highlights the transformation of the Roman, Jacobin, royalist and Napoleonic sovereign State and its public law into a system of "social services" which fulfill their task in full autonomy, subject only to a certain degree of control.

Duguit leaves nothing to the spontaneous, unorganized development of law. The organized industrial and occupational

1 Duguit, *Traité de droit constitutionnel*, 3rd ed., 2 vols. (Paris, 1927), 1:114.
2 See his works *Le droit social, le droit individuel et les transformations de l'État* (1911); *Les transformations générales du droit privé depuis le Code de Napoléon* (1912); *Les transformations du droit public* (Paris, 1921); and *Souveraineté et liberté* (1922).

313

groups now acquire a leading role in the formation of the *"droit social."* By means of a functional decentralization, the traditional state will be transformed, as Saint-Simon already predicted, from a governmental institution controlling people into a system of organized " administration of affairs." The sovereignty of the *"droit social,"* which in Duguit's account is purely constituted as a combination of socio-economic norms and manners (*"moeurs"*), will be elevated, in the individuals' consciousness of what is right, to the "highest level" of a social norm, namely to a *legal* norm, all in the interest of maintaining social solidarity.

In the final analysis this boils down to a complete replacement of classical civil private law and public law. The natural-law theory of human rights, in which the basic principles of civil private law were conceived, is then put aside as "metaphysical speculation." The concept "subjective right" is replaced by the concept of "social function" which leaves no room for the domain of freedom guaranteed in civil law.

And so also this variant of the theory of the sovereignty of law leads to the absolutization of a certain kind of law. Once again the substantive devours the adjective.

* * *

In the context of our investigation, special attention is due to a second sociological variant of the doctrine of the sovereignty of law as recently elaborated by Georges Gurvitch.[1] This author, as he works out his theory, proceeds precisely from the rich variety of legal spheres and the problem of competence entailed in this acknowledgement. He offers an original articulation of the theory of folk-law of the Historical School and arrives at a completely irrationalist and universalist conception of the sovereignty of law. In other words, in the thought of Gurvitch one finds a development directly opposite to that found in Krabbe.

According to Gurvitch the concept of sovereignty is absolutely essential both from a sociological viewpoint and from a juridical

1 It is found already in his first big work, *L'idée du droit social. Notion et système du droit social* (Paris, 1932), in his most systematic work, *L'expérience juridique et la philosophie pluraliste du droit* (Paris, 1935), p. 138 *et passim*, as well as in his *Sociology of Law* (London, 1947), pp. 197 ff., Section III: "Sovereignty and the relations of various jural orders with that of the State."

and political perspective. Viewed from a sociological and juridical standpoint, there must be a sovereign juridical structure capable of harmonizing the various particular structures of law that may come into conflict with each other. In terms of the viewpoint of the state, the latter has to dispose over political sovereignty – which Gurvitch distinguishes sharply from the sovereignty of law since it entails nothing more than the monopoly of unconditional coercion in a territory. This political sovereignty of the state encompasses all local groups brought to a unity in the state.

Gurvitch too is of the opinion that power does not deserve independent status in the problem of sovereignty. Every form of social power is merely a function of the jural order of the group within which it is exercised. He remarks: "That is why sociological analysis leads to the conclusion that the fundamental problem of sovereignty is that of law."[1] Sovereignty is then to be seen merely as a special quality of the power derived from the jural order of the group.

By contrast, writes Gurvitch, the power of the government proper always contains a non-juridical element that is not susceptible to regulation by law. For this reason he views the right of government as a deformation of the true "*droit social*," because it makes the latter serviceable to the "*droit individuel*," which is of an entirely different character.[2] Having established this, the author draws a sharp distinction between *relative* and *absolute* sovereignty. To his mind every social group (state, church, business firm, trade union, employers association, etc.) possesses a *relative* legal sovereignty over the different kinds of law that are brought to a unity in its social jural order. *Absolute* sovereignty, however,

---

1 *Sociology of Law*, p. 198.
2 *L'expérience juridique*, p. 136. Gurvitch denies explicitly that this entails a value judgment. "When I qualify the right of domination as a perversion, a deformation of the law of integration resulting from its enslavement to individual right, then it is not a question of bias . . . I do not deny that domination and subordination can at certain times in history correspond to the profound aspirations of the communities in question, and that their necessity may be sociologically and morally justified. All I affirm is that from a strictly juridical point of view the right of domination cannot be understood in any other way than as a deformation of the social law of integration as a result of its submission to the heterogenous law of coordination. . . . This is not an evaluation, but a juridical explication of structure, an explication that leads to the recognition, in subordination and domination alike, of an element that cannot be reduced to regulation by law, an element of meta-juridical power."

cannot apply to the jural order of the state, but only to the spontaneous, unorganized jural orders of the national and international folk community encompassing all particular groups as parts of this larger whole.

In contrast with the particular groups of a differentiated society, which according to Gurvitch are characterized by a single function or a variety of functions, the all-embracing groups are *supra-functional* and can therefore never be exhausted by a specific organization, such as a state or an economic organization. They are, rather, the total infrastructures of a given society. Their absolutely sovereign jural order determines the material competence of all the specific spheres of law contained within it, including the state. These material competencies are utterly *variable* and *there does not exist a hierarchy among the legal arrangements of these jural orders that would be valid for all times.*

The state in truth never possessed absolute jural sovereignty. It always exercised its political sovereignty, consisting in the monopoly of unconditional coercion, within the boundaries of its variable juridical competence assigned to it by the supra-functional folk community and community of nations. The latter constantly alter the competencies of the state and the other functional groups. Thus, for example, the supra-functional legal order of Western society from the 16th to the 19th century accorded primacy to the law of the territorial state and the right of contract to free and equal individuals. But the distribution of competencies was totally different in the legal order of medieval, state-less feudal society as well as in other supra-functional legal systems.

According to Gurvitch we are currently living in a transitional system of law, one in which the supremacy of the legal order of the state and the right of contract are undermined by the emergence of newly formed authoritative legal institutes of the economic groups of organized capitalism which still reflect a completely disintegrated economic society torn apart by class and group rivalries. On the other hand the increasing organization within the domain of international law continues to push the legal order of the state out of its dominating position. This chaotic transitional period holds out two options: (i) an autonomous legal organization of economic life (equivalent to the legal order of
316

the state) on the basis of industrial democracy, commencing with factory councils and culminating in a national economic Council, that is to say a "guided economy" personally controlled and governed by the parties concerned; or the various economic orders in a totalitarian state.

The significance of Gurvitch's sociology of law is that its theory of the sovereignty of law had a deep philosophical foundation and a many-sided sociological elaboration. It surpasses by far the theory of Duguit, who likewise broke radically with the doctrine of state sovereignty but failed to pay attention to the basic problem of every theory of sovereignty, namely the interrelation between the material juridical spheres of competence of the various societal spheres.

But what remains quite unclear in Gurvitch's theory is how one should conceive the national and international community in the sense of unorganized infrastructures as bearers of an absolute legal sovereignty. In this connection Gurvitch operates with his well-known construction of the "normative fact" as the genuine and original source of law. The national community and the community of nations are according to him social facts in which the value or the idea of law has embodied itself in its multiplicity, while the particular social groups are the "normative facts" that incorporate only certain aspects of the idea of law. This is then immediately related to the supra-functional character of these all-encompassing communities. The legal order of the latter is completely spontaneous and dynamic and comes to consciousness in the integral legal experience of its members. It does not require juridical organs endowed with competency to form law. The jural power of the organized groups is dependent upon the ultimate sovereign because it is derived from it. And so this theory carries the folk-law theory of the Historical School to its ultimate consequences: the assignment of absolute sovereignty to a "mystical" legal order of a truly incomprehensible supra-community, once referred to by Puchta as an "incertum corpus."

Universalist theories of human society have always attempted to understand society as a whole with its parts. To the

317

extent that this sociological universalism originated from an irrationalist turn in humanism's freedom motive, it always looked for the social whole in a completely non-delineated structure which it conceived, consciously or unconsciously, after the model of an undifferentiated social community.

The "folk-spirit" of the folk-community, elevated by the Historical School to be the original material source of law, is indeed, in a closed undifferentiated society, a genuine organized social community. However, it does not belong to natural communities which are by definition unorganized, but always displays, to a greater or lesser degree, an artificial form of organization and has its own undifferentiated structure.[1] As soon as the process of differentiation commences within a society, the undifferentiated folk or tribe (with its undifferentiated subdivisions such as sibs, clans, guilds, etc.) sooner or later is doomed to disappear. There is a fundamental clash between a state and an undifferentiated society. The expression "citizenry" has nothing to do with a primitive folk-community, and the term "nation," too, acquires its meaning only when the undifferentiated folk-community has disappeared.[2] The "nation," as I have explained in the third volume of *De Wijsbegeerte der Wetsidee*, has an intrinsically *political* structure and therefore lacks the character of a *natural* community.[3]

It was the fatal effect of the historicist mode of thought, whose theory of folk-law simply levelled the societal structural differences, that it lost sight of these important sociological truths and construed a continuous historical development between the undifferentiated, primitive folk-community and modern society. It began to view the state as the political organization of the old undifferentiated folk-community whose infrastructure would generate in a natural, organic way both the state and the legal order. It also levelled the structural difference between the state and the

---

1 In his book *Sociology of Law* Gurvitch identifies the primitive tribe with the comprehensive infrastructure of a folk-community which, in terms of his theory, has to be an unorganized one! Clearly, his theory here jumps the rails.

2 Nazism had an ideology of *Volkstum*, but in all the countries occupied by Nazi Germany it opposed every expression of what is *national*.

3 *WdW*, 3:407 [cf. *NC*, 3:468].

genetic natural communities grounded in ties of blood. In the end it erased as well the radical structural differences between the natural communities and the undifferentiated societal communities.

This *folk* conception, originating in Romanticism, has acquired its consistent, universalist elaboration in Gurvitch's sociology of law. Here it is fitted into a modern activist and dynamic philosophy of life, a philosophy that is likewise nourished, among other things, by the spirit of the Restoration period.[1] It proclaims the mystical infrastructures of the folk-community and the international community to be the bearers of the absolute sovereignty of law.

Accordingly, this variant of the doctrine of the sovereignty of law seems to resolve the old antinomy of humanism's concept of sovereignty, the conflict between power and law, and in a deeper sense between "nature" and "freedom." After all, in the unorganized infrastructure of society law arises spontaneously without the intervention of any power organization. But what are we to think of this theory if the "infrastructures" turn out to be no more than speculative constructions of an irrationalist universalism? Predictably, as the theory is worked out further it will automatically reveal that in the end absolute sovereignty is once again assigned to one sphere of life.

Apparently, Gurvitch himself realized that this was the Achilles' heel in his theory of sovereignty. In his *Sociology of Law* he raises the following objection against himself:

> It might, however, be objected that these considerations affect only diffuse, unorganized sovereignty of law, and ignore the problem of jural sovereignty concentrated in an organ capable of expressing it consciously and deliberately. Would not every sufficiently developed society be characterized by such concentration of the sovereignty of law?[2]

---

1 In his book *L'expérience juridique*, p. 136, Gurvitch remarks: "One can see therefore that the role I attribute to spontaneous and unorganized law in the construction of democracy does not imply any romantic belief in the special value of this law, which can be good or bad like every other empirical law and which has nothing to do with natural law." Yet Savigny would have been in full agreement with this statement in support of his own theory of folk-law.

2 Gurvitch, *Sociology of Law*, p. 200.

The answer he gives completely confirms our prediction. In practice, he replies, this problem will only arise when the structures of state law and autonomous economic law are acknowledged as of equal value by the underlying legal orders of the national and international community – something that will only happen some time in the future. When that happens, says Gurvitch, it will become necessary to organize a court of arbitration that has the competence to interpret the spontaneous sovereign law of the national and international community in a binding way. However, in periods in which juridical supremacy is assigned to a specific functional group (e.g., to the church during the medieval era, or to the state during the 16th to the 19th century), it is the group that receives the organs with the competence to interpret and represent the sovereignty of law. "This fact, however, does not mean at all," he assures us, "that jural sovereignty may be attributed to partial groups, because in any case true jural sovereignty remains diffuse within all-inclusive supra-functional societies."[1]

In all cases, therefore, Gurvitch's theory of the sovereignty of law, too, leads to the need to find a competent organ as the exclusive representative and binding interpreter of the absolutely sovereign legal order generated by the all-encompassing social infrastructures. Precisely during periods of state absolutism, in which personal freedom and the freedom of the other spheres of life experience the greatest threat, it is the state itself, according to Gurvitch, that obtains for its usurpation of the original spheres of competence of the other spheres of life its legitimation from sovereign law!

Thus, this theory once again relapses into the fundamental antinomy present in the traditional concept of sovereignty, in spite of the fact that next to Duguit's doctrine of the "*droit social*" it appeared to have made a radical break with this concept. The antinomy is already contained in Gurvitch's conception of "juridical experience" itself, in which he tries to unite in dialectical fashion autonomy and heteronomy, idea and sensory phenomena, "norm" and "fact," "nature" and "freedom." While eliminating the modal structure of the jural aspect, the idea of law is

1 Ibid.

320

approximated as a "logicization of moral values" on the basis of a generalization and qualification of the latter. This in turn entails an internally contradictory combination of the irrational and the rational, the unorganized-spontaneous and the organized, the formed rule and the unstable dynamics, positivity and ideality within legal life.[1]

Notwithstanding the fact that this view appears to take into account all sides of the process of law formation, it continues to be governed by the dialectical ground-motive of nature and freedom which does not allow for the mutually irreducible modal structures of the distinct aspects of reality.

3. The traditional concept of sovereignty and the theory of sphere-sovereignty

Surveying once more the evolution since Bodin of the concept of sovereignty in humanism's conception of law and the state, I think I may state the following: in all its variants, including the doctrine of the sovereignty of law, the concept of sovereignty implied the denial of the existence of original, materially and juridically defined spheres of competence for the state and the other spheres of life.

Original spheres of competence in this material and juridical sense can never be based on an order of positive law, because any formation of positive law as such presupposes the original competence or jural power to do so. Only derived competency can be based on positive law and consequently have a necessarily variable foundation.

No matter how far one ascends in any possible hierarchy of derived competencies formed according to the rules of positive law, in the end one will arrive at the original competency from which the said hierarchy itself has been derived. What then is

1 Cf. *L'experience juridique*, p. 65: "Juridical life, directly experienced, is essentially intermediate between spiritual experience and sensible experience as it is essentially intermediate between moral experience and the experience of logical ideas. This double tension in juridical experience, which is the cause of its intense inner contradiction, its keen drama, has as its result an extreme complexity of its immediate givens: the reality of law, the idea of justice it embodies, and the entire juridical sphere . . . I therefore seek to reconstrue in dialectical fashion this interpenetration of ideal and sensible, value and being, autonomy and heteronomy . . . "

the basis of this original jural power as the presupposition of all positive law?

This jural power can only be grounded in and materially defined by the inner nature, the internal structural principle, of the social sphere within which it is exercised. This principle is not subject to human arbitrariness. As an *original* jural power – not derived from another temporal sphere of life – it may be called *sovereign*, provided this concept of sovereignty is immediately circumscribed by adding: "within its own proper sphere or orbit." And then it becomes at once the radical opposite of the concept of sovereignty construed by humanistic theories. For, in spite of all attempts to provide the latter concept with a juridical basis or at least some legal demarcation, it could not but break theoretically through the boundaries of the original social spheres of competency, and at the same time through the modal confines of law.

"Sphere-sovereignty" is not some vague political slogan, the motto of a particular Christian political party. It is deeply rooted in the very constitution of things and cannot be ignored with impunity. It is the expression of the sovereign will and wisdom of the Creator, who created all things after their kind and set their constant structural boundaries within the order of temporal reality. And He maintains this temporal order of reality even after the Fall, to reveal it in the redemption by Christ Jesus in all its religious fullness of meaning: namely, to focus the whole of temporal reality on the loving service of glorifying God.

In other words, sphere-sovereignty is a universal ontological principle, which receives its special *legal* expression only in the jural aspect of reality.

Sphere-sovereignty reveals two different states of affairs in the structure of reality:
(i)   the mutual irreducibility of the different aspects of reality;
(ii) their indissoluble intertwinement and coherence in the temporal order of reality.
For only in their indissoluble coherence can the different modal aspects of reality reveal their irreducible uniqueness.

This holds for both the structures of *the different modal aspects of reality*, which determine in general the unique nature of the aspects, and the *typical totality structures* or *individuality structures* in which these modal aspects are united in their integral coherence and are grouped and individualized into an individual structural whole in characteristically different ways.

All jural relations – in whatever typical individuality structure of human society they may occur, such as state, church, business firm, international relations, etc. – are determined, as *jural* relations, by the modal structure of the jural aspect of reality. In this modal structure the whole order and coherence of the different aspects are expressed in an irreducible *modus*. As I set out and argued in detail in Volume II of my work *De Wijsbegeerte der Wetsidee*, this modal structure consists of a *nuclear moment* that guarantees the irreducibility of the aspect, and of a series of other structural moments. Some of these other structural moments or elements, the so-called *modal analogies*, maintain the inner coherence of the jural aspect with all those modalities that occupy an earlier position in the order of aspects. The other structural moments, the so-called *modal anticipations*, maintain the connection of the jural aspects with those modalities that are positioned later in the order of aspects. Meanwhile, all of them are qualified by the nuclear moment of the jural aspect.[1]

Among the analogical moments in the modal structure of this aspect, jural competency or jural power occupies an essential place. It is the prerequisite for all human shaping of the principles of law into concrete form, whereby these principles are elaborated into positive norms of law. Competency is *jural* power, and this strong term "jural *power*" expresses the indissoluble connection between the *jural* and the *historical* aspect of reality. For *power* (or *control*) is the modal nuclear moment, the modal "meaning-kernel," of the historical aspect, which is the aspect pertaining to cultural development.

Jural power is not power in the original sense of *historical* power. It is only a historical analogy within the modal structure of law, which is always qualified by the modal nuclear moment of the jural aspect. Yet jural power is indeed *founded* on historical relations of power and therefore can never occur apart from them.

---

1 [As mentioned earlier, Dooyeweerd later distinguished systematically between *retrocipatory* and *anticipatory analogies*.]

Jural competency or jural power is by its very nature never absolute or exclusive. It is premised on a plurality of original spheres of competency which exist in jural relations that are defined and demarcated from each other. For like every other fundamental modal concept of jurisprudence, the concept of competency, too, contains a *numerical* analogy expressive of the inner coherence between the juridical and the quantitative aspect.[1] Jural life in which only one jural subject functions is no more conceivable than jural life that has only one original sphere of competency for the formation of law. Even in a still undifferentiated society this is not the case.

From this it is once again evident that the traditional concept of sovereignty must necessarily collide with the modal sphere-sovereignty of law. No matter how many attempts have been made since Bodin to construe the exclusive sovereignty of the state (or of "the community of nations") over the formation of law, or to bind it again in the end to legal limits, all these constructions have proved incapable of transforming this (essentially unjural) concept of sovereignty into a genuine concept of *law*. This failure goes back to a theoretical conception of reality governed by the religious ground-motive of humanism's world-view, that of nature and freedom, which leaves no room for reality structures grounded in the divine creation order.

That is why a *fundamental* critique of this concept of sovereignty must start exactly here.

The humanist theories of state and law could ultimately not do without a concept of sovereignty, because they had to do duty first of all for defining the interrelationships of the competencies of the various societal spheres. The societal sphere that was declared sovereign, and so was absolutized, was accorded the exclusive, original competency, and all the other spheres were meted out merely derived competencies.

1 For this, see my recent paper for the Royal Academy of the Sciences, "De modale structuur van het juridisch oorzakelijkheidsverband" [The modal structure of jural causality], *Mededelingen der Koninklijke Nederlandse Akademie van Wetenschappen* 13.5 (1950): 93–141. Eng. trans. in *Essays in Legal, Social, and Political Philosophy* (Lewiston, NY, 1997), pp. 39–70.

Given that the very conception of reality underlying the traditional doctrine of sovereignty had no room for the modal structures of the aspects of our experiential world, this conception *a fortiori* could give no place to the typical individuality structures of human society, since individuality structures cannot be understood apart from their foundation in modal structures. As a result, the concept of sovereignty was at the same time proclaimed the essential characteristic of the state, now that the internal structural principle of the state (and with it its inner *nature*) had been eliminated.[1]

Now then, the modal structure of the jural aspect delineates the competence of a societal sphere only in a *general* sense. It is the unique individuality structure which each time gives a sphere its *typical* material content and limits and which provides the only supra-arbitrary basis for a scientific definition of the different types of law that reveal the inner nature of a differentiated societal sphere, such as constitutional law and civil private law, church law, business law, family law, international law, etc., etc.

The individuality structures of the societal spheres are typical structural *principles* that are grounded in the order of reality. They do not become become actual until man *shapes them into concrete forms*. The results of this shaping activity are the *social forms*, which always have a historical foundation and vary throughout the historical evolution of society. The typical structural *principles* of the social spheres of life, on the other hand, have a constant and invariable character, because they determine the *inner* nature of these spheres. The *inner nature* of the state or of

---

1 In Hermann Heller, the most militant champion of the traditional concept of sovereignty, the only essential characteristic of the state is indeed its sovereignty; cf. his definition: "We call the State the universal and therefore unique and sovereign entity of decision-making in a given territory." *Die Souveränität* (Berlin, 1927), p. 110. Although he too treats sovereignty as no more than a historical concept, he also draws the logical consequence from the traditional concept for the area of the formation of law, namely that the modern sovereign state has the only original competence for forming law; cf. his thesis that "for the juridical view of the modern state, the positivity of the communities incorporated in it seems to be derived from the positivity of the state's legal order" (ibid., p. 57). See also his posthumous work *Staatslehre* (Leiden, 1934), pp. 186 ff, and my critique of it in WdW, 3:345–349 [cf. NC, 3:387-396].

the institutional church does not change in the course of time, but only the *social forms* in which they are realized. These variable social forms, to be distinguished in *genetic* and *existential* forms,[1] are at the same time the nodal points of the intertwinement of the various societal spheres, even as they are entirely different from each other in their internal structure and nature.[2] Not one of the structural principles can be realized in isolation, because they are inextricably connected to each other within temporal reality.

Yet, just as each of the modal structures of the aspects in their mutual connectedness retains its modal sphere-sovereignty, so each of the typical structures of the differentiated social spheres in their mutual intertwinement maintains its typical sovereignty in its proper orbit and thus, for example in the jural aspect, it maintains its original sphere of competency in the domain of the formation of law.

The state is no exception in this respect. It too possesses no more than sovereignty within its own proper sphere. However, this does not take away from the fact that its original jural power is of an altogether unique kind.

In conformity with its internal structure, the state has the character of an institutional community of public law embracing government and subjects on the historical basis of a monopolistic organization of the power of the sword in a given territory. For, as with any differentiated social structure, the structure of the state, too, is *typified* by two modal functions located in different modal aspects, the first of which is called the qualifying or internal destination function, the second the "founding function," since the individuality type of the former is founded on that of the latter.

The destination function of the state, in distinction from that of the other societal spheres, lies in the *jural* aspect of social reality. That means that the state, acting qua state in the domain of the formation of law, can never form law that is qualified by a typical extra-jural destination function. All law that serves an extra-jural destination by virtue of the inner structure of the societal

---

1 For this distinction, see my *Tien voordrachten over sociologie* (Delft, 1947), p. 159 [Eng. trans.: *A Christian Theory of Social Institutions* (La Jolla, CA, 1986), pp. 72, 103].

2 Thus, according to its *genetic* form in civil law, a modern marriage is intertwined with the state and the nuclear and extended family, and according to its *existential* form in society it is intertwined with church, business, industry, social interaction, etc.

sphere for which it holds, such as economically qualified internal business law or pistically qualified internal church law, is *specific law, ius specificum*. In contrast, from the nature of the case, law formed by the state is communal law, *ius commune*.

In accordance with its very modal structure, all law displays a correlation of what we have called coordinational and communal relations, because this correlation is inherent in every societal relationship, regardless of its typical structure. In coordinational relations the subjects do not act as members of a whole but in co-ordination, *alongside* or even *opposite* each other. In community relations the subjects are members belonging to a whole that encompasses all of them. That is why in state law we meet with the correlation of two legal domains, namely civil private law and public community law. The first is coordinational law, based on the classic foundations of *ius naturale et gentium*; the second is community law. These are the state's two original spheres of competence, delimited in a material sense by the inner structure of the state.

The state by definition cannot form internal (typically economically qualified) business law of a coordinate or communal character, or internal church law, or any other extra-jurally qualified law. It lacks the original competence to do that. Granted, a state and a business firm, or a state and a church, can work closely together in a state enterprise[1] and in a state church (or an ecclesiastical state). But even such closely intertwined structures never change the firm or the church into *parts* of the state. A state enterprise according to its inner structure remains a business enterprise, and a state church remains a church. Only those organized communities that exhibit the inner structural principle of the state can be parts of the state.

At the same time, along with the internal sphere-sovereignty of the social structures their implicit original spheres of competence in the domain of the formation of law remain intact even in the most intimate structural intertwinements. By definition, internal business law or internal church law cannot take on the typically state character of public law or civil private law. To be sure, all non-state law as *ius specificum* creates lability in civil and public law, creating the impression that the state alone is sovereign in forming law. This false impression is reinforced if one has no eye for the inner structural principles of the social forms of life and

1 [In some jurisdictions these are known as Crown corporations.]

their typical jural spheres, and if one looks only at the formal sources of law like statute laws, ordinances, contracts, court decisions, etc. For just as social forms proved to be the nodal points of the mutual intertwinement of social spheres, so in the jural aspect the formal sources of law are the nodal points of the mutual intertwinement of the original spheres of competency.

In the world of business and commerce, a cartel agreement is the original source of economically qualified coordinational law. At the same time the agreement is incorporated by the state into civil law and possibly also into public law, that is to say, in the two spheres of competence of the state. In consequence, cartel agreements are subject to liability under civil and public law.[1] However, that does not transform internal coordinate business law into civil or public law. It retains its internal sphere-sovereignty regardless of its liability under the law.

And the same holds for the internal community law of a business firm. The moment a state in its civil contract law were to try and bind private agreements to a socio-economic destination, its legal rules would at the same time lose their character as civil private law, as *ius commune*, and could therefore not be enforced with the authority of the state. The history of our Commercial Code speaks volumes here. The civil authorities initially thought they could regulate internal business law through compulsory legislation. They tried to prescribe what are to count as commercial transactions; they tried to bind the limited liability company to an economic destination function; they tried to restrict brokers to dealing in real estate only; and so on, and so forth. On all these points their regulations were dismal failures. Business and industry blithely continued to give form to its own internal law, and time and again the legislator had to step back again from his intervention in an original sphere of competence that was not his.

However, what continues to belong to the state's inalienable competence is to guard against any competency violations on the part of the so-called private spheres of life, and to bind their

1 See my study "De sociologische verhouding tussen recht en economie en het problem van het zgn. 'economische recht' [The sociological relationship between law and economics and the problem of "economic rights"]," in *Opstellen aangeboden aan Prof. Dr. A. Anema en Prof. Dr. P. A. Diepenhorst bij hun afscheid van de Vrije Universiteit* (Amsterdam, 1949), pp. 221-265.

laws to the demands of civil and public law, each of which has its own typical jural principles.

This in broad outline illustrates the meaning of sphere-sovereignty in the domain of the formation of law and explains why the traditional concept of sovereignty could not but come into conflict with reality. For a further elaboration of this view I must refer to the third volume of my *Wijsbegeerte der Wetsidee* and my later publications devoted to the subject. However, there are still two problems that beg a solution if we give up on the traditional concept of sovereignty: (1) Does the state have any room at all for a governmental authority that is not derived from positive constitutional law? (2) What is the relation of the state to the organizations of international law, and implicitly, what is the relation of constitutional to international law?

3.1 Governments and unwritten law

As for the first problem, we have already pointed out that an original competence can never itself be derived from a positive legal order. And in our critique of the various "sovereignty of law" theories it became apparent that an original competence always presupposes an organ that is invested with this jural power.

Now all jural authority that is exercised within the internal sphere of the state as an organized community, according to the inner nature of the state, is a public-legal *governmental* authority which is typically founded on a monopoly of the power of the sword in a given territory. No other differentiated life-sphere can have a jural authority that has this unique character.

Gurvitch's position, perhaps the dominant version of the theory of the sovereignty of law, that governmental authority always contains a metajuridical element of power which is not susceptible to regulation by law, to my mind evinces a lack of insight into the modal structure of the jural and into its relation to the individuality structures of society.

With its public-legal competency, governmental authority is intrinsically jural in nature. But it has a *typical* jural nature that can never be understood apart from the historical (non-jural) power of the sword, because this connection is inherent in the very structural principle of the state. The typical structural connection between the jural and the historical aspect, however, does not detract anything from the modal sphere-sovereignty of both. For we have seen that the modal structure of the jural aspect binds competency as a *jural* power to *historical* power without eradicating the modal structural boundaries between law and power. Similarly, in every societal sphere the *typical* competency is grounded in a *typical* form of historical power-formation.

All we can say in keeping with a Scriptural, Christian understanding is that governmental authority is connected with sin, that it is instituted for the sake of sin. But this is something else than the view of Gurvitch that government is a "deformation" of genuine societal legal power.

Governmental authority can be exercised by a derived series of organs that enjoy relative independence with respect to one another and whose competencies are regulated in the constitution and further defined in so-called organic or generic laws. But original competency requires a jural organ that is indeed endowed with the highest authority within the structural boundaries of the state. Even in the case of a temporal suspension of the positive constitutional order this jural organ can legitimate itself as government because it can perform its public-legal task on the basis of the territorial monopoly over the power of the sword.

We have become so familiar with "emergency law" or acts regulating "emergency measures" that we cannot succumb anymore to the illusion of the "logical closedness" of the positive legal order. This remains the kernel of truth in both the maxim of Roman law, *"princeps legibus solutus est"*[1] and the famous theory of *"le pouvoir constituant."* Even Kelsen had to keep this in mind when he grounded positive law in an original norm that did not present itself as a positive legal stipulation but merely indicated the original organ for the formation of law.

To be sure, in the context of a democratic tradition of political life this original or highest government organ will never be able to legitimize itself without popular support. But the citizens of a state as such can never be endowed with governmental authority since they are not capable of governing. Governance will always be the task of an élite.

---

1 Heller's defense of this saying — "the ruler is not bound by the law" — against modern objectivist theories is certainly his strongest point.

The prominent French theorist of constitutional law, Maurice Hauriou, has expressed this state of affairs in a striking way (albeit in the terminology of the traditional theory of sovereignty) by distinguishing between the *sovereignty of governing* and the *sovereignty of subjection*, both encompassed by the *sovereignty of the idea of the state*.[1]

3.2 The nation-state and international law

The second problem still remaining when we abandoned the traditional concept of sovereignty was this: What is the relation of the state to the organizations of international law, and implicitly, what is the relation between constitutional and international law?

Let me state, first of all, that the entire dilemma generated by the logicistic variant of the modern theory of the sovereignty of law essentially rests on the very concept of sovereignty which that theory intended to leave behind! The variant holds, either that state law receives its validity from international law, or vice versa.

Both hypotheses dissolve themselves in internal contradictions. International law presupposes the existence of independent states with an original sphere of competence, and a plurality of states presupposes a law of nations for the juridical arrangement of their mutual relations. By its very nature international law is *inter*-state law, not *supra*-state or *intra*-state law, a situation that does not preclude the acknowledgment of other subjects of international law.[2] Realizing the idea of a *civitas maxima* would spell the end of international law.

Internatonal law, once somewhat matured, displays, like all law, a correlation of coordinational and communal functions. But even the communal nature of international law, with its current constitution in the Charter of the United Nations, differs fundamentally, both typically and structurally, from the internal law of the state as an organized community, and therefore it can never be the sovereign source of validity of the latter.

1 M. Hauriou, *Précis de droit constitutionnel*, 2nd ed. (Paris, 1929), pp. 86 ff.
2 See Gezina H. J. van der Molen, *Subjecten van volkenrecht*, inaugural oration, Free University, Amsterdam, 29 March 1949 (The Hague, 1949), pp. 12 ff.

In the first place, both the United Nations and its predecessor, the League of Nations, lack the institutional character of the state. The state is not an association or a partnership based upon the principle of free entrance and exit. Like the church and the natural communities, the state is an institution designed to embrace its members independently of their will. By contrast, an international organization can only have the character of a partnership. It cannot force a state to become a member against its will, nor force a state to stay in the partnership. Its jural power lacks the public-legal character of governmental authority because it is not founded in a monopolistic organization of the sword power on a territory. Thus a state can never be part of a union or league of nations in the same sense in which municipalities, provinces, water boards or other autonomous public-legal bodies are parts of the state. Not the traditional concept of sovereignty but rather the internal structural principles of the different organized communities give a satisfactory explanation of this state of affairs.

However, if one proceeds from the universalist idea of a natural, i.e., unorganized, community of nations of which the states are natural members, then implicitly one has introduced a constructivist view of human society leading to a fundamental blurring of all structural boundaries. Why not simply declare the state to be a natural community as well? But what will then remain of the structural differences between the various societal spheres? Surely one can't be serious about the notion that the so-called "natural community of nations" has an inner structure similar to that of a family or a marriage? A family, by definition, ends where blood ties no longer exist. The fact that man-kind sprang from one blood does not provide a basis for a structural theory of human society, for the latter can only be investigated in the *temporal* spheres of social reality. To be sure, a Scriptural view of society has to proceed from the religious root-community of the human race. But this root-community cannot be found *in* time. In temporal reality the principle of structural diversity obtains, which is eliminated by the universalist view in all its variants. The universalist idea of a natural community of states is an

332

ideological construction without foundation in the temporal world-order, just as is the idea of a natural community between different firms in the same branch of industry.

Similarly, the proper relation between international law and constitutional law can only be understood in the light of the cosmological principle of sphere-sovereignty. This principle retains its incontestable validity even amid the most complicated intertwinements within reality.

Constitutional law is enkaptically[1] bound in international law, just as international law is enkaptically bound in the internal constitutional law of states; yet this reciprocal relation does not cancel out their own proper natures and original spheres of competence.[2] The "unity of the jural world-picture" postulated by the "Normlogik" school can be realized theoretically only through a fundamental leveling of the individuality structures of human society and through a fundamental blurring of the boundaries between the original spheres of competence of the societal spheres of life.

---

1 I use the term "enkapsis" in order to designate the relationship between individuality structures that are different in principle and therefore cannot stand in a part-whole relationship.

2 When the controversial article 2, sub 7 of the *Charter of the United Nations* is understood in this sense, then the concept "domestic jurisdiction" loses its absolute character inherent in the traditional concept of sovereignty. For that matter, the reservation mentioned in the final part of this article – "but this principle shall not prejudice the application of enforcement measures under Chapter VII" – implies that international law is bound to the original competence of the state. I do not believe, however, that the statute means it would be correct to assume that international law can unilaterally establish the boundaries of a state. Article 51 alone, which explicitly acknowledges the "natural right of states to individual or collective self-defense," indicates that the Charter assumes as a matter of principle the limited competence of the United Nations, flowing from the nature of the state. On this question, see L. M. Goudrich and E. I. Hambro, *Charter of the United Nations*, 2nd rev. ed. (Boston, 1949), pp. 98–100; Hans Wehberg, "Der Nationale Zuständigkeitsbereich der Staaten nach der Satzung der Vereinten Nationen," *Archiv des Völkerrechts* 2.3 (1950): 259 ff.; and G. H. J. van der Molen, *Uitsluitend nationale bevoegdheid en gemeenschapsbevoegdheid in het volkenrecht* (Exclusive national competency and communal competency in international law), (Wageningen, 1946), pp. 26 ff.

* * *

Here I end my critical reflections on the concept of sovereignty. In the course of my analysis my fundamental objections to this concept in its traditional interpretation revealed its deeper, more general background in the total theoretical conception of reality from which the concept arose.

The theoretical conception of reality from which the different scientific disciplines take their starting point is never neutral with respect to religion but is intrinsically governed by the religious ground-motive from which the activity of scientific thought receives its central driving force.

Here lies the inner, inescapable point of contact between religion and science. As our University expands, the inner reformation of our theoretical view of reality becomes more and more urgent. For it is not horses and their riders that will lead us to victory in the effort to realize the ideal of our institution's founder,[1] but it is solely and ultimately the internal dynamic force of the Scriptural ground-motive of the Reformation – creation, fall, and redemption through Christ Jesus – that must also radically transform our theoretical view of reality if there is to be Christian scholarship that is not merely *scholastically accommodated*, but truly *re-formed*.

Postscript

After this treatise had been set in type, an important speech came to my attention. It was given at the University of Vienna by the President of Austria, Dr. Karl Renner, on the occasion of the commemoration of the fourth anniversary of the Organization of the United Nations.[2]

Renner supports those who consider the concept of sovereignty to be outlived. He states:

> The societal functions that sovereign states together were historically called to fulfill are slipping away from them, a change that is experienced more clearly every day. However, these functions are conceptual attributes of sovereignty; when they break down they lead to the phenomenon that I designate as the dissolution of sovereignty.

1 [Abraham Kuyper is the founder of the Free University of Amsterdam.]
2 Published in the *Österreichische Zeitschrift für öffentlichen Recht*, 2.3/4 (1950): 387 ff.

Renner wants to be serious about eliminating the concept of sovereignty, but when he states: "Every sphere of law and power is limited and therefore absolute force does not belong to a collective organization of nations," he remains in the grip of the historicist view of human society and consequently has no criterion for demarcating the original spheres of competence of the various societal spheres. No wonder, therefore, that at the close of his address he unexpectedly falls back again into the idea of sovereignty that he is combating. The idea of the United Nations, he remarks,

> brings the task of societal organization to its completion and at the same time confirms every member nation's own sphere of law and power, and thus also confirms the inalienable right of the individual human being. And an unbroken staircase leads from the rights of the human individual to the rights of humanity, from human rights to humanity's rights. To be sure, of this staircase the state will long be the most important step, but still only one step.

The function here assigned to the United Nations factually comes down to sovereignly defining the distinct jural spheres and spheres of competence of all other societal bodies that presumably find in this union their crowning organizational completion. Accordingly his concluding remark no longer surprises us:

> If one absolutely does not want to give up the concept of sovereignty one might say: Humanity itself finally wants to be sovereign, wants to become its own master and master of its own historical destiny.

And with that, we are back at humanism's classic confession of faith.

VI

The Relationship between Individual and Community in the Roman and Germanic Conceptions of Property[1]

1. The prevailing contrast between the Roman and the Germanic conception of property

SINCE THE SECOND HALF of the 19th century the debate about the proper relation between individual and community with regard to property right has never lost its relevance. In fact, after the Great War of 1914–18 it has entered an acute stage. It regularly happens that "the" Roman and "the" Germanic conceptions of property are sharply contrasted. In Article 625 of the Dutch Civil Code and Article 544 j° 537 of the French Code Civil the Roman conception is clearly in evidence, characterized by an individualistic conception of the will and power principle. What is considered to be typical of Roman law is the idea that an individual owner has exclusive and absolute competence to dispose of his property as he sees fit. The Roman idea was that restrictions in consideration of the rights of others or the interests of the community did not belong to the inner essence of property right as such but merely put external limits on its exercise. It is this idea that has been branded an expression of individualism.

Furthermore, the Roman conception of property supposedly displayed a uniform character, irrespective of the nature of the entity that was the object of this right. In opposition to this the Germanic view of property is said to have had from the beginning an intrinsically social character which left no room for an absolute or exclusive competency of the individual to dispose of it. It conceived of any obligations towards others and towards the community as an inherent ingredient of property and it bore a

1 Paper presented for discussion at the 9th annual meeting of the alumni association of the Free University, 19–20 April 1936 and published in 1938; republished with slight alterations, under the title "Individu, gemeenschap en eigendom," in *Verkenningen in de wijsbegeerte, de sociologie en de rechtsgeschiedenis* (Amsterdam: Buijten en Schipperheijn, 1962), pp. 149-215. [Translated by D.F.M. Strauss; co-edited by Harry Van Dyke.]

flexible character which fully took into account the differing nature of the legal object.

At this point a further step was taken. The Germanic conception was allied with the Christian conception and with the full weight of this religious accent it was then played off against the pagan conception of Roman law.

This brief summary of the contrast between the Roman and the Germanic conception of property became accepted doctrine – supported on the one hand by the intriguing way in which Jhering portrayed the egoistic and individualistic spirit of Roman private law, and on the other by Gierke's tireless campaign to establish a German Civil Code in a more social, Germanic spirit.

2. Jhering's view of the development of Roman law and its influence

In the two first volumes of his famous work on "The Spirit of Roman Law in the Different Phases of Its Development," Jhering attempted to explain the entire historical development of Roman law in terms of three basic principles: (1) the subjective will principle; (2) the principle of state-formation apparent already in Rome's ancient family and military organization; and (3) the religious principle with its influence on law and the state.

Jhering believed he could fully explain Roman private law in terms of the subjective will principle, that is, from the basic idea that individuals "find the ground of their rights within themselves, in their sense of justice and their enterprising spirit," and that "in respect of the realization of this, they rely on themselves and their own strength."[1] He assumed that Roman law had evinced this individualistic basic trait from its earliest stages. Initially this trait also showed up in the communal principle expressed in the large agnatic family relationship (the *gens*) and in the state based upon this family principle. Family and state were viewed entirely as contractual bonds between equal and self-sufficient individuals.

According to Jhering the will principle is the true source of the Roman conception of property with its hall-marks of an exclusive and absolute will-power of the individual. In no other legal order, Jhering claimed, did the idea of absolute control over an ob-

1 Rudolf von Jhering, *Geist des römischen Rechts auf den verschiedenen Stufen seiner Entwicklung*, 3 vols. (Leipzig, 1852-65), 1:106.

338

ject come to expression with such clarity as in the Roman concept of property. The latter was absolute both with respect to the protection (*reivindicatio*) and the content of the right.[1] The individualistic will or power principle, according to him, found its oldest symbol in the sword or the spear: "It is not the gods who gave the Romans their first provisions for life, unlike the God of Israel who gave the Jews the Promised Land. It was not necessary to resort to purchase and cunning, unlike Dido at the founding of Carthage. The Romans did not have any 'derived' property in the meaning of jurisprudence: derived from God or other men. Rather, they had 'something original,' where the owner is its own originator; they took it as they found it."For the Romans, acquisition of property consisted in *taking* (*capere*).

Property was what was taken by hand (*manu-captum, mancipium*) – and the owner is the one "taking possession" (*herus*). As the famous Roman jurist, Gaius (2nd cent. A.D.) informs us in his *Institutiones*: from the beginning the best form of acquiring property was to capture it from the enemy.[2]

Jhering found an exceptional confirmation of his view that the individualistic will principle already inspired the oldest Roman conception of property among other places in the famous stipulation of the Law of the Twelve Tables, which supposedly formulated the absolute disposal competence of the testator with respect to his property.[3]

Subsequent authors largely built on Jhering's theory as briefly sketched above in its main features.[4] Particularly Otto von Gierke, the famous advocate of the Germanic understanding of

---

1 Ibid., 2:149.
2 Gaius, *Institutiones* 4.16: "maxime sua esse credebant, quae ex hostibus cepissent."
3 Jhering, *Geist des römischen Rechts*, 2:148, quoting Table V.3: *uti legassit super pecunia tutelave suae rei, ita ius esto*: "as a man has provided in his will in regard to his money and the care of his property, so let it be binding."
4 Cf. e.g. Gierke's characterization of the Roman concept of property in his work *Deutsches Privatrecht* (Leipzig, 1905), 2:360: "According to the Roman conception, property is that abstract relationship by virtue of which an object falls within the sphere of control of a person. No matter what object, Roman property law thus always displays the same quality. It is purely private law. As such it is strictly individualistic in its construction. Throughout, it appears as free property right. According to its concepts it entails unrestricted power. It does not sacrifice anything through restrictions and remains the same also in the case of a temporary nullification of its content (*nuda proprietas*).

law, gratefully employed it in order to oppose the Roman "individualistic" property concept with the "social" Germanic one.[1] He held this opinion even though he did not deny that the reception of Roman law in the Germanic countries had had a beneficial effect in the area of property relationships.

To be sure, the way in which this contrast between Roman and Germanic property conceptions was constructed did not escape counter-arguments from the Romanist side. Maschke,[2] Pininski[3] and other authors attempted to construct from the sources a totally different Roman conception of property law, one in which the absoluteness and exclusivity was completely hollowed out. Maschke believed that the Roman concept of property, just like the Germanic one, allowed for a division according to competencies.[4]

Finally, in the footsteps of the famous Niebuhr and Mommsen, various authors taught that originally in Rome all possessions in land, just as was the case among Germanic peoples, was inalienable collective property of the *gens* and that the introduction of individual property with its exclusive character of property law was owing to ancient laws dating from the days when Rome had a king. Supporting this view, besides Roman poetry that spoke of a golden age when land was the undivided possession of the whole community, were mainly Roman historians like Pliny, Varro, Livy and others, according to whom the Roman king Numa took the land captured by Romulus and divided it

---

1 Many times it was not done in the spirit of Jhering! For he pointed out repeatedly that it concerned merely the abstract juridical side of Roman society; in real life the juridical will-power was subject to numerous moral and social restrictions. Jhering held that the very distinction between *"ius"* and *"mos"* demonstrated the higher development of the Roman conception of law in comparison with the Germanic one (op. cit., 2:101 ff.). He consistently defended the "individualism" of Roman law against misconceptions.
2 Richard Maschke, *Das Eigenthum im Zivilund Strafrechte* (Berlin and Leipzig, 1895).
3 Leon Pininski, *Begriff und Grenzen des Eigenthumsrechts nach römischem Recht* (Vienna, 1902).
4 Maschke, op. cit., p. 864.

among the citizens, such that each citizen was granted a plot of about half a hectare.[1]

This entire criticism, however, failed to touch the *core* of the accepted doctrine because it did not attack Jhering's research method.[2] Throughout the nineteenth century the Romanist wing generally agreed with Jhering's view of the individualistic principle of will at the core of subjective right. From the beginning the theory of the will also negatively affected the study of the sources of Roman law. This theory, dominant in the Romanist wing of the Historical Law School but eventually rejected by Jhering, was worked out especially by the German idealist philosopher Hegel.

3. The dialectical view of Hegel

What this dialectical mode of thought, as it linked up historically with Roman private law, did first of all was to posit the abstract right within an exclusive and absolute sphere of will of the individual. Next, it showed how in civil society this abstract element of the will necessarily called forth its opposite: the norm for civil and administrative law whereby the individual in spite of himself was made subject to the requirements of the community. Finally, within the state as absolute moral totality and the highest revelation of the "objective Spirit," individual and community came to a higher synthesis as the individual member was absorbed within the whole.

One finds the unmistakable influence of this dialectical Hegelian conception of law in Jhering's research method.[3] It brought him to accept, as an "ethical minimum" of the oldest phase of development of Roman law, the individual with his au-

---

1 [I.e., 2 *iugera* or 1.25 acres.] Cf. Theodor Mommsen, *Römische Geschichte*, chap. XIII. In the same sense, inter alia, August Meitzen, *Siedlung und Agrarwesen der Westgermanen und Ostgermanen, der Kelten, Römer, Finnen und Slawen* (Berlin, 1895), 1 : 252 ff. But see also Moritz Voigt, "Ueber die *bina iugera* und ältesten römischen Agrarverfassung," *Rheinisches Museum für Philologie* 24 (1869): 52 ff.

2 As far as the theory of Mommsen is concerned, Jhering too acknowledged that initially the *gentiles* did possess guarantees against the transfer of land into the ownership of a *familia* belonging to a different *gens*. He also himself pointed out certain restrictions to property right imposed by the state.

3 Cf. his particular appreciation of Hegel's conception of the essence of Roman law in *Geist des römischen Rechts*, 1:100, even though he does formulate some criticism.

tonomous will and power, while holding him in dialectical tension with the community principle in the family and the religious principle in sacred law (*fas*). He was well aware that he was thus basing his research on a hypothesis from philosophy of history that harbors the danger of misconstruing and misinterpreting the source material. "Recognizing this," he writes, "we want to approach our task of advancing insight into the oldest Roman state by asking to what extent it had already distanced itself from its absolute starting-point of history – the individual or the community of individuals – and at what points of the historically recognizable situation it still bore traces of this starting-point. Although mistakes cannot always be avoided, I reckon that it is more correct and more promising if we proceed from the assumption that *history commenced with infinitely little* and that accordingly we must try to attach an 'ethical minimum' to the first structures that unveil themselves to our observation, rather than be content to settle for the given facts of state and law."[1]

4. Primitive societies

In the meantime, precisely this starting-point of Jhering's view of history contradicts everything we have learned from modern ethnology about primitive societal relationships.[2] If Jhering's view of the origin of Roman property right were correct, the Roman people indeed would have occupied a most exceptional position among peoples by already assigning to the individual person a freedom which according to the historical record can only be the fruit of an advanced stage in a society's process of individualization and differentiation.

It therefore deserves notice that recently a totally different conception of the origin of the Roman conception of property has been gaining ground. In respect of the original form of the Roman *dominium* it does not alter the features of absoluteness and exclusivity, but instead provides a totally different interpretation of them – one which we believe is more correct from the perspec-

1 Ibid., 1:105.
2 Bonfante too was right in pointing this out; see his *Histoire du droit romain*, 3rd ed., 2 vols. (Paris, 1928), 1:186. He opposed the view that the testator's freedom in the Law of the Twelve Tables was an indication of the early recognition in Roman law of the "predominance of individualism". He called such opinions "affirmations that fly in the face of the entire Roman history of law and Roman civilization."

tive of legal history by explaining them from the initially undifferentiated structure of the Roman *familia*.[1]

5. The contribution of Bonfante

To the Italian Romanist, the late Professor Pietro Bonfante of the University of Rome, belongs the honor of having opened the way for a better insight into the development of Roman law in general and Roman property right in particular.[2] He accomplished this in various studies and in particular in his two-volume work translated into French as *Histoire du droit romain* (3rd ed., 1928).

For the research method applied by him he chose an unfortunate name which caused much misunderstanding, in particular from the neo-Hegelian authors Gentile and Croce. Bonfante called it the "organic" or "naturalistic" method and viewed it as a necessary correction of and supplementary to the critical-historical and comparative mode of research.[3]

The designation "naturalistic" all too easily calls forth an association with the naturalistic view of history, but Bonfante's view is in no way connected to the naturalistic philosophy of history à la Taine or Buckle. What then did he mean by the expression "the organic or naturalistic method"?

He defined it as a particular application of the general principles of critical-historical research. One has to discover from the institutions of legal life themselves the secret of their origination and the most mysterious phases of their development. In doing so, one has to take as one's starting-point that the older forms, also in the case of entirely changed historical conditions, will adjust to new goals, but that they nevertheless will always con-

---

1 This *familia* structure certainly did not escape Jhering's attention (cf. op. cit., 2:156 ff.). He even raised the question whether or not "the *res mancipi* alongside *mancipatio* constituted original parts of the *manus* system." But he did not pursue this promising notion any further, for then he would have had to give up his individualistic premise.

2 In his important study, "Methode und Wert des heutigen Studium des römischen Rechts," *Tijdschrift voor Rechtsgeschiedenis* 15 (1937): 130, Emilio Betti remarks: "As for Roman 'individualism,' we are now in a better position to asses it than we were in the previous century." He refers to the work of Fritz Schulz, *Prinzipien des römischen Rechts* (Munich, 1934), pp. 99 ff and 161; but he does not mention the ground-breaking work of Bonfante!

3 On this method, see Bonfante, "Il metodo naturalistico nella historia del diritto," *Rivista ialiana di sociologia* 21 (1997): 53 ff., as well as his *Scritti giuridici varii*, Vol. I (Turin, 1916), pp. 190 ff.; Vol. IV (Rome, 1925), pp. 46 ff.

tinue to reveal traces of the ends they served in an earlier phase of development.

In this, Bonfante observed an historical analogy of what is also striking in natural organic life. It is possible that this analogy brought him to his questionable characterization of his method as "naturalistic" or "organic."

In the meantime Bonfante gained a following also outside Italy.[1] In 1936, for example, an American sociologist and economist from the modern "institutional school," Reinold Noyes, published a book in which the development of Roman and English law with respect to the institution of property was investigated according to Bonfante's method of research. Noyes's research into the origin and development of the Roman concept of *dominium* fully corroborated the results of Bonfante's own research.[2]

With regard to Bonfante's conception of the exclusive and absolute character of the primitive Roman conception of property, one can trace his influence also to modern Romanists who for the rest do not regard themselves in any way as belonging to his school in the strict sense of the word.[3]

On the other hand it must be conceded that the criticism exercised on certain parts of Bonfante's theory by several leading German Romanists did point out some weak spots in them. This applies, for example, to his theory of inheritance laws which is all too much dominated by the preconceived opinion that in Rome the will predated intestate succession. It clashes both with the results of comparative legal history and the oldest Roman sources.

Meanwhile, Ernst Rabel[4] has already pointed out that this succession theory in no way involves the essence of Bonfante's theory. It is quite feasible to accept the theory about original family property as defended by Heinrich Mitteis and with him by the

---

1 In Italy itself his view became the dominant one among the Romanists.
2 C. Reinold Noyes, *The Institution of Property* (New York, 1936), *passim*.
3 See e.g. Fernand de Visscher, *Le rôle de l'auctoritas* (Ghent, 1933). In spite of his rigorous but hardly plausible distinction between the old *mancipium* as *imperium domesticum* and the *dominium*, he too essentially continues Bonfante's views. See also the intriguing study by Franz Leifer, "Mancipium und Auctoritas," *Zeitschrift der Savigny-Stiftung für Rechtsgeschichte, Romanistische Abteilung* 57 (1937): 127 and 151n, where he remarks that in De Visscher's polemic against Bonfante "the latter's influence on the author's positions is palpable at every turn."
4 E. Rabel, " Die Erbrechtstheorie Bonfantes," *Zeitschrift der Savigny-Stiftung für Rechtsgeschichte, Romanistische Abteilung* 50 (1930): 295 ff.

leading German theorists and consequently recognize intestate succession as anterior to the will without giving up the quintessence of Bonfante's view of *dominium* in Roman law.

The question whether to endorse Bonfante's theory about the origin of Roman *dominium* or instead the traditional theory is of more than mere legal-historical significance. At stake is insight into the very structure and unfolding process of human society, which is of fundamental value not only for legal history but also for legal philosophy and the politics of law.

The contrast between the "individualistic Roman" and the "social Germanic" conception of property has been turned into a political shibboleth in the full sense of the word. The moderate and well-considered attitude which Gierke adopted in his struggle for a German Civil Code in a Christian-Germanic spirit and which directly after the publication of the draft of 1889 appeared in his Viennese address on *Die soziale Aufgabe des Privatrechts* (The social task of civil law) has since the [First] World War made way among various opponents of "the Roman conception of property" for a kind of radicalism. An important role in all of this is played by lack of insight into the inner nature of civil law and a fundamentally erroneous identification of civil law and private law, an error which for that matter has confused the issue from the start.

Accordingly, now that the community idea has turned today against individual freedom in truly absolutistic fashion, and particularly while in the dictatorships of Central and Eastern Europe civil property law is gradually being undermined in a perilous way, it will be timely to form a clear idea of the true structure of property in civil law and of the development which gave this legal concept its prominence in Roman legal history.

6. The nature of civil law

Civil law proper, as it has found expression in modern law codes, is the outcome of a long-standing historical process. It presupposes a high degree of differentiation and integration of legal life and is geared to one structure in human society only, namely that of coordinational civil relationships that fall outside the internal communal and collective spheres of marriage, family, the business firm, organizations, and so on, thus to relationships in which individuals do not exercise any authority over one another.

345

On the one hand civil law presupposes the existence of a genuine state, one in which civil-legal cases are decided by an impartial judiciary and decisions arrived at by the civil judge are executed by officers of the state. On the other hand it presupposes the development of individualized private societal relationships where people participate in coordinated interaction as individual legal subjects with juridical equality. Distinct from the specific private communal law obtaining within particular societal collectivities such as the family, church, school, business, social club, etc., the sole purpose of civil law is to apply the demands of social justice in the reciprocal private interactions between individuals. In this respect civil law is also clearly distinct from constitutional law, although it is necessarily interwoven with the inner law of the state. Constitutional law, taken in a broad sense, is typically organized communal law of a distinct character: it comprehends the legal organization and arrangement of relationships of authority and compliance between government and subjects. This organization is founded on the sword power of the government and is intended to bring to expression the public-legal idea of the common good. Civil law, by contrast, regulates private coordinational relationships as such, displaying no relationships of authority and subordination. It is governed by the idea of civil private law.

In modern civil law the worth of the individual person comes to juridical expression independently of race, ethnicity, religion, membership in a specific interest group, etc. Although its legislative origin is inextricably intertwined with the state, yet civil law as such is not *communal law*[1] and cannot be made into communal law without affecting its inner nature.

Nevertheless, civil law by its very nature does not exist in isolation but only in indissoluble intertwinement with all the other jural spheres of human society: with private communal law in the distinct structures of marriage, nuclear family, extended family, church, business firm, school, voluntary organizations and associations, etc. etc. Civil law is also intertwined with the public law of the state as an organized community; with international law; with the non-civil, free coordinational law of normal social interaction.

---

1   Not even in its regulation of the external civil-legal relationships between family members, or members of other communities.

When, for example, our Civil Code makes the introductory remark regarding marriage: "The law treats marriage only with respect to its civil relationships," then it proceeds from the assumption that marriage functions in numerous other relationships and that this intimate societal form of life has an *internal* communal sphere without which the merely civil-legal relationships would not be able to function *externally*.

Civil law, according to its entire structure as a differentiated legal system, is the asylum of the individual person, the fortress for the protection of the individual person within legal life.

7. Civil law and non-civil law

Civil law can fulfill this role only in unbreakable coherence with the communal and collective jural spheres[1] in which the solidarity of the members in relationships of authority and subordination is maintained.

Within these communal and collective spheres a person is only a member of the collectivity and is not considered according to his private sphere as an individual. In civil-legal relationships, however, the government has to ensure that every person receives his due as an individual.

Precisely to prevent overstraining society's communal and collective spheres, civil law functions as a beneficial bulwark insofar as an individual's civil rights ought to be protected against infringements by collective and communal organs – including that of the state.

However, as we shall see later, civil law cannot accomplish this task alone. On the one hand it needs the counterbalance of the state's social legislation guided by the public-legal idea of community which prevents private individuals or organized communities from usurping power. On the other hand it needs the counterweight of private communities which ought to protect their internal spheres against usurpation by the state.

---

1 Every societal collectivity (*"verband"*) embraces a community, but not every community is a societal collectivity. A societal collectivity always has organs endowed with power. The family community, to the extent that it is built solely upon a cognate basis, lacks such an organ. On the other hand, a societal collectivity has relative continuity independent of changes in its membership. For that reason, for example, marriage as a community is not a societal collectivity.

When the principles of civil law are overemphasized the inevitable effect is an individualistic conception of law. But this does not justify the view that civil law itself is individualistic just because it cannot fulfill the role of a communal law.

8. Civil property right

All of this should be kept in mind when evaluating civil property right. *Civil law* should never – as so frequently happens in legal science – be equated with all of *private law* understood as all law falling outside the domain of *public law*. After all, as we have seen, private law encompasses many spheres of law which as such do not display a civil-legal character.

What falls outside the domain of civil law is all the specific law of private communities and collectivities which serve their inner structure, guided by a destination lying outside the jural domain. This is the case in internal marriage and family law, internal business law, internal associational law, internal church law, and so on. The same goes for those branches of private law which, although they do not display a communal or collective character, are typically guided by an extra-jural destination. An example would be the commercial rules that arose in society to deal directly with the economic destination of business and industry, such as conditions commonly used in the insurance business like the exclusion of particular risks, a condition that makes sense only for reasons of business economics.

Non-civil private law in real relationships must be taken into account in the formation of civil law only to the extent that it is intertwined with civil law. But then it is done solely for the protection of the sphere of civil law itself and not for interfering in the internal domain of non-civil private law.

Accordingly, Gierke's remark that "our private law must be *social* or it will not be"[1] can be positively misleading. Although he meant civil law he confused it with non-civil, private communal law. In doing so he failed to appreciate the differentiated structure typical of civil law. His mistake was not that he called attention to the intimate intertwinement of civil law with private and public communal law, but that he obscured the distinctive

1   *Die soziale Aufgabe des Privatrechts* (Berlin, 1889), p. 45.

character of civil law by equating it with the whole of private law, even though he did distinguish clearly between "social law" and "individual law."

Property right in modern civil law is differentiated subjective right which does not cover the legal concept of property according to all its facets but only according to one: the civil-legal side. Therefore it can only exist in unbreakable coherence with the communal and collective functions of property law while maintaining its own differentiated structure.[1]

The primitive Roman *ius civile*[2] did not know a civil property right in this differentiated sense. It knew only an undifferentiated element of *dominium* in which the individual competence of disposal and enjoyment was totally dependent upon the position that a person occupied within the undifferentiated societal collectivity.

The undifferentiated state of societal forms is characteristic of a more primitive, not yet disclosed cultural level of a people. An undifferentiated society does not know an independent state or church, no independent business or school community. It also is not acquainted with individualized relationships of social interaction with cosmopolitan tendencies, and it does not have societal organizations based upon free access. Primitive societal forms such as the extended family, sib or clan, the folk commu-

1 Consider the following case. A local congregation is the owner of a church building. Its property right involves both civil law and church law. Under civil law, following the principle of autonomy according to which the owner is free to decide for what specific purpose he wants to use his property, the church is perfectly free to rent out its building on Sundays to a movie theater company. Under church law, however, the matter is quite different. The main part of this building is typically meant for worship. This imposes a restriction under communal law to the freedom which the church has under civil law. However, it is a restriction that would not stand up in a court of civil law, but would have force of law only under church law. Any attempt to incorporate the communal restriction into civil law would undermine civil law itself.

2 Primitive *ius civile* as found in the *Law of the Twelve Tables* is by its content still entirely quiritary folk-law and therefore does not exhibit anything like genuine civil law. Thus one must not translate *ius civile* as "civil law." [In the original article the note continues: ". . . just as little as one may translate *ius gentium* as 'law of nations.' It is folk-law."]

nity and tribe rather fulfill in an undifferentiated way all the tasks for which distinct societal forms develop as the level of a culture opens up. In contrast to the differentiated societal forms, they are of a nature that excludes all direct power of other forms over their subordinates. Here peaceful society is *enclosed* within the strict walls of division erected by sib, clan, folk or tribal collectivity. This explains that when a culture opens up, the first to go are the partitions erected by sib or clan, folk and tribe. For world history cannot unfold in isolated groups but only in international intercourse between cultured peoples.

9. The development of the absolute and exclusive character of the Roman concept of *dominium*

Absoluteness and exclusivity were also typical of the primitive, undifferentiated structure of the Roman patrician family, the *gens*, and the quiritary folk collectivity. Here the individual person was *absorbed* within the societal collectivity. He had no civil private legal sphere that he could regard as the asylum and fortress of his personal independence as a human being. Rejection from the folk resulted, just as among Germanic peoples, in becoming a person without any *rights* and without any *peace*. Salic Law proclaimed: *"Wargus sit!"* that is, "Let him bear a wolf's head." As the wolf was outlawed, so was the member of the folk who had been declared to be "without peace."

The idea of a primitive, undifferentiated community therefore bears an *absolutistic* and *exclusive character*. It does not leave any room for a private sphere of freedom attached to the individual person. The undifferentiated collective authority here encompasses the human being in all spheres of life interwoven with the collectivity.

Now it can be shown that the formal exclusivity and absoluteness of the Roman concept of *dominium* indeed derived from this undifferentiated condition, hence cannot possibly have had an individualistic origin. The patrician *gens*[1] was probably the original primitive social unit of Roman society. Initially the Roman *civitas* then was nothing but a folk or a tribal collectivity on the basis of these *gentile* collectivities. In the gradual process by which

1 [The clause "showing similarities with the Germanic sib and the Irish clan" appeared in the 1938 edition but was deleted in the 1962 edition.]

the Roman city-state began to liberate itself from this primitive society, its first political activity aimed at breaking down the jurisdiction of the *gentes*. A definitive step in this direction was the state's promotion of dividing up the old *gens* lands among the *patres familiae*, i.e., the heads of the household communities. The *actio familiae erciscundae*, which is explicitly mentioned in the Law of the Twelve Tables, clearly points in this direction, as does the stipulation so strongly emphasized by Jhering: [*"Uti legassit super pecunia tutelave suae rei, ita ius esto"*].[1] This terminated the long-standing control of the *gens* over the family property.

To my mind Mitteis, Rabel and others have convincingly demonstrated that in the period immediately preceding the Twelve Tables there must have been a transitional period when families had communal ownership of property. Their conclusion is based on the subsequent right of inheritance of the so-called *heredes-sui*, i.e., the house heirs. But these authors, too, concede that after the Law of the Twelve Tables no trace is found of a codetermination right of the *sui* over the *familia* while the *paterfamilias* was still alive.[2]

It is the Roman *familia* or *domus* which, after the gradual decline of the larger *gentile* collectivity, emerged as the smaller, closed, so-called *private* social unit directly opposite the city-state as a *public* social unity. But Bonfante correctly points out that this opposition should not be understood in the sense of a *material* distinction between public law and private law, for that distinction emerged only at a later stage.[3] The Roman *familia* or *domus*, after all, was an undifferentiated collective societal bond which, like the state, looked after political functions within its own sphere, even though internally the structural principle of the family community fulfilled the guiding role.[4]

1 Cf. Bonfante, op. cit., 1:185, 211.
2 See also Franz Leifer, op. cit., p. 119.
3 Bonfante, op. cit., p. 165: "The distinction between *ius populi* (or *ius publicum*) and *ius privatum*, between *res publica* and *res privata* or *familiaris*, could only have been, at the beginning, a distinction between diverse spheres, never between things that are essentially different." See also Jhering, op. cit., 1:179 ff.
4 See my *WdW*, 3:295 ff. [cf. *NC*, 3:346-376].

Among *the persons* who belonged to the *familia* we find not only the agnatic (not merely cognatic) relatives as well as the housewife (at least insofar as she found herself in *manu mariti*), but also slaves, clients and those who were taken up in the family community through adoption or arrogation. Within the *familia*, all persons and properties that were unbreakably connected to the family community (the so-called *res mancipi*), were subject to the *manus* (understood in a broad sense), the exclusive and undifferentiated *dominium* of the head of the household, the *paterfamilias*.[1] Romans preferably connected the word *dominium* with *domus*.[2]

Ever since the Twelve Tables, whatever belonged to the household community belonged to the *patrimonium* of the head of the household, subject to his undifferentiated property right. But according to its inner nature it primarily bore the character of authority within an organized community or societal collectivity. As such it was therefore more an *officium*, an office, than it was a *ius*, a subjective property right, although it definitely displayed an aspect of property right as well. This *dominium* was *absolute* and *exclusive*, not in the sense of an "individualistic" civil property right, but only in the sense that it was proof against penetration by the public power of the *civitas*.

Occupying the first place among *the goods* that were subject to the *dominium* of the *paterfamilias* (and originally that may have been only the *res mancipi*) was the land with its house.

1   The way in which De Visscher (in *Studia et Documenta Historiae et Juris*, nr. II, 1936, pp. 317 ff.) argues against Bonfante that there did exist a sharp distinction between the authority in the primitive family and in the *dominium* appears to suffer from a lack of historical perspective. One should not look for abstract, differentiated concepts in primitive thought. The very competence of the *paterfamilias* to sell his sons "trans Tiberim" clearly points in the direction of an undifferentiated conception of authority that embraced at once political and property rights. De Visscher fully endorses Bonfante's notion that the *ager privatus* was the main ingredient of the *res mancipi*, since it represented "the zone in which the *paterfamilias* exercised his exclusive authority to command." But surely we are here completely within the terrain of *dominium* in its undifferentiated sense?
2   See Jhering, op. cit., 2:161. However, the etymological derivation of *dominium* from *domus* is incorrect; see Georg Curtius, *Griechische Etymologie*, 4th ed. (Leipzig, 1870), pp. 231, 233.

Mommsen's view, mentioned above, that king Numa introduced individual ownership of land, is hardly tenable because it has been discovered that the allotment of *bina iugera* (which for that matter must be considered inadequate for the livelihood of a people that grew mainly wheat) was destined for the *plebeian* class, who until that time had been landless.

However, the patrician family, just as earlier the *gens* and later the *civitas*, enjoyed a right to the land that was different from civil property right. It was a form of ownership that displayed totally different traits, thanks to its initial absolute and exclusive character. In respect of land, *dominium* had the character of a "domain" or *territory* laid out in a sacred ceremony. Within this *territory* the *paterfamilias* had an exclusive legal authority over all the people and goods within the household community. In this regard the *ager privatus* or *familiaris* showed an unmistakable connection with the *ager publicus*, the public domain of the Roman *civitas*.

The further one goes back in recorded Roman history the more private ownership displays an absolute and exclusive character. Initially no other right to land was known than property right as well as two inheritable land services (access and the flow of water), subsumed under the *res mancipi*. All other property right to land, bearing an explicit civil-legal status of a property right, was only introduced in a relatively late, more advanced stage of Roman law. It was completely unknown to the old *ius quiritium* or *ius civile*, i.e., the old folk-law of the early Romans.

The sparse stipulations contained in the Twelve Tables served to guarantee the reciprocal freedom of landholdings rather than to establish restrictions in the exercise of property right.[1]

The exclusive power over all goods present on, above and underneath the soil – a typical feature of Roman land ownership – cannot be explained with the aid of the structure of civil property right. From an economic standpoint such an exclusive power was rather absurd. This feature therefore can be understood only in the light of the primarily political structure of undifferentiated household authority.[2]

---

1 To my mind Bonfante has shown this convincingly; op. cit., 1:213 ff.
2 The analysis of the original *dominium* by Bonfante in this connection is indeed excellent; see op. cit., 205 ff.).

Moreover, only a part of the land, and certainly not the largest part, was private property. Judging by the reform laws of the Gracchi brothers, the economy in antiquity was based more upon the *ager publicus*, of which private families could acquire only a dependent ownership but no property right: a *possessio*, not a *dominium ex iure quiritium*. Compared to the modest area covered by land in the form of property, the shares of the rich patricians in the *ager publicus* were enormous.

But this *possessio* differed in principle from the *dominium ex iure quiritium*. It was a dependent proprietary right that remained subject to the *dominium* of the state, a right which the state, legally at least, could withdraw at any time. Originally the land was only handed out to the patricians for purposes of exploitation and cultivation, either in rent (*locatio conductio*), which gave no juridical proprietary right to the renter, or in genuine *ownership*. Although this form of ownership was consolidated through inheritance in the large families, it never became a free and exclusive *dominium*. Only later did agrarian laws allot to the plebeians, as compensation for their initial exclusion, small plots (at first two, later seven or more *iugera*). These pieces from the *ager publicus* were granted *in outright ownership*. But this by no means implied, as Mommsen believed, that the state thereby created private land ownership.[1] After all, this plebeian property was totally – also in the rites of *"limitatio"* – modeled after the example of the *patres*, and patrician property certainly existed already before the rise of the state. Probably only the property rights of the plebeians may be traced back to laws when Rome had kings.

10. A significant result of Bonfante's investigations

A remarkable and instructive result of Bonfante's research is his exposition of the original structure of Roman contract law. It had been customary to distinguish clearly between *actiones in rem*[2] and *actiones in personam* (actions about goods and actions about persons), alongside the development of private property law and the last will, as main arguments for the strongly advanced individualization already of the oldest forms of Roman legal life in

---

1 This is also denied by Jhering, op. cit., 1:199.
2 I leave aside the question whether *res* originally did not at all mean "thing," as Noyes believes (op. cit., p. 178), but instead referred to a legal claim before the court.

contrast to that of the other nations. Contract law, the domain of *actiones in personam*, personal lawsuits, from the beginning presumably displayed the character of an individual property right and was made serviceable to commercial purposes.

By contrast, Bonfante justifiably emphasized that the oldest Roman contract law on the whole did not display the structure of property law but rather of penal law. We note in passing that the same is true of the oldest phases of Germanic contract law.

Whereas in the early years the law of things – the *dominium* – belonged *par excellence* to family law, contract law was in sharp contrast to it. The best way to explain its role is to compare it with modern international law in the restricted sense of law for the external relations between sovereign states. In Rome, they regulated relations between the sovereign heads of households, regulations for which the oldest forms of contract law laid down only penal rules.

It is therefore remarkable to note that the entire contrast between personal law and the law of things grew stronger the further one goes back to former phases in Rome's legal development and became weaker as civil property law began to arise.

Of the known sources dating from the reign of the Emperors dealing with the rise of contracts – namely, agreements, crimes against property, and a series of legal facts which Gaius brought together under the collective name *variae causarum figurae* – only the *delicta* date back to the primitive phase of development.

The origin of modern property law contracts can be precisely pinpointed in Roman law. It was not introduced until the *Lex Poetelia* of 326 B.C., as described by Livy.[1] After this the *obligatio* as a feature of private law lost its primitive character which had entailed control, backed by penal law, over the body of the debtor, the *nexus* or *reus*, and thus indeed turned debt (from the vantage point of the debtor) into an obligation under property law.

---

1 Titus Livius, *Ab urbe condita*, 8.28: "Ep annno plebei romanae velut aliud initium libertatis factum est, quod necti desierunt ... iussique consules ferre ad populum, ne quis *nisi qui noxam meruisset donec poenam lueret*, in compedibus aut in nervo teneretur; *pecuniae creditae bona debitoris, non corpus obnoxium esset*. Ita nexi soluti; cautumque in posterum, ne necterentur." [The *Lex Poetelia* abolished bondage for debt.]

At the time of the Twelve Tables, contract law was still entirely absorbed by a system of crime and punishment, and the only distinction between private and public penalties (*poena privata* and *poena publica*) lay in the subject who imposed the penalty: either the *paterfamilias* or the *magistrate*.

11. Roman civil law and the disclosure of the meaning of law

The civil law proper of the Romans, within which the truly civil-legal concept of property developed, was not the old folk-law, the *ius civile* or the *ius quiritium*, which rested on the *manus* system of the undifferentiated family organization. Rather, it rested on the *ius gentium* which was formed for the private civil interaction with foreigners (*peregrini*).

Only with the inner absorption of this old folk-law into the *ius gentium* did a genuine process of differentiation take place between civil private law and the *ius publicum*. In classical Roman law the old institutes of the *ius civile* merely functioned as antiquated forms which began to be filled with totally new juridical content.

That we are here indeed confronted with a typical disclosure and deepening of the meaning of law appears from the fact that the strict formalism so characteristic of primitive law made room in the civil law of the Romans for the principle of equity (*aequitas*) which pointed towards morality. The *ius gentium* developed into a kind of international law in which the principles of good faith, fairness, and so on, broke through the rigidity of the old folk-law. Only at this point did legal life witness the emancipation of the individual person from the absolute and exclusive power of the primitive organized communities.

During the classical period the *familia* in its old undifferentiated structure still mounted considerable resistance to the process of differentiation that is characteristic of all higher cultural development.[1] But the old *manus* system was already starting to fall apart, particularly with regard to the housewife. And in property law the *paterfamilias* turned into a mere juridical title (*nomen iuris*), employed to designate his being an agent under civil law, abstracted from his function as representative of the *fa-*

1 Bonfante, op. cit., 1:481.

milia. In respect of classical law Bonfante remarks: "The juridical subject is concentrated in the free individual and his sovereign will, and private law no longer recognizes any social differences between men."[1]

But this statement is misleading if no distinction is drawn between *non-civil private law* and *civil private law*. It applies only to the latter but not to *private communal law*, which was not at all pushed aside by the *ius gentium* and the *ius civile* that was reformed by it.

Now it is remarkable to note the extent to which property right during the classical period of Roman civil law underwent a fundamental change.

First of all, the long-standing distinction between *res mancipi* and *res nec mancipi* – a distinction that was typically associated with the undifferentiated structure of the *familia* and with agriculture as the main source of subsistence for the *quirites* – receded into the background. The old *dominium ex iure quiritium* still maintained itself during this period, but in the new civil law it was almost reduced to a *mere form*. This provided the starting-point for the development in praetorial law of a truly civil property right, the so-called *bonitarian property* which had the character, as the name indicates, of simple property law and no longer exhibited the primitive, undifferentiated traits of absoluteness and exclusivity. Bonitarian property was acknowledged by the praetor whenever a good – in deviation from the strict forms of the *ius civile* (namely, *mancipatio* or *in iure cessio*) – was being transferred and protected by the so-called *actio publicana*. In this case the *dominium* formally remained above bonitarian property. Yet it is typical that the significance of this *dominium* practically manifested itself only when genuine *authority competencies* were at stake. This was particularly the case when a slave was set free, with regard to whom the *dominium* belonged to the one while the bonitarian ownership belonged to the

---

1   Bonfante is to the point when he remarks: "In its essential organization the Roman family continued to exist" (op. cit., 1:482). The correctness of this statement appears at once from the continued existence during this period of the *ius vitae ac necis* of the paterfamilias, a right that was exercised *more maiorum*. Only the excesses in its execution were punished by the emperors Trajan, Hadrian and Antoninus.

357

other. In this case the patronage over liberated slaves was assigned only to the former.

On the other hand, property law developed a type of proprietary right particularly from the regulations regarding numerous types of *possessio* which arose as a result of the exploitation by the conquerors of the lands of the conquered. This right of ownership in the *fundus provincialis* remained, as we saw, subject to the state's *dominium*, and was therefore anything but exclusive and absolute.

During this period, genuine family law was developing which guaranteed to the member of the household community a personal legal sphere in civil-legal relationships. Also here we find a penetration of the principles of *aequitas* dominant within the domain of property law. The competence entailed in the right of ownership of the *filius familias*, albeit in a restricted sense, was acknowledged with respect to the so-called *peculium castrense*, over which the *filius* might dispose in the case of a last will.

Similarly, to a limited extent and with the father's consent, the possibility was opened up to the *filius familias* to obligate the *pater familias* to undertake civil actions against third parties.

Dowry rules (the *dotalis* custom) acquired an important civil-legal side, while guardianship of women and minors (*tutela mulierum et impuberum*) likewise lost its primitive, undifferentiated authority structure by being brought within the scope of essentially civil-legal principles. Civil property law showed the loss of its original exclusive and absolute character especially in the rise of numerous property rights which to a significant degree restricted the owner's right to usufruct and disposal for the sake of the other owners. Contract law, too, basically became civil law and property law. Contracts, as agreements between civil-legal subjects, became the chief source of the *obligationes*.

But as the legal sphere of the individual gained recognition in civil law, a new problem presented itself: What was the proper relationship between private property and the public needs of the common good?

Public law and civil private law, which in the general differentiation process had been kept *materially* separate, now saw tensions rise between them. In a primitive society this problem

358

could not have occurred, since here individual rights were absorbed in the undifferentiated community.

In the classical period of the development of Roman law, individual freedom continued to enjoy adequate protection vis-à-vis the state. Public-legal restrictions on property right were not yet severe; chief among them were the building codes enacted during the early Empire. But throughout this period the measure so familiar to modern legal thought, *expropriation in the public interest*, was unknown. No doubt society at the time had no need of it. On the one hand, the government, especially the Emperor, had an almost unlimited number of means at hand to compel large landowners to sell portions of their land; on the other hand, the Roman citizen during this period was far more imbued with 'public spirit' than his modern counterpart. Moreover, as we saw, the state had retained *dominium* over the public lands in the conquered provinces and in addition had other vast properties at its disposal.

Above all, however, the retention of the undifferentiated solid structure of the *familia*, albeit restricted, provided the citizen of Rome with an important counterpoise to excesses of governmental power. Civil property law partially benefited from this leftover of a primitive legal condition. The *familia* continued to represent a political power that shielded property right and restrained the government from arbitrary violations of it. Indeed, this political power exerted itself in the highest college of the state itself, the Senate, which was for the greater part recruited from the *patres* of the old Roman families, the large landowners and the industrialists. Even though the Senate's real power was not significant during the classical era of the Empire – despite an expansion of its competencies through legislation – its influence as a brake on violations of civil law should not be underestimated.

However, no sooner was the position of the *familia* completely undermined during the age of the Byzantine Empire, than the innate defect in the ancient view of the state came home to roost. It rendered impossible a principled harmonization of civil property law and the common good. From its birth, this pagan view of the state was *totalitarian*. It viewed the state as the totality of human society within the territory of the *res publica*. Its concept of

359

sovereignty was exclusive, absolutistic and purely political. It did not recognize the internal sphere-sovereignty of any non-political domain.

So long as the *familia* maintained its undifferentiated structure it functioned like a kind of miniature state. In his domain the sovereignty of the *paterfamilias* was just as absolute and exclusive as the government's authority in the public domain. Private Italian land may have enjoyed political immunity, but what remained foreign in the ancient world was the idea that any non-political societal collectivity had a proper internal sphere of freedom next to the state.

The influence of individualistic tendencies, imported from Greece into Rome through the mediation of middle and late Stoic philosophy, was confined to the world of *theory*. It never penetrated popular consciousness in classical Rome. People knew only of *political* authority, supported by the power of the sword, and (next to civil-legal rights) solely of *political* freedom, expressed by participating in public affairs; but they never acknowledged any internal boundaries of governmental authority over against non-political spheres of life. The *patres* themselves had of old made up the highest state college, the *Senate;* practically no important decision could be taken without the *auctoritas* of the Senate.

Apart from the sphere of civil law, the truly Roman understanding of freedom never transcended the limits of the undifferentiated totalitarian community. During the classical period this showed up especially in the attitude taken by the state in regard to non-political organized communities in society. Private *collegia,* in order to gain legal recognition, would receive from the government an organizational form modeled after the state.

The only impenetrable bulwark against the power of the state was the *familia.* Under its shadow as well, freedom of commerce and industry managed to maintain itself in Rome. During the Byzantine era, however, this old bulwark of freedom collapsed with the influx of Oriental and Hellenistic conceptions, which did not know the Roman family structure. Civil law did not succeed in mounting a sufficient counterpoise to the emerging absolutism of the state. The Senate, the traditional college of the *patres* which before Diocletian still shared sovereignty with the Emperor, was now totally deprived of its political power. The "individual" of civil law, no longer rooted in the closed societal bond of the *familia*, became a helpless prey under the absolute sway of the *salus publica*, the scope of which was determined solely by the despotic arbitrariness of Byzantine bureaucracy.

Property law was increasingly hollowed by a flood of restrictions and violations. The immunity of the Italian private lands disappeared with Diocletian (A.D. 292) and with it the distinction between Roman property and holdings in provincial lands. The huge extension of the *iura in re aliena* during this period also clearly demonstrates that the former exclusive private legal *dominium* concept lost the last remnants of its significance.

A veritable policy of state socialism was pursued. It forced all private vocations and professions that were of common interest into the mold of public-legal organizations that had compulsory membership and were binding also for their offspring. Manual laborers and industrialists, organized in public-legal guilds, were proclaimed public officials. Bonfante writes: "Everyone became a public functionary. The huge bureaucracy and the organization of society reflected a veritable state socialism."[1] The famous edict of Diocletian, *De pretiis rerum venalium* [on the sale price of goods] must be the most extreme example of price and production controls known to ancient history.[2]

The totalitarian state at first seriously opposed the church, and after the elevation of the Christian religion to the status of state religion this state soon attempted to absorb the church. This was merely a continuation of the pagan tradition, for the Roman state carried forward this strongly undifferentiated trait of the older tribal and family bond through which it acted simultaneously as a public cult community.

1 Ibid.
2 [In the first edition of 1938, Dooyeweerd writes: ". . . the most extreme example of price and production controls known to history up to the Bolshevist experiment in Russia.]

361

What happened to civil property law during this period? For all practical purposes the state united within itself the absolute and exclusive *dominium eminens* over all private property. Civil law, in the absence of a counterpoise to state power grounded in a strong private communal life, did not provide any guarantee for the individual freedom of the human person in opposition to Byzantine state absolutism.

During the period of decline of the Western Roman Empire the weakening and disintegration of the authority of the state in the provinces, particularly in Gaul, gave birth to a new flourishing of a *private* undifferentiated property law. It was no longer the *patres familiae* but the powerful landlords who acquired a "demesne" that enjoyed a kind of immunity against urban authorities and was practically independent even of the Emperor. In practice, this *dominium*, attached as it was to the land, gave these large landowners absolute and exclusive power over all users of the land and their offspring, thus absorbing all their civil-legal freedom[1] – an analogy of the former *familia*.

The famous French historian Fustel de Coulanges has written extensively about the rise of the large *villas* of the landlords. They had serfs as well as free tenants, yet all belonged to the lord's "demesne." Noyes has pointed out how the primitive Roman property system, with its economic base in agricultural relationships, in fact experienced a revival in order to become, during the Germanic medieval period, the prototype for the juridical structure of land ownership.

12. The Germanic conception of property before the reception of Roman law

The question now is: What development did the Germanic system undergo in distinction from the system of Roman law before its reception?

Bonfante believes one can characterize this contrast in the following manner: Roman law in its classical and post-classical

---

1 Cf. Noyes, *The Institution of Property*, pp. 217-218; in his source documents he indeed came across the designation *familia* again in reference to the entire community of persons and properties enclosed within the *villa* of the new landlord. [This note corrects the 1938 edition where Dooyeweerd attributed the designation to Noyes himself, not to the original sources, adding: "... apparently in order to construe a direct continuity between the old Roman familia and the Gallic-Roman villa régime. This seems more confusing than elucidating."]

forms owed its rise to a process in which the originally exclusive and undifferentiated *dominium*, bound to the old *familia* structure, was gradually reduced to private ownership within the restricted sense of property law. Germanic property law, by contrast, developed from a gradual differentiation and individuation of a richly varied system (at least with regard to the land) of originally collective ownership relations within which the legal concept of property as *unity* and *root* was at first totally unknown.[1]

As for the old Germanic conditions at the time of Julius Ceasar, it must indeed be acknowledged that both *folk* and *sib* ties did not as yet have a firm territorial base. Consequently, an undifferentiated *dominium* concept in the sense of primitive Roman law could not of course develop during this period. The organized communities were themselves of a primitive and undifferentiated character,[2] although, as Caesar reported, they took turns cultivating the fields collectively.

Many historians are of the opinion that this situation changed already at the time of Tacitus. Every household now had its own private plot, although grazing fields and woodlands, and in general any untilled land, were retained as "commons" for the members of the *folk* community, probably for the sibs, the agnatic communities. Given the vagueness of the statements in Tacitus, however, this opinion cannot be proven.[3]

In any event, during the Merovingian period, the undifferentiated legal concept of *dominium* was found in the royal and eccle-

---

1 [The 1938 text adds: "However, in respect of the Germanic concept of property I think this historical reconstruction is not entirely correct." This sentence was deleted from the 1962 edition.]

2 During the Frankish era the domestic authority of the father over children still encompassed the power over life and death (*ius vitae ac necis*), the power to approve or disapprove marriages, the right to sell his children into slavery, and more. See R. Schröder and E. von Künszberg, *Lehrbuch der deutschen Rechtsgeschichte*, 6th ed. (Berlin, 1922), p. 351.

3 On the controversial interpretations of Tacitus, cf. the extensive discussion in E. Glasson, *Histoire du droit et des institutions de la France*, vol. 2 (Paris, 1888), 1:58 ff.; H. Brunner, *Deutsche Rechtsgeschichte*, 2nd ed. (Leipzig, 1906), 1:83 ff.; N. D. Fustel de Coulanges, *L'Alleu et le domaine rural pendant l'époque mérovingienne*, ed. C. Jullian (Paris, 1890).

siastical *latifundia* or *villae*. The only difference with the Roman system was that it was not the Roman structure of the agnatic *familia* but rather the *seigneurie* that determined the content of property right – albeit that the lord continued to designate the undifferentiated community of his *villa* as *familia*, meaning that he continued to view his authority after the model of authority prevailing in the primitive Roman household.[1] Ownership of large tracts of land at once entailed an undifferentiated authority over all people residing within the lord's domain.[2]

In setting up the large Frankish kingdom in Gaul as well as other realms in Europe, the Germanic tribes did not bring with them their own state idea. They only knew the undifferentiated *folk* and *tribe*. The Merovingian kings found a point of contact for their conception of kingship in the idea of private landholding as it already existed in practice. They viewed their *regnum* as their *patrimonium* of which they could give away pieces at will. Implicit in their land grants was the transfer of governmental authority over the subjects that had already settled there, an authority that remained subject only to royal power. The grants were in no way of a civil-legal nature. In most cases they gave ownership of property that could not be alienated without the consent of the king. The land grants came with a very limited right of inheritance and they were bound to the condition of loyal service that was typical of relations within an *organized community*.

When lords lost the goodwill of the king he could take back their land at his discretion. Thus initially the lords did not have

1 [The previous two sentences replaced the following ones in the original article of 1936: "During their subsequent invasions of Roman territory, the Germanic tribes (with the exception of the Franks in Gaul) carried out a formal distribution of the land, whereby the existing landowners had to surrender large parts of their property to the Germanic people. What was indeed soon to emerge in Germanic law was the undifferentiated legal concept of *dominium*, differing from Roman law only insofar as it was not the *familia* but land that now determined the contents of property law."]
2 Cf. Fustel de Coulanges, *L'Alleu et le domaine rural pendant l'époque mérovingienne*, p. 458: "An owner became, within the boundaries of his demesne, a kind of head of state. People called him *dominus*, a term that denoted at once owner and master. They also called him *senior* [*seigneur*].

an exclusive and absolute *dominium* over their inhabitants, but no sooner did royal authority begin to crumble and weaken, than the powerful lords were able to assert a *de facto* independence from the king and their *dominium* acquired a sovereign and exclusive character. The institution of "immunity" laid the foundation for this course of events.[1]

The same development took place with the introduction of the feudal system under the Carolingians. The *beneficium* which the vassal received from his seigneur on the basis of his promise of support (*aide et service*)[2] did not furnish free civil-legal property, but only an undifferentiated ownership linked to a specific relation to an organized community which at once entailed authority over the inhabitants of the enfeofed property.

In the age of feudalism, which dates from the breakup of the Frankish kingdom during the early medieval period, many grants and immunities turned into "seigneurial rights," that is to say, into public-legal powers. During the Carolingian era these powers had still been tied to offices that were subject to the king, but now they ended up in the undifferentiated *dominium* of the powerful lords who in turn had free disposal of them. Private persons acquired many seigneurial rights. In this connection the old division of the populace by ancient folk-law into freemen and bondmen lost much of its practical significance since it was increasingly admixed with a classification according to occupational estates as well as the replacement of personal fealty by economic dependence, a development which in many ways pushed personal freedom aside.

In the most recent literature on the subject[2] it is convincingly shown that the legal concept "freedom" during the Middle Ages in no way had a *civil-legal* content. It could acquire the most diverse contents, which would be further defined only by listing the specific relationships of dependence from which the person (or the group) was now set free.

There are cases where "freedom," for example of a rural municipality, merely meant the freedom from a certain embargo right

---

1 Cf. Maurice Kroell, *L'Immunité franque* (diss., Univ. of Nantes; Paris, 1910), chap. 14.
2 A synopsis is found in an important treatise by Th. Mayer, "Die Entstehung des modernen Staates im Mittelalter," *Zeitschrift der Savigny-Stiftung, Germanistische Abteilung* 57 (1937): 210-289, where an extensive list is found of the most recent literature on the subject.

of the lord (say, of the monopoly of giving wine as presents).[1] We read about "freemen" who were sold or pledged by their lord; in that case "freedom" meant no more than that these men no longer belonged to the tutelage of the church or a feudal lord. This alone suffices to show how little the concept of "seigneurial right" in its undifferentiated *dominium* character was compatible with recognition of civil-legal freedom.

With regard to the law of persons, family law, law of succession and process law, the medieval land rights were to a large extent governed by the principle of *Ebenbürtigkeit* or equality of birth or rank. That is to say, a whole series of legal relationships could only be entered into with people belonging to the same or a lower estate.[2] Foreigners, Jews, or people "outside the law" (i.e., persons who did not occupy a position in any estate) were in many respects delivered over to the arbitrariness of the feudal lords.

What was undoubtedly alive in the legal consciousness of the medieval period was a Christian Germanic idea of freedom which entailed the divine right to freedom for all human beings as creatures of God. The most impressive manifestation of the idea of freedom is embodied in the *Sachsenspiegel*, the famous 13th-century description of Eastphalian law by Eike of Repgow, where the conclusion is drawn, on the basis of the creation of the human being after God's image, that whoever lays claim to a human being as property is acting against divine law.[3]

This idea, thanks to its universal scope and its Christian foundation, went far beyond the conception of a general freedom present in the old Germanic folk-law. It also went beyond the way that estates were structured during the Middle Ages and as such it never had any significance in the positive law of German lands before the French Revolution.

1 Cf. Karl Glöckner in *Archiv für hessische Geschichte* (1934) and H. Wiessner, *Sachinhalt und wirtschaftliche Bedeutung der Weistümer* (Baden, 1934), pp. 75 ff.

2 Cf. H. von Minnigerode, *Ebenburt und Echtheit* (Heidelberg, 1912). F. Hauptmann, "Das Ebenbürtigkeitsprinzip in der Geschichte," *Archiv für öffentliches Recht* 17 (1904): 529 ff.

3 Homeyer ed., *Landrecht* 3.42.5: "Dar bi is uns kundlich von godes worden, dat die mensche godes belde, godes wesen sal, unde sve anders iemanne to seget danne gode, dat he weder got dut." [In the critical edition of the *Monum. Germ. Hist.* the text is the same.]

Churches and monasteries had their own manors with many serfs, and they enjoyed an undifferentiated *dominium* over these lands and persons. The lack of freedom in this condition was officially justified as belonging to the so-called relative natural law of the state of sin.

In the first volume of his standard work *Das deutsche Genossenschaftsrecht*, Gierke particularly emphasized the revival of the Germanic conception of freedom in its new form through the development of the free *Genossenschaften* (associations) since the 12th century. He interpreted the free mark associations, towns, guilds and confederations of estates as signifying a fundamental break with the undifferentiated seigneurial rights that were characteristic of the feudal era. These associations constituted an important factor in the rise of the modern Germanic state-idea which stands in radical contrast to the absolutistic state-idea of the Roman-Byzantine period.

One should certainly not underestimate the importance of these associations for the development of the modern view of freedom. In particular since the rise of the towns in the 12th century, insofar as they did not bear a patrimonial character,[1] a new freedom idea came to expression: the establishment of towns gradually ended serfdom and feudal land tenure. Hence the adage: "town air liberates."[2]

But no less should it be kept in mind that neither the free mark associations nor the medieval towns and guilds managed to transcend the level of undifferentiated societal relationships, a failure which constituted an insurmountable obstacle for the recognition of true civil-legal freedom.[3]

The free mark associations were based (at least in the Netherlands, particularly in Drenthe and Overijssel) in the free hamlets in which full-blown membership was based on the existence of

1 That is to say, insofar as they did not stand under the *dominium* of the feudal lord.
2 This is a peculiar application of the adage, "Air makes what belongs to one" (*"Lucht maakt eigen"*) which stems from the law of ownership; see Schröder-Künszberg, op. cit., p. 692 note 61.
3 [The next five paragraphs did not appear in the original article but were added in the 1962 edition.]

"eigenerfden," i.e., of freeholders who enjoyed a share in the mark's commons (the mark was merely an extension of the hamlet).

However, the *dominium* of an *eigenerfde* was not a civil-legal property right. Rather, it was an undifferentiated right. Interwoven with subjective property right, it contained the following integral parts: the right to share in the governance of the hamlet; in enacting local ordinances; and, if a hamlet's autonomy included its own jurisprudence, in adjudicating disputes.

Whoever transferred a freehold property at once therefore also transferred public-legal competencies. Thus this transfer was not completely free since it was subject to various restrictions in the charters of hamlets and marks (e.g., no transfers to crofters, and limitations on transfers or mortgages to foreigners).

Similarly, selling a share in common lands always took place with the inclusion of the governmental authority attached to that part of the common property (*cum iustitia et politia*).

The craft guilds, too, in their very nature as fraternities that included members' families, retained their undifferentiated character.[1]

The incorporation of the craft guilds as parts of the town, their compulsory membership, their monopoly over the craft, their right to impose rules and penalties (even linked at times with a predominating influence on the governance of the town) once again led to an overestimation of the community at the cost of individual freedom. Known as *fraternitates*, these guilds had an exclusive character and embraced their members with their families for all spheres of life.[2]

The whole field of personal law, law of things, family and inheritance law was permeated in the Middle Ages with undifferentiated legal relationships. For instance, on the basis of *emphy-*

---

1   These fraternities were the undifferentiated foundations for the craft guilds and must be distinguished from firms which encompassed only the participating partners.
2   [The next three paragraphs did not appear in the original article but were added in the 1962 edition.]

teusis[1] acquired from the abbess of Elten, who had been its rightful owner, Floris V count of Holland appointed a sheriff in Naerdinxlant.[2] Resulting lawsuits based on ownership and seigneurial rights invoked distinctions between manorial estate, praedial property, church assets, free private farm property (which included competency to wield authority in hamlets), etc., etc.

Many entitlements which in our modern civil law cannot be divorced from property right, such as a seigneur's rights to fishing and hunting, ferry service and tolls on navigable streams, were feudal in origin – implications of governmental authority. Tithes, as well as ancient land rents (like court fees, grain payments, parish dues), were originally ecclesiastical or lay *taxes* which gradually were consolidated into land taxes. Yet these taxes, no more than the seigneurial rights themselves, were viewed as material rights; instead they were considered unmovable immaterial goods to which sometimes were attached property rights, inheritable tenure, and so on.

Nowhere in these relationships do we find a connection to our modern concept of civil law or to the classical Roman concept as it was developed in the *ius gentium*.

13. The significance for the modern idea of freedom

There is undoubtedly a fundamental difference between the feudal system of medieval times and the state absolutism of the Byzantine bureaucracy.

The medieval Germanic formation of law was founded on the principle of *autonomy* of the colourful diversity of societal spheres. Autonomy was not delineated according to the *inner nature* of these societal relationships but was determined in a *purely formal* way by privileges and customs. The only criterion was whether or not the autonomous legal sphere could administer its own affairs without interference from a higher authority. This

1 [*Emphyteusis*: a long-term lease of land conditional upon adding improvements to it.]
2 [This historic name was recently resurrected in a proposal to give the new municipality of Gooise Meren (a fusion of Naarden, Bussum and Muiden) the name Naardingerland. The castle of Floris V, who was murdered by rival lords, is located in Muiden.]

autonomy was so stoutly defended that not even powerful royal houses were able to carry through their occasional plans for centralization. Nevertheless it safeguarded only corporate freedoms and privileges. It undoubtedly also served as a guarantee against direct interference in the property right attached to these corporations by powerful feudal lords or the imperial power. Still, a civil-legal sphere of freedom for the individual as such, independent of his membership in particular societal collectivities, could not gain recognition as long as the latter continued to display an exclusive and undifferentiated character. "Freedom" from direct subjection to the government of the realm meant at the same time an all-round dependence on the undifferentiated societal community which had drawn its members from the state and turned them into its own immediate subjects.

Even when – as happened in different regions of Germany, Austria and Switzerland – the imperial authority or the territorial princes managed in the 13th century to regain these subjects and incorporate them into their state-system by means of episcopal principalities, church wards, etc., the "freedom" which the subjects thus acquired meant at the same time that they were once again subject to the undifferentiated *dominium* of the princes. For example, the landownership of the "free" colonists in the newly cultivated grasslands fell under the supreme property of the prince. Manorial dues had to be rendered to this prince, and a part of the harvest had to be delivered to him as a tax. Furthermore, without the permission of the prince or his count, the land could not be sold.[1] And since the 15th century the reinforcement of seigneurial power over the land subjected these "free" peasants, who were not represented in the landed estates, to a position that closely approximated that of feudal serfdom.

1 Cf. Theodor Mayer, art. cit., pp. 286 ff. "Freedom meant being merged into the royal state. Granting freedom at once established the creation of a royal position of power. That was the meaning of freedom, as we observe it since the close of the 12th and particularly since the 13th century. It is intimately connected with the structuration of the new state, but it constitutes an expansion of the Stauffian policy of guardianship which more than made up for the loss of the former arrangement and had nothing to do with the old common freedom."

Even the free mark associations were not able to call a halt to the process, because as mark vassals these lords managed to secure a supreme property right to the commons, which turned the free mark association into a state resembling serfdom.[1] On the other hand, following the Peasant Revolt [of 1524] the "free" peasants in the colonized area of East Germany were in many ways made subject again to the private *dominium* of the nobles who were forced by the circumstances of the time to expand their landownership.

14. Once again the contrast between Roman and Germanic law

Those who have followed our exposition thus far will realize that the "social" character of the Germanic property concept in its contrast with the "individualistic" character of Roman law has been put in a more proper light.

In the first place, it is noteworthy that the entire fundamental contrast constructed by the Germanist side between the Roman and the Germanic conception of property insofar as it concerns the "social" character of the latter, applies only to landed property. With regard to goods that could be moved or lifted, Gierke himself had to concede: "Not removed to the same extent, the competence ascribed to owners 'to act at will with their goods and shut out the interference of others,' is given the lie by legal stipulations that state the opposite."[2]

What is indeed found in many medieval verdicts with regard to ownership of movable goods is that they affirm an individual owner's exclusive power of disposal so vigorously that an unhistorical approach could easily be tempted to consider it compelling evidence of the dominance [in Germanic law] of the

---

1 Cf. the well-known lament [from the *Schwabenspiegel*]: "Die fürsten twingent mit gewalt \ velt steine wasser unde walt \ dar zue wilt unde zam: \ den lufte toetens gerne alsam; \ der musz uns doch gemeine sin, \ möhten s'uns der sunnen schin \ verbieten, wint auch unde regen, \ man müsste in zins mit golde wegen" [The princes take with force from us / the common fields and streams and woods,/ together with the game therein / and wish to add fresh air to boot. / The princes would be mean withal, / forbid the sun to shine on us, / deny us also wind and rain, / while forcing rent in gold be paid.]

2 Gierke, *Deutsches Privatrecht*, 2:515.

individualistic will-principle that Jhering proclaimed was the source of the original Roman concept of *dominium*.

Consider the statement that an owner may tie his "fahrende Habe" (movable property) to the tail of a wild horse or a dog or throw it into the water,[1] a statement that certainly has to be understood in the same humorous sense as a custom in Aardenburg: "A man is allowed to hit and stab his wife, cut and divide her from top to bottom and warm his feet in her blood, and then sew her up again without loss of being her master, in order that she stay alive."[2]

As far as landownership is concerned, we have seen that the origin of Roman *dominium* can only be understood in terms of the undifferentiated *domain concept* which on the one hand was attached to the structure of the *familia* and on the other to the structure of the organized *folk*-community.

Now then, the medieval Germanic *dominium* with regard to immovable goods differed from the primitive Roman concept only in that it was rooted, besides the structure of the cognate family, in the undifferentiated structures of a variegated set of feudal and fraternal societal collectivities.

Thus, in order to obtain a solid basis of comparison for the history of law, one has to select the *internal* property relationships in the undifferentiated organized communal structure of the old Roman *familia*. What cannot serve this purpose is the classic civil-legal concept of property as a *differentiated property right*.[3] What needs attention is the legal concept of the *peculia* as a fundamentally dependent proprietary right derived solely from the *dominium* of the *paterfamilias*.[4] At this point a surprising parallel between the primitive Roman and the medieval Germanic sys-

---

1 Cf. Gierke, *Der Humor im deutschen Recht* (Berlin, 1871), p. 31.
2 *Rechtsbronnen der stad Aardenburg*, ed. G. A. Vorsterman van Oyen (The Hague, 1892), *Wettelychede*, par. 9, p. 201.
3 In respect of the comparison between the Roman and the British feudal property system, the first to do this was Reinold Noyes in his work *The Institution of Property*, pp. 221 ff. Particularly instructive is the way he characterizes the difference: "The Roman political organization [i.e., the state as an organized community – HD] was wholly supra-familial. The feudal system was wholly intra-familial."
4 Cf. Noyes, op. cit., pp. 85 ff.

tem can be noted (while the differences may be explained almost entirely from the pluriformity present among medieval organized communal relationships). Similar to the way in which in the Roman *familia* all ownership by those subject to the authority of the *paterfamilias* was a dependent form of ownership, while the *paterfamilias* alone disposed of absolute *dominium*, so in the feudal system all ownership was *dependent* ownership subject to the undifferentiated, organized communal authority of a lord or an association. Wherever feudal law with its established feudal hierarchy obtained and a seigneur in turn stood in a vassal relationship to an overlord, there the distinction between *private* and *dependent* ownership was altogether blurred. This situation made it impossible for an absolute and exclusive *dominium* to develop.

Gierke strongly emphasized that in Germanic law, property rights were divisible in principle in respect of immovable goods, and he contrasted this with the conception of Roman law which proceeded from the fundamental indivisibility of *dominium*.

Yet, what should not be forgotten for a moment is that the theory of divided property during the Middle Ages did not derive from the Germanic conception of law. It is a construction, rather, of the Romanist glossator school.[1]

According to this school of law, Roman law already acknowledged a dual property right with regard to the same thing, namely a *dominium directum* and a *dominium utile*.[2]

The Romanist school probably proceeded from an expression occurring in the records, the *rei petitio utilis* of the long-leaseholder and the conditional leasehold, and assumed that this action, which was granted analogous to the *reivindicatio*, was based on the conception of these rights as a *dominium utile*, that is to say, as a right analogous to ownership. From there the

---

1 Andreas Heusler makes a similar remark: "This is not a question of something that arose from the essence of Germanic law, but from a theory of the Romanist school and from students of feudalism." *Institutionen des Deutschen Privatrechts*, 2 vols. (Leipzig, 1885-86), 2:48.

2 [That is, a direct proprietary right, and a right of usufruct (to till the land and enjoy its fruits). In the original article the first part of the next paragraph read as follows: "It [the glossator school] assumed that the distinction between *actio directa* and *actio indirecta* as found in the sources was based on a division of property right into a *ius directum* and a *ius utile*."]

373

glossators moved on to distinguishing between a *dominium directum* and a *dominium utile*.[1] They then applied this distinction to feudal law[2] and to various Germanic rights of land use unknown to Roman law.[3] What is then understood under *dominium directum* is a supreme property right (the undifferentiated right of authority), while *dominium utile* is taken as referring to the dependent factual property right of the person using the soil.[4] However, it is simply impossible to demonstrate in medieval Germanic law (insofar as it was not influenced by Roman law) the existence of another conception of property next to that of the undifferentiated *dominium* or *allodium*.[5]

Remark: Gierke has not demonstrated this either. He quotes *Sachsenspiegel* 2.57, *Lehnnr.* 15.1, but in these places Eike von Repgow does not at all talk about two kinds of property. The first quotation only mentions a lord's "ledichlike Gewehre" [pure ownership], which is emphatically understood as "personal, private ownership" ("des dat gut eigen is"). In other words, both property and the dependent right of usufruct were subsumed under the typically Germanic concept of right of ownership ("Gewehre"), but that did not mean that both were understood as "property" in the same sense.

This is abundantly clear from other places, e.g., *Sachsenspiegel*

1 Cf. e.g. the gloss "Nam in suis" on "Appellatione sui accipe, sive sit dominus directo vel utiliter, ut feudatarius, emphyteuta et similes." *Justinian* Code 10.15.1.
2 That the glossators did not construct this with a view to feudal law, as Gierke believed, is argued, correctly I think, by Heusler: "These expressions surely point to the fact that the glossators did not in the first place erect their distinction on the basis of such a view, for then they certainly would have chosen other expressions for it" (op. cit., 2:49).
3 Compare Gl. ad. 1.1 C. de thesaur. (10.5); II F.8 § 1 (*tanquam dominus*), and so on.
4 Cf. Gierke, *Deutsches Privatrecht*, 2 : 370 ff. See also Stobbe, *Privatrecht*, vol. 2, § 96; Heusler, ibid.
5 Allodium originally meant "inherited family property." Only later was it contrasted with feudal property. It then often stood for "noble property," patrimony free of feudal dues, in contrast to a peasant's ownership of a property in a free hamlet, or the latter in contrast to the commons of the mark. Cf. J. Ph. de Monté Ver Loren, *De historische ontwikkeling van de begrippen bezit en eigendom in de landsheerlijke rechtspraak over onroerend goed in Holland* [The historical development of the concepts possession and ownership in the manorial jurisprudence concerning real estate in (the county of) Holland] (diss., Utrecht, 1929), pp. 299 ff.; and Melchior Winhoff, *Lantrecht van Auerissel* (1782), p. 492 n. 13.

2.43, where fief and property are contrasted: "Sve en gut eme seget to lene, unde en ander seget it si sin egen; spreket se t mit geliker were an, jene mut it bat to egene behalden mit tvier scepenen getüge, denne die andere to lene."

As for Gierke's quotation from feudal law, here too there is no reference whatsoever to divided property! On the contrary, the *de facto* ownership is simply characterized as feudal property ("*sines lenes geweren*"). On page 369 Gierke then immediately provides a much more cautious statement: "*Throughout*, we get the sense that the factual or legal ownership reserved for the lord constituted a supreme kind of property, while the right of vassals or tenants belonged to a subordinate property."[1] But this "throughout" is a matter of subjective evaluation on the part of Gierke.

It need hardly be pointed out that Gierke's appeal to urban and feudal laws that adopted the theory of the glossators is no compelling argument. Add to this that Heusler, who also according to Gierke[2] is supposed to have shown that "the idea of divided property was current throughout the Middle Ages," actually claimed, in direct opposition to Gierke's argument, that prior to the adoption of the post-glossators' theory of the legal concept of "divided property" it was absolutely unknown in medieval Germany and that even subsequently this theory was applied only to the different levels of feudal lordship and landholding. The theory of divided property in Gierke's sense did not become widespread until the 14th century.[3]

The dependent full right of usufruct was designated by its own title. The splitting up of the formal authority of the lord and the factual rights of use of his vassals *in the sense of a dual dominium* clearly shows the influence of a *theory*. For centuries, following in the footsteps of the glossators, it was believed that the theory of divided property was indeed found in the Roman legal sources. Yet we have seen how this theory, which was disproved already by Budneus and later by Thibaut, acquired to a certain extent a new follower in Richard Maschke during the latter part of the 19th century.

It cannot be contested that this theory, which was not only adopted in various imperial laws, in the laws of several coun-

---

1 Gierke, op. cit., p. 369 (ital. mine, HD).
2 Ibid., p. 369, note 3.
3 Heusler, *Institutionen der deutschen Privatrecht*, 2:49 ff.

tries, and even in some urban laws,[1] made a compelling contribution to the preparation of the development of a free civil property law.[2] Nor can it be denied that in the medieval towns a process began whereby supreme feudal property was *eroded* by "subordinate property." Yet serious objections must be raised against the method followed by Gierke and other Germanists when they proclaimed the divisibility of property to be the original *Germanic* conception of property, to play it off against the civil-legal conception of property in classical Roman law, which they then branded as "individualistic."

This is not, however, the reading of all Germanists. Duncker,[3] Gerber, Stobbe and Heusler rejected the legal concept of divided property also for Germanic law. Is their interpretation to be explained solely from slavishly following the logic of Roman law, as Gierke assumed?[4] I would deny this. Gierke posed the dilemma that one has to either acknowledge the dependent full rights of usufruct of the soil as (sub)property, or degrade them in a Romanist spirit into *iura in re aliena*. But this dilemma must be rejected. In its developed form the legal concept of *iura in re aliena* is *civil-legal in character* and as such presupposes *civil* property law.

For this reason alone they are not applicable to the medieval dependent right of usufruct of the soil. In the context of feudal law, before the influence of the classical Roman property conception and the theory of the glossators, it was known only as the undifferentiated *dominium* of a lord or as independent ownership often bound up with a right to participate in the governance of a free hamlet. In the same vein Heusler remarks: "It cannot be denied that particularly since the 13th century the charters increas-

---

1   Very extensively in the Prussian Land Act, 18.19-20; see also ibid., 8.1 as well as Austria's *Civil Code*, § 357. A broad overview is offered in J. W. Hedemann, *Die Fortschritte des Zivilrechts im XIX. Jahrhundert*, 2 vols. (Berlin, 1930), II/1:4 ff., where an example is also given of an application of the theory in the legal system of the town of Breslau. See also Gierke, *Deutsches Privatrecht*, 2:371 ff.
2   Contra Heusler, op. cit., according to whom this theory did not acquire any practical significance.
3   See his article in *Zeitschrift für Deutsche Rechtsgeschichte* 2 (1881): 177 ff.
4   Gierke, op. cit., p. 372.

ingly employed the term *dominium* as a synonym for *proprietas*. But the truly technical meaning of *dominium* in early medieval usage is indeed not that of proprietary right in the narrow sense of civil law but that of dominion, more in the sense of '*munt*'[1] than in that of property."[2]

According to feudal and seigneurial law the right of usufruct attached to the property of the dependent landowners was originally conceived neither as (sub)owning nor as *iura in re aliena*, but simply as a material property right *sui generis* with independent ownership (*Gewehre*). The abstract civil-legal concept that all rights under the law of things are rooted in proprietary rights in the sense of property law is simply foreign to the undifferentiated Germanic conception of law.

15. Reactionary political tendencies in Germany: their totalitarian consequences

The method followed by the Germanists mentioned earlier became even more suspect when it acquired a clearly *political* tendency. Following his historical explanation of the development of divided ownership, Gierke wondered out loud if this legal concept might not once again be called upon to play a future role in the distribution of land. And he answered his question in the affirmative: "Settling the broader layers of the *Volk* through internal colonization can hardly have lasting results without resurrecting the basic idea of divided property."[3]

This suggestion was[4] of some influence in Germany. Both under the Socialist government after the Great War of 1914-18 and under the National Socialist government we have witnessed a *de facto* atavism to the concepts of supreme ownership and dependent subownership of the soil. I need only call to mind the following laws: *Reichheimstättengesetz* (Reich Homestead Act) of 10 May 1920;[5] the Prussian *Bauerliche Erbhofgesetz* (Hereditary Farm Act)

---

1 [*Munt* stood for power in the Germanic household community.]
2 Heusler, op. cit., vol. 2, § 49 ff.
3 Op. cit., 2:373.
4 [From here till the end of this section, the original paper of 1936 consistently uses the present tense.]
5 On this point, see Hedemann, op. cit., II/1:157 ff.

of 15 May 1933; and the federal *Reichserbhofgesetz* of 29 September 1933.[1]

But the wheels of history did not allow for turning back to a dead past. The regime could not breathe new life into the Germanic feudal system of the Middle Ages. Nor could it undo the reality of the modern state and the differentiation of collective forms of social life.

Similarly, it was no longer possible to restore the undifferentiated *dominium* feature of the feudal period. In actuality, the new supreme property did not reflect that of the medieval Germanic situation but was rather a manifestation of the differentiated public-legal governmental authority of the State, which was organized extremely powerfully in Germany. It was a *"dominium eminens"* that reminded one more of Byzantine absolutism than of the "social" Germanic conception of property.

By dint of a federal law, about one million small farmers were excluded from the domain of civil property right and brought under a public-legal regime. Under National Socialism the agricultural sector was no longer free. Owning a "small family farm" was no longer a *civil property right* but only a reflection of an *official function*.[2] The State determined the conditions for inclusion in the agri-corporation (one had to be a farm owner, of German descent, racial purity, economic ability and "honor" as understood by National Socialism). Only the State had the competence to dispose of hereditary farms, and in cases where a farmer acted in opposition to National Socialist ideas the State could expropriate such farms through eviction.

This hereditary farm legislation was not an isolated measure but formed an integral part of National Socialism's agricultural policy, which was a regulatory system of a totalitarian type. By a federal law of 13 September 1933 the rural population was as-

---

1 Ibid., 3:361 ff.; and H. Stoll, *Deutsches Bauernrecht* (Berlin, 1935).
2 Remarked Professor Hedemann, who converted to National Socialism: "The farmer appears here most clearly as a trustee of the clan. Many therefore call farmers 'civil servants.' However, this should be understood only in a metaphorical sense" (ibid., II/2:364). Hedemann's language was typical of the way National Socialism formed its concepts: it called reality what was a mere "myth" and a "metaphor" what actually was reality.

signed to the corporation responsible for food production in the Third Reich. According to a statement by its founder and "leader," Walther Darré, the agri-corporation was characterized by three features: exclusivity, a public-legal position, and disciplinary authority. This served to bind its self-governance and responsibility to *Staat* and *Volk*.

It followed from this policy that the members of this "corporation" were bound to the soil and barred from access to the cities. The organization of the corporation, equally provided for by the abovementioned law, was accompanied by measures regulating the market and prices of agricultural products. Hedemann summarized this policy as follows: "In order to establish firm market arrangements for agricultural products, a whole series of Reich offices and mergers have been created throughout the country. On the one hand they are to ensure sufficient supply with a view to attaining the highest possible independence from foreign countries. On the other hand they are to provide for adequate and stable prices with a view to preventing market volatility and popular anxiety."

Soon to follow were price controls for meat, milk and eggs, cheese and butter, and particularly wheat. In addition to controlling minimum and maximum prices, the goal was to establish so-called "fixed prices." In order to achieve this goal it turned out to be necessary to establish a deeply interventionist coercive organization of all the groups involved: producers, manufacturers, and commercial distributors. The *forcible cartelization of mills* in 1933[1] and the organization of all subdivisions of the grain industry in 1934 were the first steps in this direction. "Up to a certain degree," wrote Hedemann, "all these organizations exist under the sign of self-determination, exemplifying their earlier demo-

---

1 It should be noted that according to the official motivation the federal law of July 1933 regarding the compulsory formation of cartels was intended merely as a "crisis-law" [i.e., a measure to combat the economic depression] and that it was not meant to become part and parcel of a "planned economy." But Mussolini, too, declared repeatedly that the means of production of individual property would be respected. Even with the introduction of the Corporative Law of 1934, which factually brought the entire industrial life under Italian state control, he declared that it was not at all his intention to introduce a planned economy. Reality corresponded little with this statement.

cratic character. But much more powerfully organized is the direction from the Ministry."[1]

Of course all this had nothing to do with the undifferentiated medieval *dominium* concept, and it also went far beyond the legal concept of the feudal and seigneurial supreme property as outlined in the Prussian Land Act. Under the feudal system of so-called divided property, the supreme and the subordinate owners stood as it were in each other's way. Neither one had free disposal of the land; in some way or other one person's authority restricted that of the other. The peasants who acted as sub-owners were not in a position either to dispose of their plot without the consent of the lord, or to weaken it by exchanging or selling parts of it. But it was no more possible for the lords to act with the peasant's land as they pleased. Among other things, severe penalties supported the prohibition against concentrating small farms into economic homesteading and consolidating the main goods.[2] These goods would be withdrawn from free exchange and become "inalienable."

But this modern application by National Socialism of the concept of supreme property well suited the theory of State supremacy regarding the government's *dominium eminens* of the land. It found its crudest application in the Prussian Land Act in the form of "economic coercion" with regard to the farmers.[3] We heard echoes here of the idea of the police state in the spirit of the teacher of Frederik the Great, Christian Wolff. These policies were also in line with the state socialism of the late Roman and Byzantine empires, which indirectly subjected peasants by law to compulsory cultivation of their land.[4]

---

1 Op. cit., II/2:370.
2 *Preus. A.L.R.* (1794), II 7 § 247.
3 *Cf. Preus. A.L.R.*, II 7 § 8 ff.: "Every farmer has the responsibility to cultivate his parcel of land economically in part to support the common needs. Thus he can also be forced to do so through coercive measures by the State; and if he persists in neglecting this duty he may be obliged to cede his parcel to someone else."
4 This was the case in the law of the emperors Valentian, Theodosius and Arcadius, from the years 388 to 392 (*Codex Justinianus* 11.59.8). By this law a person who left his land unused had to hand it over to another, more productive farmer, with the right to reclaim his land for a period of only two years, on condition he compensate the new farmer for all costs incurred.

One can clearly see how fraught with political danger it can be to contrast the "social" Germanic property conception with the "individualistic" one of Roman civil law.[1] It posed a constant threat – of an absolute State, either in centralized bureaucratic forms or in the less dangerous, decentralized form of compulsory organizations for commerce and industry, organizations endowed with autonomy and self-regulatory powers but also with public-legal competencies with respect to the internal sphere of economic life.[2]

To eliminate from the civil-legal sphere an important part of private property – the owning of land – is a fatal attack on personal freedom!

16. Humanistic natural law

The theory of natural law in the humanist tradition, as is well known, became individualistic in that it overemphasized the concept of freedom in classical Roman civil law at the cost of insight into the typical structure of private communal law.

In the school of state absolutism, these natural-law theorists ran into an inner contradiction between the idea of absolute state sovereignty or popular sovereignty and the idea of the individual's civil-legal freedom whenever this freedom was sacrificed on principle to the sovereign power.

In the other school, which defended the classic liberal idea of the constitutional state, it led, in coalition with an individualistic

---

1   Cf. e.g. Stoll, *Deutsches Bauernrecht*, p. 14. He attributes the loss of freedom of the peasant class in Germany since the 17th century largely to the penetration of alien Roman law, a process that was facilitated by the growing influence of an individualistic conception of law since the flourishing of towns, the expansion of trade, and the transition to a money economy. Even the serfdom into which many formerly free peasants fell back he explains from the use the landlords made of the Roman theory of *locatio conductio* whereby a peasant's "hereditary title" was turned into a "time-loan"! Yet, it is not possible to find a basis for "landholding rights" in the Roman *ius gentium*. Incidentally, it was quite embarrassing for National Socialism that the disqualification of Roman law in favor of Germanic law was a popular topic already during the individualistic Enlightenment period. Cf. H. Thieme, "Die Zeit des späten Naturrechts," *Zeitschrift der Savigny-Stiftung, Germanistische Abteilung* 56 (1936): 241 ff.

2   [This sentence was omitted from the 1962 version.]

economic theory, to the demand of state abstention from the entire domain of socio-economic life. The new individualistic conception of exclusive and absolute property right, introduced by this school, was utterly divorced from the historical and social background of the Roman *dominium* concept. In this individualistic version of natural law the theory of an owner's absolute and exclusive competence of disposal was translated into the "Declaration of the Rights of Man and the Citizen" during the French Revolution. All feudal and seigneurial rights were repealed. Guild monopolies and the right to put people under a ban were abolished. Even the private expropriation rights of family members, neighbors and trading partners found no favor in the eyes of the French revolutionaries. Similarly, the last vestiges of landholding rights were annihilated. Serfs acquired the land they tilled. Tenant rents as well as seigneurial dues were abolished, as were stipulations pertaining to the inheritance of feudal, seigneurial and tenant properties. The freedom to make a will was extended in the sense of Roman law to a person's entire property: the family *fidei* commissaries were forbidden.

It has frequently been pointed out that the attitude of the French Revolution was fraught with an inner antinomy regarding property. On the one hand, feudal and seigneurial rights were abrogated without precedent and without compensation, while on the other hand the sanctity and inviolability of private property was proclaimed. However, this antinomy vanishes when one realizes that the French Revolution acknowledged only *civil* property law while declaring war on all forms of non-civil property. It was precisely in the name of the sole validity of civil property law that the dispossession of all feudal and seigneurial forms of property was carried through. In future, only the state would be entitled, in the public interest, to impose restrictions on property rights. In a civil-legal sense, and independently of the will of the owner, the state was considered to be bound only by the requirement to respect the rights of others, by the stipulations of neighbor law, and by other prescriptions given through or by virtue of the law.

382

This conception of property right was also adopted by the French Code Civil and by the Dutch Civil Code. To a certain extent it was the conception of Roman law, that is to say, not that of the old primitive *ius civile* but that of the *ius gentium*. But it acquired a modern individualistic character – different from the classical Roman conception – by adopting an individualistic view of human society.

This did not entail an automatic cancellation of the Germanic legal relationships regarding the law of things. They were not terminated except if they clashed with civil-legal freedom and equality.

It is well known how this purely civil property right made itself serviceable until the end of the 19th century to unbridled economic individualism. The latter on the one hand was made possible by the total destruction of all forms of private organized communities in the area of trade and industry and on the other by the *laissez-fair* policy of the state with regard to the economy.

While fully acknowledging the destructive consequences of the almost sole reign of civil law in respect of private property and the long-standing strongly formalistic interpretation of this law, which also legitimized *abus de droit* (abuse of right), one has to understand on the other hand that this development initially represents a good deal of historical necessity. At the beginning it was important that the spirit of the individual entrepreneur should be able to stretch its wings as freely as possible. Without a large degree of freedom, modern industry, commerce and land development would never have been able to advance to the same height.

Above all, the dark side of the individualistic development of society during the 19th century should not tempt one to launch a principled attack on the legal concept of civil property as such, especially not in the name of a supposedly superior Germanic conception of property as compared to that of the Roman conception. And it is no more correct to represent the increasing influence of the principles of good faith, equity, the avoidance of abuse of power and abuse of circumstances, risk liability, etc. in our civil jurisprudence as a victory in our civil law for the Germanic communal idea. All of these principles are real principles

383

of *civil law*, which have nothing to do with what was essentially *"communal law."*

These principles threaten to be perverted and so undermine the very foundations of civil law by the doctrine of the so-called *"socio-economic" function* or *destination* of private civil rights, a doctrine that derives in part from positivist sociology and has found expression in the first article of the Civil Code of the Soviet Republics and has been defended in France by the civil lawyer Josserand.[1] However, in the Netherlands the Supreme Court, up to its most recent decisions regarding an abuse of right, has firmly rejected this dangerous doctrine. It has upheld private autonomy in determining a "reasonable interest" served by subjective civil rights.[2]

17 The continued contest between individualistic and universalistic theories

In the light of a Christian view of law and history, the differentiation of civil-legal property right out of the undifferentiated feudal and seigneurial legal relationships must be welcomed as a *deepening* and *unfolding* of the meaning of law.[3] Basic to the meaning of law is that it is to break with all *formalism* and introduce *material* legal principles for human interactions in civil society. The recognition of a sphere of individual freedom attached to the human person as such, independent of belonging to specific societal collectivities, was in Roman law still hampered to a high degree by being bound to the structure of the *familia* of which slavery was an essential component.

When humanist natural law secularized the Christian idea of personal freedom into the doctrine of innate and inalienable human rights, it undoubtedly transcended the Roman *ius gentium.* However, it at the same time overstretched the idea of freedom

---

1 [Cf. NC, 2:396 n. and 3:463.]

2 As we know, the theory of *abus de droit* has been used in Dutch jurisprudence only since 1927. Subsequent to the well-known impounding case of 2 Dec. 1937 in connection with Teunissen v. Driessen, consider the cases of 12 Jan. 1939 in connection with Nediphega v. Van Soest and that of 14 June 1940 in connection with Pope's Metal Wire Bulb Factories v. Isaac Barend and the annotation of Justice Scholten concerning this last case. Our Supreme Court has applied as a criterion of an abuse of right only the yardstick "without reasonable interest" and not that of using a right contrary to a specific purpose. See also the Court's decision of 7 June 1957 and decisions by the Court of Amsterdam of 28 Oct. 1942 and 3 Dec. 1959.

3 Cf. NC, 2:259 ff.

under civil law to the level of an exclusive conception encompassing all private spheres of life. It was this tendency that dominated the initial development of private property law during the 19th century. A reaction from both state and society was bound to occur, but in the 20th century it threatens to end in an overestimation this time of the communal idea, at the cost of civil law.

A wave of universalist perspectives on society is pushing back the individualistic conceptions, but it threatens to throw out the baby with the bathwater. The modern totalitarian idea of the state is wrapped in a variety of forms. The modern drive to shape a social order that aims at providing industry with a public-legal form of organization entails a serious danger when the fundamental, ontic differences between the various coordinational and communal relationships in legal life is disregarded.

In this context, a philosophical sociology inspired by the biblical ground-motive, by working out a more correct view of the divine structural laws obtaining for human society, has a high and extremely responsible calling to fulfill. With all the force at its disposal in this day and age, such a philosophical sociology has to engage in a battle against the blurring of the boundaries between the societal structures to which the divine world-order has guaranteed an internal sphere-sovereignty.

The issue is not to arrive at a golden mean between individualism and universalism. No, we need to acknowledge the false root of both.

Why was it that the individualistic conception, which in line with humanist natural law construed all human societal forms, foremost the state, from a civil-legal social contract and which in its classic liberal elaboration proclaimed civil property to be an exclusive and absolute right of the individual, necessarily came into conflict with the Christian view of human society? The answer is that it squarely opposed the biblical conception regarding the *root-community* of the entire human race, as it is in a pregnant sense embodied both in the doctrine of original sin and in that of the "body of Christ."

According to the divine creation order, temporal society is not made up of autonomous "individuals" conceived of as atoms. The fact alone that a human child is born from the intercourse of its parents is irreconcilable with this individualistic construction.

Furthermore, every theory which conceives property right as an exclusive and absolute civil right of the individual directly contradicts the biblical doctrine regarding God's absolute *dominium* over all temporal goods. This doctrine finds application, for example, in the Mosaic legislation with its peculiar prescriptions regarding the jubilee year, the Sabbath year, headland harvest, and so on. Though these laws may bear an exceptional theocratic character, the basic principles upon which they are built are still of fundamental significance for our present-day property relationships – also because at no time does it sacrifice the individual freedom of the owner to the private or public *dominium* of a temporal supreme owner.

18. A Christian view

But why is it, on the other hand, that the *universalist* conception is also necessarily in conflict with the Christian starting-point? The answer this time is that by proclaiming the state to be the totality of all human societal relationships within its territory, and by thus accounting for the relationship between the state and the non-political societal spheres in terms of the whole-parts relationship, the universalist view assigns to a temporal organized community the place which, according to the Christian view, can only be occupied by the religious root-community of humankind reborn in Christ – by the *civitas Dei*.

In opposition to the pagan conception of the total world-state, the Christian theory posits the totalitarian City of God which is not exhausted in any temporal societal collectivity since it lays claim to all temporal societal relationships according to the unique nature of each.

Since the deeper unity of temporal society therefore is not found in any particular societal form, it is also illegitimate, as a matter of principle, to understand the relationship between the state and the other societal relationships in terms of the schema of the whole and its parts.

No single societal collectivity of an intrinsic non-political nature can be a part of the state according to *its internal side*.[1]

---

1 Thus we must also oppose the Roman Catholic idea of the corporative state as installed in Austria on the basis of the well-known papal encyclical of 1931, *Quadragesimo Anno*. See H. Tingsten, *Den nationella diktaturen: nazismens och fascismens idéer* (Stockholm, 1936); Dutch trans., *De nationale dictaturen; de gedachtenwereld van nationaal-socialisme en fascisme* (Utrecht, 1938), esp. pp. 177-227 which deal with Austro-fascism.

To be sure, in everyday life the distinctive structural types of societal collectivities are inextricably intertwined through reciprocal bonds. However, in this intertwinement and binding, their internal sphere-sovereignty, which is guaranteed by their unique structural laws, ought to be jealously guarded.

This structural diversity within society also necessarily comes to expression in the *jural aspect* in a rich structural diversity of legal domains. Amidst all forms of mutual interlacement the internal sphere-sovereignty of these legal domains ought to be maintained.

Sphere-sovereignty in this sense differs from *autonomy*, with which, alas, it is often confused.[1] Autonomy can only apply to *parts* of a *whole*. For example, Dutch provinces and municipalities have autonomy with regard to the central government. Similarly, local congregations have autonomy in respect of the overarching church denomination.[2]

By contrast, sphere-sovereignty can only apply to the mutual relationship of societal forms which are *radically different from each other* and which for this reason can never relate to each other as parts to the whole.

Naturally, only in a differentiated society does sphere-sovereignty come to a clear manifestation. In the social schema of the Germanic medieval period, with its undifferentiated societal collectivities, only *autonomy* was acknowledged,[3] while Emperor and Pope struggled to acquire supreme authority in the Holy Roman Empire as a whole, which, according to the universalist

---

1 A case in point is found in the report *Nieuwe Organen* [New organs] published in 1931 by the commission appointed by the Dutch Labor Party. In connection with the competency [of "*publiekrechtelijke bedrijfsorganisaties*" (sectoral organizations under public law)] to enforce rules, the report states that it belongs to "the competency of an ordinance-making body to assess, freely and independently, if, how, and where ordinances will be enacted in respect of the entrusted interests, for example regarding municipal regulations within the internal affairs of the municipality." [This note was omitted from the 1962 version.]

2 [This sentence was omitted from the 1962 version.]

3 In the main, undifferentiated societal collectivities are not of a fundamentally different character, except that in the more weakly organized folk communities like clans, hamlets, guilds, etc., the *family principle* predominates, while in the more strongly organized tribal and feudal societies the political principle is paramount.

387

mode of thought of the time, was believed to encompass temporal Christian society in all its undifferentiated parts.[1]

It is wrong on principle to want to take this social scheme and in name of the "Christian Germanic conception of law,[2] carry it over – of course with adjustments – to the differentiated relationships of modern society and force the world of commerce and industry into sectoral organizations under public law with the intention to make the *internal economic life of these sectors* serviceable to the interest of the state, in keeping with the idea of the corporative state.

For the same reason it would be wrong to undermine civil property right by conjuring up the legal concept of "divided property" and to sacrifice the hard-won civil-legal freedom of the individual person to the supreme ownership of the state.

In our modern differentiated society, the acknowledgment of sphere-sovereignty can alone provide a proper solution to the problem regarding the relationship between individual and society *also within legal life.*

A form of "social binding" to particular communal-law restrictions of civil property right, which does not itself share in a communal character, is imperative, on principle; but it can only be achieved through joint action of the state and private communities. It cannot be done by degrading the private communities into autonomous and self-regulatory parts of the state. *What is needed instead is to acknowledge each community according to its own distinctive nature and peculiar structure.*

Undoubtedly the social binding of property right through private communal relationships will, to a greater or lesser degree, come to expression *externally*. For example, I cannot see why the old kinship purchase cannot be restored as a subjective civil right in respect of land. Also in the case of the intestate law of succession, Roman civil law already took into account natural family ties. Such a civil right of purchase by family members, supported by customary agricultural inheritance law, along with the existing Re-allotment Act, could for example have made a contribu-

1   [The next two paragraphs were omitted from the 1962 version.]
2   For the appeal to the "Christian Germanic idea of law" by the Austrian defenders of a Christian corporative state, see Tingsten, op. cit., p. 211, and the literature cited there.

388

tion to the prevention of farmland fragmentation without having to take recourse to removing the so-called heritable lands from the domain of civil law.

The only basis for linking civil law and public law is the "general interest" or "common good." Yet, the idea of the "*salus publica*" necessarily turns into a power slogan of state absolutism when it is not, according to its jural aspect, understood as a genuine *jural idea* that puts definite limits on the competence of the government, as determined by the inner nature of the state as an organized community on the one hand and the inner nature of the non-political societal collectivities on the other.

Although the state, like every other societal collectivity, functions within the economic sphere, still it does not have a typical economic *qualifying function* such as is found in commercial and industrial firms. Rather, in its entire structure the state is qualified as a public-legal community on the typical foundation of a monopolistic organization of the power of the sword. The state must be a *just state* in the sense of *sphere-sovereignty* or it will disintegrate into a reign of despotism over all spheres of life.

VII

Law and History

1. Introduction: The Historical School and "empirical natural law" at the end of the 18th century[1]

SINCE THE WIDESPREAD ACCEPTANCE of what may be called the "historical mode of thought", the relationship between law and history has become a second "Cape Horn" among the problems of legal philosophy.[2]

Legal philosophy was obliged to reconcile itself to this manner of thinking if it wanted to uphold its own scientific pretensions, but a latent tension persisted between "philosophical" and "historical" views of law. Did the latter, then, have no "philosophical" character? The question touches the heart of the matter! The "historical mode of thought" announced itself in legal science as a new view of the relationship between law and history, but its widespread acceptance allowed its philosophical *a priori* to remain hidden beneath a scientific, empirical method of operation. Precisely this hidden philosophical *a priori* of the "historical view of law" rendered impossible any substantial reconciliation with a view of law that had a different orientation. It nurtured an imperialism that ultimately brooked no competition and made it a dangerous figure in the field of legal philosophy.

At first sight this assessment seems unfair! Has not the permeation of the "historical way of thinking" brought to the philosophy of law a much deeper insight into the development of legal life? Did it not rescue legal philosophy from wandering in the labyrinth of the *a priori* systems of natural law and rational law and bring it into fruitful contact with the rich material of historical experience?

Since the Historical School finally disposed of natural law in the rationalistic cast that humanist legal philosophy from

1 Paper presented at the 23rd Scientific Gathering of the Free University of Amsterdam; July 13, 1938.
2 Rudolf von Jhering called the relationship between law and morality the "Cape Horn" of legal philosophy [i.e., the turbulent waters where many suffer shipwreck].

Grotius to Kant had given it, two theses have seemed beyond reproach:
1) all positive law is a historical phenomenon that cannot deny its link with the past, and
2) *next to* or *above* this historically developed law there can exist no second legal system with everlasting and immutable content, such as one might deduce in an *a priori* manner from "human nature" or "human reason."

Should we challenge these axioms of the historical view of law? And if we do, where lurks the danger they embody for legal theory?

Naturally, I would not deny that the historical way of thinking has brought great gains to the philosophy and the science of law. Nor can I deny that both these theses are held today as almost unassailable truths whose discovery is reckoned a lasting memorial of F. C. von Savigny (1779–1861) and his followers. My only claim is that this historical mode of thinking, for all its inestimable value, has also revealed a dangerous downside for legal philosophy. Overemphasizing its significance has caused confusion in the difficult borderline questions of the science of law and the science of history. Indeed, the philosophy of law has yet to find a way out of this confusion.

Let us review those two theses above that capture the significance of the Historical School for legal philosophy. The scope of the first can only be assessed if we consider the meaning which Savigny's school attached to the term *geschichtlich* (historical). If you just take it to mean "temporal," "subject to coming into being, undergoing change, passing away," then naturally, your characterization of positive law as a *historical* phenomenon brings nothing new to the debate with the learned champions of natural law. The actual difference would then only be found in the second thesis. However, the center of gravity of the historical view of law is rather to be sought in the first thesis. Place all the emphasis on the second thesis, and you will never appreciate the real meaning of the rise of the Historical School and the historical mode of thinking in general.

After all, the rationalistic systems of natural law, whose designers attempted to construe *"more geometrico"* (in mathematical fashion) a timeless, natural or rational legal order, accounted for only a short phase in the powerful natural-law tradition. They emerged in an intellectual climate dominated by the deductive spirit of Descartes. But the triumph of the method of natural science, erected on Galileo's foundations and provisionally perfected by Newton, soon generated resistance to the *aprioristic* systems even in the natural-law camp. The 18th-century Enlightenment is already largely empiricist in its thought: the genius of Newton had ousted that of Descartes.[1]

The construction *of aprioristic* systems in the school of Christian Wolff, and even in Kant and his immediate followers, enjoyed a short Indian summer, with some healthy fruit for the codification of Prussian Provincial Law and for the Austrian *Civil Code*. But the newer trend in natural law, which emerged during the last three decades of the 18th century and in which figures like Feder, Weber, Thibaut, Runde and others[2] dominated the scene, abandoned in the main any idea of a timeless, universally valid, material, natural-law order.[3]

The famous struggle for codification in Germany saw the father of the Historical School pitted against A. F. J. Thibaut (1772–1840). Savigny, although tactically directing his attack against rationalistic natural law, was in fact pleading the case against a new, dynamic, natural-law idea which was strongly attached to the empirical research method. Eichhorn would soon do the same in rejecting Runde's method of appealing to the "nature of the case."

This newer natural-law theory of the Enlightenment became a flexible, critically axiological method which claimed universality only for the method, not for its results, which varied according to circumstances.

The idea of a "natural law with varying content," later to be propagated by Rudolf Stammler and the so-called "free law

1 Cf. Ernst Cassirer, *Die Philosophie der Aufklärung* (Tübingen, 1932).
2 Up to a point one can also rank the precursor of the Historical School, Gustav Hugo, among this school; cf. F. Eichengrün, *Die Rechtsphilosophie Gustav Hugos* (The Hague, 1935), pp. 82 ff. Hugo (1764–1844) was strongly influenced by Johann Stephan Pütter (1725–1807) and Immanuel Kant (the latter in his pre-critical, empiricist phase).
3 On this school, cf. the important paper by H. Thieme, "Die Zeit des späten Naturrechts," *Zeitschrift der Savigny-Stiftung, Germanische Abteilung* 56 (1936): 202 ff.

movement," was already familiar to this new 18th-century school, albeit without Stammler's neo-Kantian elaboration. Descartes' disparagement of historical investigation was utterly foreign to it. One can even discern a remarkable link between natural law and the science of legal history in Germany.

Whereas the aprioristic natural-law systems of Grotius and Pufendorf were bound to the Roman *ius gentium* as an invariable *ratio scripta*, the dynamic, natural-law method of the Germanist C. L. Runde (1773–1849) already showed a critical historical orientation. As he attempted to construe "common German private law" out of the great diversity of particular rights with their many gaps, Runde no longer called upon the support of "natural-law rules of eternal validity" but simply appealed to the "nature of the case" within the context of specific historical circumstances.

This alone may suffice to support our claim that the true significance of the view of law introduced by the Historical School is not the demolition of the aprioristic natural-law systems. No, the new "historical mode of thought" that we know since 1892 as *"historicism"*[1] caused a radical turn-about in the very view of history itself, in consequence of which the relationship between law and history came to stand in an entirely new light.

The irrationalist idea of development, which Herder's *Ideen* [*zur Philosophie der Geschichte der Menschheit*] had already broached and Romanticism had enthroned in alliance with the new concept of culture that Enlightenment historiography had engendered, could only lead to an *intrinsic historification* of all the normative aspects of reality and appeared to leave no room for belief in extra-historical norms and standards.

The danger of this historicism was the greater because its irrationalist orientation characterized the process of historical development as "law-less."[2] All positive norms of social intercourse, language and economics, art, law, morality and faith are

---

1 According to Friedrich Meinecke in the *Historische Zeitschrift* 149 (1933): 303.
2 I.e., that history according to its subject-side is subjected to no universally valid laws. In effect, here individual subjectivity is a law unto itself.

viewed as products of an irrational unfolding of the individual historical aptitudes of a folk or a nation, or – if the notion of a *Volksgeist* ("folk-spirit") is exchanged for a broader cultural-historical viewpoint – from the unique *Zeitgeist* ("spirit of the age") of an unrepeatable cultural context.

Fichte, in his final intellectual phase, had characterized the "historical" as such as "law-less" and had identified in this feature its sharpest contrast to "natural reality,"[1] though he immediately added that one has to assume a "hidden lawfulness" in the course of history, which in a pseudo-Christian way he identified with "divine providence." This idea of a hidden lawfulness, which would be accentuated by Romanticism and introduced into the antirevolutionary conception of history by F. J. Stahl (1802–1861) using the familiar Christian expression "God's guidance in history," could never disavow its irrationalist, humanist origin. When it claimed a normative – albeit secondary – character for "God's guidance" taken in this irrationalist sense, as it did with Stahl, it could not avoid the charge that "God's hidden counsel" had come to stand in the place of "God's revealed will."

So long as humanism cherished an idealist metaphysical standpoint, it was possible to avoid the most extreme consequences of historicism. Eternal, absolute "ideas" or "values," implicit in the humanistic personality ideal, persisted as a transcendent norm for human action, a norm which in the course of history might enjoy a better or worse realization. So long as this norm was cherished, it was possible as well to uphold the idea of a normative goal in history, as laid out in Herder's idea of humanity, or in the aesthetic "educational ideal" of Romanticism,

---

1 Fichte knows only two kinds of laws, *natural laws* and the *moral law*. Cf. *Werke* (Bonn, 1834-35), 9:462-463: "Therefore the matter stands as follows: by far most of the products of freedom, present in a time-span of intuition, came into being not according to the clear *concept* of moral laws, thus not according to these laws; just as little did they come into being through natural law, since the latter is closed to its generation and since they came into being through freedom. Now, since apart from these two there is no lawgiving, they occurred *law-less*, by chance. This is actually and notoriously the object hitherto of the history of mankind." Cf. my *WdW*, 1:455-456 [cf. *NC*, 1:488-495].

or in Hegel's idea of the progress of mankind in awareness of freedom.

However, as soon as the "historicist mode of thought" had reduced this Olympian bastion of the humanist personality ideal to the level of historical determination, a twilight of the gods fell over the realm of humanist "values" or "ideas." To seek asylum in a realm of transcendent ideas seemed but an unhistorical escape from critical historical awareness when weighed against the relativistic wisdom of Goethe's Mephistopheles: "The worth of whatever exists is that it passes away."[1]

Marxism and Darwinism had undermined the foundations of idealist humanism. Conscious of this spiritual revolution-in-the-making, Ranke's pupil Jacob Burckhardt never ventured to write a "World History" in the manner of his great teacher. The imposing figures of Nietzsche and Søren Kierkegaard sounded the death-knell of German idealism. And Wilhelm Dilthey, the genius of historicism in our time, tweaked the humanist idea of the autonomy of the free personality so that "historical thought" could triumph over all forms of a metaphysical faith in reason: once freed from dogmatism by historical awareness, mankind would at last regain its true sovereignty; unburdened by any theological or metaphysical preconceptions, mankind would henceforth be able to appropriate all cultural goods of past and present in full freedom.[2] Legal philosophy, increasingly influenced by historicism, gradually had to let go of its idealistic axiology.

The Hegelian notion of the "rationality" of all historical "reality," a view that was revisited by the "objective idealist" schools in modern legal philosophy, remained rooted in an idealistic faith in reason which modern historicism has completely demolished.

The retreat of idealism to its last bastion, juridical epistemology, merely presaged its complete surrender. Kelsen's "doctrine of pure law" did not even present itself any longer as legal philosophy. The empty thought-forms of the "jural *ought*," by which

1 "Denn alles was besteht, ist wert das es zugrunde geht."
2 Dilthey, *Gesammelte Werke*, 7:290-291.

he tried to maintain the independence of the science of law, surrendered law entirely, as to content, to a historicist solution in terms of subjective power-relations.

The so-called "sociological mode of thought," in the forms in which it made itself progressively at home in modern legal philosophy, provided nothing like a deliverance from historicism, as we shall see below; it turned out instead to be one of its strongest allies. It is indeed the case that the historical conception of law turned out to be a dangerous figure in the field of legal philosophy.

2. The sociological strain of historicism

The real meaning of historicism, as we pointed out, lies in the *inner* historification of all normative aspects of human society.

Historicism is no longer able to view the "historical" as an "aspect" of reality, a functional *mode*, an internally delimited *side* of reality. Rather, it elevates the historical to become the entirety of societal reality. History in this optic embraces "concrete life in all its fullness."[1]

This view is intimately connected with the modern notion of culture.[2] Culture" is assumed to embrace all phenomena falling outside the realm of the natural. It is practically identified with human society in all of its temporal manifestations, and the *mode of being* of this culture, in contrast to nature, is conceived of as *historical development*.

---

1 Cf. the statement by a leading representative of the historical school in the discipline of economics: "History, like poetry, wants to embrace all of life" (Schmoller, *Thukydides*, p. 35). An even stronger statement is found in Karl Knies, *Die politische Oekonomie vom Standpunkte der geschichtlichen Methode* (Braunschweig, 1833), pp. 118 ff. Dilthey in particular, and those historicists who followed him, contrasted history as the "full reality of life" with the abstract "Gegenstand" (object) of natural science.

2 Cf. Heinrich Rickert, *Die Probleme der Geschichtsphilosophie* (The problems of philosophy of history) (Heidelberg, 1924), p. 80: "They (i.e., the general cultural values) constitute, in the way indicated, the concrete structures that adhere to the historical processes, such as the *real state, real art, real religion,* and *real scientific organizations.* They give these real objects those intelligible meanings which transform them into historical objects or truly historical structures. To this extent the historian always has to be a cultural historian" (emph. mine, HD).

Rickert's first attempt to reduce "culture" to a mere thought category, a synthetic *a priori* association of an "individual natural reality" with a purely ideal realm of "values," he eventually had to abandon[1] since it clashed too much with the "realistic" concept of culture held by historians. For them, "culture" is historical *reality*, not first of all the scientific product of a *mode of understanding* that is merely theoretical, individualizing and value-related, next to a "value-blind" and generalizing natural science. And within this historical totality of "culture," historicism must now first of all assign a place to the various normative aspects of reality.

With regard to the relationship between law and history it is presupposed that law in its positive form can only be a *side* of historical "reality," a limited *aspect* of "culture." This view leads, as we shall see, to a tangle of internal contradictions and owes its dangerous appearance of self-evidence to the adjectival association of "historical" with "reality." For example, to say: "Positive law is one side of *historical reality*" sounds much more acceptable than to say: "Positive law is one side of *historical development*." Why? Simply because one has to concede that "real society" (this is what is meant by "historical reality") displays many aspects besides the jural alone, whereas when using the term "historical development" the question arises what it is that *undergoes* historical development. That can hardly coincide with the development itself.

We therefore see the *historical* mode of thought joining forces from the start with the sociological, and their alliance is no *accident*. Without it, historicism would immediately reveal its inner untenability.

A sociological turn in the historicist doctrine of law is clearly evident as early as Savigny. The basic thesis of his school, which he first explained in his programmatic publication of 1814 about "the calling of our time for legislation and legal science," and which he then elaborated the following year in the opening article of the journal for historical science of law, runs as follows: "Historical development is an immanent, 'hidden' regularity of

1 See ibid., pp. 68 ff., where he makes it clear that the theoretical method of "value-relatedness" is adjusted to the historical material, which "according to its essence is meaning-fulfilled cultural life."

law which, quite independent and free from the arbitariness of a legislator, asserts itself with inner necessity and gives birth to law as a function of an organically developing cultural whole."[1] In this statement, the irrationalist "hidden lawfulness of history" replaces every form of natural law that would submit positive law to the test of non-historical, abstract, rational norms. Let us see how Savigny develops this basic concepttion!

According to Savigny, all law, just like language and customs, displays a specific character peculiar to a *nation*. Language, morality and law[2] have no independent existence; they are natural functions of one and the same nation, inseparably connected in kind and appearing as separate properties in our eyes only. What unites them is the shared conviction of the people, the same feeling of inner necessity which precludes any notion of accidental or arbitrary origin. This organic historical connection of law with the essence of a nation's character persists in its further development, which enjoys the same hidden, inner necessity. Law therefore grows with the nation, develops with the nation, and finally dies away when the nation loses its distinctive character. "The sum total of this view is therefore that all law originates in this manner, designated by a somewhat inappropriate linguistic practice as *customary law*; that is, it is first brought forth through the morals and beliefs of a people and then through jurispru-

---

1 Cf. the following statement from his opening article in the *Zeitschrift für geschichtliche Rechtswissenschaft* 1 (1815): According to the historical view "no human existence is completely individual and isolated: rather, what could be viewed as individual appears from a different viewpoint to be a member of a more encompassing whole . . . This being the case, every epoch does not for itself, at will, bring forth its world, since it accomplishes this through unbreakable communion with the total past. But then every epoch has to acknowledge something as given, which nonetheless is necessary and *free* at the same time [my ital., HD]: necessary insofar as it is not dependent upon the special will of the present; free because it proceeds just as little from a foreign will (such as the command of a master to his slave). Instead it is brought forth by a *Volk's* higher culture as a constantly changing and developing whole."

2 Applying Savigny's line of thought to the discipline of economics, Schmoller and Knies therefore also conceived of the economy as a dependent function of national life. They turned the economy into a "*Volkswirtschaft*" (folk economy) in a historical sense. Cf. Max Weber, "Roscher and Knies," *Gesammelte Aufsätze zur Wissenschaftslehre* (Tübingen, 1922), pp. 20 ff. and 142 ff.

dence, thus everywhere through internal, silently working forces, not through the arbitrariness of a legislator."[1]

Remark on Folk-Law and Jurist-Law. In his important work *Savigny und der Modernismus im Recht* (Berlin, 1914) Alfred Manigk is of the opinion that injustice is regularly done to Savigny by attributing to him the idea that the genesis of law is entirely under the influence of the national spirit. "Rather, he has the unconscious production of law in subsequent phases of development turn into a conscious production which passed to the class of jurists and elevated Science in the place of *Volksgeist* as the source of law" (op. cit., p. 79, ital. added). But precisely the words that I italicize reveal Manigk's misunderstanding. As I have demonstrated with extensive supporting quotations in the series of articles on "The Sources of Positive Law in the Light of the Cosmonomic Idea" [*Antirevolutionaire Staatkunde* (quarterly) 4 (1930): 46 ff.], Savigny never posited "science" as an independent material source of law *next to* the conviction of a people. Even in the technical phase of the formation of law, the "national spirit" remains the only *material* origin and source of the validity of positive law. The only difference with the earlier phase of development of folk-law consists in the fact (still according to Savigny) that the class of jurists now deduce the legal norms from the national consciousness in a scientific manner, whereas in the earlier phase law grew "unconsciously," without the aid of a specific "formative organ." Not until Georg Beseler was jurist-law, which accomplished the reception of Roman law, posited as an independent legal source in opposition to the Volksgeist. This caused a break in the entire historical theory of legal sources, as was immediately realized by Puchta in his sharp criticism of Beseler's work *Volksrecht und Juristenrecht* (Folk-law and jurist-law) (Leipzig, 1843). Savigny and others persistently proceeded from the fiction that jurist-law was nothing but folk-law "on a higher level."

Here, the interpenetration of the historical and sociological modes of thought is tangibly demonstrated. In Savigny, it is only by way of a detour that positive law is construed as a dependent aspect of the historical process of development. This detour necessarily follows the path of identifying "culture" with the "national community" and "history" with "societal reality."

Ultimately, this conception of law rests on an historical-sociological doctrine of reality based on a philosophical *a priori*.

1 Savigny, *Vom Beruf unserer Zeit*, repr. of the 3rd ed. (Freiburg, 1892), pp. 8–9.

Historicism has never distinguished the sociological problem ontologically from the historical one. It views law as an aspect of cultural development *because* law is an aspect of society and the full reality of this society is viewed as historical.

The danger of this "historical way of thinking" is not limited to relativizing all standards for human conduct. Historicism's view of the reality of the human community has led to the gravest consequences for human society. This is regularly overlooked in the critique of "historicism."

Since the 19th century, "the century of historical thought *par excellence*,"[1] this view of reality has become so common that modern research into the foundations of the science of history never raises the question whether or not the "historical" may be just an *aspect*, a *modality of temporal reality*. Only in a book of Huizinga's, "The Science of History," did I find a statement witnessing to a deeper insight into the *ontological* basic problem of historicism. Because of its rare nature I quote it in full:

> The 19th century became the century of historical thought par excellence. In order to understand a phenomenon one now has to see it in its origin and growth. Language, law, economy, state, religion, and society are viewed and understood historically. This brought with it tremendous intellectual gain, but it also imported great dangers. Whoever thinks that a phenomenon is nothing but history, merely a perspective of changing phases, relinquishes the principium individuationis[2] and lapses into a sterile relativism.[3]

The fact that Huizinga then actually lets this ontological viewpoint lie fallow is probably to be explained by neo-Kantian influences in his epistemological stance, according to which the historian's data consist merely of complex and heterogeneous material that can be ordered into a coherent historical whole only by the thought-forms of our mind.[4] Here Huizinga points as well to the necessary *a priori* influence of a world- and life-view.

---

1   Huizinga, *De Wetenschap der Geschiedenis* (Haarlem, 1937), p. 89.
2   What is most probably meant here is the criterion for the distinction between the various modal aspects. The so-called *principium individuationis* is something totally different.
3   Op. cit., p. 89.
4   Op. cit., pp. 44 ff.

If, however, historicism is to be challenged at its root, one must start by distinguishing sharply between *historical development* and the *theoretical investigation* of that development, and also between the *historical process* and *that which functions* in that process.

The historical can only be a modality of temporal reality; it cannot be the reality itself, which merely *functions* within history.

Human society as temporal reality displays various aspects or meaning-modalities and among them also historical development. The *identification* of society with its historical aspect is based upon an *ontological* historicism that is not surrendered but at most mitigated by accepting supra-temporal "ideas" or eternal "values."

We shall elaborate these points below but we first want to demonstrate how ontological historicism entangles scientific thought in hopeless antinomies.

3. The historical contingency of the humanistic thought-forms and ideas in modern legal philosophy and the problem of the "free-floating historical intelligence"

It is a trivial truth that *legal* history is not *economic* history or *art* history.

For ontological historicism, however, there is an immediate problem: what criterion would permit the distinction of these several domains of investigation? Whichever way you look at it, the criterion itself can never be just *historical*. Without a concept of *law* one cannot practice legal *history*. Although that concept, in its subjective theoretical character, will have a history of its own, nevertheless as *law* concept it inevitably tries to grasp in theory the constant modal structure which guarantees the jural character of legal phenomena.

Anyone who thinks that the legal historian has constantly to adapt his concept of law to the different popular opinions about law that emerge in the various periods he studies, has not yet understood the nature of the problem we are examining.

In the first place, the concept of law is an articulated scientific concept which depends on theoretical analysis of the different modal aspects of society. Popular conceptions of what is just and unjust are not theoretical concepts about the *jural nature* of legal life. Even if it were the case that a given legal system takes its rise from popular convictions, this could not in any way be true of the *modal structure of law itself.*

Besides, in the second place, reference to different popular standards of what is just and unjust presupposes in the legal historian a concept of law which he could not have derived from those popular conceptions. Only with the help of his definition of law can the legal historian distinguish the legal opinions of a people at a given time from their *economic, moral* or *creedal* convictions, because in the rather problematic popular consciousness the latter are never theoretically differentiated from people's legal convictions.

Consistent historicism undeniably rests upon a lack of critical insight.[1] A historification of the very modal structure of legal life – the very structure that makes the changing legal phenomena possible – leads to a theoretical elimination of the possibility of a legal history.

Of course, up to this point my argument has offered nothing new. Ever since the renaissance of Kantian epistemology broke the spell of uncritical positivism, the consensus is that the legal historian, no more than the scientific jurist, can derive his concept of law from the changeable "historical material of experience." Thus, so long as legal philosophy continues to bow to the dogma

---

1 In his essay *Natuurlijke waarheid en historische bepaaldheid* (Zwolle, 1935), the renowned legal historian D. G. R. Hora Siccama exemplifies a veritable dialectical struggle between *scientific* historicism and a critical mind. Right next to each other one can read these statements: "Without an *a priori* concept of law as norm of what ought to be, no research in the history of law is possible"; and: "From a scientific point of view there is no natural law [*natuurrecht*], if for no other reason than that there is no law [*recht*] but only societal customs and practices which can differ from other ones in special features but which are nonetheless purely "factual in nature" (p. 79).
— Is a science of legal history therefore impossible? According to the author it is possible; it is even the only possible science of law! From a "spectator's point of view" this "play" with "yes" and "no" is most telling!

of reason's self-sufficiency, what are its options for rescuing the concept of law from relativistic historicism?[1]

Applying the form-matter scheme of Kantian epistemology, Stammler and Kelsen attempted in different ways to reduce the modal peculiarity of jural phenomena to a transcendental thought-form. The content of positive law then exists as a kind of historical substance of experience which is ordered into logical legal categories only by the theoretical knowing activity.

The followers of the Baden school of neo-Kantians tried to construe the concept of law as an *a priori* culture concept, which can only acquire its distinctiveness from a relation to the supra-temporal value of justice. "Culture" itself, however, is in this way not regarded as a unique sphere of reality; it is understood only as the ideal "meaning" (value-relatedness) of natural reality. The neo-Hegelian legal philosopher Julius Binder went still further in defending an "objective idealism" by focusing his concept of law on the idea of a supra-personal community that finds its historical realization in the totalitarian state. He saw "culture" as a second realm of experience alongside nature, and in his later publications[2] he exchanged the neo-Kantian notion of a mere "value-relatedness" (*Wertbezogenheit*) for the Hegelian doctrine of the *realization* of the idea in the historical process!

The pupils of Fries and Heymans attempted to discover their law criterion along an "empirical-analytical" path: they looked for a hidden regularity in people's concrete acts of evaluation in terms of their sense of justice.

We could enumerate still other attempts (e.g., that of modern phenomenology) at establishing a "universally valid" concept of

---

1   Not even Savigny and Puchta attempted this. According to Puchta in his article "Gewohnheitsrecht," *Zeitschrift für geschichtliche Rechtswissenschaft*, 1:141 ff., law by definition contains two elements: (i) folk conviction, and (ii) asserting this folk conviction through the state organs as organs of the "general will." The historical conception of law also surfaces in the theory of will-power which Savigny and Puchta took over from Hegel, according to which both subjective and so-called objective law essentially are *power*, *will-power*. That "power" indeed evinces a historical meaning will be argued below.

2   Cf. his treatise "Zur Lehre vom Rechtsbegriff" (Concerning the theory of the concept of law), *Logos* 18 (1929): 26 ff.

law, but in the present context I do not intend to submit all these attempts to any closer critical inspection. In our quest for an intrinsically Christian legal philosophy we cannot follow the paths taken by these schools, if for no other reason than that they all start in the philosophical immanence standpoint which surrenders to the dogma of the intrinsic self-sufficiency of theoretical thought. In any case, they cannot help us achieve our goal.

That the humanistic thought patterns and rational ideas are "historically determined" can no longer be denied in the present day with its tremendous growth of "historical consciousness."[1] One can acknowledge the fact without becoming entangled in "historicism."[2]

The validity of a concept or a judgment cannot be decided by its historical origin, says the so-called critical philosopher, and up to a point he is right![3] But one should not forget that neo-Kantianism, under the pressure of historicism, meant to protect only the subjective epistemological thought-*form* of the judgments of law and justice from being historicized. Having chosen its starting-point in the autonomy of reason, neo-Kantianism was obliged to lift these logical forms out of their necessary historical coherence and to proclaim them "free-floating," self-sufficient, supra-temporal categories or ideas which as such have no *historical foundation*.

Yet to any deepened historical consciousness this very act of granting independence to subjective humanistic thought-forms and ideas as free-floating, supra-temporal presuppositions of experience or judgment, which are assembled in the abstract cate-

1 Dilthey emphasized "historical determinedness" already in his *Einleitung in die Geisteswissenschaften* (Introduction to the humanities) of 1883. More recently, the "sociology of knowledge" has brought to light significant historical-social connections in this area; cf. Mannheim, "Wissenssoziologie," in *Handbuch der Soziologie* (Stuttgart, 1931), pp. 661 ff.
2 Spengler betrays the truly radical nature of his historicism, particularly in his use of the word "*nur*," when he writes: "But what he [Kant] declares to be necessary forms of Western thought are still only (*nur*) the necessary forms of Western thought." *Der Untergang des Abendlandes* (The decline of the West), 15th–22nd impr. (Berlin, 1920, p. 33.
3 Up to a certain level, because *subjective theoretical insight* remains *bound* to history even though in itself it is not historical in nature.

gory of a transcendental consciousness, must appear as pure *dogmatism*.

"Historicism" will not be refuted by an epistemological "logicism." If the first position leads to inner antinomies, the second no less so. Moreover, it remains indefensible against the kernel of truth in the historicist argument that "thought-forms" themselves betray a dependence on cultural development. One need only recall the table of categories deduced by Kant, which given its historical dependence upon Newton's *Principia* is no longer up to the level of modern physics. Yet these categories and their corresponding "synthetic judgments *a priori*" were presented as "timeless, universally valid thought-forms *making possible* all experience of nature in the first place"!

Something more must be said. The subjectivist, essentially nominalist attitude of modern humanistic philosophy does not know the difference between the *subjective a priori* to which both the concept and the idea of law belong, and the *cosmic a priori structure* of the jural that makes possible and defines all concrete legal phenomena. This structure does not derive its foundational character from subjective human consciousness, but from the constant, temporal world-order that springs from God's creative will.[1] When you do not distinguish between the modal structure of legal life and our subjective *a priori* concept of it, you pass off your inevitably historically shaped and fallible subjective insight into the modal nature of legal phenomena for unchangeable and universally valid truth, thus lapsing into an uncritical dogmatism which will in turn be overtaken by the critique of historical consciousness.

The Philosophy of the Cosmonomic Idea has exposed the dogmatic bias of all immanence philosophy. The dogma of the internal autonomy of theoretical thought – the confidence that in thought itself can be found a supra-temporal starting-point absolved in this sense of all temporal contin contingency – is the fundamental

---

1   With regard to this distinction, see my WdW, 2:478–479 [cf. NC, 2:547–548].

flaw of immanence philosophy.[1] It testifies to a lack of that critical self-reflection which is only possible in the light of the divine Word revelation, because the Word alone can reveal the person to himself. The human selfhood – the *heart*, the *center* of human existence from which even theoretical thinking proceeds – is not *theoretical* but *religious* in nature. It exists only in the creaturely mode of being of religious dependence upon God. It is, by virtue of the divine world-order, non-self-sufficient! How would it ever be possible to find within theoretical thought, which is only a temporal function of human existence, an autonomous concentration point that transcends the temporal cosmic diversity of meaning?

Modern historicism believes it has finished once and for all with the dogmatic faith in reason of humanistic natural law. Dilthey proposed to replace Descartes' *cogito* (I think) with *vivo* (I live) as the starting-point for a truly critical, historical philosophy. But a basic misunderstanding is at work here. The irrationalist, "hermeneutical" approach of historicism, after all, if it wants to evade a suicidal skepticism, must find its Archimedean point within theoretical thought, even though it emphasizes the depth-layer of thought in what is *lived through*. For the absolutization of historical development is possible only by way of *theoretical abstraction*. If theoretical *analysis* is not first made absolute, the *historical* cannot be made absolute! The only difference from the Cartesian position is the shift of the Archimedean point from *mathematical* to *historical* Reason.

Within historical thought, then, one next has to find a center which in itself is not historically determined since, to pass universally valid judgments, it must be free from all dogmatic ties with particular ideologies.

---

1 It would be interesting to confront the critical method of the *Philosophy of the Cosmonomic Idea*, which approaches every school of thought immanently in terms of its own law-idea, with modern sociology of knowledge in order to discover the "aspect structures" of knowledge in its totality. There are undoubtedly important points of contact here. However, they end where the humanistic orientation of *"Wissenssoziologie,"* in order to maintain its "theoretical neutrality" with regard to worldviews, ensconces itself behind the dogmatic prejudice of a "free-floating intelligence." We shall explain this in more detail in the text.

In this regard the views of Karl Mannheim are typical. With Max Scheler he founded the modern "sociology of knowledge," which was prepared by the "critique of ideology" of Karl Marx. The alliance of historical and sociological approaches which we mentioned earlier is found in Mannheim's thought as a self-evident presupposition. The *"social* determination" of scientific judgments he actually treated as *historical* determination. Their contingency, typically designated by him as the *connection to reality (*"Seinsverbundenheit")* or as the "situational aspect-structure of knowing,"[1] necessarily limits the validity of scientific propositions, particularly in the humanities. He defined the actual task of the sociology of science as tracing this "connection to reality."

But what value has this "sociology of knowledge"? If we are to believe Mannheim, it is the critical "neutralizing" of those non-theoretical prejudices which intrude elements foreign to science into scientific research, elements that modify the form and content of knowledge and so diminish the truth status of the results.

But does the validity of this task of the sociology of knowledge not itself fall victim to historical-social determinism? Mannheim denies it. In any sociological investigation there is an element which can free itself from the non-theoretical prejudices of the "connection with reality." It is the "free-floating social intelligence" of intellectuals who because of their independent position in society can be relied upon to "summon up that social sensitivity which alone enables them to navigate dynamic rival forces."[2] It is able to recognize and neutralize the partiality of knowledge and those elements in it that depend upon "particularities of standpoint."

The attempt to offer a *historico-sociological* foundation for a "freefloating social intelligence" was not all that well conceived in terms of Mannheim's own starting-point.

Remark: In his quoted article in the *Handwörterbuch der Soziologie* Mannheim acknowledges that the "sociology of knowledge" can

1   In his article on *"Wissenssoziologie"* quoted earlier, Mannheim differentiates this historical-social "connection to reality" of knowledge sharply from "ideology" in that the latter, according to him, deliberately falsifies judgment, something the former does not do.
2   Karl Mannheim, *Ideologie und Utopie*, 2nd ed. (Bonn, 1930), p. 126.

"neutralize" the historical-social *Seinsverbundenheit* only to a limited degree. This is done by means of an increasingly abstract formalization of concrete historical situations, through which an ever more general and less particular position is attained: "But even this tendency towards abstraction to higher levels does not destroy the theory of the reality-bound nature of thinking, since the adequately accountable subject certainly is not an absolute, free-floating "consciousness in itself" but always a subject who is in the process of becoming more encompassing (in respect of the earlier, more particular and concrete, levels of the neutralizing, concrete subject)" (p. 675). Here it is in fact acknowledged that this "sociology of knowledge" with its nominalistic elimination of the *constant a priori structures of reality* does not really have a tenable defense against the skeptical consequences of historicism, even though it attempts to side-step them at all costs. After surrendering what is indeed a truly metaphysical concept of an absolute free-floating theoretical consciousness and "truths in themselves," the sociology of knowledge cannot withdraw its insights regarding the historico-social determination of knowledge – insights that are in many respects justified – from historicistic interpretation. Its historicistic view necessarily also determines its own conception of knowledge's "connection to reality." To my mind this point is too much neglected in the important study by Sjoerd Hofstra, *De sociale aspecten van kennis en wetenschap* (The social aspects of knowledge and science) (Amsterdam, 1937), p. 45.

But it is obvious that a radical historification of theoretical thought in the manner of Oswald Spengler leads directly into a skepticism that eliminates the very possibility of scientific history. To deny the peculiar laws of theoretical thought and to conceive of the science of history as a merely historical phenomenon is to rob one's own historical opinion of any claim to truth. Dilthey, in his attempt to arrive via a "Critique of Historical Reason" at the universally valid conditions for the science of history, was keenly aware of this problem. However, having rejected Kant's idealistic abstraction of a merely formal transcendental consciousness, the only option left to him was to take refuge in the idea of an *impersonal* historical empathy with the stream of cultural development, a form of *self-reflection* of cosmic historical life within the science of history. This amounts to demanding from the historian that he transcend his own individual historical determination by transposing himself mentally into an impersonal cosmic historical consciousness, which interprets without any prejudice the development of a culture in terms of its own vital core.[1]

Because this impersonal empathy, located within historical development, requires theoretical distance with regard to the individual historical contingency of the investigator, and because the hermeneutical method is explicitly proclaimed to belong to the humanities, it is clear that this notion amounts to the dogmatic, metaphysical elevation of a "free-floating" scientific historical consciousness above the "historical determination" of real society.

The "impersonal historical consciousness of cultural development" which comes to "self-reflection" only within the science of history is a metaphysical construct of the first order. The so-called "universally valid" historical consciousness, freely floating above historical development – whether or not imagined with "empathy" at its core – is indeed the only possible shelter for modern historicism against a wholesale skepticism. But its very endeavor to escape its skeptical consequences forced it to elevate the historical mode of thought to a "free-floating" and therefore "unconditioned" level divorced from all temporal cosmic coherence. In this way it relapsed necessarily into that uncritical dogmatism which it believed once for all to have conquered by the "historical mode of thought."

Historical consciousness too has its historical development. The modern form of the hermeneutical method is "historically determined": it is based upon the foundation of modern culture. Both the science of history and the "sociology of knowledge" are unbreakably intertwined with history. For subjectivistic historicism, the escape into the theoretical abstraction of a "free-floating intelligence" remains internally contradictory.

4. The need for a closer philosophical reflection from a Calvinistic standpoint on the relation between law and history

Historicism's way of thinking is based upon a historicist view of reality and human society. If we want to escape the historicist view of law but do not want to seek asylum among the subjec-

---

1 Regarding the inner antinomy contained in this requirement, see Philipp Lersch, *Lebensphilosophie der Gegenwart* (Contemporary philosophy of life) (Berlin, 1932), pp. 35–36.

tive, humanistic thought-forms and ideas, we must challenge this view of reality at its root. Calvinist philosophy has an imperative task in this regard, for even in our own circles there is anything but philosophical clarity with regard to the place occupied according to God's world-order by historical development in the temporal cosmos.

When Mr. A. C. Leendertz, in his well-known dissertation: *The Foundation of Governmental Authority within the Anti-Revolutionary Theory of the State*[1] launched a principled attack on the anti-revolutionary view of history, his charge – that the opposition of norm and fact is denied if we assign a normative significance to the "guidance of God in history" – undoubtedly rested upon an irrelevant neo-Kantian starting-point.[2] Not only does the separation of "fact" and "norm" defended by Leendertz have a religious origin in the hidden conflict between the humanistic science- and personality-ideals, but also the meaning of this opposition was not thought through; many facts (for example, A is the judge; B commits murder) can only exist within the context of norms and therefore definitely have a normative meaning.[3] But Leendertz' attack at least had the merit of exposing the danger of the irrationalist-historicist mode of thought which particularly pervaded Stahl's legal and political theory and there led to grave consequences. For example, with an appeal to *God's guidance* common law was believed to have emerged out of the historical process "without human intervention" and was therefore clothed with an aura of sanctity – in contrast to enacted law, which never enjoyed the same value because it was "man-made" law.[4] The control of the revealed

---

1 A. C. Leendertz, *De Grond van het overheidsgezag in de antirevolutionaire staatsleer* (diss. Leiden; Amsterdam: De Bussy, 1911).
2 Cf. my article "Norm en feit," *Rechtsgeleerd Magazijn Themis* 93 (1932): 155–214.
3 In the first example the fact can only be *grasped* by virtue of those jural norms that regulate the office of judge. In the second example the fact also cannot exist without the legal norm to which it is subject; how else, for example, would one distinuish between carrying out a death sentence and committing murder?
4 Cf. Stahl's statement in his work *Die gegenwärtigen Parteien in Staat und Kirche*, 2nd ed. (Berlin, 1868), p. 307: "Justice is the holier for us the more it has separated itself from laws and presents itself as something at hand, where no one thinks of its origin anymore."

moral law over historically grown law merely served in Stahl's thought to correct the inner historification of positive law, as a result of which both history and law were presented in a distorted way.

In reaction to the irrationalist appeal to "God's guidance in history," the inclination arises, particularly on the part of theology, to deny (at least within the domain of "profane" history) that historical development has any normative meaning. It is viewed as a mere "factual process" that legislators and politicians simply have to *reckon with* as the "given situation." The Christian view of history as the struggle between the *civitas Dei* (the kingdom of God) and the *civitas terrena* (the kingdom of darkness) may still be maintained, as well as the confession of God's providence in history, but one cannot say it has contributed much to a Christian *theory* of history.

To the extent that such a conception revives a scholastic way of thinking, in which the so-called natural moral law serves as the sole norm for human conduct and only requires appropriate "application" according to "time and place," it represents no advance beyond the position taken by Stahl and his followers. Both the scientific and the practical problem[1] that history poses for us are thus simply ignored and no account is given of the rich pluriformity of normative aspects which temporal reality exhibits according to the divine world-order. In addition, the moral law itself, like a metaphysical natural law, is thus lifted out of its temporal coherence with all other spheres of ordinances.

The radical unity of God's divine law truly transcends the temporal diversity of ordinances. It is revealed to us through Christ as the commandment to love God and our neighbor, a love that must proceed from an undivided heart, embrace our entire understanding, and call upon all our strength. This is the religious fullness, the fulfillment of the law, which reflects the way in which the religious concentration point of our entire

1 I think especially of the great problems in the present phase of our culture raised by national socialism and fascism, to which I shall return toward the end of this paper.

temporal existence is located in the heart. But according to the divine world-order, this unity of God's law is attuned to a rich *temporal pluriformity* of law-spheres, through which the manifold wisdom of God is revealed, just as the heart or soul of a human being is attuned to the body and understood as a created whole whose interwoven individuality structures comprehend all the functions of a person within all the spheres of temporal life. As little as the soul can be substituted for the body, so it is impossible to substitute the religious commandment of love for the pluriformity of divine ordinances in the various normative aspects of human society. The temporal moral law, which governs the moral relationships here on earth, is just *one* of the many aspects which the divine law exhibits in its refraction of meaning. The moral aspect is indissolubly intertwined with all the other law-spheres; when it is absolutized it *loses* its moral meaning.

In this sense, the moral law in its positive form is also intertwined with history, just as are legal norms, social norms, lingual norms, and so on. To deny this indissoluble coherence is to succumb to a rationalistic metaphysics of natural law; to try and reduce the positive moral law, positive legislation, and so on, to "historical phenomena" is to fall headlong into the evil of historicism.

5. Ontological historicism and the boundaries between the science of law and the science of history

The historical view of reality is demonstrably connected to the popular conception in which *history* is identified with *what happened in the past*.

In order to eliminate any misunderstanding, we must first note that prescientific thinking does not direct itself towards a theoretical analysis of the various aspects of temporal reality since it is *embedded*, rather, within full reality as it offers itself in the concrete individuality structures of things, events and societal relationships. It is not the *modalities*, the *how*, but the *what* of events that we grasp explicitly in naive experience. The *modalities*, which qualify the various *aspects* of reality, only come to the awareness of naive experience *implicitly*; they are not theoreti-

413

cally articulated. When we want to distinguish the aspects of number, space, movement, organic life, feeling, and so on, we start by abstracting from the concrete individuality structures of entities and events. The mental effort that it first takes to do this is known to everyone who has ever helped a child break free from an abacus in order to be able to make calculations. Similarly the jurist must theoretically abstract a *legal fact* as the *jural aspect* of an event from the full concrete reality of life. This never happens outside theory.

It is therefore quite natural that in everyday life, "history" – unless one means a narrative or an historical account – is identified with *what has happened*.[1] However, to deduce from this that historicism sees reality in the same way as our naive experience does is an error rather like that of the epistemologist who thinks that naive experience identifies the sensory aspect of things with the things themselves on the grounds that naive experience depends rigidly on sensory representations in forming concepts.[2]

Ontological *historicism* is not a *naive* view of reality. It is a *theoretical* view in which the concept of "history" has from the start been given a specific theoretical meaning. Since the rise of the "historical way of thinking" this meaning is summed up in the concept *cultural development* in which, as we saw, historical and sociological thinking are combined to grasp "culture" as an individual totality. In a similar way, his torical ethnography (the theory of "cultural spheres") searches for a "genealogy of cultures."

The inner historification of the various normative aspects of society (the logical, the social, the lingual aspects, the economic,

---

1 The restriction "in the past" is by no means essential. In everyday parlance, too, we connect history to the present. Consider the expression: "Today we are witnessing a historical event," or: "This is a historic moment."

2 In this respect, Hegel's ontological historicism is typically based on "the common definition of history." He opened his lecture series on the philosophy of World History with these words: "I need not comment on what I mean by history, world-history; the common definition will do and we are generally in agreement with it." *Vorlesungen über die Philosophie der Weltgeschichte*, ed. Lasson (Leipzig, 1917), p. 1.

aesthetic, jural, moral and faith aspects) is achieved by conceiving "culture" as the historical "realization of values" or, taken in a neo-Kantian fashion, as a synthesis of "fact" and "value." While idealism assigned to these "ideas" or "values" a timeless validity, radical historicism reduced them to mere "historico-psychological" motives.

It is evident that on this view of reality the very science of history as a special science is at risk. Given the lack of delineation in the understanding of "culture," what should be the distinct field of investigation of this discipline as compared with economics or law? It cannot be maintained – and indeed it is never claimed by anyone – that the historian describes the *full reality* of human society in the course of its development. Even historicism concedes that the historian has to make a "selection" from the "historical material."

But what point of view guides the selection? At this juncture the question of the *modal meaning* of the historical surfaces unavoidably, and precisely here ontological historicism fails us. To answer that the sifting of "historical material" is guided by what is *culturally important* is useless because it is precisely the distinction between what is important and what is not that requires a yardstick. Huizinga's answer – that what is considered for historical treatment depends on what a particular culture considers important – misses the point because the question concerns not the *what* but the *how* of the historian's selection. Huizinga may be right with regard to the *what* of historical importance, but his historification of the *how*, of the mode of historical selection, would lead to antinomies like those encountered in historicizing the concepts of law or historicizing theoretical knowledge.

Rickert's criterion of "value-relatedness" is no solution either because, while his "values" do encompass those of "truth," "beauty," "justice" and "holiness," what is absent in this pantheon is exactly the "muse of history."[1]

It is therefore understandable that no other criterion for demarcating history's field of study remains but that of *becoming* or *development*.[2] Thus in order to distinguish between the so-called *dogmatic science of law* and the *science of legal history*, all emphasis is laid upon the *systematics* of the former as opposed to the *genetic description* of the latter. This was already done by Savigny, and on the surface the criterion seems to be sufficient if you restrict it to the separate *branches* of the science of history which are distinguished precisely according to the various modal aspects of society.

But then what to think of the comprehensive category "cultural history"? Definition according to a specific modal point of view is lacking here as a consequence of the customary but vague concept of "culture."

The opposition between *genetic* and *systematic* reveals itself in all its weakness here. All scientific labor as such is systematic, the historian's too. Strongly oriented to history himself, the Spanish thinker Ortega y Gasset even defined history as the *sys-*

---

1   Remarkable in this respect is the approach taken by Julius Binder in his work in philosophy of law, *Philosophie des Rechts* (Berlin, 1925), pp. 1011 ff., an approach that is oriented to Rickert's conception of the "value-relating" method of the cultural sciences. On the one hand Binder writes: "The object of study both for the historical and the systematic science of law in the final analysis is actual contemporary law which as a 'meaningful structure' displays a historical essence that constitutes the unifying perspective for both disciplines of empirical law." On the other hand he acknowledges that "jurisprudence" cannot really be a historical science, even though "the essence of all law is history and therefore can only be understood historically" (p. 1011). And in an earlier context (p. 411) he distinguishes the "categories of history" explicitly from "the other categories of culture," such as those of law, morality, "religion," and so on! But these other "categories" are not seen by him as "forms of knowing" but as ideal norms deduced from specific "ideas." But then where do the specific categories of history come from?
2   Bernheim particularly emphasized this well-known definition of the science of history in his *Einleitung in die Geschichtswissenschaft*, 3rd and 4th ed. (Berlin, 1926), pp. 46 ff.

tematic science of human life.[1] Whoever fails to understand a historical phenomenon theoretically in its *historical coherence,* grasping it instead as a fact existing in and of itself, produces no scientific history but simply writes "miscellaneous news." It is only the nature of the historian's systematics that is different from the jurist's. But then, everything hangs on that difference in nature, that *modal difference!*

The same applies to the "genetic" way of looking at things. The science of law has its own genetic problem in the theory of the sources of law. The Historical School introduced a fundamental confusion into this theory by ignoring the jural character of the legal sources and interpreting the *juridical process of becoming* as a *historical process of development.* This alone explains why it did not acknowledge any jural genetic sources for "common" law and why it elevated science, owing to its historical influence upon the formation of law, to a formal genetic source of positive law.[2]

This criterion – that the science of history grasps the historical material *in succession* while the systematic science of law does so *in simultaneity*[3] – is no more useful without a closer *modal* definition of *succession* and *simultaneity.* And even in general terms the

---

1 Ortega y Gasset, "History as a System," in *Philosophy and History: Essays presented to Ernst Cassirer,* edited by Raymond Klibansky and H. J. Paton (Oxford, 1936), p. 316.
2 Cf. in this regard my extensive treatment of the issue in the series of articles cited earlier, "De bronnen van het stellig recht" (The sources of positive law) in *Antirevolutionaire Staatkunde* (quarterly) of 1931.
3 This is already found in the thought of Savigny, *Zeitschrift für geschichtliche Rechtswissenschaft* 1 (1815): 14: "The given multiplicity is twofold, viz. partially simultaneous and partially successive, which necessarily entails a twofold scientific treatment.... The treatment of a successive multiplicity constitutes the proper task of historical method." This criterion is also employed by Hermann Heller in his posthumously published work *Staatslehre* (Leiden, 1934) in order to demarcate political theory as structural theory from the discipline of *political history.* The "historical forms of human activity" (among which Heller explicitly mentions *state, church* and *economy* but which undoubtedly would also include positive law) cannot be *understood,* let alone *explained,* he writes, solely with the logical tools of the science of history, that is to say, with the category of "temporal succession." "They are to be understood only from the simultaneous being together of societal structural action, from intersecting historical currents as it were" (p. 50).

417

statement is incorrect. The historian must also be concerned to take into account the *simultaneity* of historical events, and the dogmatic science of law must reckon with the *succession* of legal facts and norms (think of concepts like "serial crime," "transitional law," "delegated law"). The confusion is complete when, as is fashionable, the systematic concepts of dogmatic legal science, such as pledging and mortgaging, renting and buying, etc., are all designated as *historical*.

The opposition between a *typifying* and an *individualizing* method is equally unhelpful to characterize the respective working methods of dogmatic legal science and the science of history.[1] The reason is that dogmatic legal science should never be satisfied with an abstract schematism of legal life, but must as its inescapable task always grasp legal norms in terms of the process of their eventual concretization in individual cases. The old scholastic wing of legal science – construing the legal rule, the case and the decision as a relationship of logical major premise, minor premise, and conclusion – certainly ought not to be resurrected as representative of the essence of the juridical-dogmatic method as opposed to the historical. On the other hand, the historian too must employ type concepts such as *renaissance, feudalism, early capitalism*, and so on.

Even less profitable is the opposition between a *normative* and a *causal* view. The jurist operates with a *jural* concept of causality and the historian with a *historical*, but neither employs a natural-science concept of causality. Once again everything boils down to the modal meaning of these concepts.

Finally, the demand that the historian pursue a non-normative kind of observation must be emphatically denied. For example, how could he speak of cultural flourishing or cultural decay – as Spengler (inconsistently) does – if he is not allowed to apply a normative yardstick for cultural development? From a radically positivist standpoint one might possibly risk the ban-

1 This corresponds with the distinction between *systematic* and *individualizing* cultural science. Rickert, for example, uses this distinction in his work *Kulturwissenschaft und Naturwissenschaft* (Cultural science and natural science), 4th and 5th ed. (Tübingen, 1921), pp. 125 ff. The distinction is still absent in his work *Die Grenzen der Naturwissenschaftlichen Begriffsbildung* (The limits of natural-scientific concept formation), 3rd and 4th ed. (Tübingen, 1921).

ning of even such normative yardsticks from the purview of historical science. But then the historian's peculiar concept of development would lose its foundation as well. For this concept definitely has, as I intend to show in more detail, a normative meaning. This is not meant in an *ethical* sense or in the sense of *steady progress* as used by philosophers of history during the Enlightenment. It has the sense, rather, of an *immanent cultural norm* of a typically historical nature, which once again presupposes a modal definition of the concept of history.

The mere distinction between *primitive* and *disclosed* cultures, which is needed to demarcate the subject matter of historical ethnology from that of historical science proper,[1] requires a normative historical yardstick. The science of history as such is not interested in primitive, closed cultures like that of Tierra del Fuego; it investigates the history of only those peoples that have been taken up in the stream of disclosed cultural development.

6. The problem when viewed in the light of the theory of modal spheres and of the individuality structures of human society

What we have come to see is that all the difficulties and self-contradictions in which historicism's view of reality entangles itself, whether in respect of the science of history or of law, result from a failure to define properly the modal meaning of the concept of *history*. In my opinion, at this point the theory of the modal law-spheres as developed in the *Philosophy of the Cosmonomic Idea* may bring greater clarity to the debate about the relationship between law and history.

I think that I may assume some acquaintance with the sharp distinction made in our philosophy between the two interconnected structures of reality, namely *modal* structures and *individuality* structures, both of which are part of the divine world-order.

Modal structures are investigated by the theory of the law-spheres. According to this theory, the distinct aspects of reality, namely those of number, space, movement, organic life, feeling, analysis, symbolic signification, social intercourse, the eco-

---

1   See my *WdW*, 3:281–285 [cf. *NC*, 3:332–337], where I show that this is also related to a difference in method.

nomic, the aesthetic, the jural, the moral and the pistical, do not find their origin in the *a priori* organization of the knowing consciousness, but in the world-order called into being by God's creative will. These aspects are enclosed in law-spheres which on the one hand are marked off from each other by their mutually irreducible *modal meaning* but on the other hand are articulated by the temporal world-order in a *constant and irreversible order* and an *indissoluble coherence*.

The modal structure of the different law-spheres displays an architectonic association of modal moments. The nucleus as the central or qualifying moment guarantees the original uniqueness as well as the sphere-sovereignty of the modal aspect. *"Analogies"* or *"retrocipations"* point back to the nuclei of the *earlier* aspects. *"Anticipations"* guarantee the temporal coherence with the aspects that appear *later* in the cosmic order; they deepen and disclose the modal meaning of an aspect and ultimately point beyond the temporal meaning-diversity towards the religious fullness-of-meaning and root-unity of creation.

This architectonic structure, in which the cosmic time-order is expressed and which therefore does not possess anything like a supra-temporal character makes it possible that every modal aspect reveals its coherence with all other aspects and that each aspect reflects, in its own modal fashion, the *totality* of modal aspects. In the theory of law-spheres, this state of affairs is designated the sphere-*universality* of the modal aspects, which is merely the reverse of their internal sphere-*sovereignty*.

This explains the apparent persuasiveness of all the *isms* in philosophy, historicism being just one among many. "Isms" originate in the immanence standpoint that is rooted in the primary absolutization – the proclamation of the self-sufficiency – of theoretical thought. It is a standpoint that compels the thinker to seek the deeper unity and coherence of the diverse aspects of experience (so far as he considers them knowable) in a particular aspect that he isolates through theoretical analysis and elevates to be the common denominator of the whole of temporal reality. The sphere-universality, which under the divine world-order properly belongs to such an aspect, is then interpreted as an *absolute* universality.

The theory of individuality structures, which treats a second main theme of the *Philosophy of the Cosmonomic Idea*, goes on to show how these modal aspects of reality in concrete entities and societal forms are grouped in a *typical way* within the individual whole of an *individuality structure*. This guarantees the typical inner nature of transient entities or transient societal forms.

Individuality structures too are grounded in the temporal world-order. They *make possible* the coming into being and passing away of things and societal relationships by providing the constant law-conformative framework for their existence. In this sense, for example, state, nuclear family and church institution, just as natural things and so-called cultural objects, have their constant intrinsic individuality structure, which is no more subject to change than the *modal* structures in which they function. Just as the modal aspects of reality are indissolubly interwoven while retaining their sphere-sovereignty, so are the individuality structures. In the case of the individuality structures, sphere-sovereignty acquired the *concrete* meaning given them in Kuyper's well-known expositions of this principle. One can also find substantial points of contact in Kuyper's work for the sphere-sovereignty of the law-spheres.[1]

If we look into the fields of investigation of the various special sciences, it appears that only "pure" mathematics and a part of mathematical natural science can completely exclude the individuality structures and orient themselves purely to the modal structure of the studied aspects. All other disciplines, if they do not want to be led astray, have to account in their empirical investigations for the individuality structures of reality. As for legal science, I will only refer to the fact that the "material" classification of law as constitutional law, civil law and civil procedure, the private law of associations, ecclesiastical law, international law, and so on, is inseparably connected to the different individuality structures of human society. The attempt to level these structural differences theoretically, as in Kelsen's "pure theory of law," had to lead to patent inaccuracies (think only of

1 Cf. in this connection the article of C. Veenhof, "*Souvereiniteit in eigen kring*" (Sphere-sovereignty) that appeared during the centennial commemoration of Kuyper's birth in the weekly *De Reformatie*, 29 Oct. 1937, pp. 35–36. Veenhof demonstrates this point with extensive quotations from Kuyper's entire oeuvre.

421

Kelsen's attempt to identify state and law in a "norm-logical" way).

In economic science, "pure economics" was guilty of similar errors in interpreting historically based international market relationships within a *merely* modal economic viewpoint. In doing so, it failed to appreciate that such market relationships are only possible in a typically historically grounded individuality structure of human society, a structure that can never be understood in a *merely* economical (i.e., in an exclusively *modal*) way.[1]

At the same time it appears that these special sciences, in spite of the need to orient themselves to the individuality structures of full reality, can only go on operating as *special* sciences if they investigate those structures in the perspective offered by a specific *modal aspect*. (Note that this does not imply that they can dispense with the services of "auxiliary" sciences.)

Sociology, in its specialization as sociology of *law*, sociology of *economic relationships*, sociology of *knowledge*, *cultural* sociology and sociology of *religion* is possible only as a philosophical theory of the structure of society which furnishes the special sciences with the required method for their investigation of the phenomena. Attempts to elevate it to the level of a "synthetic encyclopedic" empirical science are inspired by naturalistic prejudices, resulting in attempts to explain the different aspects of human society in a natural-causal way by some or other particular aspect (such as the psychical or the economic).[2] This eliminates both the modal meaning of the remaining modal aspects and, by implication, the individuality structures of society which are inseparable from the modal structures.

History as a special science cannot occupy an exceptional position that would be in flagrant conflict with the structure of its field of investigation. The fact that it is specialized as economic

---

1 Particularly Menger completely lost sight of this in his sharp polemic against Knies. [Karl Menger founded the Austrian School of economics, while Karl Knies, professor of economics in Heidelberg, was a proponent of the older Historical School.]

2 This is the kernel of truth in Georg von Below's objection to sociology as an independent empirical science; cf. *Die Entstehung der Soziologie*, ed. Othmar Spann (Jena, 1928), pp. 22 ff.

history, art history, legal history, history of language, and so on, and that it functions besides as a science of general "cultural history" in no way bears out the historicist view of social reality. Surely the same holds for other special sciences such as empirical psychology with its specializations of cognitive psychology, cultural psychology, psychology of language, psychology of law, psychology of religion, and so on, and which presses its claims besides as general psychology. Indeed, this state of affairs can only be explained by the above-mentioned *sphere-universality* of every modal aspect of reality. Unless the historical is seen as one *modal aspect* of temporal reality, no account can be given of the special character of the so-called individualizing mode of thinking of the scientific historian.

7. **Analysis of the modal structure of history. The normative meaning of history and that of law. The formation of law and historical power formation**

Law and history have different modal meanings even though within the temporal world-order they are indissolubly intertwined. Once insight into this state of affairs is gained, ontological historicism is defeated in principle.

In the theory of law-spheres I have tried to offer a theoretical analysis of the *modal meaning* of history. The method I followed was to combine this structural analysis with that of the aspects of reality that occur *earlier* and *later* in the cosmic order. It is a method that requires the greatest degree of critical scrutiny, but it delivers the proof of the pudding by showing that the discovered modal moments are indeed something more than merely subjective constructs. In the present context I can share only some provisional results of my investigation. For a more extensive exposition I refer to [Volume II of] my work *De Wijsbegeerte der Wetsidee* (1935-36).

My starting-point was a modal analysis of the concept of culture as the *pièce de résistance* of all modern epistemological investigations into the science of history.[1] It was necessary at the outset to eliminate humanism's focusing the concept of culture on "values" or "ideas." Precisely that focus has prevented its modal delineation as a concept of culture and turned it into an unqualified collective concept. My method led me to see the moment of *free formative control* as the nuclear moment of the modal meaning of history. This moment is *original* only in a *historical* sense and is not qualified by any other modal nucleus, while one does meet it in the earlier law-spheres as an *anticipation*. For example, the modal structure of the logical aspect does not display the moment of *logical control* inherent in *systematic* concept-formation until it is *deepened* or *disclosed* in theoretic thought. In pre-theoretic thought, which is still strictly bound to sensory representations, this element of logical control is absent. *Logical* control as such does not have a historical meaning. It has a logical meaning, characterized by *analysis* as the nucleus of the logical aspect. Yet it *anticipates* the historical meaning. That this is so appears from the fact that only *disclosed, scientific thinking has a history*. Naive thinking does not have a history.[2] It betrays no tendency towards the logical formative control of epistemic material.[3]

On the other hand, in the modal structure of law-spheres that *succeed* the historical in the cosmic time-order, we meet the formative moment as an *analogy* or *retrocipation,* not as an *anticipation*. We meet social *forms,* lingual *forms,* artistic and legal *forms,* moral *forms,* and so on, not only in *disclosed* but also in *primitive, still closed* societies.

---

1 From the preceding it must be clear why one cannot proceed from concepts like "becoming" or "development." Both concepts must receive all their delineation precisely from the core modal meaning of history. In 1867 the well-known historian Robert Fruin defined history as "the science of becoming"; see his oration "De Beteekenis en waarde der geschiedenis" (The meaning and value of history), *Verspreide Geschriften,* 11 vols. (Leiden, 1902–04), 9:341.

2 Of course, naive thinking does have a history with respect to its concrete social contents, but not in regard to its *logical* side.

3 It is typical of historicism to call science a "factor of culture," but not naive thought.

Here we touch on a very important point in our discussion of the relationship between law and history. It is clear at first sight that it must be precisely the formative analogy within the modal meaning of the jural that provided the reference point for proclaiming positive law to be a *cultural* phenomenon and thus assigning it a historical meaning. Positive law has to be crafted in close association with a community's historical stage of development, because legal norms, like the norms for all other spheres of life, are only given *in principle*. It is in the nature of a temporal *norm*, as distinct from a natural law, to appeal to the free rational judgment of those who are subject to it. Even the laws of logical thought in their character as norms are ordained only as *principles*. They are logical *principia* that receive logical *formation* only in *disclosed* or *theoretical* thinking.

At the same time, the formation of law as examined in the theory of the sources of law cannot as such be *historical* in nature. It displays an intrinsic jural nature and therefore presupposes *juridical competence*.

The legal historian can derive the idea of competence only from the *science of law*. Historical science does not find it in its modal field of investigation. Juridical spheres of competence may well be historically *grounded*, as is the case with governmental authority in the internal organization of the state; but this does not turn them into historical spheres of *power*, as we shall see below. When the historian ignores this jural point of view, the formation of law becomes an issue of historical power, which leads to false interpretations of source material. A textbook example is the way Fustel de Coulanges, Heinrich von Sybel and others attempted to explain popular rights during the Frankish period purely as the product of royal legislation: in the area of folk-law the Frankish kings are supposed to have been able to do whatever they wanted with absolute plenitude of power!

Records indeed mention that the first powerful Merovingians often autocratically intervened in folk-law, just as they did in church law. But in the *praeceptum* of Lothar II (AD 613), affirmed by the famous Edict of Paris of 614, the *antiqui juris norma* (norm of the old law) was explicitly restored, just as Gunthram earlier had annulled the coercive measures of his predecessor Chilperik. For the *historian* who neglects the *normative jural point of view*, there is no room left for a modal difference between *power* formation and the formation of *law*. But the juridically trained historian realizes that in this way the proper nature of the formation of law is disregarded.

Power as such is truly a historical configuration of meaning which may reveal itself in many types, relative to the individuality structures of society: the power of the sword, the power of capital, the power of science, and so on. It differs fundamentally from the power of nature or the pure emotional impact of mass psychology, because free formative control is the qualifying nucleus of the historical. Power may presuppose psychical impact but is not itself of a psychical nature, although it contains a psychical analogy. It is a *formative power* which carries with it a historical task, a normative historical calling. In this sense a legal principle or even a whole legal system may acquire historical power. A classic example of this is the reception of Roman law in the Germanic countries.

That historical development is indeed embraced within a *normative* law-sphere and that God subjected the processes of culture to distinctive normative principles comes to expression already in the creation account of the primordial cultural mandate. It seems to me beyond all doubt that this norm cannot be reduced to the moral law.

The normative character of the historical law-sphere, together with the normativity of all law-spheres that succeed the logical aspect in the cosmic law-order, is *grounded* in the normative nature of the latter.

Just as we found, within the logical aspect, its first *anticipation* to be that of the nucleus of the historical, so we find, within the modal structure of the historical aspect, the logical as its first *analogy*. Natural things and natural events cannot have a subject function within the historical aspect because they do not function as subjects in a logical sense. They can only function in an objective, passive way in historical development, and always in relation to human *historical subjectivity*.[1] Historical subjectivity

1 Think of famines or floods that threaten human culture and furnish historical grounds for cultural intervention.

or historical agency presupposes *historical accountability* in cultural action, and this accountability is only possible on the basis of the *logical principle of sufficient reason*. It is not itself of a logical nature; it is a logical analogy within the historical.

A typical *logical analogy* in the modal meaning of history is the contrast between *historical* and *unhistorical* (reactionary) activity. This distinction is possible as an evaluation only within a normative lawsphere or within the normative anticipations of a law-sphere which itself is not normative.[1] Such a distinction is typically *grounded* in the logical principle of non-contradiction, although anti-normativity is rooted in sin.

Whoever views history as a purely factual process without any normative meaning comes into conflict with his own view as soon as he meets with configurations of *reaction* and *repristination* that cannot be neglected by scientific historiography if it would understand the meaning of the historical process. One cannot refer to *reactionary* currents without implicitly acknowledging a historical norm of development against which the reaction is attempted.

I do not want to deny for a moment that, in political practice, the different party ideologies have seized upon the term "reaction" in order to disqualify every policy that does not line up with their own insight into what historical development demands. But this is not say that the concept "reaction" is merely a matter of subjective life- and world-view without any *meaning* for historical scholarship. The concept of development employed by scientific history requires the distinction between "reactionary" and "historical" simply because it is not a *biological* but a *normative historical concept*. How could the historian correctly understand the politics of the Restoration period after the fall of Napoleon without noticing its "reactionary" stamp?

1   Compare these oppositions: logical-illogical; historical-reactionary; conformity to social norms and violation of them; economic-uneconomic; beautiful-ugly; lawful-unlawful; moral-immoral; belief-unbelief. The axiological opposition healthy-ill is not biotic in the narrow sense since it has a *medical* meaning which as such presupposes a norm. The axiological opposition between "sensitive and insensitive" is also not valid for feeling in its closed meaning but only for its normative anticipations (such as feeling of love, feeling of what is just, and so on).

Ever since antirevolutionary political theory struggled free from the influence of Haller, it has recognized the reactionary nature of the counter-revolutionary Restoration politics and rejected those politico-historical currents on the basis of its *Christian historical* principles. The counter-revolutionary who did not just repudiate the revolution *principles* but also strove to lawfully restore dead elements of the *ancien régime* did not behave illegally or immorally, but none the less he acted in violation of the *normative principle of the continuity of historical development.*

Reinstating our old political estates under King Willem I was, from a juridical point of view, undoubtedly an act of law formation, as was the partial restoration of manorial rights. But the constitutional historian discerns a *reactionary* thrust – so typical of the Restoration period! – which from a *historical* perspective could have no future because the historico-political basis for estates and manors had collapsed.

The independence of the jural viewpoint from the historical, on the other hand, was clearly evident in that, on the basis of equity, long-acquired property rights were preserved without objection, even though they stemmed from historical conditions long since worn out. The historical foundation for feudal rights had practically fallen away already with the disappearance of the mobilization of vassals from the organization of the military and especially with the liquidation of the feudal political system. Any legal claim to tithes disappeared after the Reformation destroyed the secular power of the Roman Catholic Church in the Netherlands. We could go on. Yet in juridical life such configurations can last for a long time, albeit often in a denatured form, even though they provide no prospects for any new developments. So, for example, our Transition Act of 16 May 1829 upheld rights acquired under earlier legislation (but not rights explicitly terminated, such as feudal rights). From an historical standpoint one cannot speak of this as *reactionary*. Law formation will just pursue its own distinctive principles when it respects acquired rights that are not in conflict with the principles of modern constitutional law and modern civil law.[1]

It also makes no sense in this context to speak, in neo-Kantian style, of a constant juridical *thought-form* with a *historical content*. After all, positive legal institutions bear a *jural content*. The legislator cannot dictate rules to historical development any more than historical development can regulate the *jural side* of society. There simply is an indissoluble coherence between law and history, a temporal modal intertwinement embracing the two, even as each maintains its *sphere-sovereignty*. The Historical School lost sight of this when it proclaimed historical development to be a hidden law inhering in positive law.

8. Historical and juridical continuity. The problem of revolution

The principle of historical continuity is a normative modal principle of historical development which may be violated temporarily through reaction or revolutionary arbitrariness. It belongs to the *biotic* analogies within the meaning of history, since it regulates historical development and because development is an original biotic mode of time. Yet it retains its *normative historical nature*.

Historical continuity is maintained in the power-struggle between tradition and the progressive or repristinating will of the makers of history.[2] In this power struggle the subjective arbitrariness of the shaper of history ought to be made subject to the historical norm of development in order to allow the new forms

1 This cannot be said of genuine manorial rights and estate privileges! Respect for *all* acquired rights regardless of their character constitutes a demand which can only be made by a dogmatic rationalistic natural law or by a historicistic theory of legitimacy. In this regard, Stahl definitely goes too far in *Die gegenwärtigen Parteien in Staat und Kirche*, p. 309. Cf. also Ernst Beling, *Revolution und Recht* (Augsburg, 1923), pp. 37 ff. Of course claims for losses [incurred during a revolution] is a separate issue.
2 Cf. my *WdW*, 2:180–182 [Cf. *NC*, 2:241–243]. See also what Huizinga remarks in this connection (op. cit., p. 65): "The manner in which they [the cultural factors] manifest themselves is almost always in the form of conflict: armed struggles, clashes of opinion are ever the theme of the narrative of history." [In connection with the reference to *WdW*, vol. II, one should also consult *NC*, 2:229 ff., where the exposition contains important alterations and an expansion of the original Dutch text.]

to absorb the viable cultural elements of the tradition. In the historical tradition the past and present are indissolubly intertwined. Tradition is the condensed form – only partly conscious – of the cultural development of entire generations. An individual can never ignore it with impunity. For that matter, a person is himself historically fed and formed by tradition and daily draws on its riches.

The *juridical continuity* encountered in the *process of law formation* differs fundamentally from *historical continuity*. A revolution does not necessarily break historical continuity yet it cannot but entail a disruption of juridical continuity.

A revolution has sometimes been called a "juridical miracle" insofar as it might create what is just from what is unjust. However, this qualification is mistaken on principle. The unjust can never give rise to the just. It is only the positivist formal theory of law, which looks for the validation of legal norms only in their adequate juridical origin, that is compelled to arrive at this "juridical faith in miracles." But its faith only conceals the antinomy in which the positivistic starting-point entangles itself.

Juridical discontinuity interrupts only the *formal* validity of laws. The Dutch constitution of 1814 had no formal validity, yet it became the formal validation of all later legislation.

Formal validity indicates only that the jural mode of origin of a legal norm or a complex of legal norms is not *original*, but *derived*. That is to say: the legal organ accountable for determining said norms was acting within a *juridically established (i.e., formal) sphere of competence.*

The formal sphere of competence itself is the product of law formation, although it can exist only within an original *material* sphere of competence, which itself did not arise through law *formation* but much rather makes *possible* all formation of law.[1]

---

1   Cf. also E. J. Bekker, "Recht musz Recht bleiben," in *Festgabe für den Grosz-herzog von Baden* (Heidelberg, 1896), p. 39: "The primordial source of the entire developmental sequence is everywhere contained within something which itself cannot be counted as part of positive law. For otherwise, before whatever law could have been created through human action, there must have existed law created through human action."

The material spheres of competence are not grounded in human arbitrariness but in the immutable divine world-order and they are delimited by the individuality structures of the distinct societal forms. For example, what belongs to the material sphere of competence of the institutional church rests upon the inner nature – the internal law-for-life – of the church; in no way can it be established along formal juridical[1] or legal historical lines. The same applies to the material sphere of competence of government.

Both juridical positivism and relativistic historicism eliminate the constant structural laws of the transient societal forms and therefore end up having to resort to a "juridical faith in miracles." In its view of revolutionary law formation, the former is compelled to allow that what is "just" is generated from what is "unjust," while the latter considers what is "just" to originate from "power." Precisely this point demonstrates the significance of our theory of law-spheres and individuality structures for legal and political theory.

A revolution can neither breach the modal sphere-sovereignty of positive law in the face of shifts in historical power, nor put aside the constant structural principles of human society. The issue is rather this. The original material sphere of competence of government, by virtue of the individuality structure of the state community, is typically grounded in the *power of the sword*. For in accordance with its internal normative, structural principle, the state is characterized as a *public legal community* on the basis of a monopolistic organization of the sword power within a territory. Law and history, jural competence and historical power formation, are interlaced in a typical manner within this structure, while respecting each other's *sphere-sovereignty*. Thus only those are called to the original formation of law within the material sphere of competence of the state who control the power apparatus of the state. This requires, in the first place, power over persons who have to believe in the historical calling of these new leaders. The public legal community, after all, which defines the typical qualifying function of an orderly state, can exist only on the basis of historical power. A government's authority, unlike that of parents in the nuclear

---

1 That is to say, by researching what is stipulated about it in state laws and ecclesiastical rules.

family, is not typically grounded in the natural ties of blood, but is based upon a historical power organization with a typical character. In the final analysis, therefore, a break in the formal continuity of law formation through a revolution amounts to a loss of the *original* competence on the part of the previous law-formers. This removes the basis for the formal continuity of legislation from an earlier period. It must never be construed in a historicist manner as an obliteration of formal law by might, or in line with uncritical juridical positivism as the emergence of what is just from what is unjust in the course of time. If those newly in power do not attend to the *jural* office of government, they are but *usurpers* incapable of ever acquiring the material legitimacy of a government. Power is only a condition, not an inner ground, for the original competence of a government. The material boundaries of competence in legal life are determined not by might or power but by divine structural *jural* principles.

A revolution does not generate justice from injustice. A new government is not legitimated by a successful seizure of power that is unlawful according to the pre-revolution political constitution: it is legitimated by conformity to the material requirements of the competence that is determined by the inner structural law of the state. The *Gesta regum francorum* records the advice of Pope Zachary in 751 to the Franks regarding whether or not it was proper to maintain the Merovingian king Childerik who was incapable of ruling. The pope answered: *"Melius esse illum vocari regem apud quem summa potestatis consisteret"* (it is better that he who has the highest power be named king).[1] Here too the intention was merely to respect the necessary historical condition for occupying the office of government, and not at all to *equate* law and power, right and might.

The issue is essentially no different in the context of international law when *de jure* recognition is considered for a *de facto* government that came to power in a revolutionary way, or when *de jure* recognition is requested by a newly established state. In neither case does recognition in international law imply a judgment on the manner in which the new government or state was *formed*; recognizing them merely notes that they have legitimated themselves[2] in a *material* sense and that they are

1 *Gesta regum francorum*, Appendix, 751; in Bouquet, 2:576.
2 In the case of any uncertainty about the stability of this legitimation, recognition would initially be *de facto*, that is *provisional*.

qualified to take on international legal relationships with those states that recognize them.

9. Historical and juridical causality. The emergence of feudal law as a problem for the history of law

A very deep divergence has been shown above between historical and jural causality. No less a divergence is revealed when we compare further modal structural features in law and history. In both the historical and the jural aspect we can discern in the retrocipatory direction a *causal analogy* which has its modal foundation in the nuclear meaning of the aspect of motion investigated by physics.[1]

Many a theory of history still works with the naturalistic conception of a "closed" causal sequence in which the course of events is fully determined.[2] This notion of causality derives from classical physics and has been expanded by the humanistic science ideal into a cosmological *idea* of causality of universal scope – a method of explaining the world.

From Simmel[3] to Huizenga,[4] modern epistemological studies show that the historian in his "causal explanation" of historical processes can only apply the causality concept in a highly inexact manner. This is so, presumably, because the enormously complicated nature of the factors involved in bringing about an event allows for no more than an extremely deficient understanding. Causal explanations can actually incorporate only impressionistic bundles of un-analyzed connections in their developmental sequence.

It was the science ideal of rationalism that tried to reduce all events in the world to a strictly law-conforming, natural process

1 [After 1950, Dooyeweerd distinguished between the kinematic aspect of uniform motion and the physical aspect of energy-operation.]
2 The naturalistic conception of history advanced by Henry Buckle and Hippolyte Taine, but also by Karl Lamprecht, is totally inspired by this idea.
3 Cf. Georg Simmel, *Die Probleme der Geschichtsphilosophie* (The problems of philosophy of history), 4th ed. (Munich and Leipzig, 1922), pp. 96 ff.
4 Cf. his *De Wetenschap der geschiedenis* (The science of history), pp. 53 ff.; cf. pp. 47 ff. See also Raymond Aron, *Introduction à la philosophie de l'histoire*, 2nd ed. (Paris, 1938), pp. 162 ff., where he attempts to define the historical concept of causality in terms of "retrospective probability."

of cause and effect. When this science ideal lost its fascination and an irrationalist historicism started to ponder the fundamental opposition between natural science and the "humanities," the historicists understandably were inclined to ban the entire concept of "causal explanation" from the science of history. It belonged to natural science, after all, with its search for abstract *laws*, whereas historical thinking struggles to achieve an understanding of "life in its fullness," in its "creative freedom" and irrational individuality. It was in this spirit that Dilthey, Troeltsch, Spengler and Othmar Spann fought against causality thinking. According to them, the concept of causality belongs to the abstract, objective worldview of natural science which essentially reduces *time* to *static space*. In opposition to that, Spengler posited the historical understanding of "fate," the inescapable destiny that governs all history in a frightful "incomprehensibility."[1]

Max Weber, on the other hand, tried to reconcile "causal explanation" and "empathic understanding" by bringing a needed nomological classification method to the aid of historical science's individualizing praxis. His well-known "Idealtypes" are intended as rational models to assist the interpretation of human social actions. Weber's *Idealtypen* evaluate these actions as to their "possible outcomes"; they interpret them as to their "rational meaning" and causally explain them insofar as they can be understood in terms of rational motives.

All these approaches, we recall, take as their point of departure the concept of causality as used in the natural sciences and cosmologically absolutized by the humanistic science ideal. But now that modern physics itself has had to abandon the idea of a *closed* causal nexus within its modal field of investigation, this entire concept of causality has been recognized for what it was from the start: a subjective philosophical hypothesis of a naturalistic stamp.

---

1 Cf. Oswald Spengler, *Der Untergang des Abendlandes* (The decline of the West), 1:166: "Fate and causality relate in a fashion analogous to time and space." See also Ernst Troeltsch, *Der Historismus und seine Probleme* (Historicism and its problems), pp. 56–57 and Othmar Spann, *Geschichtsphilosophie* (Philosophy of history), pp. 72 ff.

Without any doubt we have to accept a cosmic causal coherence, grounded in the *cosmic time-order* and overarching the modal boundaries of the law-spheres, that is, keeping the modal causal sequences mutually connected. But this causal coherence cannot be grasped in theory any more than can cosmic time. It is the presupposition of all events. The special sciences, however, can employ a concept of causality that is bounded and delineated by the modal meaning of their respective fields of investigation. The causality concepts used in other disciplines can only render auxiliary service in this regard.

Historical causality is therefore to be understood only in the sense of *cultural development*. Causal connections in the logical,[1] psychical, biotic and physical senses lie at the foundation of the modal historical nexus of causality because the historical law-sphere is grounded in these earlier spheres. But it is a naturalistic prejudice to try and reduce historical causality to a so-called psycho-physical one.

Historical causality is qualified by the nucleus of the historical. It has meaning only within the coherence of cultural development and it presupposes, insofar as it proceeds from human actions, *the possibility of a normative attribution to responsible subjects*. Among other things[2] we find historical causality at work in the Moorish invasions with its effects on the development of the feudal system, inasmuch as it necessitated the formation of an extensive professional cavalry that could not be provided for by the old *"trustis."*

This example already demonstrates that, essentially, we are operating here with a *normative* concept of causality with a dis-

---

1   What I have in mind here is the logical causal connection of sufficient reason, which in rationalistic metaphysics is all too often identified with the cosmological idea of causality.
2   Certainly not *exclusively*, as Heinrich Mitteis has demonstrated in his excellent work *Lehnrecht und Staatsgewalt* (Feudal law and political power) (Weimar, 1933), pp. 124 ff., in opposition to the older theory of Helmut Brunner and his followers.

tinctive modal meaning.[1] One could also say that the Moorish invasions brought to light a politico-historical need to expand the cavalry within the Frankish military organization. The first Carolingian rulers *satisfied* this need in a brilliant way by incorporating into their kingdom's military organization all existing private vassalage that was in any way related to cavalry service. What is so astute about this Carolingian policy is that it killed two birds with one stone: in one stroke it neutralized the dangers to the state entailed by both private vassalage and feudal tenure, given that land at the time was the sole inducement one could offer for acquiring political support.[2]

Domestic factors too exerted a historical causal influence on the formation of the feudal system. But here again they merely placed before the Carolingians the need to take timely measures to eliminate the dangers of private military power formation.

Thus a politico-historical norm in the sense of a twofold demand was revealed in the growth of the Frankish state. It has nothing to do with the "hidden law" espoused by irrationalist Romanticism. The first Carolingians positivized that norm in the political forms of the feudal system, and by using forms already in existence they avoided breaking the line of historical continuity. The cultural norm embodied in this system was certainly not *purely modal*-historical in nature because it had the character of a *politico*-historical norm involving the structural principle of the state. At the same time it stamped as eminently historical the Carolingian policy with respect to (a) the church, which experienced a partial secularization of its property and as a result had to be indemnified; (b) the magnates of the realm,

1 I cannot accept the contrast between a "norm" and a "law of causality" that governs the historical process, nor the identification of "it ought-to-be" (*sein sollende*) with the *moral law*, as is proposed by my esteemed colleague Professor A. A. van Schelven in the volume *Historie en leven* (History and life) (Kampen, 1925), p. 32. The *nature*, the *modal* character of historical causality, renders such a contrast impossible.
2 Cf. Paul Guilhiermoz, *Essai sur l'origine de la noblesse en France au moyen âge* (Essay on the origin of the nobility in medieval France) (Paris, 1902), p. 239, and Mitteis, op. cit., p. 126. [Reference to the role of Charles Martel and his mounted warriors in repelling the Moorish invasion at Tours, A.D. 732.]

whose private power was made subservient to the public interest; and finally (c) the threat of Moorish power.

Not a single *concrete* norm could be derived from the merely *modal* meaning of the law-sphere under consideration. As we saw, this applies equally to jural and moral norms, because they too can acquire a concrete shape only within the individuality structures of temporal society. But the *historical* character of this positive cultural norm[1] was indeed derived from the constant *normative modal meaning of history.*

The historical causal factors mentioned earlier, which had to be considered in the formation of the feudal system, are, as we established, essentially factors of political *power* formation for which certain groups in the society of the time were responsible. As such they have nothing to do with psycho-physical causal connections and are therefore not at all reducible to interconnected complexes that supposedly defy complete analysis. They are, rather, normative historical *grounds* for historical *consequences.* Of course, when establishing a causal historical connection the historian cannot avoid taking into account as well any psychical, biotic and physical causal factors, no more than the *jurist* can avoid noting such factors in establishing any so-called "factual" effects of a crime. But the theory of law-spheres and individuality structures sufficiently accounts for this state of affairs by pointing to the necessary *intertwinement* of all law-spheres within cosmic time. This does not detract from the *unique modal nature* of historical causality. The non-historical causal connections are always, for the science of history, only interesting as a *foundation* for historical causality.

Naturally, these remarks are not intended to give a complete exposition of the historical idea of causality. That would require a separate treatment and would have to account in particular for the coherence between subjective and objective factors within

1   One may perhaps formulate this positive norm as follows: What the politico-historical situation of the Frankish kingdom needed at the beginning of the 8th century was to achieve political power by incorporating the feudal system within the organization of the state. This was a concrete historical guideline for Carolingian politics, a true norm of *raison d'état* taken in its proper sense.

historical causality. My intention was merely to highlight the *modal* character proper to historical causality. I also wanted to demonstrate why it is unsatisfactory to neglect this modal character by representing historical causality as an impressionistic selection from a closed or an open nexus of natural causality.[1]

So what then is *jural* causality? It is certainly not of a *historical nature*. It does not function in the developmental context of cultural powers, but in the retributive coherence of legal ground and legal consequence. It displays a modally normative character and like historical causality is not a more or less arbitrary selection from a supposedly closed, causal sequence of natural processes. It has meaning only within the *jural* perspective and is therefore qualified by the jural nucleus of *retribution*. A legal fact exerts causal effect in the world of law insofar as it functions as the legal ground for legal consequences. Even the so-called *factual* effects can only be considered within the sense of juridical attribution.[2]

It is impossible to understand feudal *law* as the jural aspect of the feudal system unless we apply the concept of jural causality. Yet one cannot speak of the emergence of feudal law until vassalage[3] and the assignment of a *beneficium*,[4] both of which had appeared already in the earliest Merovingian period, started to function in a jural causal connection of *legal ground* and *legal*

1 Equally unsatisfactory in this regard seems to me the following characterization by Huizenga, *De Wetenschap der geschiedenis*, p. 54: "The image of historical causality may never be that of links that form a chain. Instead, whoever establishes an instance of historical causality is loosely binding together a bunch of flowers: every newly added notion alters the appearance of the entire bouquet. In other words, the acknowledgment of historical causality seldom constitutes anything more than giving an account of a certain, not fully comprehensible, conditionality." See also his *Cultuur-historische verkenningen* (Explorations in cultural history) (Haarlem, 1929), p. 31.

2 Cf. the extensive treatment of this issue in my study "Het juridisch causaliteitsprobleem in 't licht der Wetsidee" (The problem of jural causality in the light of the law-idea), *Antirevolutionaire Staatkunde* (quarterly) 2 (1928): 21–121.

3 Since the middle of the 8th century, vassalage was only established in the legal form of the *commendatio* (accompanied by oath-taking and weapon-supply) derived from the *trustis*. The word *commendatio* in itself is not free of ambiguity.

4 [In the Middle Ages a *beneficium* or benefice was a position or post granted to a bishop or an abbot that guaranteed a fixed amount of property or income.]

consequence and subsequently operated in this function as an unambiguous legal form, variable only within set limits.[1]

The question *when* it is justified to speak of the rise of feudal relationships, still debated today in the science of legal history, is in essence a *legal* question. It can never be answered by the historian from a merely historical point of view. For legal history, this is of primary methodological interest. A lively controversy over the inception of genuine feudal law circles around the question how much significance attaches to the secularization of Frankish church property under the first Carolingians for the development of the benefice system as a *factual component* of feudal law.

The older theory, introduced by Paul Roth,[2] saw in this secularization the crucial point. He entertained the opinion that it brought about a fundamental alteration of the entire organization of the Frankish state. Against this, the well-known historian Alfons Dopsch argued that the Carolingian secularization measures reveal nothing *new*. He emphasized that church property had repeatedly been subjected to confiscation already earlier, under the Merovingians, and that one can find the entire technique of the later *"descriptio"* and *"divisio"* in the proceedings of the sixth-century Councils, whose decisions, directed against the *"competitores"* for church property, mark them as truly reforming synods.[3]

1 However, during the Carolingian period the term *beneficium* is also not found as an unambiguous technical legal term. It did not necessarily have the meaning of vassalistic loan, since in general it was used more often in the sense of a factual accomplishment or even in the older sense of a "benefaction" (e.g., in the expression *"per beneficium alicuius habere"*). A sharp differentiation in juridical signs will not be achieved until further study and reflection by *legal scholars*.

2 P. Roth, *Geschichte des Benefizialwesens von den ältesten Zeiten bis in das 10. Jahrhundert* (The history of the system of benefices from the earliest times to the 10th century) (Berlin, 1856), pp. 313 ff., and "Die Säkularisation des Kirchenguts unter den Carolingern" (The secularization of church property under the Carolingians), *Münchener Historisches Jahrbuch*, 1865.

3 A. Dopsch, *Wirtschaftliche und soziale Grundlagen der europaeischen Kulturentwicklung* (Economic and social foundations of the development of European culture (Vienna, 1924), 2:312 ff.). Cf. also his study "Das Lehenwesen in Verfassung und wirtschaftliche Geschichte des Mittelalters," in *Gesammelte Aufsätze* (Vienna, 1928). A similar view is already found in A. Hauck, *Kirchengeschichte,* 2nd ed. (Leipzig, 1914), 1:397 ff., 412 ff.

To my mind it is Mitteis who deserves the credit for bringing the correct methodology to this controversy. What Dopsch had done was essentially to eliminate the *jural question* by positioning the issue strictly within the context of cultural development. He emphasized the continuity of development from antiquity to the early medieval period. But everything here depends upon the first lawfully established *juridical form* under which, from the start of the 8th century, benefices were taken from secularized church property and given to the royal vassals by Carloman's capitulary of Lestinnes (A.D. 743). It is this point that Dopsch neglects here, despite his criticism of the school of Schmoller and Lamprecht for neglecting the need for sharp juridical distinctions in questions of legal history.

From a historical perspective Dopsch's argument is correct in that already during the early Merovingian period, thus under political relations quite similar to those prevailing at the beginning of the 8th century, the need arose to transfer (in quantities no longer ascertainable) crown property to the spiritual and secular aristocracy as compensation for services to the King.[1] It is quite probable as well that this practice was subject to historical influences which to some extent can be traced back to the end of the Roman period, seeing as the Merovingian kingdom, like the other Germanic realms,[2] was dragged into the "natural economic" disintegration of the Roman Empire.

But, as Mitteis rightly emphasized,[3] the *legal* historian may not, in this particular question, neglect the fundamentally *jural* difference between the Merovingian land grants and the *"precaria verbo Regis,"* the new legal form established by the Carolingians for benefices procured under legal coercion from secularized church property. The synod of Lestinnes is the great turning point in the process of law formation with respect to the feudal system, even though the *precaria verbo Regis* was of course only a transitional form.

The origin of feudal law is the jural-causal combination, according to typical legal rules, of the conscription of the vassals

1 Dopsch, *Grundlagen*, loc. cit.
2 This historical connection still contains many points that beg further clarification.
3 Mitteis, *Lehnrecht und Staatsgewalt*, p. 116.

and the fixed legal form of the *beneficium*, which thereafter, even when it concerned the royal domains, was given out exclusively as a business-like loan and no longer in restricted ownership tied to the land. The legal historian has the job of throwing the light of historical-causal coherence upon this jural-causal coherence between vassalage and *beneficium*. But it is never possible to *explain* the jural nature of a new legal institution in terms of historical causes, as the naturalistic historical conception would wish. Law formation follows its own intrinsic rules, albeit in indissoluble *coherence* with the historical. It *has* its history, but precisely for this reason it is not itself of a historical nature.

10. The process of disclosure in cultural development and legal life

In our analysis of the anticipatory moments within the modal structure of the historical, we encountered the relationship between law and history in the *disclosure* or *deepening* of culture.

The Historical School was of the opinion that conscious law formation occurs only at a higher cultural level in the form of jurist-law and secondarily in legislation, whereas *folk-law* in its primitive phase has no formal origins, growing unconsciously as it does directly from popular convictions. This irrationalistic misunderstanding sprang from the intellectual world of Romanticism. The *formation of law* is also proper to a primitive and still closed legal order as a necessary historical analogy. The only peculiarity is that most law here does not emerge directly in the form of abstract legal rules, since it is positivized in the form of case-law (verdicts, concrete decisions). *Legal norms* originate first in the *indirect* form to which we have given the infelicitous name "common law."[1]

Economic and aesthetic analogies, too, are present in the still closed modal meaning of a primitive legal order. In the form of retribution practised in a primitive context – e.g., the *talio* principle in penal law – the principle of jural economy is observed in the prohibition of excessive revenge, and there is also in such a legal system an attempt at juridical harmonization of legal interests. The lingual analogy is there on a primitive cultural level in a vivid and extremely rich *legal symbolism*, and the logical, psy-

---

1 Infelicitous, since customs in common law, as already noted by Savigny, do not constitute originating juridical forms but merely cognitive sources of law.

chical, biotical, physical and mathematical analogies as well are never missing from any primitive manifestation of the modal meaning of the jural.[1]

Nevertheless, the differentiation and individualization of legal life, which are closely linked to the higher forms of development of human society, are only encountered on a disclosed cultural level.

Primitive law fully displays the undifferentiated character of closed folk and tribal societies (and sometimes sibs[2]). It is tribal law, folk-law and sib-law, but it lacks the material differentiation, common in modern legal systems, between civil, constitutional and administrative law, church law, the internal law of associations, international law, and so on. Not until society undergoes a process of differentiation does legal life individualize itself, in the sense that a private civil-law domain of freedom is guaranteed to the individual independent of any of the organized communities that he is a member of. In a primitive legal order, the person is only looked upon as a member of a sib or a folk. The foreigner is *without any rights*; he is *hostis, exlex,* outside the law. Indeed, as we learn from Roman and Germanic legal history, initially the sib-less neighbor enjoyed practically no protection under the law.

Modern civil law, more even than the Roman *ius gentium,* serves as the legal asylum of personal freedom. It emancipates the individual juridically from the exclusive relationships of an undifferentiated society.

Only in a differentiated and individualized legal order can deepened jural principles such as *aequitas,* good faith, *iusta causa,* prevention of abuse of the law, the principle of fault, etc. etc. manifest themselves. By contrast, a primitive legal order is one of rigid juridical formalism.

---

1 [At this point the author refers to the systematic volume of his *Encyclopedia of the Science of Law,* forthcoming as Ser. A, Vol. 10 of *The Collected Works of Herman Dooyeweerd.*]

2 That the formation of sibs is not evident in *all* cases of *primitive societies* and is regularly absent precisely among the least developed primitive peoples has been demonstrated by modern anthropological research; cf. Robert Lowie, *Primitive Society,* 2nd ed. (London, 1929), p. 142.

All the deepened jural principles in question are therefore *historically grounded* in the norms for cultural disclosure. They are not abstract ideas of reason with a timeless validity that can serve as a guideline for any existing legal order regardless of its stage of cultural development.

Stammler's idea of "natural law with variable content" is *uncritical* because his conception of law is endowed with the rigid, historically irrelevant, content of the Kantian humanistic personality ideal. Against the critique of "historical reason" this idea cannot hold its ground. But this is not because the principles of modern civil law, on which alone Stammler's concept of law is focused, are themselves historical in nature. Rather, it is defenseless because the divine world-order has made the disclosure of the meaning of the jural conditional upon historical cultural disclosure.

The process of disclosure is normed by the differentiation, integration and individualization of culture. An unmistakable sign of cultural disclosure is the gradual dismantling of those undifferentiated forms of social life which were calculated to keep folk-life in a closed condition. It is just such a closure of a culture that leads to a petrifying condition – to a vegetating on the past, a mythologizing of tradition, and a rigid binding of historical developent to biotic analogies.

For all its special traits, a primitive culture exhibits a strong uniformity as the generations succeed each other.[1] When a folk as bearer of a culture ceases to be, such a culture disappears from world history without a trace.

In the process of cultural disclosure, the *social anticipation* in the modal meaning of history is inevitably correlated with disclosed social life. Only through the enriching cultural intercourse of nations does history unfold itself into world history.[2]

1 The individualizing method of the science of history proper is therefore only applicable to disclosed cultures. To the naturalistic sociological mode of thought, by contrast, precisely *primitive* cultural phases, with their relative uniformity, appeared to be a fruitful field of investigation.

2 Hegel already realized that "world-history" does not display an *extensive* but an *intensive* character. In other words, it does not presuppose that all peoples on earth are incorporated into it.

And that such cultural intercourse is a prerequisite signifies a modal historical norm of fundamental significance.

Under the influence of fascism and national socialism, symptoms of an "autarchic" cultural isolation of nations from each other have recently made their appearance again. Yet these phenomena of *repristination* stem from reactionary tendencies that ought not to be accepted, as might be done in the spirit of a positivistic historicism. Rather, we must engage them in a spiritual power struggle even as history is being formed. In intimate association with these symptoms one can detect the gravest signs of reaction operating in the *formation of law*[1]: the gradual dismantling of civil law by a totalitarian view of the state; the mythological glorification of undifferentiated, primitive, Germanic communal forms aimed at absorbing all spheres of the individual's life in the *Volk* community; the reversion to medieval forms of "shared" property; the replacement of hard-won civil liberties by a legal tie to blood and soil; and so on.

These recent trends in Western culture should drive home to Calvinists the need for renewed reflection on the relationship between law and history. To deny the unique normative meaning of history is unacceptable, already on a practical level, for all who still believe Christianity has a positive calling to be involved in the development of culture.

But the irrationalist views of Stahl and the Historical School, assigning a secondary normative significance to historical development, is equally unacceptable. The doctrine that regarded the national folk-spirit as the true source of "culture" could give no account at all of the process of *disclosed* cultural development. Hence it was a crux for the Historical School to explain the reception of Roman law among the Germanic peoples, particularly as to the "historical" origin of law. This reception could not

---

1 For this, see my extensive treatise *De Verhouding tusschen individu en gemeenschap in de Romeinsche en Germaansche eigendomsopvatting* (The relation between individual and community in the Roman and Germanic conception of property), Publications of the alumni association of the VU Amsterdam, nr. 10, 1938. [An abridged version of this treatise is found in *The Collected Works of Herman Dooyeweerd*, Ser. B, Vol. 2, pp. 91–98, under the title "The relation of the individual and community from a legal philosophical perspective." The full text of this treatise is found in Chapter VI of the present volume.]

be explained from the "German *Volksgeist*," and yet Savigny and Puchta knew no other *material* source of law than a folk's convictions.[1] Not until Jhering was the historical dimension of the reception considered in the light of the great cultural law of the community of nations and the world-historical calling of Roman *ius gentium*.[2] Beseler, by contrast, employs the very doctrine of *Volksgeist* against Savigny and Puchta in order to pillory the reception as an adulteration of the development of Germanic law.

World history cannot be understood in terms of isolated "folk-spirits." A nation's individuality is constructed precisely from the cross-fertilization of the nations of the world. A primitive culture knows no real *national* individuality precisely because it lacks any *internal* contact with disclosed cultures that have been taken up into world history. At most it has some *external* contact with them.

Positivistic historicism lacks a historical yardstick for distinguishing between *reaction* and genuine cultural *disclosure*. Hence it lapses into unhistorical constructions, as exemplified in Spengler's "morphology of world cultures."

To continue with our systematic analysis of the modal meaning of history according to its anticipatory direction, I would also have to deal successively with the *symbolical* anticipation of cultural symbolism (in the sense of pointing forward to the lingual aspect) which plays such an essential role in disclosing or unlocking historical consciousness by teaching the distinction between what is historically significant and insignificant. I would further have to point to the culturally so important modal principle of cultural *economy*, which can play a role only in an essentially disclosed history and which brands as in conflict with the divine ordinance for the disclosure of culture the dominance of any one particular differentiated cultural sphere (such as that of science or the state) at the expense of other spheres. I would want to discuss the aesthetic and jural anticipations (as manifest, for example, in *disharmony* in the process of disclosure when the norm of cultural economy is violated,[3] and in the revelation of the history of the world as the *judgment* of

1 Puchta was undeniably far more narrow-minded than Savigny in his nationalistic thinking.

2 Rudolf von Jhering, *Die Geist des römischen Rechtes* [The spirit of Roman law), 6th ed. (Berlin, 1907), pp. 1–16, 312 ff.

3 Cf. the excesses of science as a cultural factor during the Enlightenment.

the world). Above all I would elaborate on the meaningful connection between *history* and *faith,* inasmuch as the process of cultural disclosure in the final analysis does not manifest a firm direction in our eyes unless we proceed from a faith orientation. However, the scope of this presentation does not permit a discussion of all these issues. I must therefore refer to the extensive exposition of them in the second volume of my *Wijsbegeerte der Wetsidee.*[1]

In the present context, finally, I would only emphasize that the view defended above concerning the normative meaning of history in its unique modal character is not grasped until one reckons with the strict distinction between law and subject, between historical norms and the historical facts that are subject to these norms, a distinction which is characteristic of the Calvinist cosmonomic idea and which strikes at the root of both the rationalist and the irrationalist conception of history.

The accusation that the acceptance of the normative meaning of history does not reckon with *sin* is thus stripped of its force.[2]

Since Augustine, the Christian view of history has taken for its religious starting-point the confession that the struggle between *civitas Dei* and *civitas terrena* in the root of the fallen creation may also be seen in the drama of world history. This religious ground-motive is central to the idea of development in the Christian view of history.

The usefulness, however, of the Christian idea of development for the theory of history depends on focusing its religious basic conception on the unique nature or distinctive modal structure of the historical process whereby its *immanent* normative foundations are brought to light. The same must be done in legal philosophy, and I hope that the foregoing exposition has somewhat clarified the inner relationship between law and history, for all the distinctiveness of the law-spheres in which they function.

1 See *WdW,* 2:191–259 [cf. *NC,* 2:259–330].
2 *Normative* should not be equated with *norm.* In speaking of normative aspects of reality I simply mean that the subject-side of these aspects can function only in subjection to the distinctive norms of the law-spheres under consideration. A crime, for example, is a normative legal fact insofar as it can be understood only in relation to *legal norms* and can actually exist only by virtue of these norms.

Index of Names

447

449

Voigt, M., 341
Voetius, Joh., 276
Vollenhoven, D. H. Th., 12, 20, 207
Vorsterman van Oyen, G. A., 372

W

Walz, G. A., 267
Wangenheim, K. A. von, 280
Weber, M., 168, 172, 309, 393, 399, 434

Wehberg, H., 333
Wiessner, H., 366
Windelband, W., 122
Winhoff, M., 374
Wolff, Chr., 188, 278, 380, 393

Z

Zachary (pope), 432
Zasius, U., 269
Zeno, 17f, 35, 55

Index of Subjects

A

absolutism, 230, 260, 266, 269, 270, 273, 362, 381, 382; *see also* totalitarian

absolutization, 12, 64, 116, 118, *et passim*; *see also* reification

abuse of right, 126, 145, 383, 384, 442

"act" structure, 97n, 99

administrative jurisprudence, 133

aequitas, 249f, 356-58, 442; *see also* equity

aevum, 5, 19f, 22f; Thomas on, 20-22, 67

analogies, 246, 247, 420, 441

anticipations, 10f, 77, 120, 420

Archimedean point, 1, 64n; *et passim*

aspects, modal, 1-109, 120, 164, 211, 246-48, 261, 322f, 325f, 394, 397f, 402, 412-16, 419-23

see also modal aspect

autonomy

  – of reason, 405

  – of theoretical thought, 64, 156, 217, 406

see also neutrality; self-sufficiency

B

Begriffsjurisprudenz, 126, 186, 235, 280, 286, 301

blood-revenge, 132

body and soul: in Aristotle, 22; Plato, 248; Thomas, 22, 67

Bolshevism, 198, 361n

bona fide, 253; *see also* good faith

bourgeoisie: in Scheltema, 167, 173-92

budget law: Laband on, 193

bureaucracy, 273, 287, 361, 369, 381

business law, 148, 278, 313, 327f, 348

C

Calvinism, Calvinistic, 111, 114, 117-119, 121, 123, 130, 138, 408, 410, 446

capitalist society: acc. to Scheltema, 181f, 195-97

Carolingians, 365, 436, 437n, 439

causa omissiones, 141

causality

  – cosmic coherence of, 435

  – historical, 418, 433-41

  – jural, 418

  – juridical, 83, 141, 433-41

  – physical, 31, 91, 210

  – in Scholasticism, 32

central love command, 261

church, 431

  – discipline, 134f, 137

  – law, 148, 327, 348, 349n

church and state, 137, 327

civil law, 133f, 154, 167f, 181, 186, 263, 269n, 276f, 286f, 326n, 328, 345-50, 377, 448

  – modern, 163, 346f, 349, 369, 383f 385, 429, 442, 443

  – Roman, 286, 356-62, 381, 389

  – in Grotius, 277; Scheltema, 181-94; Trude, 238

  – and private law, 286, 345, 348f, 442

  – and public law, 164-66, 168, 187, 314, 328, 346, 389

classes, social, 165, 167, 182, 187, 189, 191, 194, 308, 316, 353, 365, 381n, 400
class struggle: Scheltema on, 181f, 185, 196-98
codification, 179, 181, 187, 190, 192, 193, 276, 283, 393
collectivism, 200
commercial law, 169
common good, 232, 346, 358, 359, 389
communal relationships, 125, 130f, 165, 202, 240, 296, 298, 327, 331, 346f, 373, 385, 388
see also organized communities
commutative law, 189, 237-43, 248
compensation, 131f, 141, 242, 263, 305, 354, 382, 440
concept formation, 2, 10, 14, 24, 50, 62, 151, 245, 246, 248, 418n, 424
concept and idea, 24n, 138f, 151, 406
conservatism: acc. to Scheltema, 198-200, 202
constitutional law, 186, 236, 266, 286, 288, 297, 302, 306, 313, 329, 331, 333, 346, 429
constitutional state, 287, 292, 295, 303, 382
see also just state
contract, 60, 83, 123, 127, 131, 148, 154n, 242, 263, 273, 316, 328, 358
– in Althusius, 289; Aristotle, 238, 241f, 253; Duguit, 313; Gurvitch, 316; Jellinek, 298; Scheltema, 180, 188, 190
contract law, 253, 313, 328, 354-56, 358
conventions
– constitutional, 286
– legal, 258
coordinational relationships/spheres, 125, 130f, 133n, 134, 147, 148, 151, 152, 165, 327, 345f, 385
see also partnership
corporatism, 379n, 381, 387n, 388
cosmonomic idea, 1, 14, 19, 25, 74f, 115f, 121, 123
– Calvinist, 114, 117, 118, 119, 138, 446

– humanist, 116f, 118, 119, 121, 126
– rationalist, 123
see also ground-motive
creation order, 42, 72, 231, 274, 324, 386; see also world-order
cultural dominants, 144f, 155, 156, 171, 194
customary law, 276, 283, 285n, 296, 302, 354, 389, 39
Cynicism, 212

D

democracy, 167, 169, 211, 256, 319n
– acc. to Scheltema, 190f
determinism, 29, 159, 408
differentiation, process of, 95-97, 164
– in society, 130, 163, 164, 166, 168, 180, 201, 263, 273, 301, 312, 316, 318, 326, 342, 356, 358, 378, 387, 388, 443
– within a modality, 75, 82, 135, 143, 151, 153
– of the legal order, 164, 184, 249, 263, 272, 325, 347, 348, 363, 378, 384, 442
see also disclosure
disclosure, process of, 10f, 93, 255, 262f, 441-46
– of culture, 350, 356, 441-46
– of modalities, 10f, 93, 356-62, 384
– of society, 342, 345
– of theoretical thought, 424, 425
– in ancient Greece, 256
distributive justice, 188f, 220-25, 234-37, 241-43, 247f
divorce, 146, 149f

E

economic individualism, 166, 199, 382f
economics
– science/theory of, 166, 183, 199, 277, 308, 382, 397n, 399n, 422
– and law, 328n
Enlightenment, 144, 160, 161, 166, 308, 381n, 393, 394, 419, 445n

enkapsis, enkaptic, 37n, 95-99, 101, 108, 167, 201f, 333

entities, 5, 6n, 7, 32, 34, 36f, 38, 50, 70f, 79, 82, 87-94, 135, 136, 298, 304, 325, 337, 414, 421; *see also* individuality structures

equity, 187, 252f
- in Aristotle, 225, 249-56
- in Plato, 250
- in Roman civil law, 35
see also *aequitas*

estates, medieval, 365, 366

eternity, 5, 19f; Thomas on, 20-22, 67

ethnography, 414

ethnology, 85, 342, 419

eudaimonia, 227, 248, 252

evolutionism, 161

existentialism, 29, 157

F

factual side, 4, 15, 83n, 119

fairness, 356; *see also* equity

familia, 341n, 343, 351-64, 372f, 385

folk-community, 316, 318, 319, 363, 372

folk-law, 163-65, 249, 283-87, 290, 301-04, 310, 314, 317-18, 319n, 349n, 353-66, 400, 425, 441f

folk-spirit, 92, 159, 163, 164, 293, 312, 318, 395, 444, 445; see also *Volksgeist*

form-giving, human, 14, 96, 140, 212, 249, 258-62; *see also* positivization

founding function, 326

Franks, 363-65, 425f, 437-39

freedom, 29, 157, 161, 162, 165, 168f, 192, 260, 263, 274, 275, 282, 314, 320, 342, 345, 349n, 350, 360, 362, 365-68, 369-71, 381-86, 388, 442
- acc. to Scheltema, 174, 178, 185, 198, 203, 204

- in Aristotle, 220; Dilthey, 396f; Fichte, 395n; Gierke, 294; Hegel, 396; Kant, 128, 156, 158f, 217, 281; Krabbe, 302f; Locke, 277; Rousseau, 158, 192, 279

freedom idealism, 159, 160, 282, 290, 293

freedom of association, 133n3

free law movement, 125, 188, 394

Free University, 265n, 267, 331n, 334, 337n, 391n

French Revolution, 167, 178, 366, 382

friendship: Aristotle on, 224-28, 233, 240

functiemantel, 20n

function, modal: *see* modal aspect

functionalism, 24, 32, 38, 41, 91, 136n

G

geisteswissenschaftlich, 159, 293, 298, 405n; *see also* hermeneutic

genetic method, 207, 214, 215, 222, 224, 225

good faith, 83, 120, 187, 253, 356, 384, 442

ground-motive, 28, 155, 156, 160, 170, 209n, 228, 334
- Augustinian, 446
- biblical, 231, 249, 385
- creation-fall-redemption, 171, 228, 231, 249, 334
- form-matter, 36, 179, 208-13, 216-19, 228, 231, 248-50, 254f, 257, 261, 263, 404
- humanist, 158-61, 169-70, 261, 282, 293f
- nature-freedom, 156, 159, 166, 209, 261, 274, 281f, 290, 293f, 308, 319-21, 324
- nature-grace, 171, 217, 228, 231, 249, 261, 271

guided economy, 200, 317
see also planned economy

455

- pistical: faith, 138
jural concepts, time in, 60
jural retrocipations, 128
- numerical: equality, 247; multiplicity, 140f
- spatial: jural domain, 140
- physical: causality, 433-38
- biotic: competent organ, 140f
- sensitive: intention, will, 140
- logical: consistency, 140-42
- historical: competence, 323, 329
- lingual: interpretation, 140-42, 441
- social: relationships, 9
- economic: non-excess, 83; indemnification,131
- aesthetic: harmony, 141f; proportionality, 140, 220-23, 234-42, 247
jural principles, 111-54, 258, 262, 432, 442f
- and natural law, 113, 123-30, 137-45, 261-63
just state, the, 132f, 192, 277, 389
see also constitutional state
justice
- retributive, 210, 240
- in Aristotle, 207-63; in Plato, 213
- and social ethics, 231

L

law, *passim*
- history of, 207-64, 265-89, 342n, 373, 403n, 433-41; see also legal history
- philosophy of, 169, 231, 391f, 416n; see also legal philosophy
- science of, 99, 111-54, 265-89, 392, 397f, 413-19, 425; see also legal science
law-spheres, 420
- orderly sequence of, 119
see also modal aspect

legal
- history, 343f, 345, 394, 402f, 416, 423, 439-42; see also law, history of
- philosophy, 113, 121n, 138, 176, 217, 235, 254, 258, 345, 391-97, 402-05, 446; see also law, philosophy of
- science, 111-54, 265-89, 302, 310, 348, 391, 398, 418, 421; see also law, science of
legitimacy, principle of, 166, 279f, 288, 429n
Leviathan, 276
logic, Christian, 12

M

maatschap, 127, 130; see also coordinational relationships; partnership
majority principle, 233, 304
marriage, 96, 143, 144, 153
marriage law, 147-50, 348
- in the Soviet Union, 145f, 149f
Marxism, 181, 182, 183
master race, 163
Merovingians, 363f, 425, 439, 440
metaphysics, 3, 7, 27, 29, 38, 72n, 89-92, 114, 127, 136n, 216, 225, 413, 435
modalities, 1, 4, 8, 14f, 50, 80, 84, 323, 402, 414
- irreducibility of, 8, 18, 76, 84, 93, 300, 322f;
see also sphere-sovereignty
- nuclei of, see nucleus
- time in, 5-8, 53-61
see also modal aspect
modal aspect, modality, function, law-sphere, 8, 422

457

- in Roman law, 240, 255

natural law
- and historicism, 181, 282, 391-413
- and human rights, 163, 166, 259-61, 287, 309, 314, 385
- and jural principles, 129, 143f, 258, 261f, 425
- and positive law, 126, 129f, 254-61, 392
- and positivism, 189

natural law: revival of, 118, 125, 187f

nature and freedom 156, 166
  see also ground-motive

neo-Hegelian, 169, 343, 404

neo-Kantian, 113, 168f, 176f, 262, 304, 308n, 404, 405, 411, 415, 429

nervous system, 97n

neutrality, 13, 111-17, 259, 334, 407n, 408f, 436

nominalism, 7

norm and fact, 446

nuclear family, 144, 145, 323, 326n, 346, 421, 431f

nucleus, of a modality, 10, 14, 76, 78, 81, 82, 119, 323, 420
- numerical, 8, 9, 78, 80
- spatial, 9, 10
- kinematic, 18, 77, 433n
- physical, 433
- biotic, 80
- psychical, 79
- logical, 8, 9, 11, 424
- historical, 80, 323, 424, 426, 435
- aesthetic, 247
- jural, 140, 211, 247, 248, 323, 438
- moral, 248
- pistical (fiduciary, certitudinal), 79, 81, 208n

O

organized communities, 151, 195, 287
  see also communal relationships

origin, divine: 6n, 12n, 14f, 69, 72, 84f, 263, 420

P

parliamentary government, 167, 191, 192n, 203, 278, 303

partnership, 124f, 130-34, 141f, 144, 147, 332
  see also coordinational relationships

part-whole relation, 201, 386f

paterfamilias, 351-73

penal law, 60n, 131, 132, 135, 141, 151, 180, 223, 240, 286, 355, 411

personality ideal, 29, 115, 117, 126, 128, 156, 158, 161, 162, 169, 197, 217, 274, 277, 282, 290, 294f, 395f, 411, 443

Physiocrats, 277, 308

planned economy, 379n
  see also guided economy

popular representation, 191, 203
  see also parliamentary government

popular rights, 425

popular sovereignty, 278f, 289, 292n, 304, 382

positive law, 126f, 139, 145, 296, 392
- when not valid, 146, 147, 149, 152-54, 258

positivism, 108, 309, 312, 418, 444
- legal, 129, 139, 168, 186, 189, 259, 305, 430f
- philosophical, 111, 113, 181

positivization, 113n, 122, 125, 127, 129, 132, 133, 138, 140, 144-48, 305, 306, 436, 441
  see also form-giving, human power

461

53, 55, 72, 103, 109; Spengler, 25, 53; Thomas, 20-22, 67n, 105

tort, 126, 131-33

totalitarian, 164, 200, 212f, 220, 229, 237, 359-62, 377-81, 385, 404, 444

tradition, 58, 429f
- power of, 84, 163, 176, 256, 284-86, 361, 393, 429f, 443f

trias politica, 177, 192, 278
   see also powers, separation of

truth, 71, 115-18, 221, 246, 251, 252, 409
- Rickert on, 116, 416

U

undifferentiated, 318, 349f, 384
- ancient Greek society, 209-11, 256
- ancient Roman society, 349, 359-62
- the Roman *familia*, 343, 350-64, 372
- feudal relations, 363-77
- medieval conditions, 271-74, 368-70, 387
- law, 163-66, 263, 287, 442-44
   see also primitive

universalism (sociological), 158, 201-03, 220, 273, 289, 308f, 317f, 319, 332, 384-88

unwritten law, 218, 254-60, 329-31

V

value-relatedness, 404
- in Rickert, 398, 416

verband, 127, 143, 275n, 347n
   see also communal relationships; organized communities

virtue, 246
- Aristotle on, 220-26, 236f, 240-48, 254
- Plato on, 214, 219f
- Socrates on, 249

Volk, 399n, 444; *see also* folk

Volksgeist, 92, 283, 395, 400, 445
   see also folk-spirit

volonté générale, in Rousseau, 276, 279

VU University Amsterdam, *see* Free University

W

welfare state, 169

world history, 443, 445, 446

world-order, 273, 275, 333, 406, 412f, 420, 431, 443; *see also* creation order

worldview, 111, 112, 115-17, 123, 126, 203, 298, 307, 324, 401, 407n, 434

CPSIA information can be obtained
at www.ICGtesting.com
Printed in the USA
BVHW091552181221
624303BV00004B/40

9 780888 152022